Dostoevsky and the Catholic Underground

Northwestern University Press
Studies in Russian Literature and Theory

Series Editors
Robert Belknap
Caryl Emerson
Gary Saul Morson
William Mills Todd III
Andrew Wachtel

Dostoevsky and the Catholic Underground

Elizabeth A. Blake

NORTHWESTERN UNIVERSITY PRESS / EVANSTON, ILLINOIS

Northwestern University Press
www.nupress.northwestern.edu

This book has been published with the support of the Andrew W. Mellon
Foundation.

Printed in the United States of America

10 9 8 7 6 5 4 3 2 1

Library of Congress Cataloging-in-Publication Data

Blake, Elizabeth Ann, 1971– author.
    Dostoevsky and the Catholic underground / Elizabeth A. Blake.
        pages cm. — (Northwestern University Press studies in Russian literature
    and theory)
    Includes bibliographical references and index.
    ISBN 978-0-8101-2957-3 (cloth : alk. paper)
    1. Dostoyevsky, Fyodor, 1821–1881—Criticism and interpretation.
    2. Dostoyevsky, Fyodor, 1821–1881—Religion. 3. Catholic Church—In
    literature. 4. Anti-Catholicism in literature. I. Title. II. Series: Studies in Russian
    literature and theory.
    PG3328.Z7R42236 2014
    891.733—dc23

                                                                        2013046301

To Isa, Rafe, and Ruben

Not without purpose, for many years
Did the Lord as a witness place me
And gave me to understand the bookish arts.
—Alexander Pushkin, *Boris Godunov*

Contents

Acknowledgments

The current study is the culmination of research initially undertaken in Russia at the Pushkin House and the Dostoevsky Museum in St. Petersburg (with the aid of B. N. Tikhomirov) and in Poland at Jagiellonian University (with the support of Krzysztof Frysztacki) funded by a Fulbright-Hays dissertation grant and an international travel grant from Ohio State University. Additional grants from the U.S. Department of Education and the U.S. Department of State enabled me to complete the research for the monograph at the Summer Research Laboratory on Russia, Eastern Europe, and Eurasia at the University of Illinois Urbana-Champaign. Here, I greatly benefited from the expertise of the Slavic reference librarians (especially Helen Sullivan and Jan Adamczyk), who helped me locate and obtain rare resources.

I would like to express my profound gratitude to Caryl Emerson, who saw potential in a dissertation topic on Dostoevsky's dialogue with the Time of Troubles and encouraged me to write the present monograph. This study has benefited immeasurably from her perceptive observations on multiple drafts of the manuscript. I also appreciate Robert Belknap's input on an earlier draft of the first chapter and Robert L. Jackson's support for my research on Dostoevsky and the Polish prisoners, which was published as "Portraits of the Siberian Dostoevsky by Poles in the *House of the Dead,*" *Dostoevsky Studies,* New Series 10 (November 2006).

It was my good fortune to have come to Dostoevsky studies during the publication of Joseph Frank's five-volume biography of Dostoevsky and the publication of Dostoevsky's collected works in thirty volumes, to which this present study owes a significant debt. I would also like to acknowledge the intellectual contribution of the following faculty, with whom I consulted during my graduate studies at Ohio State University: George Kalbouss for sharing his love of Russian drama and culture, Dan Collins for our discussions of Orthodox monasticism, Irene Masing-Delic and Sara Dickinson for their readings of Dostoevsky, Angela Brintlinger for encouraging my analysis of publicistics, Eve Levin for the course on Russian Orthodoxy, and Yana Hashamova for her advice on historical theory. In addition, I greatly benefited from the opportunity to share my research with students and colleagues at the Department of German and Russian Studies at the University of Missouri, Columbia and at the Departments of English, Theological Studies, and Modern and Classical Languages at Saint Louis University. Research librarian Ron Crown and the chairs of English (Sara van den Berg) and theological studies (J. A. Wayne Hellmann) particularly encouraged my research.

Acquisitions editor Mike Levine and managing editor Anne Gendler at Northwestern University Press made the publication process a positive experience, and the insightful comments by series editor Gary Saul Morson and the anonymous readers led to productive revisions of the manuscript. For their help in proofreading the monograph at various stages of production, I would like to thank Marika Whaley, Mikhail Palatnik, Jan Adamczyk, Arline Cravens, Joe Lenkart, and Urszula Biegaj. I greatly appreciate the support of my first editor, colleague, collaborator, and husband Ruben Rosario. For her mature understanding during the many years of labor on this monograph, I thank our lovely daughter Isabella, whose fascination with Greek mythology reminded me of long-forgotten texts that informed the final draft of this manuscript. Finally, I am also grateful for our brave son Raphael, whose forbearance during his own troubles was inspiring during the final editing of the manuscript.

A Note on the Text

Although the Russian text in parentheses, notes, and bibliography has been transliterated according to the Library of Congress system, elsewhere the system has been modified. For example, names ending in –ii have been shortened to –y, thus rendering Dostoevsky rather than Dostoevskii, while the use of ' and " to replace the soft and hard signs in Russian have been eliminated to make the text more readable to a general audience. Furthermore, where a standard English form of a word or name exists, it is adopted so that Aleksandr Gertsen appears as Alexander Herzen. Unless otherwise indicated, all translations from the originals are mine.

Because Russia followed the Julian calendar in the nineteenth century, dates for the Russian sources are twelve days behind the countries in western Europe that adopted the Gregorian calendar. For the most part, this study adheres to the Julian dating in the text of the chapters, unless for the purpose of clarification, Western norms are necessary for allusions to famous events, for example, the September Conference of the Peace of League and Freedom or the 1849 May uprising in Dresden, or for references to specific issues of Western journals.

Throughout the book, the following sources are cited parenthetically with the noted abbreviations:

Pss   Dostoevskii, F. M. *Polnoe sobranie sochinenii v tridtsati tomakh.* 30 vols. Leningrad: Nauka, 1972–90.

PssP   Pushkin, A. S. *Polnoe sobranie sochinenii.* 19 vols. 1937–59. Reprint, Moscow: Voskresen'e, 1994–97.

Ss   Gertsen, A. I. *Sobranie sochinenii v tridtsati tomakh.* 30 vols. Moscow: Akademiia Nauk SSSR, 1954–65.

Dostoevsky and the Catholic Underground

Introduction

"But you can't *believe* things because they're a
lovely idea.
"But I *do*. That's how I believe."
—Evelyn Waugh, *Brideshead Revisited* (1944)

FEDOR DOSTOEVSKY'S ASSOCIATION of
Catholicism with revolutionary violence was encouraged by his regular encounters over the course of his lifetime with insurgents who participated
in Catholic unrest in Italy, France, and Poland in the nineteenth century.
This century witnessed the transformation of Catholic Europe as emerging nation-states frequently sought to limit the influence of the papacy in
their national affairs. Nationalism, rather than religion, played an increasingly fundamental role in unifying people as is evident from the formation of
countries such as Germany and Italy that brought together peoples sharing
a common ethnic and cultural heritage. At the same time, secular authorities governing these nation-states no longer ceded to the authority of the
papacy. In post-revolutionary France, Napoleon negotiated the Concordat
of 1801 with Pius VII that reduced the Catholic Church from a state religion
to a religion practiced by a French majority and significantly restricted the
church's temporal authority.[1] Although Napoleon III, despite his republican
principles, subsequently committed French troops to defend Pius IX's Holy
See against various forces seeking the unification of the Italian peninsula,
the French emperor nevertheless pressured Pius IX to secularize his admin-
istration and to support liberal reforms in the papal states. Prussia in 1803
revoked the Catholic Church's privileges established under the old German
Empire and thus initiated a struggle against clerical involvement in secular matters that culminated in Otto von Bismarck's Kulturkampf against the
Catholic Church in the 1870s. Furthermore, while Franz Joseph I of Austria
had concluded a concordat with Pius IX in 1855, Austria distanced itself from
the papacy in the 1860s and renounced the concordat after the First Vatican
Council announced the doctrine of papal infallibility in 1870.

Disappointed with the failure of Catholic nations to support unequivo-
cally the temporal power of the papacy, Pius IX waged ecclesiastical warfare

by threatening those who did not recognize his sovereignty with excommunication and issuing an 1864 encyclical with the attached *Syllabus Errorum,* which condemned eighty modern errors resulting from civil authorities appropriating the responsibilities that had belonged traditionally to the church. Asserting the primacy of ecclesiastical authority, the *Syllabus* maintains that the state exists to support the mission of the church, so Catholics seeking to reconcile modern ideas (e.g., socialism or republicanism) with their faith found that the *Syllabus* represented a return to the church of the Inquisition, which exercised direct authority in earthly realms. Even though Pius IX succeeded in defining the doctrine of infallibility at the ecumenical council that he called in 1869, he nevertheless lost the temporal seat of Rome when Italian troops entered the city in 1870 and proclaimed it Italy's new capital. All the same, in the European struggle between altar and throne, the clergy and many of the faithful aligned themselves with the papacy rather than with their national governments and thereby set the stage for a confrontation between state authorities and the church.

In response to growing national control over religious hierarchies, Catholics increasingly turned to ultramontanism, which promoted the papacy's absolute authority in secular and spiritual affairs by resisting state interference in ecclesiastical matters. While the heirs of the Enlightenment were reshaping the governments of Europe, the papacy enjoyed a renewed popularity among Catholics who looked beyond national borders toward a charismatic personality who provided inspiration for socially and politically transformative movements.[2] The resurgence of the Society of Jesus, a religious order formed during the Reformation that agitated on behalf of the papacy through a large network of colleges and schools, attests to the growing appeal of ultramontanism that emerged concomitant with the diminished prestige of national churches. Owing to the Order's destabilizing influence on civil society with its promulgation of papal infallibility, both Germany and France suppressed the Society of Jesus, even while Austria-Hungary supported the religious order, which enjoyed a revival in Galicia, a historically Polish section of the empire. This significant Jesuit presence on the western edge of the Russian Empire unsettled the Russian Orthodox Church, whose concerns regarding Jesuit activities in Russian Poland (the Congress Kingdom) had already persuaded Alexander I to expel the order from the Russian Empire in 1820. Despite the closing of religious schools and monasteries in addition to the confiscation of ecclesiastical properties within the Congress Kingdom after the 1830 and 1863 Polish uprisings (against Russian tsars Nicholas I and Alexander II, respectively), Russian authorities so feared the subversive activities of the religious on the behalf of the papacy that they further isolated Russian Poland from Rome by forcibly converting members of the Eastern rite Catholic (or Uniate) Church to Russian Orthodoxy.[3] These conversions were to reclaim for the Orthodox Church those believers lost during the Catholic Reformation when the 1595 Act of Union split the West Russian church into an Orthodox Church and an Eastern rite Catholic Church (allied with Rome).

Russia's frequent conflicts with Catholic Europe during Dostoevsky's lifetime may be attributed, in part, to territorial gains resulting from military victories in the eighteenth and nineteenth centuries. The partitions of Poland among Russia, Prussia, and Austria in 1772, 1793, and 1795 brought many devout Catholics into the Russian Empire. Emboldened by Napoleon's formation of the duchy of Warsaw from historically Polish lands seized from Austria and Prussia, thousands of the tsar's Catholic subjects, with the intent of restoring an independent Poland, joined Napoleon Bonaparte's Grande Armée for its invasion of Russia in 1812. When Tsar Alexander I emerged victorious over Napoleon, the tsar gained most of the lands constituting the duchy of Warsaw, which fell under his protection as the politically autonomous Congress Kingdom of Poland, but the Congress Kingdom lost even its limited local autonomy in the aftermath of the 1830 uprising when Nicholas I eliminated its constitution and the Sejm. Although the Polish invasion of Moscow during the Time of Troubles in the early seventeenth century remained historically distant from Nicholas I's Russia, the images of Napoleon's invading army and Polish insurrectionists recalled for Russian literati a Reformation precedent to contemporary Catholic violence. For example, Mikhail Zagoskin's patriotic novels in the Walter Scott tradition, *Yury Miloslavsky, or the Russians in 1612 (Iurii Miloslavskii, ili russkie v 1612 godu,* 1829) and *Roslavlev, or the Russians in 1812 (Roslavlev, ili russkie v 1812 godu,* 1831), effectively link the two periods in the national consciousness. The subsequent Polish uprisings in 1830 and 1863 likewise encouraged prominent historians, novelists, and dramatists to depict the seventeenth-century Russo-Polish conflict as a means of exploring the long-standing ethnic and religious tensions that still divided the two nations.

In their attempts to understand revolutions reverberating throughout nineteenth-century Europe, the Russian intelligentsia joined Western political philosophers like G. W. F. Hegel and Karl Marx in their discussions of the Reformation period as a historic precedent to modern conflict. For Hegel, the Inquisition's support for the despotic power of the monarchy, the Jesuits' casuistry, and the Catholic dissociation between religious and secular interests all contributed to the French Revolution.[4] Both Hegel and Marx celebrate Martin Luther's destruction of servile faith in Rome and therefore find promise in Germany's historic emancipation from the Catholic Church and from the church's endorsement of medieval feudalism.[5] The famous university lectures by historian Timofei Granovsky in the 1840s on medieval Europe recall the Roman Catholic Church's endorsement of Western feudalism, whose Russian equivalent, that is, serfdom, Dostoevsky's contemporaries sought to abolish, even by means of rebellion. The Reformation in the West coincided with the rise of serfdom in Russia, as nineteenth-century historian Mykola Kostomarov argues in his depiction of Boris Godunov as the founder of serfdom—an image of Tsar Boris advanced in Alexander Pushkin's tragedy *Boris Godunov* (1831).[6] Hegel specifically identifies the feudal agricultural relations between lord and serf in the Slavic lands as a main impediment to the progress of the Reformation in the East, since "a fundamental sense of individuality" essential to the Reformation could not prosper where "human industry" was overshadowed by "the agency of nature" and therefore failed to appreciate "the benefits of dawning freedom."[7]

Nevertheless, the nineteenth-century Russian intelligentsia experienced the Reformation through readings of William Shakespeare, Miguel de Cervantes, Friedrich Schiller, Voltaire, Alexandre Dumas, *père,* and other Western authors who encouraged the association of Catholicism with Reformation conflict. For instance, Dostoevsky's fellow writer and sometimes friend, Ivan Turgenev, underscores the common history of two such Reformation texts in his famous 1860 speech "Hamlet and Don Quixote" ("Gamlet i Don-Kikhot") by recognizing the simultaneous creation of Shakespeare's *Hamlet* and Cervantes's *Don Quixote de la Mancha* at the beginning of the seventeenth century: "Cervantes, just like Shakespeare, was a contemporary of Bartholomew's Night, and still a long time after them the heretics were burned and the blood flowed; indeed will it sometime cease flowing?"[8] British novelist D. H. Lawrence identifies in Dostoevsky the same "crisis of Middle European history" evident in the tragedies of Shakespeare and Pierre Corneille, whose *Hamlet* and *Le Cid,* respectively, Dostoevsky particularly admires.[9] He finds that Dostoevsky's "position in the crisis of late European history" parallels the struggle found in Cervantes, Shakespeare, and Corneille between the "conscious" self that adheres to the established order of the Middle Ages and the "unconscious self" that subverts the old order in a dramatic parallel to the humanists Desiderius Erasmus and Martin Luther.[10] Dostoevsky, himself, appreciates a similar discord that he recognizes as "the spirit of centuries of the Reformation" in Alexander Pushkin's poem "The Wanderer" ("Strannik," 1835)—"a transposition" of part of *The Pilgrim's Progress: From This World to That Which Is to Come* (1678–84) by puritan John Bunyan (*Pss,* 26:146).

Granovsky's research on Western medievalism had an impact on the writings of several prominent Westernizers with whom Dostoevsky maintained literary polemics, including the socio-literary critic Vissarion Belinsky and the prolific exiled writer Alexander Herzen. For example, in his "Tenth Article" ("Stat'ia desiataia") on Pushkin's *Boris Godunov* Belinsky contrasts the failed leadership of Godunov and his successors, the False Dimitry and Vasily Shuisky, to the dramatic history of England with its fraternal struggle between John Lackland and his crusading brother King Richard the Lionheart and to Reformation France, where "the decision of one question was very important: who would govern Louis XIII—his mother Catherine de Medici or Cardinal Richelieu."[11] Furthermore, Belinsky compares Pushkin's historical drama ("a lie worth the truth for it is filled with poetry") favorably to the theater of Corneille and his contemporary, dramatist Jean Racine, whose poetic "lies" still enjoy the applause of "the most enlightened and educated nation in Europe."[12] Similarly, Herzen's discussion of the progressive history of Western thought in *My Past and Thoughts* (*Byloe i dumy*) parallels Granovsky's focused study of the role of great men and the masses in the epic conflict between Latin and German cultures in the Middle Ages. As Herzen attempts to avoid, like Granovsky and Hegel, references to fate or Providence that could define the human experience, he finds that the power of ideas, specifically an "idée fixe," to which great men commit themselves, can move history: "Such an idée fixe was Catholicism in its time, then Protestantism, science during the epoch of the Renaissance, and revolution in the 18th century" (*Ss,* 11:70). Also, Herzen's co-conspirator, the inveterate anarchist Mikhail Bakunin, alludes to the Reformation, the Jesuits, and the Catholic Church in his analysis of church-state collaborations.[13]

The Western leanings of the Petrashevsky Circle, as well as members' contact with Granovsky, Belinsky, and Herzen, encouraged the circle to explore the history of Catholic Europe. Alexei Pleshcheev, the Petrashevsky conspirator responsible for sending Dostoevsky the infamous letter by Belinsky to Nikolai Gogol, records having attended some of Granovsky's lectures and having heard three additional lectures on Henry IV, "a general sketch of the sixteenth century," and "sources for the study of this century" at the home of Petr Kudryavtsev, a history professor at Moscow University.[14] Dostoevsky's historical understanding, like Granovsky's lectures, finds the Reformation Age to represent one of those "transitional epochs" which result in "the emergence of beginnings, of new forms of life" when national histories are shaped.[15] For both Granovsky and Dostoevsky, the violence of the Reformation arises out of a clash of nationalities manifested in religious strife. Granovsky believes that Germany's desire to free itself from the "unbearable Latin yoke" induced the nation to capitalize on the reform efforts of Erasmus and Luther. Dostoevsky's oeuvre emphasizes the effects of the Catholic Reformation on Russia with frequent references to the Time of Troubles and to the presence of the Jesuit-sponsored pretender Grigory Otrepev on Russian soil.[16] His lifelong dialogue with Pushkin's *Boris Godunov,* in which Dostoevsky discovers "poetic truth" in contrast to Belinsky's poetic "lies," affirms Caryl Emerson's conclusion that Pushkin's tragedy is the "poetic source" for "numerous transpositions" of "the Boris Tale" (*Pss,* 19:9).[17] As Harriet Murav's and Lyudmila Saraskina's analyses of Dostoevsky's *Demons* (*Besy,* 1871–72) discover, the historic seventeenth-century phenomenon of imposture remains central to his poetics.[18] Dostoevsky's reading of this period reflects the influence of Slavophile historian Mikhail Pogodin, who praises the victories of brave Russians, for example, Kuzma Minin or Ivan Susanin, during the internecine strife.[19] Dostoevsky, in characterizing the historical period as one in which "Russia was saved by the all-unifying spirit of the people," echoes Pogodin's patriotic sentiments rather than the critical historical analysis of the Ukrainian Kostomarov, who believes that tradition mythologized these popular figures (*Pss*, 26:132).[20] Dostoevsky participates in this nineteenth-century Time of Troubles dialogue with his depictions of revolutionary agents and conservative masses in such novels as *Crime and Punishment* (*Prestuplenie i nakazanie*, 1866) and *Demons,* in which Machiavellian principles are attributed to the Society of Jesus, whose ethics inform the actions of murderous youths.

In Dostoevsky's literature, his heroes are fascinated by great historical men with connections to Catholicism, such as Napoleon, the Inquisitor, and Otrepev, even when the characters' hero worship exposes them to ridicule by fellow characters. Dostoevsky's linking of these historical types to the Jesuits in *The Double* (*Dvoinik,* 1846), *Crime and Punishment,* and *The Brothers Karamazov* (*Brat'ia Karamazovy,* 1879–80) demonstrates the importance of Roman Catholicism for the creation of these idealized revolutionaries. At the same time it evinces Dostoevsky's anxiety over the pervasive Catholic influence on Russian society (which many Orthodox feared) during Russia's period of reforms, a period that saw increased pressure from Westernizers seeking official acceptance of religious pluralism, which Russia did not adopt until 1905. Dostoevsky's rejection of this pluralism for Russia is evident in his *Diary of a Writer* (*Dnevnik pisatelia,* 1873–81), in which he advocates for the Kulturkampf against the Catholic Church, criticizes Orthodox believers for turning to Lutheranism to avoid the Lenten fast, and equates Russianness with Orthodoxy. His encounters with Catholics in the prison camp in Omsk, while in exile in Semipalatinsk, and during his travels in Europe convinced Dostoevsky of popular papal support throughout Europe for a policy of "militant Catholicism" that aimed to expand the Catholic monarch's sphere of influence at the expense of Orthodox believers (*Pss*, 26:13).[21] For this reason, Dostoevsky increasingly sought to counter the cultural and political influence of Roman Catholicism by exposing the moral bankruptcy "of the Roman idea" in his novels and journalistic writings (*Pss*, 21:184).

SOCIAL CATHOLICISM AND THE PETRASHEVTSY

The experience of his father's service as a military doctor during Napoleon's 1812 campaign and the loss of his maternal grandfather's fortune during the evacuation of Moscow likely established for the young Dostoevsky an association of Catholicism with destruction.[22] The family readings of *History of the Russian State* (*Istoriia gosudarstva Rossiiskogo*, 1818–24) by the imperial state historian Nikolai Karamzin may have reinforced this impression, since, as Chester Dunning notes, Karamzin "emphasized foreign interference in Russia's domestic problems as the principal cause of the Troubles, seeing Poland as the main source of the pretender Dmitry's campaign for the throne."[23] Dostoevsky's younger brother Andrei recalls precisely this historical period in his reminiscences of the family circle: "Primarily historical works were read: Karamzin's *The History of the Russian State* (we had our own copy), the last volumes of which—IX, X, XI, and XII—were usually read to us, so something from the history of Godunov and the pretenders remained in my memory from these readings."[24] Furthermore, Fedor Dostoevsky's readings of Pushkin's *Boris Godunov* and Zagoskin's novels allowed Dostoevsky to experience these historic events as what his biographer Joseph Frank defines as the "Russian struggle against invaders . . . on behalf of the Orthodox faith."[25] Dostoevsky's 1848 short story "An Honest Thief" ("Chestnyi vor") attests to such a reading, since it contains a footnote describing the character Alexander Figner from *Roslavlev* as a turncoat both for spying for Napoleon and for swearing an oath to Catholicism (*Pss*, 2:424).

Dostoevsky is critical of the Gallic influence on his education before the Commission of Inquiry investigating his role in the Petrashevsky affair, when he finds that such an influence inspired his generation's westward gaze:

> And in view of this, are we, to whom this certain degree of education was given and in whom was aroused a thirst for knowledge and science, really to be accused—Are we really to be accused of the fact that we had so much curiosity as to speak sometimes about the West and about political events, to read contemporary books, and even to study it and scrutinize the Western movement as far as possible. (*Pss*, 18:122)[26]

In the late 1840s, when Dostoevsky was "infected with the ideas of theoretical socialism," especially with those of Charles Fourier, the upheaval in France and Italy encouraged youth throughout the continent to anticipate a return to those revolutionary ideals of "Liberté! Égalité! Fraternité!" that legally had guaranteed citizens freedom from the religious persecution which previously had engulfed Reformation Europe (*Pss*, 21:130).[27] The new Roman pontiff, Pius IX, granted amnesty to political prisoners and promised reforms to the enthusiastic crowds attending his religious ceremonies.[28] Dostoevsky's friend Alexander Milyukov describes the excitement in St. Petersburg in 1848: "From the first days of the Paris February Revolution the most unexpected events in Europe followed one after the other. Uprisings in Milan, Venice, and Naples responded to the unprecedented reforms of Pius IX."[29] Thus, in the spirit of the Westernizer Petr Chaadaev, who juxtaposes "la misérable

Byzance" of Russia with "la haute pensée de la religion," members of the 1840s intelligentsia looked to the Catholic West to provide freedom from a church aligned with Russian autocracy and its feudal system of serfdom.[30] Dostoevsky's acknowledged interest in Christian socialist movements and his fascination with "the radiant personhood of Christ himself" suggest that in his early period he believed in the potential for Russia's social transformation by embracing the universal humanistic values associated with Catholicism by Chaadaev (*Pss*, 21:10).[31]

The nineteenth-century French Catholic Church gained a number of fresh converts owing to a new policy of religious tolerance—one envisioned by the church's critic Jean-Jacques Rousseau in *Du Contrat social* (*On the Social Contract*, 1762)—as the faithful looked to Rome for protection against the civil unrest prevailing in Europe.[32] One such prominent ultramontanist priest, Félicité Robert de La Mennais (or Lamennais, as he came to be known), advocated the separation of church and state in a campaign against Gallicanism, a movement that encouraged nations to assert administrative control over their churches in order to limit the power of the papacy. In his demands for freedom of worship, Lamennais solicited the support of the Parisian Polish exile community, with whom he sympathized in the immediate aftermath of the November 1830 Polish uprising. The articles published in his journal *L'Avenir* (*The Future*) in 1830–31 continue Rousseau's promotion of Polish liberation, outlined in *Considérations sur le gouvernement de Pologne et sur sa réformation projettée* (*Reflections on the Government of Poland and on Its Proposed Reformation*, 1772), which boldly announces to Poland: "Vous ne serez jamais libres tant qu'il restera un seul soldat Russe en Pologne."[33] Even after the condemnation of the rebellion by Pope Gregory XVI and after the papal criticism of religious pluralism in *Mirari Vos* (1832), Lamennais continued to support the Polish cause with the publication of his *Hymne à la Pologne* (*Hymn to Poland*, 1833) and with his *Paroles d'un croyant* (*Words of a Believer*, 1833), which was influenced by Adam Mickiewicz's *Books of the Polish Nation and the Polish Pilgrims* (*Księgi narodu polskiego i pielgrzymstwa polskiego*, 1832).[34] Despite the condemnation of *Paroles d'un croyant* by Pope Gregory XVI in *Singulari Nos* (1834) for its contributing to rebellions against the established order and sedition within empires, Lamennais continued to publish in 1848–49 on Poland in the journals *Le Peuple constituant* (*The People Constituent*) and *Réforme* (*Reform*).[35] Such publications likely encouraged a tsarist government fighting former Polish officers in the suppression of a Hungarian revolt to suspect that Dostoevsky's interest in Alexander Milyukov's translation of *Paroles d'un croyant* linked him to the current Polish unrest (*Pss*, 18:158).[36] Indeed, Lamennais's democratic Christianity and Mickiewicz's Polish messianism had recently inspired the populism of Father Piotr Ściegienny, whose intricate network of co-conspirators the Moscow authorities were still unraveling in the late 1840s.[37] Dostoevsky shared a prison term in the Omsk fortress with a prominent member of Ściegienny's followers, Szymon Tokarzewski, whose fusion of Catholic spiritual devotion and patriotic zeal shapes his prison memoirs, *Seven Years in Penal Servitude* (*Siedem lat katorgi,* 1907).

The documents collected during their official investigation indicate that "the Petrashevtsy knew well the works of Lamennais," and his writings have been discussed alongside those of Henri de Saint-Simon and Étienne Cabet, as further evidence of the young Dostoevsky's fascination with utopian socialism.[38] In his 1864–65 notebook, Dostoevsky even praises Lamennais alongside the Dominican Jean-Baptiste Henri Lacordaire, presumably owing to their advancement of personal and political freedom through Christ: "attempts to renew Christianity in the greatest representatives of Catholicism, Lamennais and Lacordaire" (*Pss,* 20:189). However, the Commission of Inquiry, like Pope Gregory XVI, understood that Lamennais's *Paroles d'un croyant,* in stating that "les frères du Christ n'avaient pas été condamnés par leur père à l'esclavage," constitutes a challenge to the feudal social structure of the Russian Empire whose stability depended upon popular recognition of the tsar's divine right to rule.[39] Pope Gregory XVI considered the tsar the defender of the faithful within his realm, even while Eastern rite Catholics were being forcibly converted to Orthodoxy under Nicholas I.[40] The letter by Belinsky to Gogol, which Dostoevsky read aloud at a meeting of the Petrashevtsy at Durov's, challenges the political and religious institutions supporting serfdom and uses terms similar to Lamennais's in asserting that as "brothers in Christ . . . a brother cannot be a slave of his brother."[41] In addition, Belinsky admires the European Catholic for he acts "as an exposer [*oblichitel'*] of unjust authority, similar to European prophets" and finds that Voltaire is "more a son of Christ" than Gogol's "priests, bishops, metropolitans, and patriarchs."[42] During the investigation, Dostoevsky appeared naively ignorant of the serious implications of such Catholic theologies of liberation, even though his co-conspirators report that the commission particularly inquired about conflicting loyalties between the interests of the state and the "welfare of man [*blago cheloveka*]"[43] as well as the group's connections to Poland.[44] Despite having been questioned himself about Mikhail Butashevich-Petrashevsky's potential ties to Kiev University,[45] Dostoevsky did not recognize the official interest in his co-conspirators' links to unrest along Russia's Western border.[46] Still, Alexander Herzen's 1851 study *Du développement des idées révolutionnaires en Russie,* published by the Polish Democratic Society (Towarzystwo Demokratyczne Polskie, or TDP), draws a connection between the commencement of "la campagne de Hongrie" and the government's decision to impart to Butashevich-Petrashevsky "les proportions d'une vaste conjuration" which resulted in the mass arrests (*Ss,*

7:123).[47] For this reason, he finds that St. Petersburg will share with Warsaw a legacy of liberty in Russia that may gain momentum sufficient enough to challenge tsarist autocracy.

Dostoevsky never alludes to the substantial Catholic presence in the Petrashevsky Circle, which aroused the suspicions of a tsarist government anxious to quell news of the European unrest.[48] Although Jan Jastrzębski was the only Polish conspirator sent to Siberia, more than a half dozen Poles attended Petrashevsky's evenings.[49] Among those arrested in connection with the Petrashevsky conspiracy, Jastrzębski and the Debut brothers (Ippolit and Konstantin), who were descended from an ancient French family, identified themselves as Catholic during their interrogations.[50] In his article "The Founding of Rome and the Reign of Romulus" ("Osnovanie Rima i tsarstvovanie Romula"), Nikolai Mombelli envisions the renewal of Italy under the leadership of Pius IX and his constitutional government.[51] In addition, the Polish question entered the politics of the circle in a variety of ways, including Mombelli's translation of Adam Mickiewicz's poem to the Decembrists "To My Muscovite Friends" ("Do przyjaciół Moskali," 1832),[52] Nikolai Speshnev's links to Polish exiles, Butashevich-Petrashevsky's plans to transform the Congress Kingdom of Poland, and Jastrzębski's discussion of Polish liberation at Petrashevsky's.[53] The circle's fascination with the Jesuits is evident from their readings of Eugène Sue's anticlerical novel, *Le Juif errant* (*The Wandering Jew*, 1844–45), *Mémoires pour servir à l'histoire du Jacobinisme* (*Memoirs to Serve as a History of Jacobinism*, 1797) by the Jesuit Abbé Augustin de Barruel, and Théodore Dézamy's *Le Jésuitisme vaincu et anéanti par le socialisme* (*Jesuitism Vanquished and Annihilated by Socialism*, 1845).[54] On the basis of such studies, Speshnev and Mombelli were shaping their own secret society, because, as Fedor Lvov explains, Speshnev believed that the "jesuitical" method of secret intrigue (endorsed by Lvov, Petrashevsky, and Mombelli) represented one means of revolutionizing Russian society.[55]

The young Dostoevsky also enjoyed *Le Juif errant*, whose presentation of the ambitious and avaricious Jesuit intriguer, M. Rodin, advanced the association of the Society of Jesus with conspiracy on Russian soil (*Pss*, 28.1:110). The romantics of this generation likely found particularly appealing Sue's criticism of Russia's post-Napoleonic suppression of Polish nationalism. In the depiction of a Polish mother and her offspring, who were exiled to Tobolsk, the Russians are described as treating the Poles as slaves (*esclaves*).[56] Already in *The Double*, Dostoevsky links jesuitical intrigue and the historic pretender Otrepev to contemporary St. Petersburg in the fantastical imaginings of his hero Yakov Golyadkin. The additional association of Golyadkin "with deception and imposture," made by his colleague Nestor Vakhrameev, demonstrates Dostoevsky's early familiarity with the type of jesuitical schemes promoted by his co-conspirators (*Pss*, 1:414).[57] The narrator's jocular commentary on his hero—"Mr. Golyadkin . . . brushes against the reputation of Grigory Otrepev"—and Golyadkin's hyperbolic language display the levity with which the young Dostoevsky regards jesuitical plans for subversive activities (*Pss*, 1:390). At the same time, Golyadkin's reference to the Jesuits, who "even set as their own principle to consider all means suitable so long as the goal could be attained," attests to Dostoevsky's early association of casuistry with the Society of Jesus, to which he returns in *Crime and Punishment* (*Pss*, 1:351).[58] This traditional portrayal of conspiratorial Jesuits strikingly contrasts with that of Speshnev, who likens the Jesuits' missions in the New World to the building of modern communist communities: "No matter how it's turned, I cannot find a great difference between the social organization of the first Christians, monasteries, and state of the Jesuits and the social organization of the communists."[59]

Dostoevsky did not embrace these Catholic political models advanced by members of the Petrashevsky Circle and failed to perceive how seriously the Third Section regarded his participation in the group. The assignment of police agent Petr Antonelli—"this swine, fittingly bearing the surname of the famous cardinal"—to the Petrashevsky Circle suggests that the Third Section noted from an early period the significant number of Petrashevtsy with Western heritage.[60] Dostoevsky was not aware that his ancestral links to Lithuanian nobility and the Catholic faith of his grandfather, a Uniate priest, *essentially* connected him to the Catholics in the group and, consequently, to some of the more politically controversial ideas expressed by the Petrashevtsy.[61] All the same, Dostoevsky's heritage, when coupled with his knowledge of Lamennais and reading of religious critiques in Belinsky's letter, led a government wary of unrest in its Western borderlands to believe him capable of fomenting treasonous rebellion against the monarchy. Dostoevsky's own naïveté attests to his inherent belief in the international humanism espoused by many in his circle, but in Siberia he began the process of learning "to hate with a political hatred" those whose concepts of nationality and nationhood conflicted with his own Russocentric weltanschauung.[62] There, the Polish messianism of his fellow inmates at Omsk and Napoleon III's attempts to enhance Catholic influence in the Holy Land motivated Dostoevsky's identification of these nations with a belligerent Roman Catholicism, whose disciples dedicated themselves to expanding the political sphere of Western Christendom by encroaching on the territories of the Orthodox East.

DOSTOEVSKY ON REVOLUTIONARY CATHOLICISM

While Dostoevsky spent approximately a third of his adult life living in involuntary exile in Siberia and Europe, he was surrounded by nationalities hostile to Russia's empire-building. In correspondence with his close friend and fellow Petrashevets Apollon Maikov, Dostoevsky concludes that Russia "is necessary for my *writing* and necessary for work" and worries that "I am losing touch with Russia. There is no Russian air and no people" (*Pss*, 28.2:204, 322). When encountering the French, Poles, and Germans, Dostoevsky transcends "the loneliness of exile" by "thumping language of national pride" while categorizing other nations according to a reductionist essentialism informed by his Russocentrism.[63] Thus, Geneva becomes "a boring, gloomy, stupid Protestant city," Poles are "ruined" by Jesuitism, and France, despite its "diverse governments" of "kings, republics, and Napoleon III" is the "1,000-year representative of Western Catholicism" (*Pss*, 28.2:252; 20:190; 21:245). This tendency dates from his depiction of the Crimean War in his ode "On the European Events in the Year 1854" ("Na evropeiskie sobytiia v 1854 godu," 1854), which presents the conflict as a religious dispute between the Slavic world and the Catholic West. In a parallel to the anti-European imagery in Pushkin's famous poem on the Polish 1830 uprising, "To the Slanderers of Russia" ("Klevetnikam Rossii"), Dostoevsky's ode repeatedly differentiates the Slavic East from Western nations with the pronouns you (*vy*) and we (*my*).[64] For Dostoevsky, Napoleonic France fights alongside the Islamic persecutors of the church while the Orthodox Russians defend the crucified Christ:

> We did not thoughtlessly lose our faith
> (As would some Western nation);
> We were resurrected from the dead by our faith,
> And by its faith lives the Slavic race. (*Pss*, 2:403)

Dostoevsky continues to give voice to anti-Western sentiment in his post-Siberian writings as he addresses the Gallomania prevalent among the Russian intelligentsia in the 1860s. Through the journals *Time* (*Vremia*) and *Epoch* (*Èpokha*), which he edited with his brother Mikhail in the 1860s, Dostoevsky promotes a rapprochement between the intelligentsia and the Russian people (*narod*) based on their common cultural heritage rooted in the Russian land, or soil (*pochva*). However, the ethnic and religious tensions exposed in the wake of the 1863 Polish uprising presented an immediate political challenge to Dostoevsky's vision of a harmonious fusion of disparate elements within Russian society. He understands the conflict as a war between two Slavic nations—"a war of two Christianities—this is the beginning of the future war of Orthodoxy with Catholicism, in other words—of the Slavic genius with European civilization" (*Pss*, 20:170). Dostoevsky claims Ukraine, or the area where "Little Russians [*Malorussy*]" resided, for the Orthodox even though he linked the "Little Russian and Polish characters" and found the former to be one of the "Lesser [*Melkie*] Slavs" (*Pss*, 21:266,

267). This essentialist approach to Western nations, in particular, encourages Dostoevsky to view contemporary European political affairs within a medieval theological context so that socialism comes to represent a nineteenth-century manifestation of Reformation Jesuitism and European revolutionaries form a transnational Catholic conspiracy.

In his 1864–65 notebook, Dostoevsky connects contemporary European agitation to Pius IX's attempt to defend his temporal realm, since "much strength in Europe will be spent on this movement on behalf of the pope and in opposition to this movement" (*Pss*, 20:189). He predicts that Europe will experience a Catholic revival "in two phases—in Jesuitism and in socialism" as a rejuvenated church joins "with the revolutionaries and with the socialists" to reshape Europe (*Pss*, 20:189). Poland, with its "artificial, aristocratic, and jesuitical" civilization, unites Catholicism with revolutionary activism so that, despite papal opposition to the Polish uprising and Pius IX's *Syllabus*, Dostoevsky views the Polish unrest as the natural consequence of papal interference in national political issues, because "the papacy has more deeply and fully penetrated *all of the West* than is thought" (*Pss*, 28.2:34; 20:190). Therefore, for Dostoevsky, the Polish insurrection becomes a modern "product of the papacy" in the tradition of "former Reformations," Rousseau, the French Revolution, and socialism (*Pss*, 20:190). Such a political analysis suggests that Dostoevsky agrees with a frequent Orthodox criticism of the expansion of papal authority, particularly during the Reformation period with the sanctioning of the Society of Jesus and in the nineteenth century with the doctrine of papal infallibility.[65] The writings of Enlightenment philosophes like Voltaire and Rousseau, whose political ideas had inspired the 1789 Revolution, share this common concern over the papacy's move "towards a centralized autocracy modeled on the absolute monarchies of the seventeenth and eighteenth centuries" in response to the Protestant Reformation.[66] Dostoevsky concludes that in their efforts to limit papal power European idealists like Rousseau seek the "dream of recreating anew the world by reason and experience" without realizing that such a world remains a fantasy: "Lie of Rousseau. . . . Historical truth. Socialists: two million heads. Poland and socialists. Banquet of Garibaldi" (*Pss*, 29.1:214; 20:189).[67] Dostoevsky's brief note reveals a common socialist link among Polish revolutionaries, Herzen's émigré circle, and agitators for Italian independence through Garibaldi's London banquet.[68] At the same time, it connects Rousseau to the Poles for a second time in Dostoevsky's notebooks and suggests his familiarity with the Herzen circle's identification with Rousseau's defense of Poland.[69] Such evidence of Catholic peoples united around the banner of socialism lends credence to Prince Myshkin's claim that socialism arises "from despair, in contradistinction to Catholicism in a moral sense, in order to replace the lost moral authority of religion with itself, in order to quench the spiritual thirst of parched humanity and save it not by Christ but also by violence!" (*Pss,* 8:451).

In this respect, Dostoevsky describes Western Christendom heretofore as historically transcendent in contrast to those influenced by a progressive historical dialectic, such as that advanced by Karl Marx. For example, while Herzen acknowledges that vestiges of Catholic ideas and institutions may impact modern behaviors, he still relegates to a bygone era the dominant influence that Catholicism and Protestantism enjoyed on the world stage, since they "ont accompli de grandes choses" but "ont dépouillé le trône et l'autel de leur prestige, sans réaliser la liberté" (*Ss,* 7:273).[70] Dostoevsky, on the other hand, repeatedly recognizes Catholicism's ability to appeal to idealists who validate the Roman church with their martyrdom during the French Revolution, the Polish uprisings, and the papal struggle against the forces for the unification of the Italian peninsula (*Pss,* 21:152; 20:99–100, 189). For him, the Franco-Prussian War (1870–71) represents yet another European clash of Protestant and Catholic civilizations, whose violence signifies "in our 19th and so enlightened century the resurrection of religious troubles, and perhaps even wars, fitting only to the barbarity of the Middle Ages" (*Pss,* 21:242). Similarly, the exchange of correspondence between the German Emperor Wilhelm I and Pius IX over the issue of papal infallibility becomes another chapter in Reformation history when the Protestant "rebels" had rejected the papal "mediator" in favor of a direct relationship with God (*Pss,* 21:207). In *Diary of a Writer,* Dostoevsky develops this historical dimension to contemporary European affairs which he depicts in terms of a clash between the German and Catholic ideas with roots in "Luther's Protestantism" and "the spirit of a pope of the Middle Ages" (*Pss,* 25:7–8). Even Ivan Karamazov participates in this theological discussion when placing his personal rebellion against God's world within the context of Reformation history, as Diane Oenning Thompson finds: "Ivan brings Christ back to earth during the worst period in the history of the Western Church, at a time of hell on earth instituted by the Catholic Church."[71]

Catholicism remains this potent force so long as the world remains in the "transitional" period of history that Dostoevsky identifies as "Civilization" in 1864–65 notes on "Socialism and Christianity" ("Sotsializm i khristianstvo") but does not exist in the final stage in human development—"Christianity"— when the ideal is achieved (*Pss,* 20:194). Hence, when frequently applying the word "civilization [*tsivilizatsiia*]" to European culture and Poland, Dostoevsky understands the term as antithetical to Christianity, as he clarifies in "The Response of the Editorship of *Time* to the Attack of *Moscow News*" ("Otvet redaktsii 'Vremeni' na napadenie 'Moskovskikh vedomostei,'" 1863): "European civilization, which is the fruit of Europe, in essence, for its own place in Europe, in Poland (maybe, precisely because the Poles are Slavs),

developed an anti-national, anti-civic, and anti-Christian spirit" (*Pss*, 20:99).
The highest human achievement of this period remains socialism, owing to
its denial of self for others, but socialism in Dostoevsky's *Diary of a Writer*,
as Denis Dirscherl discusses, becomes increasingly equated with compulsion
rather than with "consciously developed individual personalities" united in
a pursuit "of the beauty of the ideal" (*Pss*, 20:193).[72] Civilization provides
such uncertainty for the individual who has lost "the source of living life"
so that she or he looks to Catholicism, or its derivative socialism, to provide
this ideal (*Pss*, 20:192). For this reason, Dostoevsky fears that Russians like
Prince Ivan Gagarin, S. J., decide not only "to cross over to Catholicism, but
even to skip straight to the Jesuits" (*Pss*, 23:43).[73] Therefore, as Dostoevsky
comes to identify more closely the future period of Christianity with Russian
Orthodoxy in his *Diary of a Writer*, he grows increasingly critical of Catholic
influence on Russian culture.

Nevertheless, iconic Catholic figures, such as Nicolaus Copernicus, the
Inquisitor, and Napoleon Bonaparte, still appeal to several of Dostoevsky's
Russian characters, particularly those of the wanderer type, which Dostoevsky
equates with Pushkin's Evgeny Onegin as he "wanders in grief about his
native land and lands foreign" (*Pss*, 26:140). Many of these wanderers in-
fuse their speech with Catholic historical and literary references present in
the agitational writings of Dostoevsky's Russian contemporaries living in the
West, for example, Herzen and Bakunin. Dostoevsky's appropriation of these
references for his Westernized Russians, who employ them in quotidian con-
texts, suggests an emphasis on the presence of "the language of the literary" in
"public performances" as well as in "most intimate or passionate moments."[74]
Often, the aesthetic sense of Dostoevsky's displaced characters, revealed in
such moments as Nikolai Stavrogin's admiration of Claude Lorrain's *Acis and
Galatea* or Ivan Karamazov's appraisal of Dante, signals a vulnerability to a
Catholicizing influence but simultaneously celebrates "the responsiveness to
the whole world" that Dostoevsky finds characteristic of the Russian nationality (*Pss*, 26:145).[75] James P. Scanlan finds Dostoevsky's belief in "Russian universality" present in his writings of the 1860s and concludes that the concept
promotes Russians' ability to transcend "petty differences . . . in the name
of what is universally human."[76] Such responsiveness leaves Dostoevsky's
Russian characters open to exploitation by predatory types from Catholic nations (often of Polish origin) that populate Dostoevsky's fiction.

Dostoevsky does not impart to these types a sophisticated knowledge
of international literary or historical traditions that play a formative role
for his Russian personages, but instead he frequently depicts them as un-
imaginative individuals who display a proclivity for uttering stock phrases
and seek to profit financially from their encounters with Russians.[77] A focus
on the material to the detriment of the spiritual is evident in Dostoevsky's

characterization of Catholics and revolutionaries, who share a similar lack of gravitas necessary for a principled stance: "Live, drink, eat, and be merry, and do not think about the soul; thus both the Catholic and the revolutionary reason" (*Pss,* 24:175). Although types from Catholic nations frequently appear vapid and predatorily materialistic (Mlle Blanche, de Grieux, and his Polish gamblers), the types' brief allusions to political events such as the partition of Poland in *The Brothers Karamazov* or the formation of the Third Republic in France in *The Adolescent* (*Podrostok,* 1874–75) link them to a Catholic tradition of revolutionary activism, which Dostoevsky identifies with modern Jesuitism and contemporary socialism (*Pss,* 14:383; 13:350). An identification of lackeyism with Catholic conspiracy ("L'âme d'un conspirateur and l'âme d'un laquais") often informs his depictions of Polish and French agitators so that his little Polacks promote nationalist causes over drinks, and Frenchmen offer eloquent, but insipid, revolutionary rhetoric (*Pss,* 15:205).[78] Yet, these types fail to continue the Catholic aesthetic tradition that once inspired the quest of Don Quixote, which Herzen associates with the revolutionaries of his own generation. Instead, Dostoevsky's Don Quixotes (Prince Myshkin and Stepan Verkhovensky) are Russians in search of beautiful forms, while his Poles often seem preoccupied with the acquisition of wealth, particularly at the expense of the Russians they encounter. In this respect, the Poles appear as representatives of a nascent bourgeoisie in Russia and heirs to his French types in *Winter Notes on Summer Impressions* (*Zimnie zametki o letnikh vpechatleniiakh,* 1863) that exploit unwary Russian travelers. Furthermore, by limiting the Poles' speech and information about their own political biographies in *Notes from the House of the Dead* (*Zapiski iz mertvogo doma,* 1860–62) and *The Brothers Karamazov,* Dostoevsky also invalidates their principled protests, for they act as injured parties without significant motivating causes.

For those literati publishing during the reigns of Nicholas I and Alexander II, references to literary figures served as Aesopian encoding whereby textual references to well-known types, for example, Otrepev, Don Quixote, or Hamlet, disclose their authors' conservative or progressive sympathies. The presence of such types in Dostoevsky's writings throughout his literary career suggests his conscious employment of Aesopian language for "every age has its own type of words and expressions that are given as a signal to speak freely, to call things by their own names, without any mental restrictions and euphemisms."[79] However, in neglecting to establish for his characters from Catholic nations a familiarity with native traditions of subversive speech, such as the French identification with the Napoleonic hero or the Polish invocation of Mickiewicz's verse, Dostoevsky frequently leaves these personages with the fanaticism of revolutionary converts but without an educated knowledge of the history of their national political causes. Their

Napoleons, Galileos, and Copernicuses become part of the Russian revolutionary tradition in Dostoevsky's novels *Crime and Punishment, Demons,* and *The Brothers Karamazov* as his Russian intellectuals integrate them into their political rhetoric. Even the Reformation figure of the Grand Inquisitor, to whom Dostoevsky provides the space necessary to justify his revision of biblical Christianity, relies on an exegesis of only the Holy Writ despite his emphasis on the fifteen centuries of Christian suffering since Christ's former appearance on earth. Ivan, on the other hand, in this discussion of rebellion with his brother Alesha, which surrounds "The Grand Inquisitor" ("Velikii inkvizitor"), includes references to Dante, Victor Hugo, and Shakespeare to illustrate his arguments. This failure to impart to his revolutionaries from Catholic nations a grounding in their own traditions allows Dostoevsky to exploit the gap that he perceives between the ideals inspired by Roman Catholicism and the violence perpetuated by representatives of Western Christendom.

PART I

Contact with Catholics in the Journeys East and West

Yes, truly, it is a great thing for a Nation that it get an articulate voice; that it produce a man who will speak-forth melodiously what the heart of it means! Italy, for example, poor Italy lies dismembered, scattered asunder, not appearing in any protocol or treaty as a unity at all; yet the noble Italy is actually *one:* Italy produced its Dante; Italy can speak! The Czar of all the Russias, he is strong, with so many bayonets, Cossacks, and cannons; and does a great feat in keeping such a tract of Earth politically together; but he cannot yet speak. Something great in him, but it is a dumb greatness. He has had no voice of genius, to be heard of all men and times. He must learn to speak. He is a great dumb monster hitherto. His cannons and Cossacks will all have rusted into nonentity, while that Dante's voice is still audible. The Nation that has a Dante is bound together as no dumb Russia can be.
—Thomas Carlyle, *Heroes, Hero-Worship and the Heroic in History* (1841)

Chapter One

Silencing Catholic Revolutionaries
in *House of the Dead*

> "I am a dead man—dead to society, without
> the pity they bestow on those whose souls have
> passed to judgment."
> —Charles Dickens, *The Posthumous Papers of
> the Pickwick Club* (1836–37)

ALTHOUGH DOSTOEVSKY'S *House of the Dead* was
celebrated by his contemporaries for its realistic portrayals of the Russian
convicts with whom he shared a four-year term in the Omsk prison fortress,
the autobiographical novel also marks the germination of his association of
Polish revolutionaries with modern Jesuitism when his narrator Alexander
Petrovich Goryanchikov describes Aleksander Mirecki's "duplicity," "deep
skepticism," and "jesuitical adroitness and prudence" (*Pss*, 4:209).[1] The participation of his fellow Catholic inmates in conspiracies that enjoyed clerical
support in Poland, the overwhelmingly Catholic identity of Polish insurgents
in the 1840s, and witness accounts depicting the Omsk Poles' participation
in Catholic mass and celebration of Catholic Christmas attest to the spiritual
devotion of Dostoevsky's fellow Polish inmates.[2] Also, Goryanchikov's assertion that the Russian prisoners do not "reproach" the Polish political prisoners "for their origin of birth, their faith, or their manner of thinking" establishes (Catholic) faith as a shared Polish trait, which separates the ethnicity
as a group from the remaining prisoners in Omsk (*Pss*, 4:210). All the same,
in *House of the Dead,* Dostoevsky on only rare occasions explores the Poles'
political and religious beliefs, and his friend Milyukov offers an explanation
for this silence in his reminiscences when he remembers that Dostoevsky
was forced by the censors "to discard the episode about the exiled Poles and
the political prisoners from his work" but provided their circle with "not a
few interesting details" on this subject.[3] Nevertheless, the surviving depictions of the political prisoners in Dostoevsky's autobiographical novel remain
his most complex and diverse portrayals of Catholic revolutionaries but still

fail to attain the sophisticated degree of artistic achievement evident in his portraits of the Russian convicts. Although eight out of the twelve prisoners whom Goryanchikov categorizes as prisoners of his same social class are Polish—and although Dostoevsky lived in the barracks with many of these Polish prisoners—Goryanchikov does not dedicate much space in his memoirs to his interaction with these inmates. Consequently, Goryanchikov's remembrances of the Poles with whom he was imprisoned reflect in a very limited manner the encounters that Dostoevsky shared with the eight Polish political prisoners in Omsk.

Because of the remembrances written by Dostoevsky's fellow prisoners, Tokarzewski and Józef Bogusławski, as well as the thorough research of Vladimir Dyakov and Wiktoria Śliwowska, considerable biographical information about Dostoevsky's Catholic inmates, their spiritual backgrounds, and their camp experiences has been documented. Over the course of the past century, Dostoevsky scholars have approached the remembrances with caution, owing in part to Tokarzewski's liberal borrowings from Bogusławski's and Dostoevsky's texts.[4] Tokarzewski's preservation of Bogusławski's recollections after the latter's death in 1857 and editing of the recollections for their publication in the newspaper *New Reform* (*Nowa reforma*) in 1896 further frustrate attempts by Dostoevsky's biographers to supply verifiable information about the Russian author's prison term in Omsk.[5] Yet, the research of Dyakov and Śliwowska, when combined with various accounts from firsthand witnesses of Dostoevsky's Siberian period, provides valuable historical context to the Polish remembrances. Furthermore, their research on Polish exiles in Siberia demonstrates that while Dostoevsky was working on *House of the Dead* in Semipalatinsk, as Baron Alexander Wrangel recalls, Dostoevsky still regularly encountered Polish political exiles in both professional and social situations.[6] Owing to the temporal divide between Dostoevsky's prison term in Omsk (1850–54) and the publication of *House of the Dead,* both his personal history in exile and his reintroduction to the literary scene in St. Petersburg shape the writing of his autobiographical novel. The chapters depicting the Poles predominantly fall in the second part of the novel, when Goryanchikov abandons the structured chronology of the first part for an uncertain temporal progression arising from the episodic nature of his remembrances.[7] Personal histories of Dostoevsky and his fellow Catholic prisoners reveal that, even when taking into account concerns over the tsarist censor and the fragmentary nature of Goryanchikov's notebook (*tetradka*), these chapters still disclose Dostoevsky's failure to empathize with the Polish political prisoners as writers, revolutionaries, and Christians, owing in part to their espousal of a Catholic liberation theology that challenged the tsars' divine right to rule Poland (*Pss,* 4:8).

THE POLITICAL BACKGROUND
OF DOSTOEVSKY'S POLES

Although Nicholas I's repressive policies protected the Congress Kingdom from the violence spreading through continental Europe in 1848, Polish Catholic revolutionaries were emboldened in Prussian and Austrian territories to pursue the cause for Poland's liberation, which had suffered a recent setback in the failure of the 1846 uprising in Krakow. The creation of a Second Republic in France, a more liberal regime in Prussia, and unrest in Vienna encouraged Poles to agitate for independence in Poznania and Galicia and to lend support to armed nationalist movements in Italy and Hungary. Nicholas, at the request of the Austrian government, sent Russian reinforcements under the leadership of Field Marshall Ivan Paskevich, who had suppressed the 1830–31 Warsaw uprising, to crush the Hungarian rebellion, which resulted in Polish conspirators fleeing into Ottoman territory. Although Goryanchikov's narrative remains vague about the political activities of Dostoevsky's Polish inmates, biographical data on the eight prisoners shows their active participation in these subversive activities. Indeed, Bogusławski's description of an encounter with a Cossack regiment on his journey to Omsk suggests an automatic association between these rebellions and the Polish prisoners in Siberia, since upon hearing of the capture of Artur Gorgey's army by the Russians, a group of Cossacks assume that Bogusławski, Tokarzewski, and Józef Żochowski are members "from that same gang."[8] Dostoevsky, unable or unwilling to disclose their backgrounds out of political, religious, or aesthetic considerations, likely depended on this immediate association, just as he assumed the reader's familiarity with his own status as a political prisoner.[9] However, the reader, forced to draw on this cultural stereotype in the absence of historically specific information pertaining to Goryanchikov's Poles, does not obtain a clear motivation for the animosity existing between Goryanchikov and the Polish comrades noted in *House of the Dead,* or for its author's critical commentary on Polish liberation movements in the aftermath of the 1863 January uprising in Warsaw. The exile history of the Polish Catholics, whose ties to Polish and Russian conspirators aligned them with both religious and political movements to which Dostoevsky remained hostile, reveals substantial motivations for the Russo-Polish tensions evident in *House of the Dead.*

When Dostoevsky entered the prison fortress in Omsk in January 1850, he did not encounter Polish armchair revolutionaries but several active Catholic conspirators, some of whom, in a manner similar to Dostoevsky's fellow Petrashevets Durov, sacrificed their health for their political convictions. Bogusławski and Tokarzewski, who were the only Polish Catholic political prisoners to share Dostoevsky's entire prison term, were arrested in connection with two famous subversive groups—the Konarski and Ściegienny conspiracies, respectively. In 1835, Szymon Konarski had helped organize in Krakow the Association of the Polish People (Stowarzyszenie Ludu Polskiego), dedicated to liberty and brotherhood for humanity, for which the authorities had arrested him along with approximately 1,000 of his followers in 1838.[10] By the time that Dostoevsky met the Polish Catholic noble Bogusławski in Omsk, the latter was a recidivist offender who had returned to his homeland in 1845 after his first exile only to be arrested again in 1846 for his contact with Apolin Hofmeister, a member of the centrist Polish Democratic Society, and Jan Röhr, who served as an emissary for a TDP military leader, Ludwik Mierosławski, during the planning of the 1846 uprising in Poznan.[11] Mirecki, the Pole who serves as Goryanchikov's guide to prison etiquette and whom Dostoevsky recalls in his *Diary of a Writer*, shared through his co-conspirator Karol Ruprecht a connection with Bogusławski, since Ruprecht had ties to Röhr's Poznania conspiracy while studying in Berlin.[12] In addition, while Michał Janik suggests a political connection between Konarski's Association and Petrashevsky, there is also a link between the TDP and Speshnev.[13] Speshnev's correspondence with Polish exile Edmund Chojecki criticizes the theory of Henryk Kamieński, whose populism was influenced by the TDP and encouraged by the efforts of the revolutionary Catholic priest, Father Piotr Ściegienny.[14]

Ściegienny's movement encouraged Tokarzewski to agitate on his behalf in Lublin and Kielce, where Ściegienny was planning popular uprisings with the goal of establishing a "theocratic village of substantial farmers living harmoniously in the love of God."[15] Although Ściegienny was arrested in 1844 before the rebellion occurred, Tokarzewski escaped arrest until the Austrian police seized him and handed him over to the Russian authorities in 1846. Tokarzewski continued to sustain contact with his co-conspirators in Siberia, where he was surrounded with people connected to Ściegienny. Hipolit Raciborski, who had organized an excursion of Ściegienny's followers (including Tokarzewski) to Kielce, was among the convicts with whom Tokarzewski set out from Tobolsk to Ust-Kamenogorsk (a place where Tokarzewski, Bogusławski, and Żochowski served part of their term).[16] Ksawery Stobnicki, who was forcibly conscripted and served in Tomsk for his role in the conspiracy, met the prisoners on their way to Ust-Kamenogorsk and later sent Tokarzewski a letter, which was found by the authorities and gave them cause to send the three Poles to Omsk where they could be observed more closely.[17] While in Omsk, Tokarzewski served time with fellow Ściegienny conspirator Ludwik Korczyński (unnamed in *House of the Dead*), who arrived at the fortress in July 1850 for a four-year term.[18] Tokarzewski's dedication to the Polish liberation movement encouraged him to continue to maintain contact with Polish exiles while in Omsk.[19] In addition, Tokarzewski discusses in a general manner that owing to a prison work detail, he was able to discuss his homeland in the houses of Omsk merchants who hired the Polish prisoners to paint: "We were asked about Poland, about our customs, about our religion, and about the entire social and cultural system in our land."[20]

Żochowski, the last of the four Polish political inmates residing in Omsk when Dostoevsky arrived at the prison, had been sent to Siberia for his speech in support of the Poznanian rebels, which he had delivered at the Cathedral of St. John in Warsaw at the grave of the prominent Polish statesman Stanisław Małachowski.[21] Żochowski's background as a former member of the Piarist Order, who had established contact with communist priests and had participated in the 1830 uprising, contributed to the severity of his sentence, which was initially one of capital punishment before its commutation to ten years hard labor in a fortress.[22] Żochowski met Bogusławski and his former student Tokarzewski in the prison at Tobolsk, from whence they began their journey to Ust-Kamenogorsk, where the authorities determined that he should be sent on with Tokarzewski and Bogusławski to Omsk for his "notes written in the style of the apocalypse."[23] By the time that Dostoevsky met Żochowski, he was an invalid, owing to a flogging he received upon arrival at the Omsk fortress at the order of the commandant of the prison, Major Krivtsov, whom Dostoevsky describes in an 1854 letter to his brother as a "petty barbarian," "drunk," and "everything rotten one could only imagine" (*Pss*, 28.1:169). Because he was in the prison hospital, Żochowski was questioned along with Dostoevsky and Durov during an 1850 official inquiry into the hospital's violation of regulations that forbade political prisoners from writing during their convalescence. Petr Martyanov identifies this as a moment of solidarity between the Russians and Poles, for the latter "held their answer in unison with the Russians" so that the investigator failed to discover anything incriminating.[24] Since Żochowski died in the prison in December 1851 and Mirecki was released from prison in November 1851, Dostoevsky spent only two years of his incarceration with these two prisoners, who represent a significant part of Goryanchikov's discussion of the Polish prisoners.

Although Dostoevsky served the same approximate amount of time with Mirecki and Żochowski as he did with the two Poles—Józef Anczykowski and Karol Bem—who completed two-year sentences at Omsk, Goryanchikov devotes little space to the latter two conspirators. The Polish noble Anczykowski, a former participant in the 1830 uprising, who escaped official notice by living under an assumed name, was found agitating among the peasants for armed rebellion in 1846 and fled to Galicia, where the Austrian authorities seized him.[25] Bem, who is remembered primarily as a talented painter by his fellow inmates, was arrested by Austrian authorities for his participation in the 1846 uprising in Krakow. Also, Jan Musiałowicz (not named by Goryanchikov), who was sentenced to a four-year term for his participation in armed insurrections in 1846, arrived along with Anczykowski, Bem, and Korczyński at the Omsk prison in July 1850. These four latecomers also do not figure prominently in Tokarzewski's and Bogusławski's discussions of Omsk, which, like *House of the Dead*, focus more on the early period of their imprisonment when Major Krivtsov's maltreatment of the political prisoners posed a more serious threat to the well-being of the Poles.[26] However, the presence of Bem's name in the notes to the Polish scenes of *The Brothers Karamazov*, in which a Pole bears a Russified version of Musiałowicz's surname, suggests that Dostoevsky's experience with this later group shapes his caricatural portraits of Polish revolutionaries, especially since Musiałowicz's dedication to the Polish cause resulted in his 1863 arrest and a second term of exile (*Pss*, 15:296).[27] Such a tendency indicates that Dostoevsky's unusual opportunity in Omsk to observe Polish nationalists in close quarters provided the basis for his subsequent fictional portrayals of Poles in his novels.[28]

DOSTOEVSKY'S ENCOUNTER WITH THE POLISH CATHOLIC EXILE EXPERIENCE

Bogusławski's and Tokarzewski's remembrances offer insights into the nature of the political discussions in the fortress, since they continue what Stanislaw Eile identifies as the Polish romantic tradition of portraying Siberia as "the national Calvary": "The sinister aspect of that land followed the apocalyptic images of persecution and deportations in Mickiewicz's *Dziady* [*Forefathers' Eve*], as did the ethics of moral elevation through suffering, since the Siberian hell usually appeared as breeding grounds for patriotic exaltation and sainthood."[29] In a letter to his older brother written soon after his release, Dostoevsky complains of Jastrzębski's similar tendency to exaggerate the hardships of their Siberian journey while traveling from St. Petersburg to Tobolsk: "I was enjoying myself, Durov chattered incessantly, and Jastrzębski envisioned some unusual future terrors" (*Pss*, 28.1:167). This gentle mockery of his co-conspirator's anxiety reveals both a familiarity with and a critical evaluation of the Polish Siberian narrative owing to its hyperbolic presentation of suffering to heighten martyrdom. Goryanchikov's allusion to Bogusławski's "paradoxical notions" and his aforementioned observation that the Russian prisoners did not reproach the Poles for their faith or manner of thought suggest that the Poles in Omsk communicated political and religious ideologies to the Russian inmates, as witness testimony indicates (*Pss*, 4:216, 210). A comparative examination of the firsthand accounts reveals that since the Polish inmates directly challenged the Russians among whom they lived, Dostoevsky was exposed in Omsk to Christian theologies of liberation whose rhetoric necessarily conflicted with his own vision of an Orthodox Russian Empire.

By all accounts, Żochowski was the Polish inmate most clearly identified with the Christian tradition, so that his death in Omsk reads in the Polish remembrances as the fate of a martyr. Martyanov names him a "fanatic of the Polish idea" who tells officials during the aforementioned hospital investigation: "No we don't write anything, we only pray and God's angels in heaven write for us."[30] Tokarzewski and Goryanchikov note his continuous praying for which the other prisoners respected him, but Goryanchikov finds his ideas so incoherent that he concludes Żochowski "was somewhat damaged in the mind" (*Pss*, 4:211).[31] Since Żochowski and Dostoevsky both spent time in the prison hospital, Dostoevsky knew of the elderly Pole's fervent belief in Catholicism as "the religion of the ages and that another real religion never was and is unlikely to be in the future, since in the state of fallen nature there can not be a religion without a mediator, and you have no other mediator than Jesus Christ, because only he was God-man."[32] Indeed, the presence of his study *The Life of Jesus* (*Życie Jezusa Chrystusa*, 1847), which focuses on Jesus as the spiritual messiah, in his court file suggests that Żochowski's faith contributed to the severity of his sentence.[33] Since Dostoevsky took David Strauss's controversial analysis of the historical Jesus, *The Life of Jesus Critically Examined* (*Das Leben Jesu kritisch bearbeitet*, 1835–36), from the Petrashevsky Circle's library, the topic of Żochowski's final publication would have interested him, even though Goryanchikov mentions only the failure of the elderly Pole's published astronomy research (*Pss*, 4:211).[34]

Żochowski's flogging, known throughout the local community, is an important factor in establishing the adversarial relationship at Omsk between the Polish political prisoners and the Russian military authorities, at whom Bogusławski and Tokarzewski primarily direct their animosity throughout their narratives. Already from their first encounter with the Major, Tokarzewski and Bogusławski discuss his particular hostility toward the Poles. Upon meeting the prisoners in their bedraggled condition owing to the lengthy journey on foot to the fortress, the Major screams: "What is this? What is this? Can these be the fortress convicts? The hard labor convicts? In civilian clothing? Unshaven? With beards and mustaches? What about the regulations? How can this be?"[35] When Żochowski responds with "a look of indignation" that he is "a prisoner of the state," the Major becomes enraged and orders that Żochowski immediately receive 300 lashes for his impudence; the Major then turns to the remaining two arrivals and threatens: "I will teach you; I will show you what service is."[36] Dostoevsky's decision to include Żochowski's history with the Major, even though he does not witness the event with his own eyes, may be motivated by his desire to refer to an infamous affair, which involved the Major. However, Goryanchikov's emphasis on the extraordinary nature of the flogging indicates that Dostoevsky himself is attempting to limit the incident's significance for the Siberian martyr narrative: "It is necessary, however, to state the whole truth: from this example one should by no means judge the Siberian authorities' treatment of the exiles from the nobility, no matter who these exiles are—Russians or Poles" (*Pss*, 4:211). Instead, in Dostoevsky's description of the scene, Goryanchikov isolates mitigating circumstances for the Major's behavior by finding that the "rather dull and perhaps unpleasant" Żochowski, "then having badly understood Russian and having thought that they were being asked: who were they? vagabonds or robbers, answered: 'We are not vagabonds but political prisoners'" (*Pss*, 4:210–11). The presence in *House of the Dead* of this flogging account attests to the author's familiarity with the nature of the Polish Siberian martyrology, which is suffused with Polish Catholic messianism.

Since Tokarzewski appears more effusive than the other Polish prisoners in the Polish reminiscences and shared a barracks with Dostoevsky during part of their imprisonment, the Russian novelist could not have avoided completely his fellow prisoner's irrepressible outpouring of Polish nationalism. Throughout his account of his first Siberian journey, Tokarzewski makes frequent references to patriotic poems and songs shared by the exiles, such as Mickiewicz's poem "To the Polish Mother" ("Do matki Polki," 1830), the Polish national anthem "Poland Has Not Yet Perished" ("Jeszcze Polska nie zginęła"), or a revised version of an Eastern liturgical prayer which substitutes the line "Have mercy on us" with "Have mercy on misfortunate Poland."[37] Indeed, when accounting for the decision of the Poles to break with Dostoevsky, Tokarzewski takes refuge behind Mickiewicz's verse: "to conceal joy and anger / And to be, like an abyss, in thoughts unattainable."[38] To describe life "in the Omsk Gehenna" with Major Krivtsov as "Lucifer incarnate," Tokarzewski follows a transnational trend in prisoner literature of invoking Dante but cites a verse from the poem "Dawn" ("Przedświt," 1843) by his fellow countryman Zygmunt Krasiński, famed for his play *The Undivine Comedy* (*Nie-Boska komedia*, 1835): "Like Dante in life, I passed through hell!"[39] In this manner, Tokarzewski borrows from a poem and poet celebrated for expressions of Polish Catholic messianism to describe a national hell rather than from the popular Alexandre Dumas, *père*, whose Edmond Dantès shares the hunger of "l'enfer de Dante," or from Dostoevsky's Goryanchikov, who enters the prison bathhouse hell (*Pss*, 4:98).[40]

Tokarzewski's various remembrances indicate that he perpetuated the Polish image of Siberian martyrdom and fused Catholicism with Polish history to demonstrate the necessity of liberating his native land.[41] As Nina Perlina observes, his conflict with Dostoevsky arose out of "the same inseparable identity of the land and the faith of one's forebears, but the substantial meaning of the two ontologies was different: Polish motherland and Catholic faith, and Russian motherland and Russian Orthodox Christianity."[42] Yet, Tokarzewski's participation in the Ściegienny conspiracy, as well as in the uprising of 1863 in Warsaw, establishes a militant tendency in his faith, for which Dostoevsky does not advocate. Tokarzewski embraces this faith by the sword as a Polish tradition in *By a Thorny Path* (*Ciernistym szlakiem*, 1909) in reply to a Russian who observes: "'In your nation, reigns a strange confusion of ideas,' he said. 'You identify religious concepts with the idea of your sovereignty. . . . To die for God and a death suffered for your native land are altogether the same, according to your ideas.'"[43] Tokarzewski, demonstrating his affinity with the traditionalism of the Sarmatian Polish nobility (*szlachta*), confirms this with a historical anecdote:

> That's exactly it! For many centuries, we were the "Bulwark of Christianity." Our Jan III Sobieski (1629–96) from the military action at Vienna hastened to the plea of the papal nuncio: "King! Save Christianity." Every time we met the infidels on the fields of victory, this many times we fought under the motto "pro Christo!" as well as for the idea "pro patriae [*sic*]!" Thus, it has already entered us in our blood, in our brain, and in our heart, and is rooted there until today.[44]

Tokarzewski's celebration of the military exploits of this "warrior-king," whose reign saw a decline in religious tolerance in the Polish-Lithuanian Commonwealth resulting in the Polonization of Lithuanian and Ruthenian nobility, shows the Polish inmate's accord with a Catholic expansionism in service to Poland's national interests.[45] Tokarzewski's Polonization of Dostoevsky according to the practice of physiognomy ("his Polish descent unfortunately! was visible from his features and surname") suggests that this celebration of Polish heritage belongs to his Omsk period as well.[46]

Yet, Tokarzewski does not counter Dostoevsky's imperialism during the Crimean War based on religious grounds, even though Napoleon III's decision to press the Ottomans for recognition of Catholic authority over Christian places in the Holy Land provoked Russia to respond with a show of force that resulted in the war. Rather, Tokarzewski focuses on the political conflict by mocking Dostoevsky's patriotism: "Once Dostoevsky recited his work to us: an ode celebrating the eventual entrance of the conquering Russian army into Constantinople. The ode was really lovely, but none of us was quick with our praise, and I asked, *And do you not have an ode for the return trip?*"[47] Both Tokarzewski and Bogusławski trace Dostoevsky's Russocentrism to his faith in the tsar as God's civil representative, which is a reflection of the Byzantine ideal of *symphonia* whereby the emperor receives his authority as earthly guardian of the faith directly from God and peacefully coexists with an ecclesiastical authority that assumes responsibility for spiritual affairs. This vision of the emperor presupposes an Orthodox nation and supports empire-building, since it draws on a "realized eschatology" acknowledging the advent of the universal kingdom of God.[48] Such a perception of the tsar's authority motivated Dostoevsky's hostility toward Polish nationalist aspirations and his denial that Ukraine, Lithuania, and Poland existed independently of the Russian Empire. Instead, Bogusławski maintains that Dostoevsky "always held that it was Russia's ancient property, that the hand of God's justice handed all this over to the authority of the tsar only so that the people be enlightened by the paternal blessed rule of the tsar."[49] Twenty years later, Dostoevsky expresses similar sentiments about the fate of a "New Poland liberated by the tsar" in his *Diary of a Writer,* so Bogusławski seems to provide an accurate summary of Dostoevsky's assessment of the Polish question (*Pss,* 26:58).

Yet, as historian Jerzy Kloczowski indicates, in Poland a fear of absolutism had established "the old right defended by the [Catholic] Church to dismiss a tyrant who abused his power" so that the "dethronement of Nicholas I by the Polish Diet on 25 January 1831, signed by four bishop-senators (more or less of their own accord), followed this law, supported by the authority of St. Thomas Aquinas."[50] Churches subsequently became centers of opposition for rebels whose insurrection was legitimized by a Catholic faith under attack by the Russian state, which closed Polish monasteries, sent soldiers to arrest worshippers in Warsaw, and exiled their priests to Siberia. In the prison camp, however, the right to worship was protected, as Goryanchikov describes in connection with Isai Fomich's Sabbath ritual. On the occasion of a mass celebrated when a priest arrived at Ust-Kamenogorsk, Tokarzewski describes the personal significance of the service at which Bogusławski and Żochowski served as ministers: "With what uplifted spirit we prayed at that holy mass, received holy communion, and sang 'Beloved Mother' ['Serdeczna Matko'], 'Whosoever Surrenders to the Care' ['Kto się w Opiekę'], 'Supplications' ['Suplikacye'], and the Old Polish 'Song About God's Providence' ['Pieśń o Opatrzności Boskiej']."[51] Bogusławski credits these services with introducing the Catholic prisoners to Polish sympathizers in the surrounding community, who invited them to lunch after services and lent them Polish and French reading materials.[52] Thus, the Catholic mass served as not only sacred but Polish space, with parts of the service in the Poles' native tongue, and the priest's blessing of their martyrdom with "our motto 'For Faith and the Fatherland,' "[53] which effectively allowed the prisoners to find "mystical consolation in messianism."[54] Such remembrances establish Catholic faith as integral to Polish identity in the ideology of several of Dostoevsky's fellow inmates.

The Christmas Eve celebrations in the prisons also served to connect the Poles to their homeland, as Bogusławski reveals in his final account of

Omsk: "Neither I nor my comrades tasted the food; our thoughts ran far away, to the West, to our homeland, where our families broke the wafer—without us" (*Pss*, 4:95–96).[55] Tokarzewski emphasizes in the scenes from Ust-Kamenogorsk that these holidays divide the Russians and Poles, for while the common inmates enjoyed drinking and debauchery during the Orthodox Christmas, "we assembled in a most secluded little nook and recalled what kind of Christmas Eve we had this year" and "when the first star glittered in the sky together we began to sing the carol 'The Angel Said to the Shepherd' ['Anioł pasterzom mówił']."[56] Tokarzewski notes, when the Russian convicts respond by screaming and rattling their fetters, that his environment is removed both from the civilized world and from religious feeling. When Bogusławski, Żochowski, Tokarzewski, Mirecki, Bem, Anczykowski, Musiałowicz, and Korczyński sat down to Christmas Eve supper in 1850, to which all Catholics in the prison had been invited, the Polish remembrances indicate that a similar separation between the Poles and the Russian convicts occurred, despite the apparent celebrations of solidarity during the Russian Easter and Christmas holidays depicted in Dostoevsky's *House of the Dead*.

Since this celebration took place after the Major had allowed the Poles to live together in one barracks with bunkmates of their own choosing, they had room to spread out an elaborate meal of soup, fish, meat, butter, and kasha, to which they invited Isai Fomich, the Circassians, and the Karbadians with whom they shared the barracks. Bogusławski attributes the formation of this "association [*towarzystwo*]" to a common Russian enemy ("they made out instinctively that we are sons, like they, of an oppressed people") and thereby angers Pavel Aristov, who was excluded from the association despite Mirecki's advocating for his membership.[57] Aristov, serving a sentence for false denunciations of political conspirators, worked as an informant for the Major and made trouble for Mirecki by reporting to the Major critical observations about Omsk which Mirecki confided to him. Furthermore, Aristov spread rumors about the Poles' collaboration with the Major among the general prison population so that Tokarzewski concludes: "The brigands resolved a long time ago to realize their schemes of revenge at our Christmas Eve supper. Aristov showed them an opportune moment."[58] As a result, as Bogusławski relates, on Christmas Eve "an entire mass of convicts sentenced to hard labor began to force its way to the middle of our barracks," but the supper was saved by the Circassians who pushed back the convicts until armed soldiers arrived to control the situation.[59] Prior to his description of this feast, Bogusławski had clarified that the Circassians habitually helped the Poles in the fortress: "From long ago, no one was surprised that sometimes a Circassian goes out together with a Pole, and that a Circassian sometimes helps Poles finish assigned work, and finishes it not for a reward but only out of sympathy."[60] Therefore, this Catholic holiday feast underscored for the

Poles their need for isolation from the Russian prisoners, not excepting those of the privileged class.

Bogusławski notes that Dostoevsky, "by the end of the imprisonment," was one of those whom they excluded, "since he threatened us with denunciation and with the publication of our former conversations."[61] Bogusławski seems concerned about the information he disclosed to Dostoevsky during their shared work detail, owing to the latter's attempts to ingratiate himself with the tsar by earning a promotion to officer in Semipalatinsk and by writing a poem dedicated to Tsar Nicholas. For this reason, Bogusławski presents a politically charged portrait of Dostoevsky in contrast to his portrayal of the Petrashevets Durov, who simply bores the Poles with his frequent anecdotes about St. Petersburg and repetitive references to his illustrious family connections. Bogusławski blames Dostoevsky's education "in the cadet corps," in which "he absorbed every evil that nestles in such institutions," for his Russian imperialism, which Bogusławski describes within the context of the Crimean War.[62] He recalls Dostoevsky's "glowing face" in reaction to the advancement of Russian forces, his dreams of Russia's annexation of Turkey for the sake of Constantinople, which would become "the blossom of the Russian Empire," and his disappointment at the retreat of the troops, with massive casualties, from beyond the Danube.[63] Dostoevsky depicts similar visions in *Diary of a Writer*'s chapter "Utopian Understanding of History" ("Utopicheskoe ponimanie istorii"), in which he declares that "Constantinople must sooner or later be ours" as he anticipates the union of the former Byzantine and Russian empires (*Pss*, 23:48). Dostoevsky's evident support for Russian expansionism, with its spiritual roots in Byzantine universalism, clearly antagonized the Poles and motivated their rupture with the Russian author, who was not, as they initially had believed, a conspirator agitating for democracy. Instead, Mirecki, Tokarzewski, and Bogusławski came to regret that they had discussed their political views with Dostoevsky, who so strongly advocated for "the right of national leadership always and everywhere."[64] Dostoevsky's note, soon after the appearance of the *House of the Dead*'s final installment, that "between us and civilization is *faith*. The Catholic origin and the Byzantine," evinces that their distinct religious identities remain for the author a fundamental source of conflict between Russia and Poland (*Pss*, 20:171).[65]

THE CATHOLIC LITERARY TRADITION IN *HOUSE OF THE DEAD*

This conflict is embedded in *House of the Dead* in its dialogue with literature informed by Catholic tradition, which is present in such disparate texts as the Holy Writ, Hugo's *Notre Dame de Paris* (1831), or Dumas's *Louise de la Vallière*. Despite Goryanchikov's early disclosure that a book the Poles shared with him "produced in him a strong, strange, and particular impression," Dostoevsky does not directly reveal the Russocentrism that informs his literary analysis, according to the remembrances of his Catholic inmates (*Pss,* 4:54). Instead, he assigns a knowledge of Western literature to various Russian convicts and repeatedly advances Goryanchikov as the textual authority in the prison, not only due to the latter's engagement with French and Russian literature but also through his conscious development as a writer who tends to reduce "the diversity" of the prison "into categories" (*Pss,* 4:197). His authority remains unchallenged in part because the other four authors in the narrative, at least three of whom—Durov, Tokarzewski, and Żochowski—were taking notes while in Siberia, are not discussed as writers in *House of the Dead.* Dostoevsky would have known about their activities, because not long after their arrival at Omsk, Durov, Dostoevsky, and Żochowski were officially interrogated about their current writings, which were forbidden by the terms of their imprisonment.[66] Furthermore, the special places reserved for the Polish nobility and Dostoevsky at the theater performance indicate that the Russian convicts recognized the Poles' cultivation of the arts (*Pss,* 4:120).[67] Nevertheless, the paucity of information about the political prisoners' readings in *House of the Dead* and Goryanchikov's expressed doubts about the Catholic prisoners' education encourage the perception that the Poles remain unfamiliar with the Catholic literary tradition.

In some respects, the Poles' lack of literary knowledge appears to address a prison dispute, to which Tokarzewski attests in his memoirs, that note a tendency toward imperialism in Dostoevsky's belletristic analysis, when the Catholic conspirator summarizes the novelist's aesthetics: "The literature of other nations, in comparison with Russian literature, is simply a parody of literature. I remember, when I said that in our homeland in 1844 a subscription to a translation of *Le Juif errant* was issued, at first he did not want to believe it but then openly accused me of lying."[68] Tokarzewski's reference to the discussion of Sue's novel among himself, Durov, and Dostoevsky links the Russo-Polish tensions in Omsk to a politically subversive novel popular amongst the Petrashevtsy. Sue's wanderer type is symbolically connected to Russia's exile history already in the prologue, in which the wanderer represents Siberia in a meeting across the divide of the Bering Straits with his sister who signifies America: "Sur le cap sibérien, un homme à genoux étendait les bras vers l'Amérique avec une expression de désespoir indéfinissable. Sur le promontoire américain, une femme jeune et belle répondait au geste désespéré de cet homme en lui montrant le ciel."[69] Dostoevsky's self-identification as "a real Wandering Jew" in a melancholic Siberian letter in 1855 displays his internalization of the politicized type, so alternative readings of Sue by fellow prisoners must have alarmed the increasingly nationalistic Dostoevsky, as he came to realize the international appeal of French literature for European liberation movements (*Pss*, 28.1:188). Yet, he retains for Russians the ability "to study the spirit of every foreign language down to its last detail" which does not exist "in European peoples, *in the sense of a national universal capacity*" (*Pss*, 18:55).

Although Bogusławski's assessment of Dostoevsky's literary knowledge is informed by his own hostility toward the latter's Russocentrism, it also reveals that literature played a polarizing role in their political discussions: "As an author, he liked to discuss literature of every nation of which he was incapable of knowing aside from his own and a little French. All of it, according to his comparison with Russian literature, wasn't worth a damn."[70] Since Bogusławski attributes Dostoevsky's arrest to his love of "progressive French authors," presumably the prison dispute over *Le Juif errant* was not a singular incident:

> In what way, someone could rightly ask, could such a man as Dostoevsky, who received a military education, descend to labor in the fortress? The thing is simple. Some works of progressive French authors fell into his hand. The truth, which he read there, forced itself as far as the abode of his reason; he could not understand it . . . it properly awakened him and showed the whole falsity of his conduct and life. He then longed for improvement.[71]

In *House of the Dead*, Dostoevsky retains for the Russians, particularly for Goryanchikov, a familiarity with French novels and distributes literary allusions throughout the text to reinforce the Russo-French connection. Furthermore, the absence of Mirecki's history as a French tutor following his release and the failure to disclose literary discussions with Tokarzewski and Bogusławski allow Goryanchikov to maintain textual authority in the prison, particularly since Durov remains an unnamed shadowy figure in *House of the Dead*.

Dostoevsky's preference for Russian literature is evident in *House of the Dead*, in which Goryanchikov compares the observant Jew Bumstein to Nikolai Gogol's Cossack-friendly Yankel rather than to Mickiewicz's Jankiel, who is "intended to demonstrate the compatibility of Jewishness and Polish patriotism."[72] Since Bumstein's Gogolian comparison appears following Goryanchikov's description of the Pole's preferential treatment of Bumstein, Gogol's character seems less appropriate than Mickiewicz's Jankiel, who is famed in *Pan Tadeusz* for having brought the national anthem "Poland Has Not Yet Perished" from abroad. Tokarzewski's citations of Mickiewicz and repetitive singing of the anthem suggest that Dostoevsky was conscious of the choice between the two authors. To emphasize the fact that the Poles' association with Bumstein was based, not on a political or aesthetic affinity, but on his ability to amuse them, Goryanchikov employs poultry imagery from Gogol to make Bumstein look ridiculous rather than creative like Mickiewicz's Jankiel. At the same time, Goryanchikov's pointed reference to Gogol's *Taras Bulba* (1842), which uncharacteristically for Dostoevsky includes the author, the name of the work, the character's name, and a description of a scene, reminds the Russian reader of a native work of historical literature that depicts Jews in Warsaw aiding the legendary Cossack warrior for the Orthodox faith, Bulba, against the abusive Polish Catholics. This literary reference, therefore, reflects the author's resentment of Bumstein for choosing Polish rather than Russian comrades for protection in Omsk and, at the same time, recalls the tragic fate of Jews during the Catholic Reformation in which Gogol's tale is situated.[73]

In the inmates' readings of sacred scriptures, a hierarchy of religious experience further prioritizes the Russian Orthodox faith at the expense of Catholicism and Judaism. Ostrozhsky, identified in *House of the Dead* as a noncommissioned officer and Polish acquaintance of Mirecki and Bogusławski, similarly combines "indecent and most coarse gestures" with the Catholic faith, for Goryanchikov also remembers Ostrozhsky's continual reading of "the Catholic Bible" (*Pss*, 4:159). By contrast, the mad Russian prisoner, who obsessively reads his Bible, is considered "some sort of holy fool" who "did not wish anyone ill and wanted only to suffer" (*Pss*, 4:29). The two Poles with acknowledged religious education—Ostrozhsky and Żochowski—were elderly men suffering from age-related dementia. Also, Goryanchikov dismisses the Old Believers in the prison as "dogmatists and literalists" for their narrow reading of old religious texts and finds Bumstein's Sabbath celebration ritualistic, pedantic, and even comical (*Pss*, 4:34, 95). However, Goryanchikov's New Testament, like Dostoevsky's, is rooted in the political history of Russia, since he received it at the departure point of Tobolsk from "those who also suffered in exile and counted its time already by decades and who already had been long used to seeing a brother in every unfortunate" (*Pss*, 4:67). Since it was the only book prisoners were permitted to keep, it became further radicalized as a clandestine purveyor of money (and likely other secret papers) pasted into the binding. For Goryanchikov, it also serves to enhance his status as a man of letters, since he tutors the Muslim youth Alei in Russian, "the literary language [*knizhnyi iazyk*]," with the New Testament (*Pss*, 4:54). Goryanchikov reports that at the end of two months "our writing also went extraordinarily well," because Alei had become a writer of Russian, owing to practice with paper and pens that he had procured in prison (*Pss*, 4:54).

Dostoevsky's distribution of literary allusions, in addition to the description of prison performance art in theater and song, also allows him to

reserve for the Russians in Goryanchikov's narrative an aesthetic sense denied to Bumstein and the Poles. The Polish memoirs and Martyanov's reminiscences clarify that reading materials were available to the political prisoners, and Martyanov specifies that the cautious Dostoevsky "only twice was
interested in *David Copperfield* and *The Posthumous Papers of the Pickwick
Club*" whereas Durov "with particular eagerness threw himself into the
French novels, like, for example, *La Reine Margot* [*Queen Margot*], *La Dame
de Monsoreau* [*The Lady of Monsoreau*], and *Le Comte de Monte-Cristo*
[*The Count of Monte-Cristo*] by A. Dumas and *Les mystères de Paris* [*The
Mysteries of Paris*] and *Le juif errant* by E. Sue."[74] Such reading materials
enter into *House of the Dead* in brief references to various French novels
that enhance his portrayals of the Russian inmates, sometimes at the expense
of Catholic culture. For instance, his labeling Aristov a "moral Quasimodo"
renders the duplicitous aristocratic informant poetic in his cruel bestiality
(*Pss*, 4:63). Although Goryanchikov apposes Quasimodo to a "monster,"
Dostoevsky, in an 1862 introduction to the translation of *Notre Dame de
Paris* in *Time*, endows the hunchback with a greater cultural significance
as "the personification of the despised and cowed medieval French people,
voiceless and disfigured, and gifted only with terrible physical strength, but
in which finally is awakening love and a thirst for justice" (*Pss*, 20:28–29).[75]

In other words, Quasimodo represents the potential for a nation's
moral regeneration envisioned in what Dostoevsky terms Hugo's "formula,"
which proposes "Le laid, c'est le beau" (*Pss*, 20:28).[76] Therefore, Dostoevsky's
discussion of Hugo's *Notre Dame de Paris* suggests that he can aesthetically
appreciate Aristov as a cultural type, which may yet redeem itself through a
pursuit of justice, even though Goryanchikov's portrayal of the person underscores Aristov's depravity. As an artist, the handsome, somewhat educated, and talented Aristov, whom the Major believes to be "almost another
Bryullov," still compares favorably to the Polish house-painter Bem, who
practices not an art but a trade, as Goryanchikov highlights: "This was a
coarse, petty-bourgeois soul with the customs and manners of a shopkeeper
grown rich by overcharged kopecks. He was without any kind of education
and was interested in nothing outside of his trade" (*Pss*, 4:63). Aristov, on the
other hand, enjoys a connection to literature that Dostoevsky finds historically transcendent because it "expresses the striving and characteristics of its
time as fully and eternally as, for example, *The Divine Comedy* expressed its
epoch of Medieval Catholic beliefs and ideals" (*Pss*, 20:29). Thus, instead of
linking the Poles, who discussed this Catholic literary tradition in Omsk, with
French and Italian medievalism, Dostoevsky chooses Aristov as the representative of this Western tradition in *House of the Dead.*

Some of *House of the Dead*'s Russian inmates follow Durov's example
by reading Dumas, as is suggested from Goryanchikov's reference to the mar-

quise de Brinvilliers, whose story is found in Dumas's series *Crimes célèbres* (*Famous Crimes*, 1839–40) and Petrov's discussion of a volume of *Le Vicomte de Bragelonne* (*The Viscount of Bragelonne*, 1847), *Louise de la Vallière*, which he specifies as "Dumas's work" (*Pss*, 4:84). The invocation of the marquise de Brinvilliers in concert with the marquis de Sade to describe the pleasure of flogging a victim ascribes this Russian practice to a Western sensuality, which Dostoevsky later links to Catholicism: "*Catholicism (strength of hell)*. Celibacy. Relation to women at confession. Erotic illness. There is here some delicacy, which can be grasped only by the most underground constant lechery (Marquis de Sade). It is remarkable that all lecherous books are ascribed to lecherous abbots, who have sat in the Bastille" (*Pss*, 20:191). The secrecy of Catholic priests and their connections to the Bastille further enter *House of the Dead* through Dumas's *Louise de la Vallière*, in which the musketeer Aramis exploits a connection with the Society of Jesus that he shares with the governor of the Bastille to secure access to a prisoner, who is later identified as the twin brother of Louis XIV. In this novel about the court of the Sun King, Dumas continues to explore the church's attempt to influence the French royal succession, famously portrayed in his novel *La Reine Margot* (1844–45), which Durov obtained from the guards in Omsk. Since *La Reine Margot* focuses on the events surrounding the St. Bartholomew's Day Massacre, it recounts the intrigues of the devout Queen Mother Catherine de Médicis in support of the future Henri III of France, who during the novel receives the crown of Poland in Paris from Polish ambassadors (including a bishop), whom Marguerite de Navarre addresses in Latin.

Yet, Petrov's reference to *Louise de la Vallière* does not highlight the religious dimension to French political strife. Instead, directly preceding the mention of the novel, Petrov alludes to the issue of succession with a question about the relationship between Napoleon Bonaparte and his nephew, the then president of the Second Republic of France, Louis-Napoleon Bonaparte. This provides Goryanchikov with an opportunity to comment on Louis-Napoleon's imperial pretensions with an assessment of his decision to dissolve the National Assembly in 1851 and to establish a new constitution in 1852, which gave Louis-Napoleon de facto imperial powers. However, Goryanchikov describes only "what kind of president he was" and then informs Petrov "that maybe soon he would be emperor" (*Pss*, 4:83). Goryanchikov's subsequent confirmation to Petrov that Dumas's *Louise de la Vallière* is simply "made up" further establishes Goryanchikov as the authority on French culture, since he dismisses the historical value of Dumas's novels that circulated in Omsk, particularly among the military (*Pss*, 4:83). Similarly, Dostoevsky recalls that soldiers and "other people" to whom he read from Dumas "stopped me and requested from me explanations of various historical names, kings, lands, and military leaders" in his 1861 article "Book-reading and Literacy" ("Knizhnost' i gramotnost'"; *Pss*, 19:53). Dostoevsky's association of the ridiculous General Ivolgin with Dumas's musketeers in *The Idiot* further attests to the Russian author's knowledge of Dumas's popularity among the military, whose members enjoyed the romanticized histories about the king's loyal guards—despite the French author's subversive reputation owing to his novel *Le maître d'armes* (*The Master of Arms*, 1840), which was banned in Nicholas's Russia for its depiction of the Decembrists (*Pss*, 8:92). Also, in his Siberian novel *Uncle's Dream* (*Diadiushkin son*, 1859), Dostoevsky provides the provincial society lady, Marya Alexandrovna, with a romantic sensitivity that appreciates the "grandiose" scandals of *Le Comte de Monte-Cristo* (1844) and "one of the windbags from the times of the regency, which Dumas portrays" (*Pss*, 2:357, 382).

Dostoevsky again refers to Dumas in a description of a painting, *Party of Convicts at a Halt* (*Partiia arestantov na privale*), which he criticizes for its melodrama in an 1861 article about an art exhibition (*Pss*, 19:151–52). In the same article, he compares Dumas to the Russian master of seascapes, Ivan Aivazovsky, for their similar speed of composition, unusual "fairy-tale" subject matter, and predictably banal finishes (*Pss*, 19:161–62). His invocation of the musketeers Aramis, Porthos, and d'Artagnan recalls the court of Louis XIV, which Goryanchikov disparagingly connects to a popular novel by Madame de Genlis about Louis XIV's mistress, *La Duchesse de la Vallière*, in a description of a young inmate who was "literate, from the clerks" and had read "*La Duchesse de la Vallière* or something of the sort" (*Pss*, 19:162; 4:180). Goryanchikov's reference seeks not only to connect Dumas to popular literature but to remind the reader of Gogol's Chichikov, who remained in his room where he read one of the duchess's volumes as the townspeople grew increasingly alarmed about his identity. The allusion to Gogol's scene links his political satire to Omsk, since the ending of his play *Inspector General* (*Revizor*, 1836) resembles the description of the inmate who has just announced the impending arrival of an ineffectual government inspector to the prison. As a result, the presence of Dumas's historical novels in *House of the Dead* plays a limited role in highlighting the inadequacy of French and Russian government officials but does not accurately reflect the novels' important entertainment or educational value for the soldiers and inmates in Omsk.

Thus, although reading is periodically acknowledged to be a pastime of the Catholics, the peasants, or Alei, Goryanchikov retains his literary authority unchallenged throughout *House of the Dead,* in contrast to the portrait of Omsk provided by Tokarzewski and Bogusławski, who disclose their tense literary discussions with Dostoevsky. Goryanchikov affirms the importance of the written word in his recording of Alei's writing, the Poles' books, Petrov's reading of Dumas, and the Old Believer's "manuscript book" of prayers, because, as he observes to Alei, many in the prison are "literate" (*Pss*, 4:34, 53). Goryanchikov's commentary on the Old Believer's "torment for the faith" or the mad Russian's biblically inspired suffering demonstrates a recognition of Christian martyrdom in Omsk, but the Poles do not share in these self-sacrificial acts (*Pss*, 4:33). Instead, Bogusławski's "irritability . . . to extreme intolerance and caprice" causes a rupture in his relationship with Goryanchikov, who is divided from these fellow literate Christians with whom he shared a prison sentence (*Pss*, 4:209). As Wacław Lednicki discerns, Dostoevsky's Poles in *House of the Dead* are "opposed to his Christian pity and humility" even though Dostoevsky "was able to extend his goodwill to such a degree as to defend before the Russian reader those 'poor Poles' whom suffering had made morbid, bitter, and unsociable."[77] Perhaps this opposition accounts for why a narrative, which includes scenes about the Jewish, Muslim, and Orthodox faiths, does not provide many details about the "faith" or "manner of thinking" of Tokarzewski or Bogusławski, with the notable exception of their contempt for the Russian peasant convicts (*Pss*, 4:210). In some respects, through his depiction of the tense relations between the Russian inmates and the Polish nobility, Dostoevsky advances a common Russian critique of the popular romantic image of the Polish Sarmatian noble, whose belief in the Christian mission of Poland (at times informed by notions of chivalry) and maintenance of a privileged position for hereditary gentry (distinct from the peasantry living in Polish lands) antagonized Russians in support of the tsar's agrarian reforms. In the wake of the 1863 Polish uprising, in a letter to Turgenev Dostoevsky concludes that Polish national pride in its European civilization informs the Polish aristocratic contempt for the Russian "barbarians" (*Pss*, 28.2:34). Thus, his presentation of the Polish political prisoners' evident aversion to Russian convicts corresponds to his aforementioned conviction that such a Western civilization reflects an "anti-Christian spirit."

RUSSO-POLISH RELATIONS AND THE PEASANT QUESTION IN *HOUSE OF THE DEAD*

The overwhelming presence of Dostoevsky's *Siberian Notebook* (*Sibirskaia tetrad'*)—a collection of phrases, proverbs, and songs that he recorded in Omsk—in *House of the Dead* demonstrates the significance of his prison experience for the book. He writes to his brother in 1859 about his intent to include "expressions written by me *in that place*" in order to realize "the portrayal of characters never *heard of* in literature" in his presentation of "serious, gloomy, and humorous things, and common peoples' conversation with a particular convict nuance" (*Pss*, 28.1:349). Still, his creation of a fictional narrator suggests a desire to maintain a degree of separation between his own life as a political prisoner and Goryanchikov's experience as a condemned murderer. With this narrator Dostoevsky can play on the text's "double status" as memoir and novel as he provides his narrator both with his own status as a political prisoner and with the identity of a murderer.[78] This dual identity is particularly problematic for his portrayal of the Poles, since Goryanchikov, as a prisoner sentenced for a murder, does not share the political prisoners' dread of being further implicated in conspiring against the tsar. For this reason, the scenes depicting Russo-Polish tensions in *House of the Dead* render suspect its "authenticity" as autobiography and Goryanchikov's close identification with Dostoevsky.[79] All the same, the novel reflects Dostoevsky's resentment of the Polish Catholics through his conscious engagement with a prominent political issue in the early 1860s: the Polish nobility's reaction to the issue of agrarian reform following the liberation of the serfs.

As Georgy Chulkov notes, Dostoevsky's novel, appearing in "the so-called years of peasant emancipation, when the problem of a free person was, if not decided, then in any case posed by the Russian public with great acuity," reflected the intelligentsia's determination to resolve the peasant question.[80] However, as *Time* illustrates in 1862 with the article "A Note on One Newspaper's Article: On the Polish-Ruthenian Question" ("Zametka na odnu gazetnuiu stat'iu: Po povodu pol'sko-rusinskogo voprosa"), Russia's agrarian issue could not be resolved without addressing tensions in the Congress Kingdom of Poland where the process of peasant emancipation was complicated by the nationalities issue. The article traces the question to "the history of oppression of the Russian nationality" in the Congress Kingdom, where the Polish nobility for centuries attempted to Polonize and Catholicize the peasantry, who retained the Russian language, customs, and "a firm consciousness of union with the rest of Rus."[81] This image of class warfare between the contemptuous Polish Catholic nobility and the victimized Ruthenian Orthodox peasantry was a commonly expressed justification for Russia's occupation of the Congress Kingdom. Dostoevsky's 1863–64 notebook shows his support for the Ruthenian peasants in Poland at the expense of the Polish landowners: "Freeing the peasants in Poland and appropriating land for them, Russia already gave Poland her thought, imparted to it her character, and this thought is the chain with which Poland is inseparably bound to Russia" (*Pss*, 20:176). However, the article in *Time* overlooked that the very announcement of the emancipation had been overshadowed in the Congress Kingdom by Polish reaction to the Russian military's firing on civilians in Warsaw in February 1861. As Herzen writes in response to another incident a month later, the shootings damaged Alexander II's reputation as a liberal tsar:

We looked forward with hope and anticipated with emotion our proposed meeting, prepared to drink, for the first time in our lives, the health of the emperor, Alexander II, liberator of the peasants. . . . But our hand fell, our toast was chocked with the blood at Warsaw. The crime was too recent, the wounds still bled, the corpses had not had time to become stiff. (*Ss*, 15:76)

The uncertainty surrounding the agrarian reforms contributed to the turmoil in Warsaw, where political exiles (including Tokarzewski), having returned from Siberia owing to the general amnesty of 1856, agitated for Poland's independence. Herzen's journal *The Bell* (*Kolokol*) supported the conspirators, ranging from Catholic conservatives to the socialist left, by regularly publishing articles advocating Poland's independence, even at the expense of Russian blood. After Bakunin, having fled from Siberia, arrived in London in December 1861 to contribute to the journal, *The Bell* became identified even more closely with the Polish cause. Yury Borisenok's historical analysis of Bakunin's involvement with Polish conspirators in the 1840s effectively establishes Bakunin's early ties to the TDP, Mierosławski, and Karol Libelt, so he likely shared mutual acquaintances with Mirecki and Bogusławski.[82] Bakunin's dedication to the Polish liberation movement intensified during his exile in Tomsk (1857–59) where he encountered the Petrashevets Felix Toll, through whom he met his future wife, Antonia Kwiatkowska.[83] While Bakunin was in Tomsk, there were several conscripted Poles serving in the Siberian corps, as well as those in exile, such as Stobnicki and Tomasz Kraśnicki, whom Bogusławski fondly remembers meeting in Tomsk on the road to Ust-Kamenogorsk.[84] Bakunin's clandestine correspondence with at least one contact in Semipalatinsk in 1862, when he and Herzen were meeting in London with Polish revolutionaries to agitate for regime change in Warsaw, further attests to the likelihood that he maintained lasting friendships with Siberian political conspirators known to Dostoevsky, who concluded his five-year residence in that Siberian town only in the summer of 1859 (*Ss*, 11:360).[85] A. V. Dulov finds that the Petrashevtsy became sympathetic to the Polish exiles but cites Baron Wrangel's recollection that Dostoevsky did not have close acquaintances among the Poles.[86] Yet, since Dostoevsky allowed Józef Hirschfeld, who had been conscripted for his connection to the Union of the Polish People (Związek Narodu Polskiego), to visit, he did not reject contact with all Polish exiles.[87] Hirschfeld could even claim a connection to Tokarzewski and Bogusławski, who had met him on their journey from Ust-Kamenogorsk to Omsk.[88] Baron Wrangel also mentions an army doctor named Lamotte (a former student at Vilnius University) on whom Dostoevsky relied for an excuse from service (*Pss*, 28.1:215).[89] Still, Dostoevsky generally shunned contact with political exiles, since he desired to restore his noble rights and to build his writing career. Therefore, serving in the army with conscripted Poles and living in close proximity to exiles, some of whom were former officers in Gorgey's army, did not inspire in him the feelings of empathy for Polish exiles that Baron Wrangel expresses in an 1854 letter to his father:

> Those for whom I have even more pity are the unfortunate Poles-politicals; there are many—all educated youth—brought here now. Thus, for example, yesterday they brought Count Janiczewski from Warsaw. The noblemen are brought here to Tobolsk and from here, shackled to murderers, they are dispatched to their destination on foot at any time of year. What must it be like to walk some thousand versts, in winter even, to Eastern Siberia.[90]

Dostoevsky's desire to separate himself from Polish Catholic political exiles is reflected in the relatively little space that he devotes to them in the first part of *House of the Dead*. In a narrative celebrated for its colorful illustration of the offenses committed by convicts, the history of the Poles' transgressions remains conspicuously absent. Instead, Goryanchikov frequently depicts the Poles as a collective group in his first impressions of the prison, in which he emphasizes their exclusive nature: "In our barracks, besides the Circassians, we had an entire heap of Poles who formed a completely separate family and hardly communicated with the other prisoners" (*Pss*, 4:54). These passages attest to Lednicki's claim that the image of Poles' "typical exclusiveness" and "national and social aloofness" permeates the novel.[91] While Goryanchikov iterates the Poles' hostility toward the Russian inmates during the first part of the novel, he at the same time discloses some sense of camaraderie with them: "Some of them were educated; about them I will speak particularly and in detail subsequently. From them I sometimes, in the final years of my life in the prison, got some books" (*Pss*, 4:54). Goryanchikov appears particularly close to Mirecki, since he shares Mirecki's samovar, cites his superior knowledge of prison life, and depends on his assessments of the camp as a guide. Still, Mirecki's brief appearances affirm Goryanchikov's observation that the Poles hate the Russian inmates: "They get angry at you because you are a gentleman and not like them. Many of them would like to pick on you. They would very much like to insult and humiliate you. You will see still many unpleasantries here. Here it is horribly difficult for all of us" (*Pss*, 4:32). At this point in the narrative, Goryanchikov concurs with Mirecki's characterization of the peasants, as he indicates in the last sentence of the chapter: "In a few minutes his words came true" (*Pss*, 4:32). Yet, as Goryanchikov's relationship with the Polish prisoners becomes progressively strained in *House of the Dead,* he distances himself from the Poles by supplying the reader with additional details about his disagreements with specific Polish prisoners.

Although the Polish accounts corroborate the growing estrangement between Dostoevsky and the Poles, Goryanchikov's narrative detailing alienation from the group does not correspond chronologically to Dostoevsky's experience in Omsk. For example, Tokarzewski's memoirs clarify that they procured books, not only in Dostoevsky's final years in Omsk but also during Major Krivtsov's tenure at the fortress, when Tokarzewski recalls that the wife of the commandant of the fortress, Anna de Grave, provided reading materials to the political prisoners.[92] Also, Dostoevsky limits the mutual acquaintances shared by himself and the Poles in this early part of the novel. For example, Goryanchikov's encounter with Nastasya Ivanovna in the sixth chapter, for whom Natalya Krzyżanowska serves as a prototype, fails to mention Krzyżanowska's acquaintance with the Polish political prisoners whom she and her husband Karol had met on the Poles' march to Omsk (*Pss*, 4:67, 304).[93] Karol, whom Tokarzewski characterizes as "one of our older brethren," fell ill and died in the Omsk prison hospital in 1850, but his wife stayed and helped the political prisoners whom she visited at their work sites.[94] Tokarzewski's memoirs reveal that her "poor lodgings," which Goryanchikov visits after his release, were a refuge for Polish exiles, where they met to discuss national politics and their related personal histories.[95] Furthermore, the Poles' reluctance to join the theatrical festivities in Goryanchikov's account appears unmotivated in the absence of any description of the 1850 Christmas mêlée or of the recollection of Żochowski's flogging, which Goryanchikov recalls only in the eighth chapter of the second part.[96] Instead, a reference to the Poles' "fastidiousness" for their reluctance to attend the performances until the final evening affirms their pattern of discriminatory treatment of the Russian convicts (*Pss*, 4:120).

In chapter 7 of the second part, Goryanchikov returns to his first summer in the prison to recall the inmates' protest against the food rations. This scene contains the only exchange of dialogue between Goryanchikov and the two Catholic inmates who recorded their remembrances of Dostoevsky: Tokarzewski and Bogusławski. The appearance of two chapters on Polish political prisoners in the last part of the book intimates that the deteriorating political situation in the Congress Kingdom encouraged Dostoevsky to write about Polish-peasant relations. Following the 1861 decree, confusion over the terms of liberation sparked unrest in the Kingdom, so that Aleksander Wielopolski was forced to create a Peasant Committee to outline agrarian reforms. Because large property owners, whose influence was intended to promote stability, guided the reforms, Wielopolski's implementation of the conversion of peasants' labor services to monetary value occurred at a rate

advantageous to the gentry. Dostoevsky's familiarity with these public policies is evident in the pages of *Time,* in which published stories appeared on
peasant refugees and Ruthenian peasants in 1862. The polarization of the
Poles and Russians during the convicts' protest thus resembles the social
struggle between the nobility and the peasants taking place in Warsaw. The
episode for Goryanchikov underscores his outsidedness as a bystander to
the conflict between political prisoners of privilege and the inmates from
the lower classes in a confrontation that assigns him the status of a political
prisoner.

In an earlier episode, Mirecki similarly hints at a political status for
Goryanchikov when presenting his class-conscious analysis on peasant-noble
relations: " 'Yes, sir, they do not like the gentlemen,' he remarked, 'especially the politicals; they would gladly devour them and no wonder, sir. First,
you and the common people are different; you are not like them. Second
formerly they were either their landowner's or were conscripted. Judge
for yourself whether they could love you, sir'" (*Pss,* 4:28). In "Grievance"
("Pretenziia"), Tokarzewski more directly links Goryanchikov to the political
prisoners by warning him as a political prisoner that he must distance himself
from the grievance brought by the common criminals: "Do you really not
know? They are registering a complaint. They will not succeed of course.
Who will believe convicts? They will begin to search for the instigators and
if we are there, of course, they will shift the blame for the revolt to us first.
Remember why we came here. They will simply be flogged, but we will be
put on trial" (*Pss,* 4:203). With the phrase "Remember why we came here"
Tokarzewski places Goryanchikov in solidarity with the Polish political prisoners, three of whom had arrived from Ust-Kamenogorsk less than a year
before, owing to an informant implicating them in subversive activities. In his
letter to his brother upon his release from Omsk, Dostoevsky understands his
own precarious position as a former political prisoner serving in a Siberian
battalion, and writes that: "It is possible to fear only one thing: people and
tyranny" (*Pss,* 28.1:172). Still, Goryanchikov, having already refused to con-
duct himself like the Poles who close themselves off "in cold and inaccessible
politeness" for protection, does not identify with their instinctive tendency
toward self-preservation, even though Martyanov assigns this asocial behavior motivated by fear to Dostoevsky (*Pss,* 4:77).[97]

In this novel, in which Poles rarely speak, Goryanchikov directly records how Tokarzewski, Bogusławski, and Mirecki oppose his desire to join
the mass protest. Mirecki, like Tokarzewski, warns him by referring to the
likely consequences: "We would risk a hundred times more, if we were to
go out; and for what? *Je haïs ces brigands.* And do you really think for one
minute that their complaint will go through? Why do you want to poke your
nose into this nonsense?" (*Pss,* 4:204). Because such arguments by the Poles

persuade Goryanchikov to stand with them, removed from the common protest, they can be held partially responsible for the breakdown in communication between Goryanchikov and the peasant convicts, a breakdown which haunts the former throughout his narrative. His frustration, as Karla Oeler recognizes, arises from the inmates judging him against the backdrop of his social class: "The convicts direct their attention away from Gorianchikov's behavior as an individual. . . . When the prisoners overlook Gorianchikov's individuality, focusing instead on his once-elevated position within society, they fail to do him justice since, as an individual, he morally opposes their oppression."[98] Even though Nancy Ruttenburg concludes that his "principled estrangement" in the narrative subverts "the constructive destabilization of his class identity," Goryanchikov's expressed desire to transcend his class identity remains an important distinction between himself and the Polish political prisoners in *House of the Dead*.[99]

In their memoirs, neither Tokarzewski nor Bogusławski hesitates to disclose an aversion to the Russian convict with his revealing "marks testifying to the crime he committed" and his "ironic smile of satisfaction, of a certain ridicule, and of some savage delight."[100] Bogusławski's description of the formation of their "Polish-Karbadian association [*towarzystwo*]" arising from a common experience of oppression attests to the Poles' desire to remove themselves from the Russians.[101] The use of the terms *towarzystwo* or *towarzysze* (comrades) to refer to this group in both Tokarzewski and Bogusławski reveals how they employed them to differentiate themselves from the other prisoners. Therefore, the title "Comrades" ("Tovarishchi") for the *House of the Dead* chapter with the most extensive depiction of the Polish political prisoners may ironically highlight the exclusivity of the group, given Dostoevsky's and Goryanchikov's contentious relationship with the Poles. Goryanchikov's additional disclosure at the beginning of "Grievance" about his simultaneous envy and hatred of "this association [*tovarishchestvo*] from under the lash and rod" underscores the political significance of the term "comrade" for Dostoevsky (*Pss,* 4:197). Although Goryanchikov expresses understanding for the Poles' hardships with a reference to their lengthy prison terms far from their homeland, he distances himself from their disdain for the convicts with the observation: "They saw in the convicts only brutality and could not, did not even want, to discern in them a single good trait or anything humane" (*Pss,* 4:210).[102] While Goryanchikov recalls in the second chapter of the book that the Russian prisoners observe the Poles' "aversion to them" and "repaid them in kind," in "Comrades" he resents the prisoners' respectful treatment of the Poles: "The convicts treated our Poles even with respect, much more so than us Russians, and did not touch them at all" (*Pss,* 4:210). Goryanchikov's commentary on the Russian treatment of the Poles and defensive account of Żochowski's flogging later in the chapter intimate that

Dostoevsky here attempts to counter accounts of Russian cruelty, which were published in *The Bell* frequently in 1862 before Dostoevsky published this chapter on the Poles, which appeared in January 1863 (*Pss,* 4:278).

For example, because Dostoevsky was abroad in June 1862, he likely encountered Herzen's discussion of Rufin Piotrowski's *Memoirs from a Stay in Siberia* (*Pamiętniki z pobytu na Syberii,* 1860–61) in the June 15 issue of *The Bell,* especially since he met Herzen in London less than a month after its publication date. Piotrowski, a conspirator with known ties to the TDP, was arrested in 1843 but fled Siberia in 1846. Herzen knew Piotrowski's memoirs from the excerpts translated into French by Julian Klaczko and published as "Souvenirs d'un Sibérien" in the *Revue des deux mondes* in 1862. In Klaczko's evocative introduction, Siberia appears as a place of no return, and Piotrowski represents a heroic emissary motivated by sentiments of "religious charity" to return to Poland from emigration.[103] The selection resembles the Polish prison narratives by Tokarzewski and Bogusławski in that it depicts the experience of exhaustion, celebrating Christmas in the prison, the weight of the chains, and concerns over torture. In his review, Herzen is pleased that the devoutly Catholic and aristocratic Piotrowski "speaks without the smallest disgust, even with a warm feeling, about the Russian people," who treat him with respect and help him with the heavy work (*Ss,* 16:114). From this account, Herzen concludes that the memory of the seventeenth-century pretenders and their destruction of "sacred places" is far removed from the contemporary peasant consciousness, since the people now stand alongside the Polish Catholics as victims of the knout wielded by the Orthodox-Protestant Germans occupying the throne (*Ss,* 16:113).

Herzen provides ample evidence of the knout in his lengthy citation of Piotrowski's narrative about the Omsk conspiracy (1833–37) in the June 1 issue of *The Bell.* Piotrowski had already succeeded in linking Omsk to Russian brutality in his published memoirs of 1846.[104] Herzen cites from Piotrowski's discussion of the monk Jan Sierociński, who was arrested in connection with the 1831 uprising, subsequently conscripted into the army, and reassigned to the military school in Omsk. There, he conspired to take over the fortress with a view toward liberating Polish exiles in Siberia, for which crime he was sentenced to 7,000 lashes according to Piotrowski. The description of the flogging differs strikingly in its severity from those floggings portrayed by Goryanchikov, since no doctor ordered a division in the execution of the sentence:

Sierociński only once passed through the formation, i.e., received the 1,000 lashes. He fell senseless and bloodied in the snow. In vain they tried to stand him on his feet; then they tied him *to a sleigh, prepared in advance, so that his back was placed under the blows and in this way he was drawn through the formation.* At the beginning of the second thousand his groans were still heard; they grew weaker but he died only after the fourth thousand. The remaining three thousand fell on a corpse. (*Ss*, 16:111)

The grave site of the five conspirators who died from the floggings is described by Bogusławski, who used to visit it often and recorded his own version of the conspiracy. Owing to Dostoevsky's fascination with the floggings at the fortress and his relationship with Bogusławski, the Russian novelist must have already known many details about the conspiracy. The fact that one of the Siberian Poles in *The Brothers Karamazov* shares the surname Wróblewski with one of the conspirators who died in the hospital following his flogging further indicates Dostoevsky's familiarity with the conspiracy.

This punishment of flogging was an experience common to the Polish political prisoners and the Russian convicts, which united them in solidarity against the military authority. The scarred backs that Goryanchikov saw in Omsk included those of soldiers, peasants, and political prisoners, but he only briefly mentions Mirecki's light sentence of 500 lashes, highlights the singularity of Żochowski's corporal punishment, and neglects to mention Tokarzewski's flogging altogether. Perlina proposes that Tokarzewski's account of his punishment was too persuasive and so "the writer resorted to inadequate substitutions" with the accounts of Mirecki and Żochowski.[105] Still, Tokarzewski indicates in his remembrances that the convicts took particular interest in his knowledge of corporal punishment in the West. He explains to a friend among the Russian peasants, Fiedko, that far from Russia, corporal punishment takes the form of a hanging or guillotining, to which Fiedko replies: "Then it is better in our country, because if a guy's head is cut off or hung in the gallows, then it's all for nothing! But he can endure penal servitude and then the guy can leave the fortress for the world."[106] Since Fiedko disseminates Tokarzewski's report around the prison, the Polish inmate must confirm to a brigand that a typical sentence for murder is beheading or hanging. The brigand, echoing Fiedko's sentiments, responds: "Well! The devil take them! Then it is better in our Russia!"[107] Such discussions of corporal punishment point to a camaraderie among flogging victims that excludes the Russian noblemen, like Goryanchikov and Dostoevsky, whose class privilege protected them from the lash. Nevertheless, the appearance of a similar conversation in *The Idiot* (*Idiot*, 1868) between Prince Myshkin and General Yepanchin's servant attests to Dostoevsky's interest in the prisoners' comparison of Western and Russian forms of punishment. Like the Russian convicts, Prince Myshkin finds physical torture more humane than the guillotine, since at least the illusion of survival is preserved (*Pss*, 8:20–21).

While Dostoevsky and Goryanchikov share an estrangement from the convicts owing to class and from the Poles owing to ethnicity and religious tradition, Dostoevsky suffered from further isolation because of his status as a former military officer. He notes this in an 1856 letter to General Eduard Totleben, a hero of Sevastopol and brother of Dostoevsky's classmate at the Engineering Academy. Dostoevsky describes his years in the prison, with an emphasis on his hardships owing to social stratification, as part of his request to be released from service: "I endured hunger, cold, sickness, work beyond my strength, and the hatred of my robber-comrades, who revenged themselves on me, because I was a gentleman and an officer" (*Pss*, 28.1:224). Martyanov's portrait of the convict Dostoevsky alludes to his military training: "F. M. Dostoevsky had the look of a strong, stocky, heavy-set worker straightened out and well provided by military discipline."[108] His memoirs also discuss various privileges from the guards that Dostoevsky and Durov enjoyed, such as reprieves from work, reading materials, and conversations about the latest news. The other convicts noticed that the doctor I. Troitsky allowed him to convalesce in the army hospital and that he enjoyed light assignments such as performing clerical work for the engineers.[109] Dostoevsky's military background, his status as a political prisoner, and his reputation as an author earned him privileges that he does not extend to Goryanchikov the nobleman-murderer.

Instead, Goryanchikov remains trapped in the prison with the hostile convicts who prefer the Poles to the Russian noblemen, while the Poles enjoy special favors such as a light work detail when they help Bem paint houses. Goryanchikov resents that, while they avoided the Russian convicts, the Poles affably approached the Tatars, Bumstein, and the Circassians, that is, precisely those with whom Bogusławski recalls sharing a barrack. Goryanchikov's description of Tokarzewski's good-naturedness, popularity among the convicts, and compassionate care of Bogusławski is difficult to reconcile with his accompanying general assessment of the Poles as "sickly, exclusive, and intolerant to the highest degree" (*Pss*, 4:209). Goryanchikov, in applying the ethno-religious slur "jesuitical deftness" to Mirecki, participates in intolerance, which is evident in Martyanov's text as well: "The Poles humbled themselves in a jesuitical manner" (*Pss*, 4:209).[110] Such expressions reveal an essentialism characteristic of Dostoevsky's speech after the 1863 uprising, when he considers Jesuitism and jesuitical behavior attributes of Polish civilization. Furthermore, Goryanchikov's mistrust of Mirecki seems fueled by resentment at his early release, for Dostoevsky betrays a similar antipathy toward the "criminals-Poles" pardoned by the tsar at Paskevich's request while he remained in Semipalatinsk (*Pss*, 28.1:215). Such a bias validates the Poles' need for separation and Mirecki's caution in his interaction with Russians in the camp. Yet, Dostoevsky participates in marginalizing the Poles by providing Mirecki with the phrase "Je haïs ces brigands" twice within the same paragraph in *House of the Dead* and in *Diary of a*

Writer, thereby reducing the inmate to a Polish stereotype representative of the West (*Pss,* 4:204; 22:46, 50).[111] Dostoevsky intimates in the closing words of the entry "The Peasant Marei" ("Muzhik Marei") that Mirecki's hatred of the "brigands" is a national trait, a result of his isolation from the Russian peasantry: "I met Mirecki again that night. The unfortunate one! He could not have had remembrances of any Mareis or of any other view of these people except for 'Je haïs ces brigands'!" (*Pss,* 22:49–50). Such sentiments indicate that, for Dostoevsky, the estrangement between Poles and Russians commences in their childhood, owing to their differing relationships with the Russian Orthodox peasantry, who represent a majority within the empire as well as within the prison walls.

Goryanchikov's presentation of these comrades thus challenges Herzen's vision of Polish-peasant solidarity by describing the animosity between the Poles and Russian convicts in Omsk. Whereas Herzen, speaking in terms of historical movements, concludes that the Polish and peasant questions are united in their opposition to the knout, Goryanchikov, based on an experience with a small group of Polish political prisoners, finds that the political concerns of the Poles remain distant from the lives of the Russian people. Because Dostoevsky does not provide many examples of Polish criticism of Russian authority figures, which the reader frequently encounters in Bogusławski and Tokarzewski, the Poles' animosity toward Russians is linked primarily to the convicts. Goryanchikov recalls Mirecki's anger at being lashed but does not identify the Russian authority figure at whom it is directed. Tokarzewski's fear of the Major's wrath serves as an opportunity for Goryanchikov to highlight his own sympathy for the Russian convicts in contradistinction to the isolationist Polish prisoners. Still, whereas Goryanchikov leaves the prison with few comrades and concludes that they part with him as they would with a master (*barin*), Tokarzewski distances himself from this title in the prison by encouraging them to call him by his given name and patronymic rather than by the appellation "barin" (*Pss,* 4:231).[112] When Goryanchikov departs the prison, he leaves for a life of freedom in the town with unnamed acquaintances or gentlemen (*gospoda*), but Dostoevsky left for further military service in Semipalatinsk, where he remained while his fellow Polish inmates returned to their homeland after the amnesty (*Pss,* 4:231). The fact that conspiratorial Poles, like Tokarzewski and Bogusławski, had left Siberia while Dostoevsky remained in exile further contributed to the latter's grievances and to a resentment that the Poles received preferential treatment—a resentment manifested in Goryanchikov's portrayal of Russo-Polish interaction.

Dostoevsky's ode "On the European Events in the Year 1854," written in the year of his release, further underscores the tensions between the Catholics and the Orthodox in Omsk, since it may reveal the author's own sentiments about his former Polish inmates who chose to associate with Circassians and Karbadians instead of Russians, in a parallel to the Crimean conflict during which Catholics allied with Muslims against the Orthodox. For Dostoevsky's oeuvre, the ode marks a point when religious identity becomes cause for ethnic polarization in his writings. The Poles, unlike Dostoevsky, must have rejoiced when their former governor-general of Western Siberia, Petr Gorchakov, suffered defeat in the Crimea. Russia's setbacks in the Crimea emboldened Polish patriots and their Russian sympathizers in the West, who prepared to seize power in Warsaw and to plan for a popular rebellion in Russia. Meanwhile, after its loss in the Crimea, Russia was forced to sign a treaty that agreed to multilateral regulation of Serbia and the Danubian Principalities and to renounce Russia's right to protect exclusively the Orthodox Christians in those areas. Hostilities on both sides of the conflict over "the Eastern question" renewed in the European consciousness the significance of the Crusades for the modern era, as Elizabeth Wormeley Latimer observes in her discussion of the Crimean War:

> Every war that affects Turkey seems like an annex to the Crusades. . . . Apart from their religious aspect we have learned to see how great were the advantages to civilization and learning in western Europe promoted by those wars, and most sincerely to regret that no subsequent crusade followed up the work begun by Godfrey de Bouillon and his successful crusaders.[113]

Yet, as Latimer recognizes, "ever since the Turks established themselves in Constantinople" Russia also staked a claim as the protector of Christians against the Muslim invaders of the Byzantine Empire.[114] Consequently, the Crimean War stoked religious conflict between the East and West characteristic of the medieval period, as evidenced by the poem "The Council of Clermont" ("Klermontskii sobor," 1854), written by Dostoevsky's fellow Petrashevets, Apollon Maikov.

Maikov's poem, named after the council that inaugurated the Crusades with Pope Urban II's request for troops to protect the holy land, recalls that: "For the honor of Christ's Gospel / Sons of Saint Louis / Indeed did not come to aid Byzantium."[115] After further illustrating Russia's own past crusades against the Horde, he concludes that the West fears Russia's power, which will enable it "to finish what the West began" owing to the fact that "we under the banner of the cross / do not play the hypocrite, do not barter, / And with a pharisee's kiss / Do not kiss Christ."[116] In Dostoevsky's praise of the poem in an 1856 letter to the author, the former admires the way in which its "idea was illuminated magnificently and fully in the national spirit and with chivalry" (*Pss*, 28.1:208). Then, Dostoevsky embraces "the Russian people" including the convicts, "my brothers in misfortune," by identifying with them ethnically, while distancing himself from those in Russian society influenced by "an influx of French ideas" and characterized by "exclusivity," which is a criticism Goryanchikov launches at the Poles in *House of the Dead* (*Pss*, 28.1:208). Dostoevsky here discloses a concern about Western and Catholic influence "on that part of society, which thinks, feels, and studies" that will motivate his post-Siberian critical evaluation of French literature published in *Time*. As the following chapter will show, the journal's promotion of native-soil conservatism (*pochvennichestvo*), defined by the fusion of the Russian people (*narod*) with the educated elite, results in its censure of the Russian intelligentsia for its Gallomania and in the frequent inclusion of anti-Catholic and anti-papal articles in its issues.

Chapter Two

The Generation of Dostoevsky's Catholic Types in the 1860s

> That which as a *man* I am not able to do . . .
> I am able to do through *money.*
> —Karl Marx, *Economic and Philosophic*
> *Manuscripts of 1844*

IN THE NARRATIVES *Winter Notes* and *The Gambler* (*Igrok,* 1866), which Dostoevsky wrote about his experiences abroad, as well as in the novel *The Idiot* (which he wrote while living in the West), Dostoevsky presents an array of Catholic types from avaricious and seducer priests to the stalwart church-going bourgeoisie, whose "code of morality" includes the accumulation of wealth, as defined by the "catechism" (*Pss,* 5:76).[1] Such bourgeois attention to materialism creates a culture in which desires are satisfied by acquisition of goods, eloquent speech, formal elegance, and brief vacuous encounters with nature à la Rousseau, "l'homme de la nature et de la vérité" (*Pss,* 5:94, 275). The narrator of *The Gambler,* Alexei, critically assesses this new French national type, that provides an *essential* connection between the pre-revolutionary French aristocracy and the French of the Second Empire: "The national form of the Frenchman, i.e., the Parisian, began to come together in its elegant form when we were still bears. The Revolution inherited the gentry. Now the most vulgar little Frenchman can have the manners, devices, expressions, and even thoughts entirely elegant in form" (*Pss,* 5:315). Through this type, with aristocratic expressions but bourgeois values, Dostoevsky begins to explore the "lackey" soul, with which he identifies both the French bourgeoisie and Polish opportunists. At the same time, the lure of French mannerisms and of Western society, for example, the gaming halls of Roulettenburg, continues to appeal to his Russian characters, especially his women. Through the character of Marya Alexandrovna in *Uncle's Dream,* Dostoevsky associates Russian women not only with a love for the French elegance of form but also with a fascination for "this medieval life" with "all that is chivalry," for example, its "castles," "troubadours," and "tournaments" (*Pss,* 2:343). Such romantic visions merely render the provincial Marya Alexandrovna ridiculous in Dostoevsky's Siberian novella, but by the end of the 1860s, similar chivalric fantasies shared by Aglaya Ivanovna in *The Idiot* leave her vulnerable to seduction by a Polish émigré count and to conversion by a famous *pater* (*Pss*, 8:409).

The presence of duplicitous, even predatory, priests in the aforementioned works of the 1860s, Dostoevsky's anti-Catholic comments in his notebooks from the period, and the criticisms of French and Polish Catholicism found in the pages of *Time* and *Epoch* suggest that Dostoevsky continues to identify these cultures with a Roman church hostile to Russia's interests. An 1873 entry to *Diary of a Writer* accounts for his post-Siberian transformation from a disciple of Belinsky's socialism, shaped by the French progressives George Sand and Pierre-Joseph Proudhon, to a Russian nationalist with appreciation for the empathy of the Decembrist wives and love for the Russian people whom he encountered in Omsk (*Pss*, 21:12). *Time's* frequent criticisms of Napoleon III's policies ensured that when Dostoevsky undertook his inaugural journey through Europe in 1862, he was prepared to resist both the attractions of Paris and the charm of the French bourgeoisie he observed abroad. In satirical portraits in *Winter Notes*, Dostoevsky mocks not only the clergy but also different strata of Parisian society, for example, *Jacques Bonhomme* and the couple *bribri* and *ma biche* for their sacrifice of freedom in exchange for stultifying security, order, and prosperity.[2] In *Notes from the Underground* (*Zapiski iz podpol'ia*, 1864), the Underground Man adds to these French types with his scorn for French romantics who "though the ground crack beneath them and though all France perish at the barricades, they would all the same (even out of propriety they would not change) sing their starry songs, as they say, to their dying day, because they are fools" (*Pss*, 5:126).

The French and Polish types in *The Gambler*, whose "use of recently lived events" renders the work "less of a novel artistically than *Crime and Punishment*," reflect Dostoevsky's enmity for Catholic France and Poland after his travels to Europe in the summer of 1863.[3] During this period, Russia's tensions with the West, linked to the unrest in Poland, fueled Dostoevsky's patriotic spirit, as is evident in his letter to Turgenev: "I do not know whether there will be a war, but all Russia—the army, society, and even all its people—is in a patriotic mood, just as in the year –12!" (*Pss*, 28.2:35).[4] Here, Dostoevsky plays on the popular connection between the Polish invasion of Russia in 1612 and the Napoleonic invasion of 1812 to implicate two Catholic peoples in past and present hostilities toward Russia. In the wake of the 1863 uprising, as Dostoevsky comes to identify more closely with the Russian conservatives like Ivan Aksakov or Mikhail Katkov, his Russian wanderers (patterned after the Chatsky "type of our Russian European") continue to encounter Catholic types, which Dostoevsky introduces in order to present the transformation of the West after revolution (*Pss*, 5:61). Unlike revolutionaries such as Herzen, Bakunin, or Marx, who share Dostoevsky's disappointment in the former Louis-Napoleon Bonaparte (now Napoleon III), Dostoevsky does not view this as a historical phase through which the West must pass. Instead, Catholicism, republicanism, socialism, and Napoleonism together attest to a dearth of Western spirituality and become conflated into a romanticized materialism, whose allure continues to draw Dostoevsky's Russians westward.

FRENCH NATIONAL TYPES IN *WINTER NOTES*

Because of Dostoevsky's accumulated foreknowledge of European charms, the impressions of his first journey abroad in 1862 are not the work of an enamored or sorely disappointed youth.[5] Instead, they reflect the maturity of a middle-aged critic who understands that Parisian divertissements cannot amuse him as they do the "young flibbertigibbets" who "flock abroad in droves" (*Pss*, 18:47). Just the previous year, Dostoevsky wrote in a letter to his friend Yakov Polonsky about the concern that before long, age and infirmity would prevent him from appreciating a European journey: "Will I really not succeed in traveling through Europe while strength, ardor, and poetry are still left" (*Pss*, 28.2:19). Indeed, when Dostoevsky left to journey through Prussia, Belgium, France, England, Switzerland, Austria, and Italy, he went both to receive treatment for his failing health as well as to take in the splendors of Europe.[6] Coping alone with his illness and strained resources in a foreign country contributed to a petulant mood that shapes his scornful portrayal of the French bourgeoisie and Catholic clergy. Their portraits signify Dostoevsky's effort to highlight the otherness of Western peoples through the *pochvenniki*'s literary process of typification, that is, the process by which a writer takes a national type from real life and reduces it to its essential characteristics. As Wayne Dowler discovers, this process "made the identification with literature and life possible" since "archetypal representations of living people" both "reflected" and "conditioned the development of social reality."[7] Dostoevsky's meditations on Catholic nationalities allow him to illustrate in *Winter Notes* his aversion to the bourgeoisie in Napoleon III's France and his strong opposition to the 1863 uprising in Poland.

Prior to Dostoevsky's imprisonment, his dreamer in "White Nights" ("Belye nochi," 1848) freely merges disparate multicultural visions of St. Bartholomew's night, Ivan the Terrible's taking of Kazan, Danton, and Cleopatra, but such universalism disappears from Dostoevsky's later fiction (*Pss*, 2:116). Before his first European journey, Dostoevsky remains more open to Western culture in his discussions of literacy in *Time*, published under the title "A Series of Articles About Russian Literature" ("Riad statei o russkoi literature," 1861), in which he envisions Russian peasants reading about "Alexander of Macedonia, Napoleon, Columbus, and Byzantium" (*Pss*, 19:41). Although he prioritizes native literature and celebrates "the Russian spirit in Pushkin" with references to "Otrepev, Pugachev, the patriarch, the monks, Belkin, Onegin, and Tatyana," Dostoevsky nonetheless recognizes that the novels of Dumas, especially *Bontekoe*, are the type of popular stories necessary to promote literacy among the Russian people (*Pss*, 19:15, 53). Yet, he also acknowledges a shift in the French literary tradition, discussed by F. Shcheglov's article in *Time*, "The Working Class Family in France" ("Semeistvo v rabochem klasse vo Frantsii"). Shcheglov concludes that writers concerned with the horrific living conditions for the average working-class family, like Victor Hugo, Eugène Sue, and Pierre-Joseph Proudhon, no longer dominate France's literary scene.[8] Still, Dostoevsky maintains his interest in Western literature's portrayal of "pauperism or *proletarianism*" of the working class, as evidenced by his introduction to the translation of Elizabeth Gaskell's *Mary Barton,* a novel about the lives of British textile workers (*Pss*, 19:212).

Dostoevsky's Russian protagonists still identify with French literature from previous eras rather than with the emerging art under the Second Empire, which Dostoevsky depicts as jejune after his return from abroad. In *Winter Notes* Dostoevsky presents the bourgeois melodrama and vaudeville created by French "lackeys" who "always flatter" the power of the bourgeoisie (*Pss*, 5: 96). He notes that the Catholic bourgeoisie's taste for noble sentiment has infused the lackeys' melodrama with moral instruction, which the new moneyed class considers a "most sacred and most necessary duty" (*Pss*, 5:95). For his Russians, Dostoevsky reserves a more sophisticated and elitist knowledge of European literature when he agrees with Herzen's observation in *Letters from France and Italy* (Pis'ma iz Frantsii i Italii, 1847–52) that "we [Russians] know Europe bookishly and literarily . . . according to questions occupying the upper stratum of life" (*Ss*, 5:219). Such an aesthetic sense can connect Dostoevsky's protagonists to a literature shaped by Catholic conflict, such as the Reformations or the Jansenist attempts to counter the perceived moral laxity of the Jesuits in the seventeenth century. For example, in *The Gambler* Alexei's characterization of Jansenist dramatist Jean Racine as a "great poet" establishes his appreciation for a period that Dostoevsky identifies with the height of French eloquence in the court of the Sun King (*Pss*, 5:315, 85). Therefore, Dostoevsky's first inaugural visit westward highlights for the author his nation's distinctive aesthetic differences with Napoleon III's Empire.

Before this visit, Dostoevsky already demonstrates a reluctance to accept modern French conclusions about Russian society, because he believes that their writers are either incapable of understanding a culture other than their own, or they do not thoroughly examine Russia's complexities. Prior to his arrest, he argues with a French tourist's characterization of St. Petersburg as "an amusing caricature of some European capitals" (*Pss*, 18:24). Dostoevsky concludes that such a traveler succeeds in reaching only as far as the Kremlin, visions of Napoleon's glory, and a good tea, because "he already knew in Paris what he would write about Russia" (*Pss*, 18:44). Dostoevsky rejects what he understands as a French model of class conflict, which he accuses French litterateurs of applying to Russia: "To this day you (at least all your viscounts) are convinced that Russia consists of only two classes: *les boyards* and *les serfs*" (*Pss*, 18:49, my italics). He also mocks French literature about Russia, for example, Dumas's *Impressions de voyage en Russie* (*Travel Impressions in Russia*, 1858–59) and the Time of Troubles drama, *Le Faux Démétrius* (*The False Demetrius*, 1852), by the French Russophile Prosper Mérimée, because they do not coincide with his native understanding of Russia.[9] After this literary analysis, Dostoevsky reminds the reader of political tensions between the two countries and the hatred for Russia expressed "by both scoundrels and people highly esteemed, in both prose and verse, in both novels and histories, both in the front pages of Parisian presses and from the oratorical platforms" during "the recent discord," that is, the war in the Crimea (*Pss*, 18:45). Such commentary reveals Dostoevsky's emphasis on the alterity of contemporary France to Alexander II's Russia and justifies why Russia must generate a new political solution, "a neutral ground" on which "all classes are merged peacefully, in harmony and brotherhood" (*Pss*, 18:49).

This vision of France differs strikingly from his early admiration of the French Republic in the 1840s, because the Second Empire had accepted certain limitations on liberties in exchange for order and tranquility. In his youth, Dostoevsky had experienced the heady days of the young republic when communists and utopian socialists joined with impoverished peasants and oppressed laborers to celebrate the end of the elitist regime of Louis-Philippe's July Monarchy. Dostoevsky followed the events unfolding in France, for example, the discontent of the peasants, unrest fomented by the workers, and a leftist propaganda campaign that enabled the nephew of Napoleon Bonaparte, Louis-Napoleon Bonaparte, to ascend to the presidency of the republic in December of 1848. While Dostoevsky was in prison, the republic came to an end, largely because of the conservatives in the National Assembly, who, fearing the power of the socialist left, voted to limit a cornerstone of the republic—universal suffrage. The opposition was crushed with the arrest of republican protesters and the government troops sent to control crowds of disgruntled peasants and workers. By suppressing public political debates with censorship of the press, manipulating national elections, dominating the new legislative branch of the Senate, and supporting the Catholic Church, Napoleon III maintained imperial control over France. In *Time* Alexei Razin follows Napoleon III's defense of Catholic interests both in Syria where French troops arrived to protect Catholics against the sultan and in Italy where Napoleon III continued to support Pius IX's temporal powers at the expense of Italian unity. Because of Razin's hostility toward the industrialized West for its exploitation of Russia's raw materials and his pro-populist stances, he champions the cause of the Italian nationalist Giuseppe Garibaldi against Napoleon III throughout 1861–62 in *Time*.[10] Only the Polish uprising of 1863 supplants Razin's interest in the Franco-Italian conflict as Poland represents for him both a Slavic nation vital to Russia's national interests and another Catholic nation in whose affairs Napoleon III wanted to interfere.

Razin's first article noting French and Italian support for the uprising appears in the February 1863 issue of *Time* along with the first installment of Dostoevsky's *Winter Notes*.[11] Razin's regular column "Political Review" ("Politicheskoe obozrenie") in the March 1863 issue of *Time*, in which Dostoevsky publishes the completion of *Winter Notes*, presents a Reformation reading of geopolitics by concluding that Napoleon III desired an independent Poland to secure a new Catholic ally with which to counterbalance Protestant England and Germany.[12] Such a dated presentation of a modern European conflict reflects the influence of Herzen's *Letters from France and Italy*, traces of which Joseph Frank and Arkady Dolinin find in *Winter Notes*.[13] Herzen links political strife in Italy to desperate attempts by the Roman church to draw on support from Catholic countries like Spain and France to defend papal temporal authority, which Germany had threatened since Martin Luther's protest and the Reformation (*Ss*, 5:83). In the April issue of *Time*, Razin concludes that papal power may benefit greatly from the cooperation of France and Poland in his discussion of the Empress Eugenie: "It seems to her majesty, that the triumph of the Polish uprising will be the new triumph of papal power, the new light which will shed a significance, universal in its expanse, for papal power."[14]

In dialogue with these concerns about the expansion of Catholic Europe, Dostoevsky recalls his summer impressions about the West, which he reached by means of the new St. Petersburg–Warsaw Railroad.[15] The Catholic presence in the narrative is evident from the first chapter with references to the pope in Rome, Notre Dame in Paris, and the cathedral at Cologne, a city that Herzen associates with feudalism and "a collegium of Jesuits and somber monk-warriors sullenly standing on the borders of papism and the Reformation" (*Ss*, 5:20). Like Herzen, Dostoevsky demonstrates that Catholicism, as an institutionalized religion, thrives in the Second Empire. Before Dostoevsky presents the avaricious hermit-fathers in France, he discusses a Catholic priest type in the chapter "Baal," after an encounter with a Catholic missionary in Haymarket Square. Dostoevsky's portrayal of the machinations of Catholic priests differs strikingly from that of the proud rich Anglicans, who are censured merely for their indifference to the plight of London's poor, their "obtuse moral virtue," and orderly "organized alms-giving" (*Pss*, 5:73–74). In *Crime and Punishment*, Katerina Ivanovna's scornful response to the hollow words of comfort offered by the priest at her husband's deathbed links Russian Orthodox clergy to a similar apathy toward the poor (*Pss*, 6:144). Yet, for Catholic clergy in *Winter Notes*, poverty serves as an opportunity to exploit the desperate, since the priest "will feed, clothe, and warm up everyone, and he will begin to heal the sick, buys the medicine, becomes a friend of the home and by the end turns everyone to Catholicism" (*Pss*, 5:73). Thus, Dostoevsky presents an early prototype of the Grand Inquisitor who willingly gives in to the first temptation of the spirit in the wilderness—buying obedience with bread.

A return to this theme of Catholic clerical materialism in the Parisian segment of *Winter Notes* describes how the Roman church obtains these generous funds, which it uses to manipulate the faithful. The pursuit of money situates the hermit-fathers comfortably within Dostoevsky's general assessment of the commercial values defining bourgeois Paris. Dostoevsky further links the Catholic clergy to the bourgeoisie, to conspiracy, and to the Napoleonic dynasty through his reference to Abbé Siéyès, the author of a manifesto of the French Revolution "Qu'est-ce que le tiers état?" ("What Is the Third Estate?" 1789) who helped to bring Bonaparte to power. Dostoevsky cites Abbé Siéyès's accurate prediction that France's third estate, to which the bourgeoisie belonged, would become dominant, but also recognizes that its prosperity came at the expense of the revolutionary ideals of liberty, equality, and freedom and produced a culture of "a lot of innate servility" that fosters "masterly spying, spying by vocation, having reached an art form with its own scientific methods" (*Pss*, 5:82). Meanwhile the bourgeois couple *bribri* and *ma biche*, expiating their sins through toil, equate financial success and social respectability with divine favor so that the wandering narrator makes a national issue out of a Frenchman's appreciating Garibaldi for his scrupulous management of government funds.

The hermit-fathers contribute to this financial theme their frequent lawsuits over inheritances brought before the French courts, since the fathers conclude that "a little capital is better than everything" as the accumulation of money leads to power (*Pss*, 5:88). The hermit-fathers face little public opposition during the scandalous proceedings, because the bourgeoisie, recognizing the power of the fathers, "is surprisingly well-behaved" (*Pss*, 5:88). However, in order to procure funds successfully in this case, they "with lengthy, crafty, even scientific (they have a science for it) accusations burdened the soul of a beautiful and extremely wealthy lady" and "enticed her to go live with them in the monastery" where they drove her to hysterics and "to idiocy [*do idiotstva*]" (*Pss*, 5:88). This imagery of seduction, which Dostoevsky associates with Catholic priests' sexual advances toward women, underscores material wealth as the highest virtue of Catholicism. The linking of Catholicism and commercialism is further evident in his portrayal of the Gothic cathedral at Cologne, which "is contaminated by the spirit of capitalism" when the narrator is "assaulted by customers of the *parfumier* Jean-Maria Farina shouting the words 'Eau de Cologne ou la vie!' "[16]

In Paris, Dostoevsky focuses on another Catholic edifice, a church dedicated to Saint Genevieve, the patron saint of Paris. Following the 1789 Revolution, the National Assembly in France had converted the church to a Pantheon with the inscription "Aux grands hommes, la patrie reconnaissante" and had laid its heroes, such as Voltaire and Rousseau, in its crypts.[17] Yet, by the time that Dostoevsky visited in 1862, the restoration of the church of Saint Genevieve had helped Louis-Napoleon advance to the throne, as Victor Hugo maintains in *Napoléon le Petit:* "il a enfoncé un clou sacré dans le mur du Panthéon et il a accroché à ce clou son coup d'état."[18] The French Christian tradition and its patriotism became intertwined in the new basilica, in which the relics of Saint Genevieve were ceremonially transported, and ushered in a new era for the Pantheon. New Christian art, such as E. H. Maindron's sculpture representing Saint Genevieve's saving Paris from Attila, was installed.[19] A photograph of the interior circa 1860 shows an altar with a tabernacle over which hangs a painting of Christ in his heavenly garments, accompanied by patron saints of the Catholic Church.[20] Despite Dostoevsky's failure to elaborate on the building's ecclesiastical significance, this architectural fusion of a Catholic church with a Pantheon dedicated to the "saints" of the republic undoubtedly informs Dostoevsky's connection of Rousseau and the French revolution to the Catholic tradition in his aforementioned notes on the Polish uprising (*Pss*, 20:190).

For this reason, the narrator uses his tour of the "Church crypts" in the Pantheon to contrast the eloquent oratory of Jules Favre, champion of freedom of the press in the Second Empire, with a rote recitation on Voltaire, Rousseau, and Marshal Lannes by a Jacques Bonhomme.[21] The tragicomic image of this "decrepit and venerable invalid" with missing teeth singing the memorized praises of heroes of the French Revolution renders ridiculous the formula "l'homme de la nature et de la vérité" repeatedly applied to Rousseau, with satirical origins in Heinrich Heine's critique of Rousseau's claim to record truthfully his autobiography.[22] When "l'homme de la nature et de la vérité" reappears in *Notes from the Underground,* he is an ideological deceiver who cloaks his self-interested "vengeance" in the guise of "justice" and vainglorious orations as candid public confessions (*Pss*, 5:104, 122). Therefore, this invalid Jacques Bonhomme may represent a victim of his nation's love of "eloquence for eloquence's sake," which the narrator of *Winter Notes* postulates is the lasting legacy of the French Revolution (*Pss*, 5:90). The Underground Man, à la Napoleon, plans to manipulate such romantics with "beautiful forms of existence, completely ready-made and forcibly stolen from poets and romantics" in order to crush "the reactionaries under Austerlitz" and to realize the dreams of Italian nationalists by driving the pope from Rome (*Pss*, 5:133). Although this credulous Jacques Bonhomme does not populate Dostoevsky's subsequent writings, Russians deceived by Napoleon's legendary feats remain central to several of Dostoevsky's novels, most notably *Crime and Punishment*.

Early in the narrative of *Winter Notes*, the Catholic tradition is portrayed as antithetical to Russianness, when the narrator refuses to discuss Russians "who settled there [Europe] definitively and forget their language and begin to listen to Catholic paters" (*Pss*, 5:63). Although this reference could apply to any number of Russians abroad, including Chaadaev, whose name appears in the preceding chapter, Herzen's 1861 publication of Father Vladimir Pecherin's "The Triumph of Death" ("Torzhestvo smerti") in *The North Star* (*Poliarnaia zvezda*) suggests that this is an allusion to Herzen.[23] During his brief visit to London in 1862, when Dostoevsky met twice with Herzen, he "then acted very tenderly" toward the exile.[24] Arkady Dolinin demonstrates well how Herzen's composition, plot, and themes, which are shaped by the Slavophile-Westernizer conflict, pervade Dostoevsky's early chapters, as both writers strive to find something "new, still unknown, unsaid" to write about Europe (*Pss*, 5:46).[25] In addition to expounding on Herzen's scathing comments on French bourgeois theater and marital bliss, Dostoevsky shares his scorn for the virtuous bourgeoisie's love for order, authority, and money.[26] Dostoevsky even borrows Herzen's image of Baal and echoes his comments on the moral purity of Protestantism from *Endings and Beginnings* (*Kontsy i nachala*), most of which appeared in *The Bell* immediately before *Time* published *Winter Notes*.[27] Herzen's presence in *Winter Notes*, when coupled with its frequent Catholic images, brings Dostoevsky's summer impressions into dialogue with the Polish conflict, especially given the citation of Gavrila Derzhavin's poem, "Canto to Catherine II on the Victories of Count Suvorov-Rymniksky" ("Pesn' E. I. V. Ekaterine na pobedy grafa Suvorova-Rymnikskogo 1794 goda," 1794) in the third chapter (*Pss*, 5:55).

The narrator mentions lines from Derzhavin's poem when he is passing through Russia's Western lands on approach to the border town of Eydkuhnen, so the landscape likely evokes his meditations on Russia's "European suspenders" (*Pss*, 5:55). In *The Idiot* Dostoevsky similarly uses apparel—Prince Myshkin's sleeveless coat suitable for Swiss or Italian winters—on the same railroad to present a contrast between Russia and the

West. Yet, in *Winter Notes,* the suspenders, along with the French kaftan, are linked to a Russian cultural tradition traced to Denis Fonvizin and found currently manifested in "our extremely progressive party" (*Pss,* 5:55). In the midst of his discussion of Fonvizin, the narrator recalls Derzhavin's praise of Suvorov, "our Hercules" from "Canto to Catherine II," with two verses underscoring his military might in the advance on Warsaw: "He lies down on the mountains, the mountains crumble" and "The Towers he throws beyond the clouds" (*Pss,* 5:55).[28] The placement in *Winter Notes* of a poem praising Suvorov's harsh suppression of the Warsaw insurrection of 1794 may serve then as a word of caution to the latest Polish insurgents, who, responding to the involuntary conscription of Polish urban youths into the tsarist army, attacked Russian garrisons in Warsaw in January 1863. The reference to Catherine's military victory recalls the partitions of Poland and highlights Poland's historic failure to defeat Russia's powerful military. The assurances by the narrator of *Winter Notes* that "this was only a metaphor" and that he is "really speaking now only about literature and namely about belles-lettres" further underscore the political implications of his literary analysis (*Pss,* 5:55).

Furthermore, Świderska observes a conflation of Polish and French nationalities when a Polish phrase, "I fall at your feet / Your humble servant [*padam do nóg*]," in Russian transliteration is used to highlight "false servile sycophancy" as a French national trait, owing, in part, to a reverence for Napoleon III (*Pss,* 5:83).[29] This conflation is characteristic of Dostoevsky's tendency to identify similar national traits in various ethnicities, such as his linking of Polish and Russian nobility to a common aristocratic "borrowed European civilization" that will not merge "with the broad Russian spirit" (*Pss,* 20:98). Dostoevsky's usage of the phrase "padam do nóg" dates to his *Novel in Nine Letters* (*Roman v deviati pis'makh,* 1847), but in *Winter Notes* the phrase is included in the aforementioned discussion of the bourgeoisie's innate "servility" to which he attributes widespread espionage in France (*Pss,* 1:231).[30] Complaints about police spies in Napoleon's Second Empire were common; Karl Marx even links them to the clergy whom he characterizes "as anointed bloodhounds of the worldly police."[31] Since the narrator in *Winter Notes* writes in an earlier passage of his encounter with the secretive police, who observed him closely on the train, the discussion of espionage represents an ongoing anti-Russian theme. Then, the placement of *padam do nóg* within the discussion of French servility and espionage links the shared attribute of bourgeois servility to contemporary French and Polish nationalities. Dostoevsky's repetition of the phrase marginalizes the Poles, who are dismissed "as fundamentally un-Russian, part of Roman Catholic Europe."[32]

Catholic support for treasonous activities in Russia's western borderlands had been in the press recently owing to the protests in Catholic churches (mentioned by Razin in the February issue of *Time*) in the Congress Kingdom of Poland in 1861–62.[33] Mikhail Gorchakov had succeeded Paskevich as viceroy of Poland in 1856, but Gorchakov had been unable to quell the public unrest, which was exacerbated by the Catholic Church's opposition to Alexander II's 1861 decision to place Aleksander Wielopolski in charge of religion and education in the Congress Kingdom.[34] In Warsaw, at funerals of public figures or on national anniversaries, such as the celebration of Tadeusz Kościuszko's death, crowds assembled in churches to display nationalist sentiments.[35] Dostoevsky's presentation of Catholic types in *Winter Notes* therefore complements the political discussions in the pages of *Time*'s 1863 issues, in which Razin and Nikolai Strakhov repeatedly attribute the violence in Poland to the Poles' Roman Catholic heritage. Dostoevsky's decision to introduce Catholic types from two European countries (England and France) in which the Polish cause for independence found vocal support, further allows his reader to connect the journal's discussions of the 1863 uprising to his depiction of the dissemination of Catholic influence throughout Europe, from the slums of London to the courts in Paris. He places a general condemnation of violence justified by the Holy Writ in *Winter Notes* in a critique of chivalry (following Derzhavin's poem), which concludes that the Europeanized Russian "will begin to defend the necessity of the slave trade with Scripture like the North American from the Southern states" (*Pss*, 5:57).

THE CHALLENGE OF THE POLISH QUESTION FOR NATIVE SOIL CONSERVATISM

The circumspect anti-Roman sentiment apparent in *Winter Notes* becomes markedly more pronounced in Dostoevsky's 1866 portrayal of his European travels, *The Gambler*. Dostoevsky here participates in what Strakhov describes as a conservative shift in Russia during this period: "How did the liberal renaissance come to an end? Suddenly proclamations calling for rebellion and destruction began to appear, after the proclamations followed the fires, after the fires—the Polish uprising, and three years later—the attempt on the Sovereign's life."[36] The success of Katkov's *Moscow News* (*Moskovskie vedomosti*) and the simultaneous decline of Herzen's progressive journal *The Bell*, which became closely identified with the Polish independence movement, demonstrate a general trend toward heightened nationalist conservatism in the 1860s. As Vera Nechaeva finds, the Dostoevsky brothers' journal *Epoch* identifies with the conservatives in its frequent criticism of Poland, because *Time* was closed by the tsarist censors in 1863 for its publication of Strakhov's controversial article "The Fateful Question" ("Rokovoi vopros").[37] Nevertheless, the final issues of *Time* already exhibit a growing anti-Polonism that logically follows from Dostoevsky's native soil conservatism in contrast to Herzen's liberalism, in which "exclusive patriotism" has no place in the new society that follows the "coming revolution" (*Ss*, 5:211–12). Dostoevsky understands the conflict between Polish nationalism and universal humanism from his experience with the Petrashevsky Circle, so he recognizes the threat posed by the Polish unrest to his proposed reconciliation of all segments of Russian society.[38] Katkov more directly discusses this danger when describing how "Polish agitators formed our domestic revolutionaries and, despising them in their souls, are able to make use of them."[39]

In keeping with its presentation of a peaceful unification of all Russians within the empire, *Time* marginalizes the insurrectionists by underscoring that they are not ethnically Russian. In defense of the Russian nationalities in the Congress Kingdom and the western provinces, *Time* asserts that Poles are a minority amidst a majority population with Russian heritage.[40] A further statistical breakdown of religious affiliation finds that a negligible number of Russians belong to the Catholic Church, whose parishioners in western Russia are overwhelmingly Polish and Lithuanian. Consequently, the minority Catholic Polish nobility, or *szlachta,* represents a Westernizing and Catholicizing force alien to the masses of people of Russian heritage who populate these lands. Therefore, in the aftermath of the uprising, the sociopolitical analysis of western Russia in *Time* resembles the Slavophile tendency to find that "the distinguishing mark of any culture was the religious faith that underlay it."[41] For instance, Slavophile Alexei Khomyakov directly attributes to Roman Catholicism Poland's resistance to unification with her Slavic brethren: "Poland considers itself more obliged to the royal title of its sovereign, to the spiritual leader of all Christendom, than to the secular master of only one part of the Christian world."[42] *Time's* position on the uprising echoes patriotic sentiments from Aksakov's conservative journal *Day* (*Den'*), which speaks to the cultural incompatibility of the Polish and Russian nations in a March 1863 article "What Is the Force of National Character?" ("V chem sila narodnosti?"): "There is no doubt . . . that Poles almost do not have an independent Polish culture, that the educational beginning of civilization in Poland, brought from Rome, was alien to her Slavic element and produced only artificial, but internally rotten, fruit, brilliant in external appearance."[43] Similarly, Dostoevsky anticipates that since Polish "civilization was not of a national nature," "was not Slavic," and contained "no kind of distinctive feature," the organic Russian spirit will overwhelm this foreign borrowing (*Pss*, 20:98).

In Strakhov's article "The Fateful Question," published in the April 1863 issue of *Time,* Strakhov cites Ivan Kireevsky's conclusions as evidence of Polish stubborn pride in her learned, yet unproductive, Catholic civilization that sustains her in perpetual idealistic rebellion against the Russian

Empire.[44] Dostoevsky evidently concurs with Strakhov, because when the tsarist censor closed *Time,* he attempted to protect Strakhov against accusations of treason (brought by the *Moscow News* and the *Russian Messenger* [*Russkii vestnik*]).[45] In a written response, Dostoevsky outlines how Strakhov traces the source of Poland's discontent to her European civilization, which cultivated "Catholicism, Jesuitism, and aristocratism" in defense of which the Poles "burned and stripped the skin off Russians" (*Pss,* 20:99–100). Dostoevsky remains convinced of Polish attempts to Polonize and Catholicize Russians, because Poland is "a nation that does not consider people of another faith as people, does not respect anything as highly as itself and its faith, and consequently, is capable of using everything in order to convert everyone to its faith" (*Pss,* 20:100). Nevertheless, he does not advocate forceful conversion of the Poles to Orthodoxy but believes that they display a potential for rehabilitation through reeducation: "One should not by force make Russians of Poles and Turks, but it is necessary to assimilate them with the development of the Russian spirit (native soil ideas)" (*Pss,* 20:203). For this reason, he does not join voices calling for Russia "to untie the knot" and abandon Poland but continues to address the problem of Russo-Polish reconciliation.[46] Furthermore, his notes during this period suggest that he envisions future Russian expansion, since he not only advances the controversial claim that "all our artificial borders (Finland and Poland) are natural and acquired instinctively" but also decides that: "We have our world and we need, therefore, Turkey" (*Pss,* 20:203).

Dostoevsky's imperialistic and paternalistic approach to the Polish Question is evident in the pages of *Epoch,* which appeared in the first months of 1864, after Russian troops had quelled successfully the Polish rebels, whose insurgent government had disintegrated owing to an absence of anticipated Western military support. The debate over the reformation of the Congress Kingdom raged in Russian journals, as the government prepared to adopt further Russification measures for the western edge of the Russian Empire. Rather than view this political step as retribution for the uprising or Realpolitik required for Russia's internal stability, *Epoch* characterizes the reforms as an opportunity for peasants in Poland to reconnect with their Slavic roots. In a three-part translation of F. Smith's "History of the Polish Uprising and War of 1830 and 1831" ("Istoriia pol'skogo vosstaniia i voiny 1830 i 1831 godov"), the author sympathetically recalls Poland's naive reliance on the false promises of freedom from the West, for example, from Napoleons I and III, as well as her rejection of the conciliatory efforts made by Tsars Alexander I and II. The series "Our Domestic Affairs" ("Nashi domashnie dela") repeatedly stresses how the reforms, implemented at great sacrifice to the Russians, deliver the peasants in the Congress Kingdom from the destructive forces of the Polish aristocracy and Catholic clergy. In the

April 1864 issue of *Epoch,* the tragic hero Tanin in Yakov Polonsky's drama *Discord: Scenes from the Last Polish Uprising (Razlad. Stseny iz poslednego pol'skogo vosstaniia)* reflects this Russian paternalistic attitude toward the Poles' rebellion. This Russian military leader, stationed in Russian Poland, feels frustrated by the Polish gentry's animosity and by the superstition with which the peasants regard the Russian forces, or *Moskali.*[47] Tanin pities the young noble nationalist Slavitsky for his belief in French promises of liberation and his sister Katerina for her ardent faith in Catholicism, particularly after a priest refuses her last rites for loving a Russian Orthodox soldier. Poland's Roman Catholic tradition, specifically the historic arrival of the Jesuits in the sixteenth century, continues to be isolated as a main source for Poland's contemporary troubles as is evident in several articles, including "What Are the Polish Uprisings" ("Chto takoe pol'skie vosstaniia").[48] Articles on Jesuitism, the papacy, and German Reformation history more generally link Roman Catholicism to a history of violence and therefore provide the impression that a historic and widespread religious movement, hostile to Russia's interests, continues to thrive in Europe.

Through his advocacy for the Russian peasant and national spirit, Dostoevsky supports Alexander II's attempts to Russify the Congress Kingdom, even though they include a punishing redistribution of wealth seized from exiled insurgents to the Russian peasantry. This policy, which alleviated for the Russian nobility some of the economic burden of liberating the serfs, forced Russian progressives to choose between improving the living conditions of the peasantry and supporting the Poles' right to self-determination. Ironically, the Russian journal most equated with the cause for Polish independence, that is, *The Bell,* eventually supports the redistribution plan, much to the anger of the younger generation of radicals who accuse it of abandoning the Poles.[49] Dostoevsky, who himself had experienced a similar deprivation of property and subsequent impoverishment of exile, shows no empathy for the displaced Poles with little financial means whom he encountered in Europe.[50] Instead, the Polish characters struggling with the impoverishment of exile in his fiction appear as "impostors, tricksters, thieves."[51] Dostoevsky's second wife's influence on his later works, starting with *The Gambler,* may have encouraged this tendency, since in her 1867 diary she makes derogatory comments about Poles, for whom she shows little tolerance, particularly when she thinks one of them may be "a little Jew."[52] However, a passing remark made by Wrangel about a Russian counterfeiting scheme directed by Polish nobility, suggests that Dostoevsky's association of Poles with the financial exploitation of Russia dates as far back as their shared exile in Semipalatinsk: "Do you remember our conversations? Is it possible that I was not right, having spoken about the Russian nobility, when its leaders—the chosen, the crème de la crème—befriend the enemies of the motherland—

the Poles, the Jews, and the Armenians—in order to rob their brethren and demolish the credit of Russia under the guise of false coiners!"[53] Wrangel's letter reminded Dostoevsky in 1865, that is, the year before he wrote *The Gambler,* of the Polish exiles and their Gallophile Russian friends with whom he had shared his Siberian experience.

SIBERIAN AND EUROPEAN CATHOLIC CONNECTIONS TO *THE GAMBLER*'S HELL

In this story about international monetary exchange, Dostoevsky draws on his experiences with Catholics in Siberia and in the West to depict Russians' disastrous encounters in Roulettenburg, a world shaped by a bourgeois desire for acquisition and an aura of aristocratic exclusivity. The self-fashioning of exile, which Goryanchikov critically assesses in *House of the Dead,* remains a cross-cultural phenomenon, as Poles become counts, Praskovya is called Polina, and Mlle Blanche du Placet ends the story by taking a married name that she has to abbreviate to "madame la générale de Sago-Sago" (*Pss,* 5:310). Although a pursuit of material wealth dominates the identity of the Poles and French, the narrator Alexei provides a Catholic-Orthodox apposition for *The Gambler,* which grounds the story in the 1863 tensions between Russia and the West over Poland, when he observes that "in the present summer it is almost completely impossible to dine in hotels at tables d'hôte," because "in Paris and along the Rhine and even in Switzerland at the tables d'hôte there are so many little Poles and their French sympathizers that there is no opportunity to utter a word if you are only a Russian" (*Pss,* 5:210).[54] This international conflict is embedded in the narrative through its contrast of bold Russian (especially Alexei's) risk-taking with calculated French seduction and lackeyish Polish cardsharping.

Since *The Gambler*'s Schlangenberg, or Snake Mountain, has a Siberian parallel in Zmeinogorsk (a Siberian region known for its silver mining operation that Dostoevsky visited with Wrangel), the narrative's focus on Russian pursuit of wealth may have links to his Siberian period.[55] In his description of a Zmeinogorsk mining town, Wrangel emphasizes that since most of the miners were well-educated with advanced foreign degrees (from a famous mining academy in Fribourg), their wives, who came from St. Petersburg or abroad, had Parisian toilettes, carriages, cooks, and champagne in abundance, because "receiving colossal amounts of money, they lived extraordinarily broadly."[56] Wrangel's description of the entertainment—picnics, dances, and performances by musician-miners—provides a portrait of an international aristocracy who enjoyed wealth drawn out of the damp imperial mines by Russian workers. Charles Cottrell's recollections from 1840–41 reveal that the mining operations were directed by a German whose workers included "convicts in irons" and state peasants.[57] Also, Bogusławski's memoirs attest that governmental officials and exiles frequently passed through this region, and he describes nearby settlements of Old Believers who had been brought from Poland under Catherine II and were marginalized according to nationality:

> The residents there are called "Poles," although none of them speaks Polish. They are all so-called "Old Believers"; they are always called Poles, because they are the descendants of those who, being persecuted for supposedly moving away from Orthodoxy, in the first half of the past century sought refuge in that part of Poland, which after the first partition of our country passed under the domination of Russia.[58]

In the nearby region of Tomsk, Cottrell identifies Poles in the mining operations: "We know that among those who work in the gold-washing establishments for their daily bread, there are many, and these are principally Poles, who have seen better days, and belonged to a very different class of society than that fate which they are here thrown."[59] Cottrell's observations as well as the history of Polish exiles suggest that these Poles were likely former political prisoners from the *szlachta* who earned a living in the mines while they awaited return to their homeland. Because Dostoevsky's fellow political prisoner Jan Musiałowicz had studied mining and, after his flight from conscription, had worked in a coal mine, Dostoevsky may have gained some knowledge of the operations from this young revolutionary. This type of multinational operation exploiting Russia's subterranean mineral resources shares several attributes with Dostoevsky's society of Roulettenburg, which as Robert L. Jackson observes, "lies in the shadow of Schlangenberg."[60] Dostoevsky's impression of Siberian mining operations, which he witnessed while visiting Zmeinogorsk and Barnaul, may be discerned from the conversation between the meddling, self-centered Khokhlakova and Mitya Karamazov, when, in response to a desperate request for 3,000 rubles, she destines him for the gold mines: "I will tell you your idea: you will track down mines, acquire millions, return and become an active figure, will set us in motion, heading toward the good" (*Pss*, 14:348). In an ironic parallel, Mitya tells his brother at the end of the novel that he is heading to Siberia to work "under the earth with some sort of hammer," presumably as unfree labor in the mines instead of as the well-compensated management above the earth (*Pss*, 15:34).

Dostoevsky, himself, connects *The Gambler* to his Siberian experience through the *House of the Dead*: "If *House of the Dead* drew the public's attention as a representation of convicts, which no one had graphically portrayed before *House of the Dead,* then this story certainly will draw attention as a GRAPHIC and most detailed representation of the game of roulette" (*Pss,* 28.2:51). In a further explication of the comparison to *House of the Dead,* he claims that *The Gambler* is "a description of its own type of hell, its own type of convict 'bath'" (*Pss,* 28.2:51). Perhaps this motivates Dostoevsky's decision to provide the reader again with notes (*Zapiski*) from a tutor-narrator, who serves as a personal guide navigating another of Dostoevsky's hells. Alexei's narration imparts effectively the disparity of Roulettenburg's varied gaming halls, which belong neither to *Winter Notes'* underworld of Baal's casino—a dive frequented by drunks and prostitutes—or in the festive Hades of William Thackeray's Rougetnoirbourg in *The Kickleburys on the Rhine:* "Hades is not an unpleasant place. Most of the people look rather cheerful. You don't see any frantic gamblers gnashing their teeth or dashing down their last stakes."[61] *The Gambler's* hell does not display the aristocratic ambiance of its English literary predecessor but the overcrowded, intoxicating atmosphere of the common prison bath. Like Goryanchikov, the tutor-narrator of *The Gambler* lives in exile, but Alexei's exile is voluntary, since he resides outside of his homeland among various European nationalities hostile to Russia's interests in order to play roulette. For Jackson, Alexei's "craving for risk" resembles the unbridled "delirium" of the murderer depicted in *House of the Dead:* "In his delirium, in his craving for risk, the gambler, like the raging murderer or rebellious convict challenging their fate-bound universe is overcome by the same passion for the abyss."[62] Jackson finds that Alexei's decision to take the metaphoric leap off the peak of Schlangenberg by submitting to Polina's demands symbolizes "his renunciation of free will" and "an act of despair," but the abyss for Russians in Dostoevsky does not necessarily signify resignation.[63]

In *Winter Notes* this appetite for risk is characteristic of his Russian abroad and is attached to the lovelorn wanderer Chatsky who is a "nice type—ecstatic, suffering, and appealing to Russia, and to the soil—but meanwhile having left all the same again for Europe, when it was necessary to find, 'Where there is a little corner for an insulted sensitivity'" (*Pss,* 5:61).[64] Although thwarted in love, this Europeanized Russian type from Alexander Griboedov's *Woe from Wit* (*Gore ot uma*) remains a bold Russian in Dostoevsky, who owns: "We do not like labor; we are not used to walking one step at a time, and it is better to fly directly in one step to the goal or to fall like Regulus" (*Pss,* 5:62). Similarly, in *The Double* the abyss actively "pulls" Golyadkin to his downfall, while in "The Meek One" ("Krotkaia," 1876) the pawnbroker suggests a certain inevitability to the fall: "They say that those standing on a great height are seemingly pulled by themselves downward into the abyss" (*Pss,* 1:142; 24:21). Mitya's moral leap "into the abyss . . . directly, with my head down and heels up" reveals his ability, as a

Karamazov, to embrace actively the abyss by reveling in the aesthetic appeal of degradation (*Pss*, 14:99). In other words, the leap into the abyss is linked to Russianness in Dostoevsky's fiction, a Russianness that he celebrates in *The Gambler* with the leitmotif of the leap off Schlangenberg. Such a leap empowers Polina and Alexei to move boldly through the story by taking personal and financial risks to pursue happiness in the midst of foreigners, who resemble in several respects the Catholic bourgeois types that Dostoevsky establishes in *Winter Notes*.

Europe in the summer of 1863 could not offer a Russian youth, such as Chatsky or Alexei, a refuge, since an armed clash between Russia and the West over Poland seemed an imminently distinct possibility. The diary of Dostoevsky's lover during this period, Apollinaria Suslova, affirms this with its conversations with Poles about the Polish Question.[65] Already in the first chapter of *The Gambler*, Alexei grounds his narrative in a similar international conflict not only with his declaration about the difficulties for Russian travelers but also with the we-they apposition that marginalizes Roman Catholics, owing to his hostile encounter with an abbot at the Holy Father's embassy in Paris. This recollection of the papal embassy serves to organize the nationalities competing for prominence in the novel, especially since Alexei introduces the story with the intention of avenging his maltreatment at the hands of the "dried-up and frosty-faced" fifty-year-old "little abbot" in the embassy (*Pss*, 5:211). His anger at the abbot's preferential treatment of the Austrian guest of a Catholic monseigneur and cardinal emphasizes both the exclusivity of Catholics as well as their contempt for the Russian Orthodox. Alexei implicates the abbot in intolerance by twice (once in French) relating perceived stereotypical accusations launched against Russians by the West: "Then I responded to him that I am a heretic and a barbarian, 'que je suis hérétique et barbare,' and that these archbishops, cardinals, monseigneur, etc. . . are all the same to me" (*Pss*, 5:211).

The multiple oral recitations of the event are acts of national aggression, because Alexei seeks to offend the Catholic types represented in his given audience, for example, the "fat Polish *pan*, the man most hostile to me at the table d'hôte" or the marquis de Grieux with whom he is sharing the General's table (*Pss*, 5:212).[66] Alexei underscores the French Catholic–Orthodox Russian divide when he reads in front of the abbot the "most dreadful cursing of Russia" in the Bonapartist *Opinion Nationale* (*Pss*, 5:211). His additional story about a French huntsman who shot a child in 1812 just to discharge his gun highlights a historic dimension to the contemporary hostilities in a narrative designed to offend the French. As Świderska concludes, such moments in the text highlight the European tensions emerging in the aftermath of 1863, particularly owing to the presence of Alexei's French and Polish audience.[67] During the summer of 1863, the papacy was widely criticized by conservatives in Russia when Pius IX sought to mediate the Russo-Polish conflict by sending to the tsar "a papal nuncio who in the capacity of a representative of a foreign power would stand as a mediator between the Russian crown and her Catholic subjects."[68] Russian conservatives became suspicious of papal representatives, accused the papacy (as well as the Catholic countries over which the pope exercised his influence) of aligning with Poland, and described the Catholic Church as "a de facto Polish national institution."[69] These political concerns may partially account for Dostoevsky's animosity during his visit to the embassy, upon which he draws to create Alexei's similar encounter with the priest.[70]

Dostoevsky's second wife, Anna Grigorevna, who worked as his stenographer on *The Gambler*, identifies Dostoevsky's voice with that of his protagonist: "Fedor Mikhailovich was entirely on the side of 'the gambler' and said that many of his feelings and impressions he himself had experienced."[71] As Dostoevsky writes, the gambler's all-consuming pursuit of his base, yet poetic, passion for risk requires him to remain abroad, since "playing at the watering-places, in fact concerning Russians abroad, has some (maybe not unimportant) significance" (*Pss*, 28.2:51). In depicting an international aristocracy at play, Dostoevsky anticipates Turgenev's *Smoke* (*Dym*, 1867), which engages such topics as the Russian knout, the emancipation of the serfs, and Slavophilism in Baden-Baden. Yet, Dostoevsky takes pains to exhibit the falsity of the aristocracy, whose acquired titles are exposed by the resentful narrator, Alexei, who is frequently addressed by the appellation *ouchitel*, or tutor. Alexei, like Dostoevsky, is drawn westward because of his competing passions for a Polina (Suslova) and roulette. Dostoevsky frenchifies his own relationship with Suslova, who ran off with a Spanish lover Salvador, to provide Alexei's Polina with the French deceiver de Grieux, and thereby introduces another seductive French type into his fiction of the 1860s.

As Frank indicates, "Dostoevsky ironically gives him the name of the passionate lover in Prévost's *Manon Lescaut*," thereby emphasizing the distance between the prosaic reality of Polina's duplicitous marquis and the idealized chevalier des Grieux (singled out for holy orders by a bishop) in the novel written by the former Benedictine, Antoine-François Prévost d'Exiles, better known as Abbé Prévost.[72] Polina shares Marya Alexandrovna's taste for French chivalry, since the former creates a romanticized vision of de Grieux, based on his château, his nationality, as well as his title. Indeed, Marya Alexandrovna's enjoyment of Dumas, in whose son's *La dame aux Camélias* (*The Lady of the Camillias*) the novel *Histoire du Chevalier des Grieux et de Manon Lescaut* (*The Story of the Chevalier des Grieux and Manon Lescaut*) provides a physical link between a courtesan and her young lover, further connects the romanticism of Polina to Dostoevsky's Siberian period. In the novels of Dumas, *fils*, and Abbé Prévost, the heroines Marguerite and Manon, respectively, are kept women dependent on the income they receive from lovers, but respectable young men (Armand Duval and des Grieux) nevertheless pursue their exclusive favors. By assigning Polina's lover, to whom her father owes money, the name de Grieux, Dostoevsky leaves the role of chevalier open for either the Englishman Mr. Astley or Alexei, who vie for the role of this faithful suitor. Alexei, in his passion for Polina, his willingness to gamble to secure their future fortune, and his respect for Racine, more closely resembles the chevalier whose reason could not suppress his desire for the charming but inconstant Manon.[73] Yet, when he partially cites from Don Rodrigue's promise (in Pierre Corneille's *Le Cid*) to avenge his father in a seduction scene with the available Mlle Blanche (who feeds him the line "Mon fils, as-tu du coeur?"), Alexei trades chivalry, idealized by French neoclassicism, for a fleeting sexual encounter with the French gold-digger.[74] In this respect, the French chevalier-type from *Winter Notes* is debased in "The Gambler," in which Polina is abandoned by two potential chevaliers despite the literary precedents of Abbé Prévost's chevalier des Grieux and Corneille's Don Rodrigue (*Pss*, 5:56).

Mlle Blanche, the former Mlle Selma, has none of the charm or emotional complexity of a Marguerite or Manon, but she moves rapidly from one benefactor to another, and in one visit to Roulettenburg progresses from an Italian prince to a Polish count, and then to a Mr. Fider (*Pss*, 5:247–48). Mr. Astley's characterization of "traveling," rather than émigré, Poles ("all traveling Poles are counts"), as well as his reference to "the third year," links Mlle Selma's history to a period when Dostoevsky publishes *Winter Notes* and visits Europe for a second time (*Pss*, 5:247). The purpose of his travels— to enjoy his liaison with Suslova—may have aroused an interest in European sexuality, but *Winter Notes* already openly discusses *ma biche*'s Gustave and *bribri*'s Camelia. Dostoevsky's Camelia is not the tragic courtesan but *bribri*'s gold-digger on the side: "Take the money, deceive me well, that is, fake your love—that is what is demanded of Camelia" (*Pss*, 5:93). Her practiced deception resembles the modus operandi of Mlle Blanche, whose titillating history related by Mr. Astley includes a seduction of a Pole by "having ripped her dresses and having scratched her face like a cat with her beautiful hands washed in scent" (*Pss*, 5:247). Siberian imagery surrounds Alexei's fascination with Mlle Blanche and her "swarthy, healthy, marvelous shoulders," because their spree in Paris displays Alexei's Russian or Tatar preference for living as a nomad "in a Kirghiz tent" rather than worshipping "at the German idol" of the steady accumulation of wealth (*Pss*, 5:301, 225).[75] When he seeks "to debauch himself in the Russian style or to make a pile at roulette," Mlle Blanche admiringly describes him as "un vrai russe, un calmouk!" (*Pss*, 5:226, 308).[76] All the same, Alexei's willingness to run through his winnings with such a contemptuous bourgeois opportunist signals his complete abandonment to Western capitalism, as is indicated by his new nickname *bibi* bestowed upon him by Mlle Blanche. She, however, remains the calculating French materialist of *Winter Notes* by profiting from gambling while minimizing risk through the practice of lending money to gamblers, and by chasing wealthy men until she marries the Russian general to obtain "un château, des moujiks," and "mon million" (*Pss*, 5:309). Thus, Dostoevsky discloses the French bourgeoisie's desire for the trappings of feudal France and its dependence on Russian peasants to provide this wealth.

Still, the vulgar pursuit of riches by the French seems respectable when compared with the comportment of the thieving Poles, who line their pockets at the gaming tables with money stolen from the aged Muscovite noblewoman, Antonida Vasilevna. Anna Grigorevna's diary suggests that Dostoevsky associates certain nationalities with luck at gambling, since he attributes a gambling loss to "a rich Pole" who annoyed him by relating his strategies to an entourage of "Polacks" but believes an Englishman brings him great fortune.[77] Yet, a general observation about the Petrashevtsy by Bogusławski indicates that this tension with Poles over cards may date to Dostoevsky's Siberian period: "All, with little exception, were like one another and none was lacking in education but everybody was of weak character and was passionate either when drinking or also when tanking at cards."[78] The agent Antonelli confirms Petrashevsky's obsessive need to win at cards and even believes that Petrashevsky forced him "on purpose" to play cards "in order to get to know my character."[79] Dostoevsky discloses a familiarity with gambling at cards during this period in his written explanation to investigators: "The very fundamental beginnings of a society threaten every minute to collapse and carry away the entire nation in their fall. Thirty-six million people every day literally risk, as if on a card, their entire future, estate, and existence—theirs and their children's" (*Pss*, 18:122). All the same, Wrangel, almost defensively, insists that Dostoevsky did not play cards in Siberia, even when they visited the commander of a Cossack regiment, at whose house "a convert, a little Polish Jew [*pol'skii evreichik*]," conducted music while guests engaged in "frightful gambling."[80] Instead, Wrangel dates the gambling to a later period and recognizes Dostoevsky's obsession with roulette in connection with his visit during the summer of 1865.[81]

Nevertheless, throughout Dostoevsky's writings frequent encounters with various games of chance provide his personages with the opportunity to mingle with a diverse group of social classes and Western (including Polish) nationalities. Already in *The Insulted and the Injured* (*Unizhennye i oskorblennye*, 1861) Dostoevsky associates losses at cards with Russian misfortune, since Nikolai Sergeich Ikhmenev loses much of his inheritance at cards while the licentious Prince Valkovsky, who traveled to Poland to secure a countess's daughter as a suitable wife for his son, enjoys the game: "I love consequence, rank, a hotel, and an enormous stake at cards (I awfully love cards)" (*Pss*, 3:179, 365). In *Winter Notes*, Dostoevsky pursues the gambling abyss (*bezdna*) in his portrayal of London's Haymarket district: "I remember that I once stopped by a 'Casino.' There music thundered, dancing went on, and an abyss of people thronged" (*Pss*, 5:71). Already on his second journey to Europe in September 1863, Dostoevsky writes his brother about a winning system but tracks both wins and losses (*Pss*, 28.2:45). His desperate pursuit of money, out of which he intended to provide for his extended family, seriously concerned his brother, to whom Dostoevsky applied for additional funds when his recklessness in Baden-Baden cost him a considerable sum. Suslova confirms the desperate circumstances in which the writer found himself: "Fedor Mikhailovich has gambled away all his money and is somewhat concerned that there is so little money for our trip."[82] Dostoevsky subsequently provides Arkady Svidrigailov, who is linked to Polish history, with the identity of a gambler, even though he objects to this characterization: "No, what kind of gambler am I? A cardsharper is not a gambler" (*Pss*, 6:359).[83] Then, in *The Brothers Karamazov*, Polish noblemen at Mokroe, a town which shares a name with an area of Omsk where Durov resided, use a marked deck to cheat Mitya Karamazov (*Pss*, 14:385–89).[84] Therefore, *The Gambler*'s Antonida Vasilevna, who loses a fortune that she intended to spend on constructing a stone church on her estate, follows an established pattern of Russian losses at games of chance in Dostoevsky's works.

Antonida Vasilevna suffers these significant losses not only because she takes on too much risk but also because predatory foreigners—several with links to France and Poland—exploit her age-related confusion for their own profit, thereby subjecting her to social exposure: "All the visitors to the watering-place, of all nations, the ordinary and most famous, streamed in to look at 'une vieille comtesse russe, tombée en enfance' who had already lost 'some millions'" (*Pss*, 5:283).[85] Unlike Polina and the General, who overcome the dislocation of life abroad through assimilation, as evidenced by their pursuit of wealth and fondness for the French, Alexei retains a sense of alienation from his foreign surroundings. Since he remains trapped in the foreign city of Roulettenburg, Alexei's isolation from Russia fuels the gambling impulse: "There is something special in the sensation, when alone, in a foreign country, far from your homeland, from your friends, and not knowing what you will eat today, you stake your last, your very, very last guilder!" (*Pss*, 5:225, 318). While de Grieux, Mlle Blanche, Mr. Astley, and the Poles crowding the casino also reside outside their homelands, they do not share Alexei's outsidedness to Roulettenburg. Rather, as the narrator, Alexei takes the opportunity denied him at the tables d'hôte to express empathy for his fellow Russians, even though he concludes at the end of the story that Russians in Roulettenburg would never redeem him from prison unlike "there in our

Russia" where "the Orthodox redeem the Orthodox" (*Pss*, 5:313). Antonida Vasilevna's direct arrival from the ancient capital of Russia provides him with an Orthodox ally, who echoes Alexei's critique of the General's assimilation of Western values, like "Russians abroad" who "are too cowardly and horribly fear what is said and how they are regarded" (*Pss*, 5:238). Alexei's delight at Antonida Vasilevna's arrival and belief that she "will now turn the whole hotel on its end!" suggest that he endows her with the powers of a deus ex machina, who comes to avert the impending impoverishment of her relatives at the hands of the French (*Pss*, 5:250).

After having been forced to implement the strategy of "that goat's beard" and "buffoon" de Grieux (whose advice causes her to lose 15,000 roubles), Alexei distances himself from her reckless roulette playing and can only report: "The next day she lost everything," since he "was not present at her game" (*Pss*, 5:278, 253, 282). His account depends upon the eyewitness testimony of her Russian servant Potapych, who embeds a binary Russia-West apposition into his narrative when longing for the environs of Russia while lamenting their decision to travel westward: "If only we could hurry to our Moscow! And what don't we have at home in Moscow? Garden, flowers (of the sort not found here), air to breathe, apples ripening, open space—no, we had to go abroad!" (*Pss*, 5:281). In Potapych's narrative, Dostoevsky concentrates the bitter animosity arising from the Russo-Polish conflict of 1863 into an elderly Russian matriarch's encounter with Polish pickpockets at a roulette table. Because the Poles abroad appear without reference to their backgrounds and with limited speech filtered through multilayered narration, the reader primarily receives Alexei's summary of Potapych's impressions of the Poles' outward appearance and comportment. By choosing to portray the Poles through the inexperienced gaze of the Moscow servant, new to life abroad, Dostoevsky authentically motivates the narrative's failure to connect these Poles to their nation's political history to which Alexei alludes elsewhere in the text.

Alexei attributes the most serious accusations against the Poles directly to Potapych, as Alexei breaks his summary of Antonida Vasilevna's losing streak to underscore Potapych's contribution to the narrative account: "The unfortunate Potapych told me all this through tears that same evening after the losses and complained that they stuffed their pockets with money, that he himself saw how they unscrupulously stole and continually thrust it into their pockets" (*Pss*, 5:282). As Zbigniew Żakiewicz indicates, in this account "the little Polacks [*Poliachki*]" emerge "as an organized group which controls Grandma Antonida Vasilevna, who is absorbed by gambling, by stealing from her and passing her on from hand to hand with the goal of future exploitation."[86] Świderska implicates Potapych in this depersonalization of the Poles owing to his "naive vernacular way of speech (i.e. skaz)," which remains distinct "from that of the I-narrator himself," and believes that the lackeyism attributed to the group is derivative of the *padam do nóg* attributed to the French admirers of Napoleon III from *Winter Notes*.[87] Yet, they also remain derivative of the French aristocratic type beloved by the Russian ladies that Alexei names "the cock [*petukh*], le coq gaulois," since the Poles scream "exactly like two cocks caught in hand" when forced to leave the gaming tables (*Pss*, 5:230, 283). Antonida Vasilevna's additional commentary about a potential duel to the General, "All men are cocks, so they fight. As I see it, you are all fools who cannot support your native land," further denigrates Westerners and Westernizers found in *The Gambler* by emasculating them and the duel, their game of honor (*Pss*, 5:258).

The label "honorable" furthers Franco-Polish links in *The Gambler*, since de Grieux, who wishes to be accepted as a "gentleman [*zhantilom*] and honorable man (gentilhomme et honnête homme)," shares a questionable honorability with the "'honorable [*gonorovii*]' *pan*" who offers his services to Antonida Vasilevna: "There appeared a third Pole, already having spoken in perfectly clear Russian, dressed as a gentleman [*dzhentl'men*], and yet, all the same, smacking of a lackey with an enormous mustache and with honor [*gonor*]" (*Pss*, 5:290, 283). With the utterance of the phrase "honnête homme," Dostoevsky parodies a common trope of seventeenth-century French theater.[88] In *Winter Notes*, these combined characteristics of lackeyism and honor are applied to the French, that is, honest people who lost their honor and "act servilely, not knowing what they are doing," thereby displaying a "bad symptom in the life of a nation" (*Pss*, 5:84). Dostoevsky's use of the Russian transliteration of the Polish word for "honor" allows him to apply its Russian significance, which carries with it an exaggerated sense of a person's merit or self-worth, to this Polish gentleman. The more "depraved" but less "contemptuous" type in *Winter Notes*, that is, the "scoundrel [*podlets*]" who yet retains his "honor," clashes with this servile type in *The Brothers Karamazov*, when "the scoundrel [*podlets*]" Mitya Karamazov mocks a Polish gambler with a similar word-play: "As if a Polish gambler would give you a million! . . . Forgive me, gentlemen, I am guilty, guilty again; he would give, he would give a million on his honor [*gonor*], on his Polish honor [*pol'ska chest'*]. See how I speak Polish, ha, ha!" (*Pss*, 5:84; 14:385). With Alexei maintaining "merit [*dostoinstvo*]" as a Russian quality and associating its (false) appearance with the elegant French manner of expression, the Polish gentleman is left with neither honor nor the appearance of it (*Pss*, 5:230). Potapych's narrative underscores this not only with the above physical description but with the assertion "that 'the honorable *pan*' winked" at "the little Polacks" and "even put something in their hands" as Antonida Vasilevna, to whom Alexei refers sympathetically with the familiar appellation grandmother (*babushka*), loses her fortune (*Pss*, 5:283).

Nevertheless, whereas de Grieux's broken Russian fails to impress upon Antonida Vasilevna the need to gamble by calculation, the Polish gentleman's ability to understand Russian and to *babble* "in a mixture of three languages" enables him to manipulate Antonida Vasilevna (*Pss,* 5:280). A similar preoccupation with Poles' mixture of languages—French, Polish, and Russian—appears in the narrative of *House of the Dead,* in which Goryanchikov criticizes Żochowski's broken Russian and cites Mirecki's catchphrase "Je haïs ces brigands" (*Pss,* 4:209, 204, 216). Since Dostoevsky knew of Mirecki's job as a French tutor for the famous Kapustiny daughters in Omsk after his imprisonment, Goryanchikov's recollection of Mirecki's words seems to highlight how the French language separated him from the Russian peasantry while promoting his communication with the Russian nobility, including the narrator himself (*Pss,* 4:204, 216).[89] Also, the importance of Mirecki's phrase is suggested by its threefold repetition, which frames Dostoevsky's fond remembrance of the peasant Marei. *The Gambler* presents a modified image of this peasant-Pole relationship by allowing the servant Potapych to express his disdain for the predatory Polish gentleman. The latter's appearance amidst the group of "little Polacks" stealing the Russian grandmother's money reverses an evident ethnic divide in the Omsk prison fortress, in which Dostoevsky shared an ethnicity with the masses of Russian convicts, known for their thievery, while the Polish prisoners were primarily of the noble class.

In *The Gambler* Dostoevsky Russifies the Polish Siberian martyr narrative by presenting his own Żochowski in the form of Antonida Vasilevna, who shares with him some age-related mental limitations, a tendency to speak out inappropriately, and a victimization by a member of a hostile ethnic group. Although she, like Żochowski, does not long survive the humiliating encounter, the experience forces some of her compatriots in Roulettenburg, for example, Polina and Alexei, to reevaluate their understanding of Russianness. For example, de Grieux's rejection of the Gallophile Polina in the wake of Antonida Vasilevna's gambling losses encourages Polina to turn to Alexei for financial help. Her financial need thereby stimulates Alexei's passion for the gaming tables so that he discovers her love for him only after he has become completely addicted to roulette. Mr. Astley demonstrates that Alexei's pursuit of this "Russian" game represents not just a personal but a national tragedy, for Alexei renounces duty to his "fatherland" for his gambling obsession (*Pss,* 5:315, 317). Alexei claims that the tendency to plunge headlong with his last guilder signifies an active response to the isolation of exile as he remembers his native land (*Pss,* 5:318). *The Gambler*'s invocation of exile motifs following a Russo-Polish conflict fraught with ethnic, religious, financial, and social tensions anticipates the conclusion to *The Idiot,* when Lizaveta Prokofevna recognizes that her daughter's pursuit of a false Polish Catholic count represents "only a fantasy" of life abroad: "All this abroad, all this Europe of yours, all this is only a fantasy, and we, abroad, are only a fantasy" (*Pss,* 8:510).

AGLAYA IVANOVNA'S ATTRACTION TO
THE CATHOLIC TYPE

In *The Idiot* Dostoevsky continues to present a variety of Catholic types, as religious figures, French dignitaries, and a Polish nobleman appear in narratives related by various Russian characters in the novel. For example, Ivan Petrovich tells Prince Myshkin that his benefactor Nikolai Pavlishchev was almost convinced by the wily Jesuit Goureau to join the Jesuit order but died before his conversion to Catholicism. Like the hermit-fathers in *Winter Notes*, Goureau appears motivated by money, since he attempted to lay a claim on Pavlishchev's estate (*Pss*, 8:449). In one of Lukyan Lebedev's colorful accounts, a cardinal, serving as papal nuncio, becomes sexualized as he places "little silk stockings on the little legs" of Louis XV's favorite, the Countess du Barry, whose cry for "encore un moment" before her public guillotining evokes Prince Myshkin's compassion (*Pss*, 8:164).[90] Lebedev's monks are plump medieval types, fed at the expense of the feudal serfs, who slavishly built tall stone castles into the steep mountainsides of Switzerland for the benefit of ancient knights (*Pss*, 8:313). General Ivolgin's Napoleon, who includes Polish uhlans in his inner circle, considers conversion to Orthodoxy and the liberation of Russian "slaves [*raby*]" in order to secure public support for his occupation of the Russian throne (*Pss*, 8:415). Yevgeny Pavlovich's letters narrate how in a Catholic confessional, a "famous pater" seized the mind of the naive young Aglaya Ivanovna "to a frenzy" and, together with the help of an émigré count, caused a rupture between Aglaya and her family (*Pss*, 8:509). Unlike the "scoundrel" de Grieux, whose appeal lies in his appearance to Polina "under the halo of an elegant marquis," Aglaya's count, who "is not even a count, and if really an émigré then one with a dark and ambiguous history," has no pretense to elegance but depends upon his narrative of political victimization to seduce the impressionable Aglaya: "He captivated Aglaya with the unusual nobility of his soul tormented by the sufferings for his native land and so captivated her that she, already before the marriage, had become a member of some committee abroad for the restoration of Poland" (*Pss*, 5:316; 8:509). This conclusion to Aglaya's story thereby demonstrates that the association of Catholic figures and nations with violence, rebellion, oppression, and deception in *The Idiot* does not prevent Aglaya from turning to western Europe and the chivalric tradition, to define the ideal for which she will sacrifice herself.

With her knowledge of Cervantes's *Don Quixote* and Pushkin's "There Lived on Earth a Poor Knight" ("Zhil na svete rytsar' bednyi"), she creates a chivalric vision of Prince Myshkin, owing in part to his experience abroad, which piques her interest as she meets with him "in order to ask everything about abroad" (*Pss*, 8:358). He becomes a part of her desire to escape the banality of Russian home life with visits to Gothic cathedrals in Rome and study in Paris. However, to force Myshkin to fit her chivalric image she must do violence to the texts of both Cervantes and Pushkin in her application of the type to the living example of the Russian prince. Dostoevsky remains conscious of Don Quixote as a type, since he singles out the knight-errant "from all of the beautiful characters in Christian literature" (*Pss*, 28.2:251). In a discussion that compares Don Quixote to Dickens's Pickwick and Hugo's Jean Valjean, Dostoevsky identifies these characters with the ability to connect with the reader, who feels compassion for them, because they are mocked by the crowd or forced to face social injustice. Petrashevsky's identification with Don Quixote and Herzen's frequent references to his contemporary revolutionaries as Don Quixotes in *Ends and Beginnings* taught Dostoevsky the appeal of this Christian literary figure for politically active idealists.[91] Aglaya participates in this literary tradition when she, while reading *Don Quixote,* applies the label "poor knight" to the prince, as Kolya exposes in a deconstruction of the Yepanchina sisters' literary discussions (*Pss*, 8:205–6). Yet, Aglaya's reading does not appreciate the comic element of Cervantes's text that Dostoevsky finds so essential to the reader's connection with the knight-errant but rather romanticizes his quest for the ideal by conducting a parallel reading of *Don Quixote* with Pushkin's vision of the "poor knight": "'Poor Knight'—this is Don Quixote, but only a serious and not a comic one" (*Pss*, 8:207). Her application of the "immense concept of the medieval chivalric platonic love of some pure and lofty knight" to Prince Myshkin requires a rewriting of Pushkin's text, as she changes in her recitation of the poem the letters on the knight's shield to read N. F. B. (a reference to her rival Nastasya Filippovna) instead of the A. M. D. (*Ave Mater Dei*) in Pushkin's original (*Pss*, 8:209).

Aglaya's powerful recitation of Pushkin's poem with her "evident convulsions of inspiration and rapture" and shining eyes resembles in its passion Sonya Marmeladova's emotive reading of the Lazarus narrative (*Pss*, 8:209; 6:251). Aglaya thereby celebrates "the romance of Cervantes" like the romantic historical novelist Walter Scott, who in his Edward Waverley discovers not a quixotic "perversion of intellect" that fails to apprehend "objects actually presented to the senses" but a mind that provides them with "a tincture of its own romantic tone and colouring."[92] Her belief in the value of Paul de Kock's popular novels for educational purposes attests further to the role that naïveté plays in her European fantasies about Myshkin, particularly since Alexei while gambling abroad uses the same novels as empty reading from a "local trashy bookshop" when he wishes to avoid "a serious book" (*Pss*, 8:358; 5:282). At the same time, Aglaya's reading of the poem with its "hidden meaning" shocks Myshkin because of the "beautiful feeling" combined "with such patent and spiteful mockery" that Aglaya expresses "with such innocence and naive simplicity" (*Pss*, 8:209).[93] Myshkin, thus, recognizes in

Aglaya her potential for spite when threatened with the loss of her ideal, that is, the Prince, who represents her gateway to Europe and flight from Russian banality. Her confrontation with Nastasya Filippovna over Prince Myshkin exposes this weakness, since Nastasya Filippovna reveals that Aglaya's snide comments about the former's virtue are motivated by jealousy. When the Prince fails to defend Aglaya's honor by momentarily siding with Nastasya Filippovna, Aglaya abandons the "poor knight" for her poor Polish count and retains her fantasy of life abroad.

Prince Myshkin's connection to chivalry continues through the end of the novel, when his failure to protect Nastasya Filippovna constitutes yet another stain on the reputation of the "poor knight." His groomsman Keller connects him to the chivalric line of the Knights of Rohan discussed in humorous anecdotes in *Winter Notes*, when Keller reveals his wish that Myshkin marry "no other than the Princess of Rohan" (*Pss*, 5:56–57; 8:486). The Prince's discovery soon thereafter of an open edition of Gustave Flaubert's *Madame Bovary* in Nastasya Filippovna's rooms maintains the chivalric leitmotif through the end of the novel. As Robin Feuer Miller concludes, "the image of Don Quixote overshadows the first parts of the novel" but "the image of *Madame Bovary*," which represents a "diminished version of *Don Quixote*," then "hovers over its final pages."[94] Flaubert's heroine is raised in a convent where she is exposed to ideals in songs from a bygone era and in novels smuggled to her by a relic from pre-revolutionary French nobility. Emma Bovary grows to admire the novels of Walter Scott and to follow the tragic histories of such great women as Mary Stuart, Joan of Arc, and Heloise from the medieval and Reformation eras.[95] As Soledad Fox recognizes in *Flaubert and "Don Quijote,"* "Like Cervantes with his fondness for chivalric romances, Flaubert would always feel a kinship with the sentimental (Romantic, in the sense of the literary vogue of his youth) romances."[96] Flaubert learns from Cervantes to reproduce "the collision course between the hero's extravagant ideas (poetic, Romantic) and the vulgarity of the material world (prosaic, real)."[97] As with the demise of their potential literary doubles, Catholic culture indirectly contributes to the destruction of Prince Myshkin and Nastasya Filippovna. Nastasya Filippovna's reading of Emma Bovary's tragedy likely helped to inspire her imbalanced self-fashioning, whereas a precedent for Prince Myshkin's final descent into idiocy may be found in the hysterics and idiocy suffered by the wealthy lady tormented by hermit-fathers in *Winter Notes*, particularly given the Prince's previous epileptic reaction to the revelation about his benefactor's Jesuit connections.

Remnants of the chivalric theme survive in Dostoevsky's later works as Linda Ivanits's analysis of the chivalric dimension to Stepan Verkhovensky and Nikolai Stavrogin in *Demons* demonstrates.[98] Dostoevsky continues his discussion of *Don Quixote* in *Diary of a Writer,* in which he dismisses "the absurdity of the existence of wandering knights for the good of humanity" (*Pss,* 26:26). This criticism anticipates Dostoevsky's later analysis of the aristocratic Russian wanderer, who professes to hate serfdom but heads "to the barricades in Paris" without liberating his serfs, since "all the same money is needed in the cushy place in Paris, even while taking part in the barricades, so the peasants' quitrents were sent off" (*Pss,* 27:158). The association of the knight with this type of Russian wanderer is also apparent in Katkov's writing when he ironically applies the label "Noble knight [*Blagorodnyi rytsar'*]" to the spendthrift Bakunin in an article discussing the émigré's appeal to young Russians.[99] Dostoevsky's Underground Man analyzes a similar type in his discussion of Russian romantics, who are not the aforementioned French fools on barricades or the "stupid starry-eyed Germans," for the foolish Russian romantics "preserve their jeweller's bagatelle" and settle "over there, more in the Weimar or in the Black Forest" (*Pss,* 5:126). In spite of his self-identification as a "spiteful man [*zloi chelovek*]," the Underground Man does not censure these émigrés with a betrayal of Russianness, but he celebrates the "many expansive natures" of different types of Russian romantics who remain dedicated to "the beautiful and the sublime" even in the face of adversity (*Pss,* 5:99, 126). In the writings of the more mature Dostoevsky, Russians' contact with the West often results in the importation of dangerous Catholic political contaminants into his homeland. Dostoevsky therefore seems to recognize that the progress that brought the railroad also increased the exchange of subversive ideas, since Russian borders became more porous and the heart of Russia became increasingly accessible to citizens from the borderlands who participated in the West-East flow of information.

PART II

The Catholic Dimension to Dostoevsky's Russian Revolutionaries

It was the best of times, it was the worst of times, it was the age of wisdom, it was the age of foolishness, it was the epoch of belief, it was the epoch of incredulity, it was the season of Light, it was the season of Darkness, it was the spring of hope, it was the winter of despair, we had everything before us, we had nothing before us, we were all going direct to Heaven, we were all going direct the other way—in short, the period was so far like the present period, that some of its noisiest authorities insisted on its being received, for good or for evil, in the superlative degree of comparison only.

—Charles Dickens, *Tale of Two Cities* (1859)

Chapter Three

The Casuistry of Revolutionaries
in *Crime and Punishment*

> "Napoleon is a Catholic of prime example;
> The Pope anointed him after all."
> —Adam Mickiewicz, *Pan Tadeusz* (1834)

DOSTOEVSKY DREW ON his literary knowledge, encounters with Catholics, and discussions of the Roman church published in the aftermath of the Polish uprising to provide his most famous Napoleonic hero, Rodion Raskolnikov, with a casuistic dimension in *Crime and Punishment.* Casuistry refers to an ethical case-reasoning with origins in Aristotle's *Nicomachean Ethics* that examines moral issues on a case-by-case basis with consideration for individual circumstances instead of relying on the general application of universal principles. Raskolnikov's casuistry displays commonalities with the Catholic tradition of casuistic literature generated by the church's codification of canon law, the scholastic inquiries of Saint Thomas Aquinas, the decision by the Fourth Lateran Council (1215) to regulate the sacrament of confession, and the formation of the Society of Jesus (1540) during the Reformation era.[1] While sixteenth-century Protestant theologians drew on Aristotle's ethics to explore casuistic moral philosophy in the Reformed tradition, the Society of Jesus's probabilistic reasoning, which prioritized the subjectivity of intention rather than the nature of the act performed, advanced its public identification with casuistry, particularly owing to its taxonomies of *casus conscientiae.*[2] Blaise Pascal's seventeenth-century defense of the Jansenists in *Les provinciales* (*Provincial Letters,* 1656–57), which satirically depicts the Society's endorsement of verbal equivocation and moral laxity, so furthered an automatic association between the Jesuits and casuistry that the popular Machiavellian maxim that the end justifies the means came to be attributed to the Society of Jesus.[3]

Dostoevsky's acceptance of this stock portrayal of the Jesuits' casuistry is evident from similar language in his 1864–65 notebook, which contains a reference to "Catholics" who "will allow *all means* (after the fall of power) and by this alone will already accept and introduce Jesuitism," as well as from Fedor Pavlovich's assessment of the moral equivocation of the "stinking [*smerdiashchii*] Jesuit" and lying "casuist" Smerdyakov in *The Brothers Karamazov* (*Pss,* 20:190; 14:119). In the same notebook, Dostoevsky connects Jesuitism to contemporary revolutionary movements in a discussion of how the Catholic Church will undergo renewal and "will be united directly with the revolutionaries and socialists—in the sincere representatives sincerely and in the insincere like a bandit (like the one now helping the plunder in Italy)—but otherwise in both cases introducing Jesuitism to the revolution" (*Pss,* 20:189–90). Already in the 1840s, Dostoevsky had demonstrated more than a passing interest in the frequent European and Russian association of Jesuitism with subversive activity, through his connection with the Petrashevsky Circle and in his editing work for an encyclopedic entry on Jesuits, which concludes that the "mission" of the Society is "to do and to allow [*dopuskat'*] all that will direct wisdom for the dissemination of the Catholic religion 'in majorem Dei gloriam' (the motto of the Order)" (*Pss,* 28.1:141–42).[4]

While Dostoevsky was drafting *Crime and Punishment,* Yury Samarin published in *Day* letters to the Jesuit convert Father Ivan Martynov, which linked the history of Jesuit intrigue in Russian political affairs to revolutionaries like Otrepev, Napoleon Bonaparte, Napoleon III, and Polish rebels of 1863 in an effort to illustrate how the activities of the Order encouraged civil unrest in Russia, thereby resulting in multiple invasions of Moscow and uprisings in the provinces.[5] The publication of Samarin's letters followed the two-volume history of Catholics in Russia, *Le Catholicisme romain en Russie* (*Roman Catholicism in Russia,* 1863–64), written by the subsequent procurator of the Holy Synod (1865–80) and minister of education (1866–80) Dmitry Tolstoy. Tolstoy's history traces the presence of the Jesuits on Russian soil beginning with the reign of Ivan IV and devotes considerable space to Latin clerical propaganda under Alexander I.[6] Dostoevsky's own discussion of the Jesuitism and casuistry of modern revolutionaries as well as the inclusion of references to Otrepev and Napoleon in his works invoking the Jesuits demonstrate that the role-playing of Golyadkin and Raskolnikov, which embraces the use of "all means suitable, so long as the goal could be attained," has roots in the Catholic casuistic tradition (*Pss,* 1:351).[7] Indeed, Scanlan alludes to *The Double* when concluding that what Dostoevsky identifies as the " 'Jesuit' notion that 'the end justifies the means' " is "a dominant theme in both *Crime and Punishment* and *Demons.*"[8] Raskolnikov's exploration of casuistry extends the course of the novel as he comes to reject its application for the justification of Dunya's self-sacrifice, Sonya's prostitution, the Napoleon-styled murders, and flight from justice. The decisions by this young offender to reject casuistic equivocation and to accept responsibility for the murders he commits thus prevent him from becoming a revolutionary like Napoleon and therefore necessarily alienate him from the Polish inmates (reminiscent of Dostoevsky's Catholic comrades in *House of the Dead*) with whom he shares his prison sentence in Siberia.[9]

EARLY INTEREST IN CASUISTRY, TYRANNICIDE, AND PRETENDERSHIP

Dostoevsky's notes on Jesuitism and revolution betray a knowledge of the Order's implication in the practice of tyrannicide owing to its support for the deposition of usurpers (and even legitimate rulers) by their subjects when warranted by despotic behavior. Indeed, a history of the Order with several accounts of regicide was found in the room of Anton Berezowski, who attempted to assassinate Alexander II in 1867.[10] Jesuit casuist Emmanuel Sa clarifies this point in a 1595 guide for confessors:

> Someone governing tyrannically, but who has acquired his position of authority (dominum) justly, cannot be deprived of it without a public judgement: once sentence has been passed however, anyone at all can execute it. He can also be deposed by the people, even if it had sworn him perpetual obedience, if he is unwilling to mend his ways after due warning. And any member of the people may kill someone occupying the office tyrannically [i.e., a usurper], if there is no other remedy; for he is a public enemy.[11]

Pierre Zaccone's *Histoire des sociétés secrètes, politiques et religieuses* (*The History of Secret, Political, and Religious Societies*, 1847), which was on Petrashevsky's subscription list, refers to this Jesuit promotion of tyrannicide when revealing the popular acceptance of the Society's participation in the assassination of Henri III of France and in an attempt on the life of his successor Henri IV.[12] Dostoevsky's familiarity with *Le prêtre, la femme, et la famille* (*The Priest, the Woman, and the Family*, 1845) by the anticlerical historian Jules Michelet informs the former's understanding of French priests' participation in the revolution "for tobacco and for a bottle of wine," and therefore Dostoevsky likely appreciated Michelet's linking the reigns of the Bourbons Henri IV and his grandson Louis XIV through the Jesuit intrigue that dominated their seventeenth-century courts (*Pss*, 20:191, 383).[13] Meanwhile in England, Protestant critics of the Jesuits joined with the Jansenists in attributing to the Order political conspiracies against the crown, as is evident in Titus Oates's *A True Narrative of the Horrid Plot and Conspiracy of the Popish Party* (1679). Russia's experience with similar conspiracies begins in the same century, when, during a period of internecine strife, pretenders endorsed by Catholic (sometimes Jesuit) authorities sought to unseat Orthodox tsars from the throne in Moscow. Dostoevsky's early references to one of these impostors, Otrepev, and the Jesuits attest to his interest in this Catholic agitation during Russia's Time of Troubles.

Militant Catholics in neighboring Poland were heartened by their kings, who encouraged proselytization by the Jesuits in historically Russian lands, and by the advance of the Roman church with the establishment of the Catholic Eastern Rite (Union of Brest, 1596), even while the Russian throne sought to expand the Orthodox sphere of influence by securing the status of patriarchate for the Russian Orthodox Church (1589). As early as Lope de Vega's 1617 *comedia, The Grand Duke of Muscovy and the Hunted Emperor* (*El gran duque de Moscovia y emperador perseguido*), narratives credited conspiring Catholics with the first False Dimitry's rise to power.[14] Alexander Sumarokov's eighteenth-century classical drama *Dimitry the Pretender* (*Dimitrii Samozvanets*), which equates Polishness with popery in a presentation of Dimitry's desire to bring Russia under papal domination, sets the stage for the Catholic-Orthodox apposition characteristic of popular nineteenth-century Time of Troubles narratives, such as Karamzin's *History of the Russian State*, Pushkin's *Boris Godunov*, and Zagoskin's *Yury Miloslavsky*.[15] In these later narratives, Sumarokov's image of Catholicism as a movement led by cunning impious leaders preoccupied with wealth and power continues to be linked to varying degrees with the pretenders attempting to capture the throne in Moscow. Although this binary reading does not account for the multitude of religious traditions represented by the reformers who entered Russia in the early seventeenth century, it is this vision of pretendership upon which Dostoevsky draws in *The Double, Crime and Punishment*, and *Demons* in dialogue with Pushkin's *Boris Godunov*.

Dostoevsky and Pushkin share an admiration for nineteenth-century narratives displaying nationalist sentiment characteristic of this historical period. Pushkin praises Zagoskin's portrayal of patriots in *Yury Miloslavsky:* "Zagoskin carries us back precisely to 1612. Our good people, boyars, Cossacks, monks, and unruly traitors—all of this was divined, all of this acts and feels how it must have felt in the troubled times of Minin and Avraam Palitsyn" (*PssP,* 11:92). Dostoevsky, likewise, appreciates Pushkin's Time of Troubles types, especially Pimen and Otrepev, from *Boris Godunov,* and celebrates the era as one of national unity in introductory notes to his famous 1880 Pushkin speech (*Pss,* 26:132). Their similar appreciation for the Russian people during the country's internecine strife may account for why Pushkin's tragedy to a great extent informs Dostoevsky's vision of the Time of Troubles, as evidenced by his admiration of Pushkinian types in the 1860s and the citations of *Boris Godunov* in his novels.[16] Indeed, Dostoevsky's literary dialogue with *Boris Godunov* begins early in his career, according to the reminiscences of A. E. Risenkampf, who remembers Dostoevsky reading his own non-extant drama by the same name at a farewell party for his older brother: "Fedor Mikhailovich, of course, was here, and he read passages from two of his dramatic experiments [very likely inspired by readings of Schiller and Pushkin]: *Mary Stuart* and *Boris Godunov*."[17]

Both Schiller's and Pushkin's dramas share a central theme of Catholic claimants vying for political power in the midst of the religious conflicts of the Reformation period. Although little information exists on these early dramas, they were written during a period of Dostoevsky's romantic fascination with heroic personages such as those found in the dramas of William Shakespeare and Friedrich Schiller, to which a Schillerean "ardent dreamer," Ivan Shidlovsky, introduced the young Dostoevsky (*Pss*, 28.1:68).[18] Such a romantic focus also accounts for why Andrei Dostoevsky recalls reading the drama with "youthful ecstasy" while the author Fedor dismissed it as "childish nonsense."[19] Assuming the romantic dramas' similarities to those by Pushkin and Schiller, Dostoevsky likely focuses on the papal-sponsored pretenders Maria Stuart and Grigory Otrepev who legitimize their claims to the throne by maintaining that God's justice demands that they unseat the usurpers (Elizabeth I and Boris Godunov, respectively) who unlawfully wield their power. While Schiller sympathetically portrays the Catholic Mary as truly pious and martyr-like, his characterization of the coldly ambitious Protestant Elizabeth, who signs the order for Mary's execution, shows that he attributes tragic consequences to the combination of religious fervor and power politics. In Pushkin's *Boris Godunov,* in spite of the fact that Otrepev initiates the imposture out of a desire to see that the murderer Boris escape neither "earthly judgment" nor "God's judgment," his pretendership ultimately becomes merely "an excuse for dissension and war" against the Russian Orthodox on the part of the Polish king and the pope (*PssP,* 7:23, 64). Samarin, in clarifying the threat that Jesuits pose to Russia, refers precisely to the Jesuits' support for this politically motivated criminal act to demonstrate how material rather than spiritual considerations motivate the Order:

> The Jesuits undoubtedly knew that the False Dimitry was not the son of Ivan, they consciously served him precisely as *an Impostor.* . . . as soon as he left the scene, they immediately attached themselves to another Impostor, known under the name of the thief of Tushino. And so, they forced their way through, bringing with them as their standard a living lie and deception personified.[20]

As Mikhail Alekseev discerns, these dramatic portraits of "Godunov who killed Dimitry and Elizabeth who puts Mary Stuart to death" already anticipate "the problem of power" that Dostoevsky investigates more fully in his great novels.[21] Dostoevsky's subsequent decision to link jesuitical intrigue and pretendership in the context of contemporary St. Petersburg attests to his fascination with spiritually motivated internecine strife that undoubtedly shaped his own *Boris Godunov* and *Mary Stuart* (*Mariia Stiuart*).

In Pushkin's *Boris Godunov* and Dostoevsky's *The Double*, both Otrepev's and Golyadkin's role-playing is associated with the intrigue of the Jesuits but for the purpose of social advancement. From the beginning of Pushkin's tragedy, Otrepev casuistically appeals to his own conscience, in appointing himself the avenger of the martyred child-tsarevich as a means of justifying his appropriation of the deceased's persona:

> Boris, Boris! All before you tremble;
> No one even dares to remind you
> About the sacrifice of the unfortunate infant—
> And meanwhile a hermit in a dark cell
> A terrible denunciation of you writes:
> And you will not escape from the world's judgment,
> As you will not escape the judgment of God. (*PssP,* 7:23)

Otrepev's insistence that secular judgment reflect that of the divine causes him to violate Pimen's charge to record history rather than actively shape the affairs of the "sinful world" (*PssP,* 7:20). His conversation with Marina Mnishek demonstrates that he draws his authority from his perceived public persona as "a devout adopted son of the Jesuits," "a noble knight," or "a tsar's son" (*PssP,* 7:64). Otrepev "proudly" admits his casuistic challenge to the usurper during these historically exceptional circumstances, which may demand that he "fight with Godunov" or "outwit [*khitrit'*] a court Jesuit" (*PssP,* 7:64, 65). He does not seek the sanction of any church official—Orthodox or Catholic—but looks to a revealed historical necessity (the divinely fore-ordained dynastic succession by adoption) for his justification:

> The shadow of the Terrible adopted me.
> Named me Dimitry from the grave,
> Rallied the peoples around me,
> And doomed Boris to be sacrificed to me—
> I am the Tsarevich. (*PssP,* 7:64)

Understanding that he remains vulnerable to the caprice of the crowd ("ruin or the crown / awaits my head") that haunts his dreams, he nevertheless looks only to the dictates of his own conscience as he undergoes a transformation from an impostor to Dimitry according to Pushkin's changing appellations in the scene (*PssP,* 7:64).

Golyadkin's decision to draw on Otrepev's example of pretendership earns him the ridicule of both his colleague as well as the narrator in the

1846 version of *The Double*. At the beginning of the fourth chapter, the narrator playfully relays to the reader that the Jesuits are responsible for Golyadkin's social success with the disclosure that "with the help of the Jesuits" Golyadkin "finally achieves his goal" (*Pss*, 1:348). Then Golyadkin, "having reassured himself" with the Jesuits' modus operandi, engages in intrigue at Klara Olsufevna's party for the purpose of social advancement (*Pss*, 1:351). Here, he exploits this Jesuit image as a way of ethically distancing himself from the "ruses [*khitrosti*]," "intrigues [*intrigi*]," and "masks [*maski*]" so distasteful to him, as the narrator recognizes: "Mr. Golyadkin, of course, was not an intriguer and not a master of boot-licking. . . . It had already happened. Besides, even the Jesuits were somehow mixed up in it" (*Pss*, 1:352). Ill-equipped to face public exposure, Golyadkin flees "headlong [*stremglav*]" from social humiliation only to encounter his double—that is, a new social persona for Golyadkin—who is capable, like Otrepev, of using cunning "to outwit [*khitrit'*]" others and "intrigue [*intrigy*]" to ensure upward mobility (*Pss*, 1:355, 369). In an attempt to dissociate himself from his double's plotting, Golyadkin bombastically identifies his alter ego not only with imposture but with Otrepev himself, as the narrator indicates: "Mr. Golyadkin awakes, writes a letter, and slightly touches upon the reputation of Grishka Otrepev. Mr. Golyadkin begins the intrigue" (*Pss*, 1:390).

Nevertheless, the aforementioned business letter written by his colleague Vakhrameev clarifies that it is the socially inept Golyadkin who enjoys a public association with the impostor's historic reputation of jesuitical deceit even though Vakhrameev, using Golyadkin's own rhetoric, confirms: "Finally, you write, my dear sir . . . of imposture in our business-oriented and industrial (primarily because of steamships and railroads) century, and it is not possible, as you were so kind as to correctly confirm, that Grishka Otrepev could appear another time" (*Pss*, 1:414). This letter further identifies a legalistic motivation for Golyadkin's exploitation of "the precious history of our fatherland" as Vakhrameev accuses him of "alluding to famous individuals, attributing to them all of your crimes, and thereby trying to save yourself from the inexorable severity of the laws" (*Pss*, 1:414). This contrast between Golyadkin's romantic historical sensitivity and Vakhrameev's admiration for science, progress, and the law exposes a subcultural clash between the dreamers and the bureaucrats in Dostoevsky's St. Petersburg that anticipates the tension between Raskolnikov and Luzhin. By thus endowing Golyadkin's inflated sense of self with historical pretensions, Dostoevsky portrays the failed application of casuistry in extremis in contemporary Russia. This jesuitical dimension to social intrigue, present in both the words of *The Double*'s narrator and Golyadkin, demonstrates that the invocation of Jesuitism in Dostoevsky represents not merely cunning or duplicitous behavior but also a historical tradition of political conspiracy. At the same time, Golyadkin's failure to demonstrate an exploration of conscience or any discernment of divine will before acting with the help of the Jesuits suggests that already in *The Double* Dostoevsky doubts the sincerity of the Jesuit tradition and the motivation underlying its moral reasoning.

SEVENTEENTH-CENTURY CONNECTIONS TO RASKOLNIKOV'S CASUISTRY

By providing the protagonist of *Crime and Punishment* with the name Raskolnikov, derived from the word meaning schismatic (*raskol'nik*), Dostoevsky furthers the connection between nineteenth-century St. Petersburg and seventeenth-century socio-political unrest with this allusion to the schism in the Russian Orthodox Church between the Orthodox accepting the Nikonian reforms and the believers choosing to remain with the old rituals (Old Ritualists or Old Believers).[22] This naming is not incidental (as the presence of the schismatic Mikolka in the novel attests), especially given Dostoevsky's acquaintance with Old Believer traditions from his incarceration in Omsk and from residing in Semipalatinsk near their settlements.[23] Furthermore, *Time* published several articles on their history, including Afanasy Shchapov's "Zemstvo and the Schism: Runners" ("Zemstvo i raskol. Beguny"). It is particularly appropriate that the discontented Raskolnikov resides in Peter's city, because the Westernizing tsar was considered by many sects of Old Believers to be an illegitimate tsar or even the Antichrist, deserving of tyrannicide.[24] *Time* recognizes the anti-authoritarian response of the Old Believers who rebelled like Razin, Pugachev, or royal impostors in popular opposition to centuries of oppression.[25] This tradition attracted the attention of Russian liberals like Petrashevsky, Herzen, and Bakunin who intended to capitalize on this anti-tsarist sentiment to foment popular uprisings.[26] Therefore, by providing his Raskolnikov with the heritage of the schism, Dostoevsky ties his hero to contemporary Russian revolutionary protest rooted in a historic tradition that casuistically advocates even murder in the name of the divine will but with a temporal benefit for the common weal.

As Molly Wesling discerns, Old Believers in nineteenth-century Russia represented only one group of social malcontents who co-opted Napoleon's legacy: "Napoleon reemerged [after the 1812 campaign] as a symbol of protest against various forms of oppression in Russian life. Peasants, Jews, Old Believers and the young officers who joined secret societies to work for social reform, all had reason to appropriate the myth of Napoleon as liberator."[27] During his Siberian experience, Dostoevsky no doubt observed, for example, that schismatics shared common causes with other dissidents seeking democracy for Russia or independence for Poland and Ukraine in that they desired liberation from the central control of the tsar and were willing to use force to achieve this aim.[28] An 1866 report by the Third Section confirms Napoleon I's popularity among the discontented populace in Siberia, some of whom carried a portrait of the general on their belts.[29] Dostoevsky recognizes the ability of Napoleon's revolutionary image to transcend generations, even while desiring its demise, as indicated by his hope that with France's defeat by Prussia "the Napoleon surname will by this time be insufferable" (*Pss*, 29.1:138). Many of his dreamers—Mr. Prokharchin, Mr. Golyadkin, the Underground Man, and the senile Prince K—fall prey to this hero worship, and in *Crime and Punishment* the confrontational police inspector Porfiry Petrovich enjoys challenging Raskolnikov with the emperor's persona when the latter maintains "I do not consider myself a Muhammad or a Napoleon": "'Well, absolutely, who among us in Russia does not consider himself a Napoleon now?' Porfiry suddenly uttered with dreadful familiarity. This time, there was even something particularly distinct in the intonation of his voice" (*Pss*, 6:204).[30]

Raskolnikov's repeated invocation of Napoleon's name, as a means of attesting to the existence of the "extraordinary man" in accordance with his criminal theory, connects this schismatic protagonist not only to rebellion but to a historical endorsement of tyrannicide, with which Napoleon was associated in the Russian consciousness as Pierre Bezukhov from Lev Tolstoy's *War and Peace* (*Voina i mir*, 1863–68) indicates: "The people gave him power only so that he could deliver them from the Bourbons and because they saw in him a great man."[31] This link to tyrannicide is furthered by Dostoevsky's association of Russian Hamlets with schisms, since Bakunin's unpublished article on Shakespeare's seventeenth-century tragedy about regicide contains a binary criminal theory that parallels Raskolnikov's extraordinary-ordinary juxtaposition. For Dostoevsky, such Hamlets suffer a mental bifurcation causing one half to suffer from melancholy and torment while the second half observes and describes the spleen of the first (*Pss*, 20:136).[32] Characterizing this melancholic contemplation in 1864 may have encouraged Dostoevsky to recall, soon before he began drafting *Crime and Punishment*, his youthful fascination with *Hamlet* at a time when Bakunin and Belinsky were studying the tragedy.[33] Since Dostoevsky's first mention of Hamlet's "stormy and wild speeches" dates to this period, he may have enjoyed Bakunin's politicized portrait of Hamlet, which was likely discussed at Belinsky's while Dostoevsky frequented the writer's circle in the 1840s (*Pss*, 28.1:50).[34]

S. F. Udartsev identifies the underlying Hegelian foundation (one shared by Raskolnikov's theory) to Bakunin's discussion of crime and justice in his analysis of Shakespeare's tragedy: "Not everything in reality may be rational [*razumno*], as Mikhail Aleksandrovich says, but the rational beginning, justice [*spravedlivost'*] triumphs all the same, even if for it, one may need to resort to violence."[35] This juxtaposition of the rational and the just, which encourages the justification of suspect means to achieve a beneficial end, parallels the "casuistry" that Dostoevsky attributes to the Jesuits in *The Double* and in *Crime and Punishment*. When Raskolnikov assesses Sonya's calculated sacrifice of her body in exchange for the happiness of her family members, he compares her moral reasoning ("Is it rational?") to that of the Jesuits: "We will probably learn for a while from the Jesuits and will console ourselves, convince ourselves that it is necessary this way, really necessary, for a good purpose" (*Pss*, 6:38). However, Bakunin limits himself to a discussion of the inner workings of the conscience in relation to the individual criminal act and does not explore the historic deeds enacted by Hegel's great men, for example, Alexander the Great (also invoked in *Hamlet*), Julius Caesar, and Napoleon Bonaparte, whose experience provides the basis for Raskolnikov's extraordinary man theory. In this respect, Bakunin's criminal theory has greater, potentially universal, applicability:

> Every criminal, unwittingly and unconsciously confessing its [justice's] unlimited power, hands himself over to trial; one, having submitted to the verdict of his conscience, freely and consciously removes himself from the crime; another, defeated by temporary fear or belated shame, does not heed the punishing voice of this inner judge and strives to muffle it and to conceal forever and from everyone the crime he committed.[36]

Bakunin finds that Hamlet similarly suffers while he remains unable, despite the supernatural revelations of the ghost of his father, the former king of Denmark, to undertake with moral conviction the act of revenge by murdering his fratricidal uncle in a way that ensures that the murder signifies justice, not a second crime. Yet, Bakunin affirms in the Hegelian tradition the importance of human agency in the search for justice, which may require casuistic endorsements of criminal acts, here tyrannicide, for the pursuit of a just end.[37]

A Hamletian punishing conscience haunts the Napoleonic Raskolnikov whose obsessive behavior suggests a mental bifurcation, despite Dostoevsky's arming him with a revolutionary's casuistry and the radicals' peasant ax to signal his place within Russian conspiratorial history widely discussed in the 1860s (*Ss*, 14:238–39).[38] Although the day before the murder he criticizes Sonya's casuistic self-sacrifice, justified only by a jesuitical barter of "conscience" at "the flea market," Raskolnikov nevertheless relies on the casuistic reasoning of his own conscience to justify the pawnbroker's murder, as the narrator reveals in a mocking tone similar to that of his predecessor in *The Double:* "And moreover, it would seem that the entire analysis, in the sense of moral solution to the question, was already finished for him; his casuistry was sharp, like a razor, and he could no longer find within himself any conscious objections" (*Pss*, 6:37–38, 58). The narrator's direct citation of Raskolnikov's thoughts on the development of the proper "will [*volia*]" and "judgment [*rassudok*]" necessary to commit a crime shows that Raskolnikov desires to follow the example of Bakunin's first criminal who submits to the verdict of only his own conscience: "Having come to such conclusions, he decided that . . . reason and will would remain essential all during the fulfillment of that conceived, solely for the reason that which was conceived is 'no crime'" (*Pss*, 6:59). Raskolnikov's emphasis on the conscience's perception of an act as a determining factor in its criminality parallels the Jesuits' moral reasoning on sin, which frustrates Samarin, because "at every step" the Jesuit theologians contradict each other: "One calls the deed a mortal sin, another a venial sin, and a third no sin at all."[39]

To build a necessary case for good intentions for the sake of his own conscience, Raskolnikov imparts supernatural significance to a series of chance encounters before the murder and thereby subordinates Providence to his moral reasoning, as he observes later in a moment of self-deprecation: "For an entire month I bothered all-good Providence, calling on her as a witness that it is not for myself that I take on, as they say, flesh and blood, but I have in mind a magnificent and welcome end . . . ha, ha!" (*Pss*, 6:211).[40] Raskolnikov places himself within the Jesuits' casuistic tradition when demonstrating that an act represents "the emanation of the will of God, which is accessible to human understanding from Revelation and from Nature, God's creation, knowable by reason."[41] For example, he discerns "predetermination of his fate" in his decision to walk through Haymarket Square, where he obtains the knowledge that the pawnbroker will be alone the next evening—knowledge that provides "an obvious step toward the success of this scheme" (*Pss*, 6:50, 52). Then, the tavern conversation containing the student's "utilitarian-altruistic justification" for the pawnbroker's murder ("Kill her and take her money provided that with its help one then dedicates oneself to the service of all humanity. . . . One death and a hundred lives in exchange") exercises such "an extraordinary influence" on him that he concludes the encounter was the result of "predestination" (*Pss*, 6:54, 55).[42] Under this influence, Raskolnikov accepts the student's argument that a well-intentioned murder may soundly appeal to "conscience" and thereby advances Samarin's thesis that "admitting all kinds of means suitable for their goal, the Jesuits themselves do not inspire crime so much as they make it morally possible for the human conscience" (*Pss*, 6:54).[43] Confident in his ability to maintain "all my will and reason" and emboldened by the coincidental availability of the ax ("If not reason, then the devil!"), Raskolnikov sets off to murder the widowed pawnbroker, a petty tyrant who beats her meek sister Lizaveta and financially exploits desperate students (*Pss*, 6:60).

At the same time, various clues evident already in the narrative reveal that Raskolnikov's reasoning and conscience falter even though he does not confess until the fifth part of the novel that he killed out of egoistic desire for greatness: "I wanted, Sonia, to kill without casuistry, to kill for myself and for myself alone" (*Pss*, 6:321–22). His mental reservations cause him to act not decisively but "mechanically" and "as if someone took him by the hand and dragged him behind irresistibly, blindly, and with unnatural force" (*Pss*, 6:58). His material poverty contributes to a mental fragility, making him susceptible to superstition and suggestion, and evidence of this fragility at his trial is introduced to ensure leniency in his sentencing. The "trifles [*melochi*]" that continually distract and agitate him recall the aphorism, "Peu de chose nous console, parce que peu de chose nous afflige," coined by Pascal, whose infamous criticism of the Jesuits' reasoning in *Les provinciales* Stepan Trofimovich paraphrases in *Demons*: "On trouve toujours plus de moines que de raison" (*Pss*, 10:51).[44] Pascal, who alongside Copernicus, Johannes Kepler, and Galileo, successfully challenged scholastic medievalism, may appeal to Raskolnikov because of their mutual interest in the Scientific Revolution's advancements in physics and mathematics, which Dostoevsky himself studied at an early age.[45] When outlining the argument of his article "On Crime" ("O prestuplenii"), Raskolnikov begins his discussion of the rights of extraordinary men with the examples of Sir Isaac Newton and Johannes Kepler, who had the "right" and were even obliged "*to remove*" those "ten or a hundred men" who might hinder their discoveries (*Pss*, 6:199). In his admiration of their deeds, Raskolnikov shares a youthful idealism quantified by *The Idiot*'s Ippolit Terentev with a citation from Pascal's *Pensées*, "Les extrémités se touchent [et se réunissent à force de s'être éloignées, et se retrouvent en Dieu, et en Dieu seulement]" and by Ivan Karamazov with his disclosure that despite his "earthly Euclidean mind" he, too, wants to view "the moment of eternal harmony" when "the parallel lines come together"—the end of eternity or absurdity as perceived by the human mind (*Pss*, 8:338; 14:214–15).[46]

In his youthful idealism and use of casuistry, Raskolnikov resembles the young novice Otrepev from Pushkin's *Boris Godunov*, whose pretendership begins with Otrepev's refusal to accept Boris's reign out of a prioritization of earthly justice common to both protagonists. Like Raskolnikov, Otrepev has been influenced by the Jesuits, who play a direct role in his affairs, since the tragedy takes place amidst the Catholic Reformation.[47] References to the Jesuits in the mouths of young male protagonists casuistically contemplating criminal acts (even tyrannicide) further justify the fears of the Order's critics that it manipulates the young under the guise of education: "The Jesuits loudly extolled their system of education, assuring that it would turn the youth of the Western border into the most trustworthy and true subjects of the sovereign; meanwhile, a portion of the pupils of their Polotsky academy, upon the entrance of Napoleon into Russia, crossed over into his army."[48] Yet, despite their engagement in casuistic reasoning, the consciences of Otrepev and Raskolnikov are not fully convinced of the righteousness of their deeds, as evidenced by the disquieting premonitions they suffer. Otrepev, in contrast to the old man (*starik*) Pimen who sits peacefully writing his chronicle, awakes from his "accursed" dream and must be calmly reassured by the chronicler:

> I dreamt that a steep staircase
> Led me to the tower; from its height
> Moscow appeared to me like an anthill;
> The people on the square raged below
> and pointed at me, laughing,
> And I felt ashamed and became frightened—
> And, falling headlong, I awoke. . . (*PssP,* 7:18, 19)

Although Dostoevsky reserves a similar dream for Raskolnikov until after the murder, on the way to the pawnbroker, he already fears a premonition which he "quickly extinguished": " 'It is probably thus for those who are taken to execution; their thoughts stick to all sorts of subjects, which they encounter on the road,' flashed through his head but only flashed, like lightning" (*Pss,* 6:60).

The publication of Nikolai Chaev's drama *Dimitry the Impostor* (*Dimitrii Samozvanets*) in the January 1865 issue of *Epoch*[49] likely brought the historical personage of Otrepev to Dostoevsky's mind when he patterned the dream of Raskolnikov's "*decrowning*" after the impostor's prophetic dream in Pushkin's *Boris Godunov.*[50] Yet, in Chaev's drama Dimitry appears as an ineffective ruler owing to his inability to challenge his wife, the Polish Catholic Marina, and to defend himself against Shuisky's condemnations, including: "Every humiliation to our Orthodox faith is committed in the Kremlin; near the sacred place, they sing the Latin Mass; the tsar married an unbaptized Polish woman, gave her communion, and even crowned her without having baptized her. . . . Where this day stand our holy churches, in their places any day now we will see Polish Catholic churches."[51] Pushkin's Dimitry, on the other hand, derives strength from his Polish alliances in the intellectually and aesthetically stimulating world of Renaissance Poland from which he derives a talent for role-playing.[52] The Europeanized Otrepev easily adapts to the Western culture of the Polish aristocrats, for he effectively strategizes with the leader Mnishek and successfully exploits the political ambitions of Catholic officials so as to enable his usurpation of the throne by the end of the tragedy.[53] For this reason, Dostoevsky's search for a literary ancestor for his Napoleonic pretender-hero leads him not to Chaev's drama but to Pushkin's, in which Otrepev succeeds in overcoming several challenges to his political legitimacy.

Mikhail Bakhtin discovers in an affirmation of "the fantastic logic of dreams" and "ambivalent logic of carnival" that Dostoevsky associates his protagonist with Otrepev in *Boris Godunov* when Raskolnikov's dream of the laughing crowd appears in dialogue with the aforementioned prophetic vision by Otrepev in Pushkin's drama.[54] Whereas Otrepev juxtaposes Pimen's tranquil manner with his own recurring "devilish reverie [*besovskoe mechtan'e*]," Raskolnikov is driven by "rage [*beshenstvo*]" instead of by political ambition "to beat the old woman" who frightens him, because "with each blow of the ax" her laughter "resounded more strongly and more audibly" (*PssP*, 7:18; *Pss*, 6:213). The staircase (*lestnitsa*) by which the dreaming Otrepev ascends to the heights of Moscow above the laughing crowds on the square (*na ploshchadi*) below (*Vnizu*) reappears in Raskolnikov's nightmare, when he is trapped in a crowded hallway (*PssP*, 7:19). In his dream, Raskolnikov does not rise above his crowd but panics in their midst: "He tried to run, but the entire hallway was already full of people, the doors to the stairs were wide open, and on the landing [*ploshchadka*], on the stairs [*na lestnitse*], and there below [*vniz*]—all the people, head after head, all were looking, but all were lurking and waiting in silence" (*Pss*, 6:213). Although Otrepev's dream accurately foretells his ambitious rise to power, Raskolnikov's nightmare, as Deborah Martinsen clarifies, underscores "his shame . . . because he believes that his crime was a failure" owing to his having killed "his dream of greatness."[55] The placement of Raskolnikov's dream after the murders further underscores his defeat (Otrepev's decrowning being only foretold but not experienced within the drama's historical time frame), since it signals his inability to embrace fully his extraordinary theory out of fear of exposure before the masses, as he explains to Sonya: "Do you know what angers me? I am annoyed that all these stupid, bestial mugs now crowd me, their eyes will aim right at me, will give me their stupid questions which it will be necessary to answer" (*Pss*, 6:403).

The dream thereby reinforces Raskolnikov's feelings of failure with a "communal act of comic *decrowning on the public square,* and a falling *downward,*" which anticipate his conclusion that his troubled conscience reflects his mind's inadequate assimilation of the Napoleonic theory: "If I had already tormented myself for so many days, 'Am I a Napoleon or not?', then really I already clearly felt that I was not a Napoleon" (*Pss*, 6:321).[56] While the possessed laughter of his victim links Raskolnikov to another of Pushkin's failed Napoleons—Germann from *Queen of Spades*—the silent throng "lurking and waiting in silence" below recalls the silent populace of the 1831 text of *Boris Godunov*, which withholds an endorsement of Otrepev's seizure of the throne by refusing to cheer for Tsar Dimitry Ivanovich (*Pss*,

6:213).[57] Caryl Emerson and Chester Dunning emphasize that precisely this ending to the tragedy "whether read to oneself, acted out, or mouthed silently to the audience—has been allowed to define the play, its author, the virtues of the Russian folk, and the teleological shape of Russian history."[58] Therefore, Dostoevsky's inclusion of a crowd silently witnessing the murder of the pawnbroker in Raskolnikov's dream draws on the culturally significant dramatic image of Pushkin's crowd refusing to cheer the murder of Fedor Godunov for the sake of (the False) Dimitry's rise to power. Here, the crowds exercise the right, granted by Raskolnikov, of the masses to reject the deeds of the extraordinary, but he must decide either to disregard the judgment of the crowd à la Napoleon and Otrepev or to consider the reaction of the ordinary masses in deciding his future fate.

NAPOLEONIC CASUISTRY AND THE ROMAN CASE FOR MURDER

Napoleon's coronation at Notre Dame in the presence of Pope Pius VII established a legitimacy to his ascent to the throne of France that threatened the inherited monarchies of Europe who ruled by divine right. Owing to his fondness for Dumas and for prison literature, Dostoevsky could not have failed to encounter in Alexandre Dumas's *Le Comte de Monte-Cristo* (1844) M. de Villeforte's discussion of Napoleon as "le type de l'égalité" in response to a marquise who denies the Bonapartists the enthusiasm and devotion of the royalists: "Oh! madame, ils ont du moins quelque chose qui remplace tout cela: c'est le fanatisme. Napoléon est le Mahomet de l'Occident; c'est pour tous ces hommes vulgaires, mais aux ambitions suprêmes, non seulement un législateur et un maître, mais encore c'est un type, le type de l'égalité."[59] Napoleon's ability to inspire "supreme ambitions" as an egalitarian type appeals to Dostoevsky's Raskolnikov, who also likens the emperor to Muhammad in his discussion of the rights, responsibilities, and abilities of extraordinary men (*Pss*, 6:200).[60] Yet, the presence of Lycurgus, Solon, and Napoleon in Raskolnikov's theory suggests that his article also draws on the portraits of these lawgivers in Hegel's *Lectures on the Philosophy of History* (*Vorlesungen über die Philosophie der Geschichte*, 1822–23), especially since Hegel, like Raskolnikov, understands Napoleon as a leader who challenges the classical acceptance of Fate.[61] Hegel introduces his section on "The Roman World" by paraphrasing Napoleon, who maintains that the modern world differs from the ancient in that the modern no longer endorses "destiny to which men are absolutely subject" but concludes that "policy occupies the place of the ancient Fate [*La politique est la fatalité*]. This therefore he thought must be used as the modern form of Destiny in Tragedy—the irresistible power of circumstances to which individuality must bend."[62] Hegel's conclusion that "such a power is the *Roman World*" which promotes "an abstract universality of power" resonates with Dostoevsky's conception of the "Roman idea" governing nineteen centuries of French history (including Napoleon III's reign), for France "constantly continued to stand in its politics for Catholicism, for Rome, and for the earthly dominion of the pope" (*Pss*, 21:184).[63]

Napoleon's attempt to unite Europe under a single French standard and the Concordat of 1801, recognizing the Roman Catholic Church as a majority religion in France, advanced this characterization of Napoleon as representative of a Roman world (including a Roman church) whose quest for universal dominion required policies that could respond to individual circumstances. While Dostoevsky identifies the Jesuits (well represented in France) with casuistry, Hegel names Julius Caesar, "a paragon of Roman adaptation of means to ends," for he achieved "universal sovereignty" with "the conquest of the whole Roman world" and "held together the Roman world by force."[64] The similar conceptualizations of Rome in Hegel and Dostoevsky, in addition to the likelihood that the latter read *The Philosophy of History* in Siberia, suggest Dostoevsky's concept of the "Roman idea" of dominion contains within it an understanding of Caesar's and Napoleon's forcible occupations of Europe, which may account for the presence of their names in the notebooks for *Crime and Punishment*. Their Roman legacy informs Raskolnikov's article about the extraordinary man, "On Crime," in which he finds that pursuit of an "idea" rather than an encounter with circumstance may require "relative and multifarious" legal crimes, but not necessarily immoral deeds, based on the process of case-reasoning: "But if it is necessary for him, for his idea, to step over a corpse or through blood, he within himself, according to his own conscience, can, in my opinion, give himself the permission to step through blood—depending, though, on the idea and its weight—note this" (*Pss*, 6:200).

After Hegel's comparisons of the French Revolution to the Roman Republic, Russian literati compared the reigns of Napoleon and Julius Caesar who seized control of the French and Roman republics, respectively.[65] For example, in the 1858 brochure *La France ou l'Angleterre* (*France or England*), Herzen considers both the Bonapartes and Caesars to be "protuberances on the lungs of a Rome that has had its day" (*Ss*, 13:240). Also, Dostoevsky may have encountered a Hegelian image of Caesar in an 1862 issue of *Time* in which "T. N. Granovsky's Lectures from Middle History" ("Lektsii iz srednei istorii T. N. Granovskogo") builds on the German historian's discussion of "great men" to characterize Caesar's legendary political legacy which is shaped by both his humanitarianism and his *transgression* of the law: "Certain of them regarded him as a man having rendered great services to the Roman world; others as a transgressor of the law, having sacrificed personal ambition for all that is good for the citizen and the person."[66] By focusing on Caesar's altruistic aims and overlooking the human cost of his rise to power, Granovsky avoids a discussion of Caesar's moral right to violate the social norm by seizing power, that is, to realize the "particular rights of great men," which so occupied Napoleon III in his history, *Histoire de Jules César,* and subsequently the novelists Tolstoy and Dostoevsky, in *War and Peace* and *Crime and Punishment,* respectively.[67]

The subject of Napoleon's appeal continued to haunt Dostoevsky's generation, as the thick journals' response to the fiftieth anniversary of the 1812 campaign, the publication of Tolstoy's epic novel, and Russian criticism of Napoleon III's history indicate.[68] The controversy surrounding *Histoire de Jules César* likely encouraged the critical portrayal of Napoleon in both *War and Peace* and *Crime and Punishment* in consecutive editions of the journal *The Russian Herald (Russkii vestnik)* in 1866, since parts of Napoleon III's theory on the geniuses of history appeared in *The Moscow News* as early as February 1865. Tolstoy explores several causes of the general's successes, including a providential reading of Napoleon's actions as the novelist summarizes: "He, destined by Providence for the sad unfree role of executioner [*palach*] of nations, convinced himself that the goal of his action was the good [*blago*] of nations and that he could govern the fates of millions and by means of authority do good deeds."[69] Napoleon III's preface to *Histoire de Jules César,* by contrast, encourages primarily the image of Bonaparte as a promoter of human progress, since "la Providence" plays only an inspirational role for men like Caesar, Charlemagne, and Napoleon, who must use their genius to trace with the people a path that allows them to "accomplir en quelques années le travail de plusieurs siècles."[70] Unlike Pushkin's parvenu Otrepev, Napoleon III does not hint that the actions of such movers of history enjoy exclusive divine endorsement. Whereas Otrepev appoints himself a divine agent with the goal of ensuring Boris's temporal judgment, Napoleon III apposes history and religion: "La vérité historique devrait être non moins sacrée que la religion."[71] He turns to embrace the *logic* of historical perspectivalism: "Si les préceptes de la foi élèvent notre âme au-dessus des intérêts de ce monde, les enseignements de l'histoire, à leur tour, nous inspirent l'amour du beau et du juste, la haine de ce qui fait obstacle aux progrès de l'humanité."[72] In this rejection of providential politics in the name of human progress, or "the love of the beautiful and the just," as perceived by genius, Napoleon III continues in the Hegelian tradition of associating Napoleon with "Policy" rather than with "Destiny" or "Fate," whose dominant role in Racine's tragedies in the classical tradition links them to the Jansenist Catholic tradition defended by Pascal.

As Samarin's reference to Napoleon attests, the emperor's 1812 campaign earned him an association in the Russian consciousness with the

Society of Jesus, some of whose members sought refuge in Russia after Pope Clement XIV suppressed the Order in 1773 with the papal brief *Dominus ac Redemptor.* The Society's restoration in 1814 by Pope Pius VII, in the wake of Napoleon's defeat, renewed concerns over its clandestine and subversive activities, even though the Jesuits were expelled from the empire in 1820. Tolstoy draws on the reputation of the Jesuit-educated Bonaparte, when his Gallophile Hélène, whose name recalls Napoleon's isle of exile Saint Helena, decides to follow Napoleon's example of obtaining the right to divorce and remarriage by securing the aid of a Jesuit. Believing that she is accountable to only "God and my conscience," she meets with "un jésuite à robe courte" and her "future directeur de conscience" Monsieur Jobert, who conveys her to a Catholic church where an "abbé à robe longue" hears her confession, whereupon she is received into the church.[73] These Napoleonic links to the Society of Jesus suggest that Dostoevsky was motivated by his visions of revolutionary Jesuitism to attach to Raskolnikov's extraordinary man theory the image of the conquering French general, whose conscience seemed to have given him permission to use any means necessary to realize his egalitarian ideal. Tolstoy's Pierre Bezukhov recognizes this tendency in Napoleon's actions when concluding: "For the common good [*obshchee blago*] he could not stop for the life of one man": "'The execution of the Duke of Enghien,' said Pierre, 'was a civil necessity, and I see the greatness of his soul precisely in that Napoleon did not fear to take on himself alone the responsibility in this action.'"[74]

Although Raskolnikov's theory originates in a moral justification for the potential sacrifice of life required by Newton's and Kepler's discoveries, his explanation quickly advances to focus on the bloodshed of "the lawgivers and regulators of humanity":

> Every single one was a criminal in that by giving the new law they thereby destroyed the ancient one, passed on by their fathers and revered as sacred by society; and of course they did not stop at blood, provided the blood (sometimes completely innocent blood heroically being shed for the ancient law) could help them. (*Pss*, 6:200)

Dostoevsky understands that concerns over political legitimacy haunt Napoleon's heir, who must therefore employ force to ensure the future of the dynasty: "Emperor Napoleon III throughout his reign was forced to direct all his efforts at consolidating and implanting his dynasty in France" (*Pss*, 21:200). This issue of dynastic legitimacy likely motivates the prominence given to blood sacrifice in the novel, which is required to achieve what Napoleon III characterizes as genius: "It is even remarkable, that the greater part of these benefactors and founders of humanity were especially dreadful blood-shedders" (*Pss*, 6:200). Invoking the name of Napoleon, both "the great and the present one," the Underground Man likewise views them as civilized "blood-shedders" next to whom "all these various Attilas and Stenka Razins did not hold a candle" (*Pss*, 5:112). Thus, the Underground Man's image of Napoleon also contains the violence with which Dostoevsky associates both medieval and modern Catholic civilization.

This emphasis on the brutality of benevolent Bonaparte echoes Herzen's portrait of the general who espouses high ideals while leading bloody campaigns:

> Bonapartism acts only with the help of death. His glory—all from blood, all from corpses. In him there is no creative force, no productive activity; he is completely barren. Everything created by him is only an illusion, a dream. . . . The reality is the Spanish land manured with French corpses; it is the sands of Egypt sown with French bones; it is the snows of Russia stained crimson with French blood. (*Ss*, 13:240–41)

Dostoevsky's understanding of Napoleon's genius, like Herzen's, is more cynical than his protagonist's vision of the emperor as "the benefactor of humanity": "Napoleon I revealed himself, and really in his idea there is probably no longer anything from love of humanity" (*Pss*, 6:322; 24:311). Still, neither Russian author denies Napoleon's widespread appeal, evident in Herzen's discussion of the glorious emperor's ability to inspire "illusion" and "dream." Raskolnikov shares the fanaticism of Napoleon's disciples, described by M. de Villeforte, as his level-headed friend Razumikhin discovers when witnessing the explanation of Raskolnikov's article "On Crime." Razumikhin reacts strongly to the moral justification of executions "*according to conscience*," since he discerns in the theory of his ambitious friend: "What is really *original* in all this—and really original to you alone, to my horror—is that you allow bloodshed *according to conscience*, and, excuse me, with such fanaticism really" (*Pss*, 6:202–3). Then, Razumikhin repeats his characterization of Raskolnikov's theory as "this permission for bloodshed *according to conscience*" and finds such bloodshed "more dreadful" than "the official permission to shed blood legally" (*Pss*, 6:203). The Jesuits' liberal acceptance of bloodshed in good conscience (for self-defense, protection of property, and preservation of honor) similarly raises concerns for Pascal in his fourteenth letter of *Les provinciales*, in which he records the public servants' fear of casuistry: "Ce n'est pas seulement l'intérêt général qui les y engage, mais encore le leur propre, puisque vos casuistes cités dans mes lettres étendent leur permission de tuer jusques à eux."[75] When Porfiry expresses a similar fear of mass murder, Raskolnikov maintains that the state has sufficient means of control with only a hint at its sanctioning of bloodshed and without reference to the executions depicted in bloody detail in *House of the Dead* and *The Idiot*: "He (he nodded toward Razumikhin) said just now that I permit bloodshed. So, what of it? Society really is too well protected by exile, prisons, court investigators, and penal servitude, so what is there to worry about?" (*Pss*, 6:203).

Hence, bloodshed in good conscience rather than legal bloodshed remains the focus of Raskolnikov's theory and anticipates the Grand Inquisitor's defense of his tyranny, which requires the bloodshed of the rebellious few for the sake of a harmonious (and obedient) society. For both the Grand Inquisitor and Raskolnikov, the bloodshed on their own consciences is balanced against great humanitarian ideas—a balance that is quickly discounted by Alesha Karamazov ("this is the worst of Catholicism—the Inquisitors, the Jesuits!") and dismissed by Svidrigailov as *une théorie comme une autre*" (*Pss*, 14:237; 6:378).[76] Still, these great Catholic men remain sympathetic characters in Dostoevsky's novels, because at least those shaping their images—Ivan and Raskolnikov—find that they are geniuses with exceptional ideas who suffer deeply for the blood they have shed: "Suffering and pain is always obligatory for the broad consciousness and profound heart. Truly great people, it seems to me, must feel on this earth great sorrow" (*Pss*, 6:203). Raskolnikov's conscience, therefore, differs from those of Porfiry, Razumikhin, and Dunya, for whom the pangs of conscience preclude consideration of benevolent bloodshed (*Pss*, 6:203, 378). On the other hand, Raskolnikov's sorrowful consciousness distinguishes him from Svidrigailov, whose easy conscience allows him to deceive the former about his intentions toward Dunya, while telling Raskolnikov "my conscience is completely calm"–a dismissive phrase that sounds similar to his denial of any involvement in Marfa Petrovna's suspicious death: "My own conscience is in the highest degree calm on that account" (*Pss*, 6:223, 215). Raskolnikov echoes a similar phrase, "My conscience is calm," only after he temporarily gains an "embittered conscience" following his confession that refuses to recognize a moral crime in the killing of the pawnbroker (*Pss*, 6:417).

Raskolnikov's conscience, which questions whether Luzhin should be allowed to live and execute his vile deeds, accepts the murders more readily than that of pious Sonya, since she does not appreciate the "accursed questions [*prokliatye voprosy*]" of this Russian Hamlet but characterizes his moral reasoning as "empty questions [*pustye voprosy*]" and forthrightly exclaims: "And you killed! You killed" (*Pss*, 24:167; 6:313, 322). Their conversation clarifies that Raskolnikov views bloodshed as more commonplace than Sonya, since he asserts that others "themselves destroyed millions of people and considered it a virtue. Rogues and scoundrels they are, Sonya!" (*Pss*, 6:323). In this violent view of world history, the masses are empowered with the right to "execute" and "hang" the extraordinary as part of "their conservative function," despite the likelihood that successive generations of ordinary men will recognize the talents of the extraordinary by placing "the executed on pedestals" (*Pss*, 6:200). In this sense, he envisions history as "the eternal war [*la guerre éternelle*]" between the masses and liberal revolutionaries, between "the masters of the present" and "the master of the future," as the ordinary and extraordinary engage in a constant battle for power until the dawn of the apocalyptic New Jerusalem (*Pss*, 6:201). In endowing both his categories of people the inalienable right to participate in an epic struggle of brutality, Raskolnikov deftly avoids granting either the ordinary or the extraordinary an exclusive providential role in history. Raskolnikov's suspicion of the masses suggests that he agrees with Hegel on the transitory nature of popular support, since "as soon as any of these great men had performed what was needed, envy intruded—*i.e.*, the recoil of the sentiment of equality against conspicuous talent—and he was either imprisoned or exiled."[77] Therefore, the hostile crowds of Raskolnikov's and Otrepev's dreams parallel Napoleon's own erosion of mass appeal, even among fanatics of "le type de l'égalité."

In spite of Porfiry's attempts to introduce God into the historical equation, Raskolnikov does not grant his extraordinary men an endorsement from the New Jerusalem, God, or the resurrected Lazarus. Instead, in keeping with the practice of casuistry, Raskolnikov denies the great men of history both divine and popular sanctification while insisting that such a man examine his own conscience to find this "permission to step through blood" (*Pss*, 6:200). In refusing Napoleon such a providential role in history, Raskolnikov tries to avoid the mockery of Porfiry and Zametov ("Really wasn't it some future Napoleon who bumped off our Alena Ivanovna last week with an ax?") who seem to dismiss the murders as derivative of a debased Napoleon (*Pss*, 6:204). Raskolnikov, on the defensive, works to escape the ridiculous image of a failed Napoleon after his first encounter with Porfiry, when Raskolnikov senses that he has not succeeded in attaining the stature of an extraordinary man. He knows by the time that he confesses to Sonya that "I did not kill so that, having received the power and the means, I could make myself the benefactor of humanity. Nonsense! I simply killed; for myself I killed, for myself alone" (*Pss*, 6:322). This confession indicates that he has not effectively assimilated the convictions of Dostoevsky's Catholic revolutionaries like Napoleon and Otrepev, whose consciences "allow *all means*" in service to their benevolent aims so that they freely violate legal and social norms. Therefore, Raskolnikov's suffering does not originate in a genius consciousness but rather from a knowledge that he remains "a louse" who could not rise above the masses but was "dragged" by "the devil [*chert*]" or "perished" according "to the decree of blind fate" (*Pss*, 6:322, 417).

SVIDRIGAILOV AND THE TEMPTATION OF CASUISTRY

The presence of Napoleon and of Pushkin's Polish-sponsored pretender from *Boris Godunov* in Dostoevsky's novel reminds the reader of more recent threats to Russia's stability from her western borderlands during the invasion of 1812 and the insurrections of 1831 and 1863, which were inspired, in part, by Napoleon Bonaparte and Napoleon III. This common revolutionary history of France and Poland, when considered along with Alexei's commentary on "many little Poles and their little French sympathizers" in *The Gambler,* demonstrates that in the aftermath of the 1863 uprising, Dostoevsky increasingly conflated these Catholic European nations into an inimical *other* image (*Pss,* 5:210). The association arises naturally from their shared history of sponsoring Catholic invasions of Moscow that encouraged the populace to challenge the absolute authority of the Russian Orthodox tsar. For their mutual preoccupation with issues of legitimacy, Emerson links Raskolnikov to Boris Godunov through Napoleon in a discussion of Belinsky's "Tenth Article" on Pushkin (1843): "Anticipating Dostoevskii's Raskol'nikov, Belinskii calls Boris Godunov a 'failed Napoleon,' and this, he says, is fatal: 'A parvenu must be a genius, or fall.'"[78] Yet, Raskolnikov's nightmare with the threatening silent crowd reveals a more profound connection with Pushkin's parvenu Otrepev, who joins Napoleon, as J. Douglas Clayton observes, in a "path of self-naming (*samozvantsvo*) or self-empowerment (*samovlastie*)" informed by "a certain cynicism."[79] As Raskolnikov's nightmare fades with the vision of the silent crowd, it gives way to the image of the casuist and self-appointed benefactor of Dunya and Sonya—Svidrigailov who remains at Raskolnikov's threshold: "But it was strange, somehow the dream still continued on; the door was wide open, and on the threshold a complete stranger stood and looked intently at him" (*Pss,* 6:213–14). At this moment, two choices stand before Raskolnikov: he may follow Sonya's advice to embrace the verdict of the crowd by accepting his punishment as prescribed by law or he may seek escape by convincing his conscience to endorse the casuistic justification of flight recommended by Svidrigailov.

Gary Rosenshield observes that "as part of Svidrigaylov's attempt to win over Dunia" he proposes the same "solution of escape" to Raskolnikov that Alesha offers to his brother Dmitry (Mitya).[80] Alesha submits to his innocent brother, who had just been found guilty of parricide, that his future moral regeneration may justify an escape from the law, but Dmitry rejects his reasoning ("After all, the Jesuits talk like this, right?) and laughs at his brother's plan: "So I've caught my little Alesha like a Jesuit!" (*Pss,* 15:186). Raskolnikov, on the contrary, entertains the idea of flight, despite Porfiry's conviction that while "a Pole will escape abroad," a Russian criminal will not leave his homeland (*Pss,* 6:262). The prison break by the "moral Quasimodo"

Aristov and with the help of a Polish guard Koller described in *House of the Dead* may have encouraged this association of Poland with flight, especially since the "spy" Aristov appears as a precursor to Svidrigailov in the notes to *Crime and Punishment* (*Pss*, 7:93, 136). This Jesuit-Polish solution of escape from the law belongs to the biography of several of Dostoevsky's fellow Polish inmates in Omsk, including Tokarzewski and Anczykowski. Still, the more recent public discussion of the 1865 flight by a former member of the Warsaw Central Committee, Jarosław Dąbrowski, likely inspired Porfiry's comment. Not long before Dostoevsky's arrival in Wiesbaden in the summer of 1865, Dąbrowski published two letters in a July issue of *The Bell*, one of which taunts Katkov for writing in *Moscow News* that "I [he] would immediately be caught, since I [he] would not find refuge in Russia."[81] Dąbrowski's reply assures Katkov that the former enjoyed many freedoms during his voluntary six-month stay in Russia, required to organize his affairs: "I so little feared all of your kinds of police—secret, obvious, and literary—that, paying full justice to the abilities of your police, I was, however, your neighbor for a long time and saw you very often."[82] Thus, Porfiry's celebration of his astute ability to track Russian criminals, to take "measures" to prevent their escape, and to trap them *"psychologically"* (in spite of the Poles who escape) may be read as a response to Dąbrowski's public boast (*Pss*, 6:262).

In contradistinction to Porfiry, Svidrigailov, who shares traits with both Dostoevsky's Poles and Jesuits, promotes this Polish option both to Raskolnikov and to Dunya. Svidrigailov's exploitation of Raskolnikov's confession for the seduction of Dunya shares similarities with a confessional scene recounted by Ivan Karamazov's Devil, who plays on archetypal images of Jesuits abusing the sacrament. Ivan's Devil recalls the Jesuit *pater* who "fixes an evening rendezvous through the little hole" after hearing the confession of a young blonde who continually falls with men because "ça lui fait tant de plaisir, et à moi si peu de peine" (*Pss*, 15:81).[83] Svidrigailov also hopes to capitalize on Raskolnikov's confession of sin by persuading Dunya to yield to his forceful sexual proposition in exchange for her brother's escape abroad where he "can still do many good deeds so that he will make amends for all this" (*Pss*, 6:379). Svidrigailov admits that "rape is a vile thing" but assures Dunya that "absolutely nothing will stay on your conscience, if even . . . if you even wanted to save your brother voluntarily, as I am proposing. So you simply yielded to circumstances, well force [*sila*] finally, if it's no longer possible without this word" (*Pss*, 6:380–81). Svidrigailov's appeal to Dunya's conscience not only includes a casuistic invocation of circumstances but also an allusion to "the fate of your brother and your mother" on which her decision rests that may mitigate Dunya's moral culpability by addressing the issue of intent (*Pss*, 6:381).

Svidrigailov thus touches upon a central theme of the novel—women's casuistic justification for commodifying their bodies in order to secure the happiness of their families. In an early indication of his discomfort with such sexualized casuistry, the "prude" Raskolnikov rejects any such sexual bartering for his sister Dunya and for Sonya when equating Dunya's sacrificial marriage to Luzhin and Sonya's prostitution at the beginning of the novel:[84]

> Indeed, why here, perhaps, we would not refuse even Sonechka's fate! Sonechka, Sonechka Marmeladova, eternal Sonechka, while the world stands! This sacrifice, this sacrifice have you both taken full measure of it? Have you? Under force [*sila*]? For whose benefit? Is it rational? Do you know, Dunechka, that Sonechka's lot is not a bit worse than your lot with Mr. Luzhin. (*Pss*, 6:38)

Later in the novel, Svidrigailov equates the marriage to Luzhin with his proposal to live in St. Petersburg with Dunya: "Marfa Petrovna then got that most despicable clerk Luzhin and almost manufactured a wedding—which, in essence would have been the same thing that I proposed. Wouldn't it?" (*Pss*, 6:367). Although Raskolnikov objects to such calculated casuistic sacrifices for the "good purpose" of family harmony, he still partly motivates his murder of the pawnbroker with the consolation that it will save his sister from marriage with Luzhin, who also ultimately regrets failing to be Dunya's "providence" (*Pss*, 6:38, 277). Ironically, her brother's welfare compels Dunya to agree to this meeting with Svidrigailov, during which the latter aggressively confronts her with the proposition to exchange casuistically sex for the welfare of her brother.[85]

Svidrigailov's rootedness in the Jesuit tradition is further enhanced by his Polish connections, which Dostoevsky highlights by endowing him with a name similar to that of the fifteenth-century Lithuanian Prince Švitrigaila (Svidrigailo in Russian). Švitrigaila exploited tensions between the Orthodox and Roman Catholics for political power in the disputed borderlands of fifteenth-century Russia, Poland, and Lithuania.[86] His collaboration with the Teutonic Knights furnished them with the logistical aid essential to their military successes in Russia and helped to establish temporarily his rule over the regions of Vladimir, Kiev, Volhynia, and Podolia. Viewed as a schismatic for his cooperation with both the Orthodox and Catholics and as a "perennial pretender to the Lithuanian throne," Švitrigaila provides for his namesake in *Crime and Punishment* an identification with historic opportunism,[87] with which Dostoevsky was familiar from having read about the prince in his childhood reading of Karamzin's history. Karamzin recalls that "flippant and haughty" Švitrigaila received generous land grants from Vasily I, because Vasily I had believed that aligning himself with "the brother of [the Polish king] Jagiełło" would ensure the presence of enough allies in Lithuania to negotiate a successful peace with the country.[88] Karamzin's account of Švitrigaila emphasizes his treachery against his cousin, the Lithuanian Grand Prince

Vytautas, since "Švitrigaila sought traitors in vain in the Lithuanian camp" and therefore forced Vasily I to conclude a peace with Vytautas to whom Vasily, "preserving his honor," refused to hand over the traitor Švitrigaila.[89]

The name of Švitrigaila likely generated particular interest in the Dostoevsky household, since the family name comes from a small village, Dostoevo, awarded to a sixteenth-century ancestor, and this village in the region of Pinsk (in modern Belarus) neighbors Švitrigaila's fifteenth-century seat of power in Lutsk (Łuck in Polish), a prominent region of Volhynia.[90] However, Dostoevsky may have encountered his name in the heated political discussions with his fellow prisoners in Omsk, during which ethnic tensions arose as a result of his denying, according to Bogusławski, the right of Lithuania, Poland, Podolia, Ukraine, and Volhynia to exist independently from Russia.[91] This recollection demonstrates the likelihood that Dostoevsky understood that the name Švitrigaila evoked a historic era and a geographic region rife with nationalist and religious tensions, especially since after the 1830 Polish uprising Nicholas I adopted increasingly stringent measures to suppress nationalists' aspirations in these regions. Nevertheless, in Dostoevsky's lifetime and particularly after Russia's loss of the Crimean War, many from these areas (like his Polish fellow inmates) continued to seek independence for Russia's borderlands. In addition, the recent discussion of Napoleon's campaign in Tolstoy's novel may have reminded Dostoevsky of the success that rebels hostile to Russia such as Švitrigaila, Napoleon, and, more recently, Konarski, enjoyed among Polish sympathizers residing in proximity to the Vilnius region.

Svidrigailov's presence in the novel therefore brings to the narrative a history of ethnic and religious unrest, particularly as he shares with Raskolnikov an association with religious schism and with Jesuitism. The decisions of Svidrigailov, who easily justifies his choices with reasoned arguments, appear more closely aligned with the Jesuits than those of Raskolnikov, who vacillates between Sonya's example of confession-absolution (connected through her to the Russian Orthodox tradition) and Napoleonic ethics. Raskolnikov continues to struggle between two schismatic traditions outlined by Afanasy Shchapov in *Time*—the moral-mystic movement and that of violent rebellion—which are represented in the novel by Mikolka from the schismatics [*iz raskol'nikov*], who chooses confession out of a need to accept suffering, and Svidrigailov, who embraces rebellion by adopting the blend of violence (his suicide) and benevolence (to Sonya and his fiancée) in the Napoleonic tradition of Catholic revolutionaries.[92] By characterizing his final exit as a trip "to America," Svidrigailov connects his suicide to the same flight that he once proposed to Raskolnikov, a flight similar to the cowardly abandonment of Russia shared by Napoleon and Švitrigaila (*Pss*, 6:373).[93] Raskolnikov's departure from the police station without his intended confession upon discovery of Svidrigailov's suicide suggests that this idea of escape remains a temptation for him. Yet his return to the station after having witnessed Sonia's despair indicates his rapprochement with Mikolka and Sonya's ethics rather than with those of Napoleon and Svidrigailov.

In submitting to the law, Raskolnikov loses his potential to become a new lawgiver as an extraordinary man through revolution like Otrepev or Napoleon, because he fails to embrace the modern view of policy, as opposed to Destiny, that enables Hegel's Napoleon to respond to circumstance with genius and thereby to perpetuate the Roman legacy of dominion. In failing to retain the resolve of a Julius Caesar when committing the murders, Raskolnikov loses the ability to shape both his present and future, since he concludes the novel as a prisoner to the state, much as Napoleon ends his days, as Wesling posits in her reading of Raskolnikov's Siberian experience "against the conventional images of Napoleon's exile on the island of St. Helena."[94] In his captivity, Raskolnikov encounters other unfortunate heirs to Napoleon's legacy, in the form of Polish political exiles. Their lives, wasted in the remote regions of Russia, reinforce Siberia's reputation as the place of residence for failed Napoleons, from the Decembrists exiled after 1825 to the Polish insurrectionists seized in the wake of the 1863 uprising.[95]

THE LEGACY OF REVOLUTION IN THE OBLIVION OF EXILE

The association of Poles with escape from the law is not incidental but lies at the heart of the novel's portrayal of self-sanctification, linked to Catholics in *Crime and Punishment* through the themes of pretendership and revolution as well as through Raskolnikov's references to casuistry.[96] When Raskolnikov confesses that he killed for himself alone, he reveals casuistry to be a practice in self-deception that advocates violent engagement with the world for the purpose of achieving a higher goal but with the end of realizing only the individual will. He thereby anticipates Dostoevsky's later direct association of Jesuits with papal designs for revolution in *Diary of a Writer*, in which the writer explains: "Jesuit revolutionaries cannot act legally, but precisely *exceptionally*. This black army stands outside of humanity, outside of citizenry, outside of civilization, and the army emanates entirely from itself alone. This *status in statu*, this army of the pope, it needs only the triumph of *its one* idea" (*Pss*, 25:162). Although Dostoevsky describes here a realpolitik more cynical than the casuistic reasoning of Raskolnikov, the latter's reasoning and Dostoevsky's characterization of this papal army both highlight the self-sanctification of Catholic revolutionaries, embodied in the Napoleonic extraordinary man in *Crime and Punishment*. While Raskolnikov abandons this revolutionary persona with his voluntary confession to the police and submission to the verdict of the law court, this Napoleonic motif carries through to the end of the novel in the image of the Poles in the Siberian prison, whose conscious separation from and disdain for Russian peasants recalls the elitism of the Polish Catholic political prisoners from the nobility in *House of the Dead.*

Examining Napoleon's cultural impact on Russia, Wesling and Dmitri Sorokine demonstrate effectively that the political connection between Napoleon and nineteenth-century Polish revolutionaries antagonized the Russian intelligentsia. Indeed, Dostoevsky concludes in *Diary of a Writer* that "the war with Napoleon ended to Europe's benefit—Alexander freed the Poles" (*Pss*, 21:268). In discussing Russians' perception of Polish involvement in Napoleon's invasion, Wesling recalls the letters of the Russian noblewoman Maria Volkova who unquestioningly accepts eyewitness accounts ascribing the worst of atrocities during the seizure of Moscow to Poles and Germans.[97] Sorokine examines the period of Dostoevsky's youth to discover that Zagoskin's historical novels and Pushkin's poetry evoke conspiratorial images of Poles who are associated with Napoleon's standard. For example, in Zagoskin's historical novel *Yury Miloslavsky* "the patriotic atmosphere and the war scenes are not the product of a novelist but a testimony whose subject has been transplanted from 1812 to 1612" since "the warriors, the peasants, and the Cossacks, who are described by Zagoskin and who, in this first novel, fight against the Polish invaders and chase them from Moscow, are those that he had seen fight against the Grande Armée in 1812."[98] Sorokine also links Pushkin's famous poetic warning to the West not to interfere in Russo-Polish affairs ("To the Slanderers of Russia") to his poems on Napoleon from the same year (1831): "Before the Sainted Tomb" ("Pered grobnitseiu sviatoi") and "The Anniversary of Borodino" ("Borodinskaia godovshchina").[99] The references to Napoleon and the 1830–31 Polish conflict in these poems reveal a patriotic poet whose admiration for Napoleon is tainted by Western support for the Polish insurrectionists, who draw their inspiration from the general's freedom fighting rather than their liberation by the Russian army. Dostoevsky himself seems to recognize the power of these Polish nationalist aspirations in connection with Bogusławski's depiction in *House of the Dead* when the narrator refers to the Polish inmate's "paradoxical" and "exclusionary" ideas for which he paid "such a dear price" that to abandon them would be "too painful" (*Pss*, 4:216). Such empathy in *Crime and Punishment*, however, is reserved for Raskolnikov, who receives a Siberian sentence, because he, too, "was ready to give up his existence for an idea, for hope, even for a fantasy" (*Pss*, 6:417).

In this later novel, *House of the Dead*'s comparatively complex depictions of various Siberian Poles are reduced to a brief passage referring to the ethnic group whose members "regarded all these people as ignoramuses and serfs [*khlopy*] and despised them with disdain" (*Pss*, 6:418). The sentiments that Raskolnikov attributes to the Polish prisoners echo those that Dostoevsky assigns to the Poles in a defense of Strakhov's article "The Fateful Question": "They, passionately committed and believing in their (aristocratic and Catholic) civilization, must be pompous about it, take pride in it before us, whom, to this day, they consider serfs [*khlopy*] and barbarians" (*Pss*, 20:100). Embodying a national exclusivity of aristocratic class and Catholic civilization, this Polish collective is defined in *Crime and Punishment* by its condescension toward Russian peasants, which parallels Mirecki's hatred of "the brigands" in a later recollection of Omsk, "The Peasant Marei." The categorization of Raskolnikov's fellow Polish convicts as "political prisoners" recalls Goryanchikov's "comrades" from *House of the Dead* in which the Polish prisoners pattern themselves after Napoleon, by following his example of remaining a "lonely and anguished exile."[100] Their determined isolation parallels Raskolnikov's Napoleonic aversion to "these stupid, bestial mugs" whose judgment he fears before his arrest (*Pss*, 6:403). Thus, Raskolnikov like Goryanchikov underscores a class division apparent in prison life, which Raskolnikov attributes to the competing nationalist loyalties of the Polish prisoners and peasant convicts, while overlooking the feelings of self-preservation that likely motivate the Polish politicals' decision to separate themselves from the other prisoners. Since no such loyalties divide Raskolnikov from the other inmates, he struggles against his separation from the Russian prisoners, even though "it appeared that they and he were of different nations," and tries to overcome the "impassable abyss" that divides him from the others (*Pss*, 6:418). He ascribes to the Poles the prison's class conflict even though in his pre-Siberian conception of *la guerre éternelle,* such tensions arise inevitably out of the historic struggle between the extraordinary and ordinary. The Poles, therefore, help to expose the flaws in his binary historical theory, since their conviction in their civilization's superiority—a belief (for Dostoevsky) stemming from its Western orientation and Catholic religion—is challenged by Raskolnikov, who defends the ordinary Russian convicts: "He saw clearly that these ignoramuses were much smarter in many things than these very Poles" (*Pss*, 6:418). Here, Raskolnikov abandons the Polish politicals, that is, the ordinary categorizing themselves as extraordinary, to live in perpetual estrangement with their revolutionary ideals so that they share the fate of other exiled Napoleons. In so doing, Raskolnikov reflects Dostoevsky's tendency to assign interethnic class antagonism to specific Catholic ethnic groups.

The Orthodox identity of the peasant convicts is evident from their praying, fasting, and attendance at services for Easter, and their anger at Raskolnikov's participation in these Easter preparations attests to the authenticity of their spiritual devotion: "'You are an atheist! You don't believe in

God!' they yelled at him. 'You should be killed'" (*Pss*, 6:419). Dostoevsky highlights the chasm between his protagonist and the prisoners with the mockery of his ax ("You shouldn't have gone at it with an ax; that's not at all the work of the nobility") through which Dostoevsky undermines the Russian radicals' advocacy of the revolutionary's ax as a political solution (*Pss*, 6:418; *Ss*, 14:239). Since brutal acts of murder committed without remorse are connected to the peasantry in the notes to *Crime and Punishment* with the phrase "A peasant kills [*rezhet*] and does not repent," Raskolnikov's moralizing over the murders signals his lack of identification with the peasant convicts, who, like Dostoevsky, sense that "our democrats are insufficiently democratic. (Freedom with a garland in hand. The people are not the people's)" (*Pss*, 7:160). With this obvious divide between Raskolnikov and the other convicts, Dostoevsky illustrates the conviction that "it is not possible to live a life in common with all humankind" (*Pss*, 7:165). Nevertheless, even in prison Raskolnikov continues the search for a viable political system as is evident from his dream about people infected with microbes, each of whom is seized by a madness that convinces the person that "in himself alone the truth was contained" (*Pss*, 6:420). Hegel notes a similar tendency with the advance of democracy, which saw the diminished importance of the oracles, Socrates's reliance on his "Daemon," and people increasingly turning toward "their individual convictions in forming their decisions."[101]

In his chronicle-novel *Demons,* Dostoevsky returns to this association of madness or demon-possession with a self-defined ethics as he considers the detrimental impact of Western revolutionary movements on Russian youth who engage in jesuitical activities, because they, like Raskolnikov, wish to become extraordinary. Although Prince Myshkin warns against "slavishly being caught on the Jesuits' hook," he nevertheless acknowledges that Jesuitism appeals to the Russian temperament: "If one of us goes over to Catholicism, then without fail he will become a Jesuit, and even of the most underground sort" (*Pss*, 8:451–52). The various revolutionaries in *Demons* reflect the Catholic-atheist continuum established by Prince Myshkin, who likens Russian Jesuits to Russian atheists for the way in which they proceed "from spiritual pain, from spiritual thirst, from ennui to the highest cause, to the firmest shore, to a native land, in which they stopped believing" (*Pss,* 8:452). The historical practice of Catholic pretendership in Russia, which in *Crime and Punishment* constitutes only a theoretical motivation to criminal activity, occupies center stage in *The Demons,* in which it becomes equated with the violent deeds of young conspirators in the Russian countryside. In this novel, Dostoevsky explores his fears concerning Russian radicals, who empathize with Polish exiles, the resurgence of socialism, and the increased secular power of the papacy, by further investigating the Catholic dimension to revolutionary activities on Russian soil.

Chapter Four

Dostoevsky's Portrayal of Transnational Catholicism in *Demons*

> "And take my advice, which is never take up
> with actors, who are a privileged people."
> —Miguel de Cervantes, *Don Quixote de la
> Mancha* (1605)

DEPICTIONS OF CATHOLICISM in Dostoevsky's novel written abroad—Myshkin's merging of socialism with the Roman faith, the near-seduction of Pavlishchev by the archetypal Jesuit Goureau, and Aglaya's succumbing to an émigré count (along with his *pater* confessor)—attest that Dostoevsky's encounters with revolutionaries from Catholic nations during his 1867–71 European sojourn inform his impressions of Western Christendom. The importance of the Roman faith for *Demons* may be gleaned from the Catholic connections of the novel's lead conspirators, Petr Verkhovensky and Nikolai Stavrogin, as well as from the allusions in *Demons* to the seventeenth-century Catholic-Orthodox conflict, the Time of Troubles. Not long before the novel's publication, Dostoevsky considers another East-West spiritual encounter in his unrealized novel *The Life of a Great Sinner* (*Zhitie velikogo greshnika*), between Chaadaev, who informs the novelist's linking of Jesuitism and revolution, and Saint Tikhon of Zadonsk in a monastery—a meeting that prefigures a similar exchange between Stavrogin and Tikhon in *Demons* (*Pss*, 20:190; 29.1:118). In his novel about Sergei Nechaev's conspiracy, about Nechaevs (*Nechaevy*) and Nechaevists (*nechaevtsy*), Dostoevsky repeatedly underscores the influence that Catholics and Catholicism exert on Westernized Russians, since the Moscow *barin* and landowner "drew the quit-rent in order to live on it in Paris . . . and to end with Chaadaev's or Gagarin's Catholicism" (*Pss*, 11:87). This link may arise from his tendency to reduce the hundreds of Russians he met abroad to a few types such as old socialists in the tradition of Belinsky (e.g., Herzen and Bakunin) and Russians-turned-Jesuits, like Ivan Gagarin, S.J. (*Pss*, 23:43).[1] Dostoevsky unites these types more explicitly in an 1871 letter to Strakhov in which he finds that Belinsky, Granovsky (a prototype for Stepan Verkhovensky), and "all this riff-raff" will make of Russia "a vacant nation, capable of becoming at the head of the common humanity [*obshchechelovecheskii*] cause. Jesuitism and the lie of our progressive movers it would take up with pleasure" (*Pss*, 29.1:215).

The jesuitical behavior of the revolutionaries, allusions to the Roman pontiff, as well as a comparison of the Chaadaev figure, Stavrogin, to Otrepev, attest to a Catholic presence in Dostoevsky's novel. The Catholic interest is multi-generational, since the circle of Stepan Verkhovensky, who declares "I do not wish to be a Jesuit," discusses the role of the pope in the new Italy: "For the pope we ages ago foresaw the role of a simple metropolitan in a united Italy and were completely convinced that all this 1000-year question in our age of humanity, industry, and the railroads is only a trifling matter" (*Pss*, 10:33, 30). Such a discussion of the age resonates well with Vakhrameev's letter in *The Double*, which similarly finds that Grishka Otrepev could not appear "in our business-oriented and industrial . . . century" (*Pss*, 1:414).[2] Yet, both Otrepev and the pope play a role in the conspiracy in *Demons* organized by the Nechaev figure Petr Verkhovensky, and in his 1875–76 notebook, Dostoevsky himself discloses that the pope's pretension to "universal dominion" (i.e., the new decree on papal infallibility)—that "idea of ancient Rome"—through which the pope intends to unite with the people is "the idea I expressed before all others in the novel *Demons*" (*Pss*, 24:149). This note accounts for the theocratic proposal by Petr Verkhovensky to Stavrogin:

> You know, I thought to return the world to the Pope. Let him come out, the Pope, discalced and on foot, and show himself to the mob: "Look what they've driven me to!" And they will throng him, even the army. The Pope is at the top, we are around him, and under us—*Shigalevshchina* [equality in slavery]. We need only for the *Internationale* to agree to the Pope. . . . the Pope will be in the West and we will, will have you! (*Pss*, 10:323)

Petr, therefore, draws on the papal model to create for Stavrogin the position of a dictatorial Russian leader, "with a halo of a victim in hiding," who maintains his power by appealing to the aesthetics of the masses (*Pss*, 10:326). A similar merging of communism, Christianity, and the papacy in *Demons* also appears in the aforementioned notebook, in which Dostoevsky describes a France, "deceived by Christianity," but bearing the idea of "communism": "In a word, this is church, religion, and temple, but without Christ. Only they forgot that this is all only utopia. . . . Meanwhile all Europe is filled with it. And our children see it. And won't the Pope be off. I said this in the novel *Demons*" (*Pss*, 24:160). Ivan Shatov, in a discussion of France's modern atheist socialism, advances similar conclusions by drawing on Stavrogin's former belief that Rome had succumbed to the third temptation of the devil. Summarizing an idea that Ivan develops more fully in "The Grand Inquisitor," Shatov associates Rome with the conclusion that "Christ without an earthly kingdom on earth cannot stand," so "if France torments itself, then it is solely the fault of Catholicism, because she rejected the stinking Roman God and did not find a new one" (*Pss*, 10:197).

In *Demons* Dostoevsky explores concerns that religious sects, Jesuits, and Catholicism may appeal to Russians like Shatov, who during the modern period characterized by "disharmony" are tempted to follow the European example and "vacillate [*shataiutsia*]" between ideological extremes (*Pss*, 24:161). He finds that "Russians abroad," for example, those "Turgenevs, Herzens, Utins" about whom he intended to write a novel, are particularly susceptible to these Catholic, socialist, and revolutionary forces, so he provides several main characters with such émigré connections (*Pss*, 28.2:210).[3] In his notes to *Demons*, Dostoevsky alludes to Nechaev's cooperation with Herzen's circle, well publicized during Nechaev's trial for murder of a co-conspirator, by affiliating his modus operandi with that of the famous émigré. Dostoevsky's Nechaev admires the "Herzen device [*priem gertsenovskii*]" of lying in proclamations about the government and endorses such "jesuitical" deception, because "the Jesuits are an extraordinarily intelligent Order, and in them, if you wish, there is truth [*istina*]. Otherwise you will not survive in the world" (*Pss*, 11:103). Here, Nechaev does not represent an organized Catholic movement, such as the pope's "black army" acting *exceptionally* but merely ascribes to a Jesuitism, which Dostoevsky implicates in the bartering of Christ's body (*Pss*, 24:150). Given his extended residence abroad, Dostoevsky was likely familiar with the accusations launched against Nechaev's co-conspirator Bakunin by Nikolai Utin, who proposed that Bakunin be expelled from the Genevan section of the International Workingmen's Association (IWA) for endorsing Nechaev's political program of "jesuitical discipline" as the "sine qua non" for a revolutionary victory.[4] By similarly attaching Catholic references throughout *Demons* to leaders of the progressive conspiracy, Dostoevsky implicates the Genevan exiles in the historic tradition of Catholic conspiracy on Russian soil.[5]

ENCOUNTERS WITH CATHOLIC CONNECTIONS TO HERZEN'S CIRCLE

Herzen's writings display a detailed knowledge of Catholic Europe—its revolutionaries and spiritual leaders—about which Dostoevsky had read for decades before he departed for his lengthy sojourn in Europe. Already in the sixth letter of *Letters from France and Italy*, Herzen is intrigued by Pius IX: "I saw Pius IX several times; I wanted to read in the face of this man, placed at the head of not only the Italian movement, but the European one, some thought, in a word, something, and I read nothing besides genial flabbiness and dispassionate serenity" (*Ss,* 5:90). Dostoevsky's characterization of the aged pontiff as a "squashed, dying being, weak like an insect" but yet with colossal "pretensions" to power strikingly contrasts with Herzen's early impressions of the Holy Father (*Pss,* 24:149). However, Herzen's surprise at peaceful Catholics carrying rifles, swords, bayonets, sabers, and pikes in church may provide a foundational image for Dostoevsky's vision of Catholic violence and theology: "Catholicism concedes that they must go with the sword (and in this is all the difference)" (*Pss,* 24:150). Herzen attaches Catholic imagery to his revolutionary acquaintances from Catholic nations, so a *carbonari* and leader of the Republican brotherhood "Young Europe," Giuseppe Mazzini, under Herzen's pen becomes "like a Pope of old in Avignon" and his Italian revolutionaries become heroes ranking "among the martyrs of Christianity and the Reformation" (*Ss,* 10:66–67). Still, the most potent blend of Catholicism and modern liberation movements appears in Herzen's portraits of his many Polish comrades, since he concludes after the 1863 uprising: "Poland presented the chivalric tradition in a new formation for European nations, in its combination with the revolutionary tradition. Full of age and youth, full of idealism, heroism, and Catholicism, she touched at once both the Middle Ages and 1789, the Crusades and the Grande Armée" (*Ss,* 18:302). From his reading of *The Bell,* his interaction with the Herzen circle while abroad, as well as from the volumes of *My Past and Thoughts* gifted to him by Herzen's cousin Ogarev, Dostoevsky gained an intimate knowledge of the exiles' interaction with such "Catholic" revolutionaries.[6]

As the progressive editor of the leading émigré journal *The Bell* (mentioned in *Demons*), Herzen, when he joined with the Central National Committee (Komitet Centralny Narodowy, KCN) in 1862 to endorse rebellion in Warsaw, affiliated himself with a motley group of Polish nationalists, ranging widely in political persuasions from monarchists to communists (*Pss,* 10:328). Prince Adam Czartoryski and his circle of Poles at the Hotel Lambert in Paris as well as the more centrist Siberian exile, Agaton Giller, were among those Catholics who closely supported Herzen's agitation (*Ss,* 11:367–72).[7] Even though Herzen records his objection to "Catholic phrases" in the Poles' writing, the KCN members defend them in the name of the people who "ardently love their persecuted mother—the Latin Church" (*Ss,* 11:136). In his *My Past and Thoughts,* Herzen concludes that *The Bell*'s Russo-Polish alliance was destined to fail owing to a conflict between Russian "realists" and Polish "mystics," with their "crucifix before which they can pray in moments of weariness and difficulty," so he finds that vestiges of Catholic feudal "Old Poland" destroyed the rebellion (*Ss,* 11:128). Unlike

Herzen, Bakunin supports the Polish revolution "even if she is the most antipathetic, jesuitical, aristocratic, monarchical," because "if she only shook the foul strength of the All-Russian Empire, she would be for us useful and redeeming."[8] He further maintains the superiority of "every Pole, even the most inveterate Jesuit or aristocrat, going to death or Siberia for his convictions" over "we who wear obediently the tsar's livery and in the hands of the accursed state play the role of executioners against all foreigners and against our own people."[9] His disciple Nechaev studies the Jesuit-inspired Polish revolutionaries, especially the Polish nationalist Anton Berezowski who failed to assassinate Alexander II in 1867. In his 1869 proclamation "Principles of Revolution" ("Nachala revoliutsii") and his *Catechism of a Revolutionary* (*Katekhizis revoliutsionera*), Nechaev draws on the Jesuitism of Berezowski, formed in part from Sue's *Le Juif errant* and Zaccone's *Histoire des sociétés secrètes, politiques et religieuses*, and on the secret society of the Catholic revolutionary Jozafat Ohryzko, who was sentenced to Siberia after the 1863 uprising.[10] For this reason, Nechaev celebrates the "Polish revolution" and mocks the "Russian inquisitors" in the first issue of the journal that he publishes with Bakunin, *Popular Reprisal* (*Narodnaia rasprava*).[11]

In *Demons* Dostoevsky merges the Jesuitism of Nechaev and idealism of Herzen's Polish revolutionaries, whether inspired by the papacy or the Internationale, in his presentation of Petr and Stavrogin. Dostoevsky had likely encountered this union of papal and socialist politics in conservative analyses of the Polish uprisings, which credited broad-based support, ranging from foreign revolutionaries to local priests, with stoking Polish "fanaticism": "This union of atheism with fanaticism is good! The Catholic Church constantly teaches that outside of her there is no salvation: from this we have St. Bartholomew's night, the horrors of the inquisition, the bloody machinations of the Jesuits, and today's events in Poland."[12] Katkov implicated an international circle of "virtuoso-conspirators" in the "crafty jesuitical intrigue—jesuitical in origin and in character" in Poland: "These networks were prepared and positioned with astounding adroitness, with jesuitical consistency, with contempt for everything sacred (worthy of the most criminal Italians of the sixteenth century), and with the idealized treason of Konrad Wallenrod."[13] Before arriving in Geneva, Dostoevsky was reminded of the most recent uprising in Vilnius, where the insurgents had suffered disproportionately owing to the repressive policies of "The Hangman [*Veshatel'*]" Mikhail Muravev.[14] In Vilnius, Dostoevsky and his new wife, Anna Grigorevna, visited a sight celebrating the "suppression" of the 1863 rebellion, that is, the Alexander Nevsky chapel on St. George's Square, which was dedicated to the Russians who died in the uprising.[15] Soon thereafter in Dresden (May-June of 1867), Berezowski's attempted tsaricide confronted Dostoevsky with the danger posed by the pro-Polish sympathies of Russian political exiles, as Anna

Grigorevna reveals: "A new assassination attempt, having followed so soon after the Karakozov attempt, clearly showed my husband that a network of political conspiracy penetrated deeply and that danger threatens the life of the emperor, whom he respected so much."[16]

Berezowski's trial in Paris furthered Dostoevsky's conviction that the Catholic nations of France and Poland remained hostile to Russia: "The events in Paris shook me horribly. Those Parisian lawyers, crying 'Vive la Pologne' are fine! Ugh, what is with this vileness, and more important— stupidity and bureaucratic formality! I am even more convinced of my former idea: that it is even beneficial for us that Europe does not know us and that she knows us so vilely" (*Pss,* 28.2:206). Here, his repetition of "Vive la Pologne"—a battle cry used, among others, by the Parisian mob of May 1848—serves to highlight the generations of European anarchists and so-cialists (including his fellow Genevan residents) supporting Polish visions of independence. Yet Dostoevsky reserves his harshest remarks for those progressive Germanized Russians residing abroad on wealth collected from Russian estates, whom he characterizes as a Polish breed, that is, "some sort of Pomeranians, querulous and squeamish," for their support of the Poles and criticism of Russian nationalists such as Katkov (*Pss,* 28.2:207). Maikov's correspondence with Dostoevsky from 1868 confirms this criticism of the Herzen circle, since Maikov isolates the "socialist idiocy of the Herzenists" as the group responsible for supporting "the division and weakening of Russia" and for the fact that "Polish nihilist movements are flourishing."[17]

In his above-mentioned letter Dostoevsky also accounts for his rupture with the Germanophile Turgenev, whom the former famously caricatures in the portrayal of Karmazinov in *Demons.*[18] Turgenev's established connections to the Herzen circle and his sympathy for Polish liberationists likely con-tributed to Dostoevsky's animosity toward the Russian novelist, whose novel *Smoke,* which touches upon the Polish Question, is criticized by Dostoevsky in the letter. Turgenev's sympathy for the Polish intelligentsia had been es-tablished by his petitioning Alexander II for the release of Jozafat Ohryzko, the editor of the St. Petersburg-based Polish newspaper *Word* (*Słowo*) who had been arrested for *Word's* 1859 publication of a letter by a Polish revo-lutionary exile, Joachim Lelewel. These connections to Lelewel, who had associated with Bakunin and Marx in the 1840s, and to Ohryzko further link Turgenev to the cause of Polish nationalism. Owing to the 1867 publication of N. V. Gogel's *Jozafat Ohryzko and the Petersburg Revolutionary Régime in the Last Revolt* (*Iosafat Ogryzko i Peterburgskii revoliutsionnyi rzhond v dele poslednego miatezha*), which recognizes the influence of Jesuitism in service to Polish liberation, Ohryzko's clandestine activities were widely known in Russian circles.[19] Dostoevsky adeptly introduces similar Russo-Polish links to his Nechaev, Petr Verkhovensky, by providing him with two potential fathers: the 1840s romantic Stepan Verkhovensky, discussed alongside the names "of Chaadaev, Belinsky, Granovsky, and Herzen, who had then just started out abroad" and an unknown "Polack" who may have impregnated Petr's mother (*Pss*, 10:8, 240). Turgenev's tolerance of the West, however, encourages Dostoevsky in his letter to categorize his fellow novelist as another Russian exile with pro-Catholic sympathies, as he indicates when telling Turgenev "to send for a telescope from Paris" in order to better view Russia (*Pss*, 28.2:211). Dostoevsky's choice of verb "vypisat'" which means both "to send for" and "to subscribe to" highlights his allusion to the Parisian journal *Telescope,* in which Chaadaev published his first philosophic letter.[20]

When Dostoevsky then arrived in Geneva in August, he encountered an international gathering of Catholics and atheists, communists and Republicans, socialists and anarchists, who were preparing for a meeting of the Ligue de la Paix et de la Liberté (League of Peace and Freedom).[21] The league attracted a disparate group of Italian, French, Polish, and Russian patriots, many of whom were seeking regime changes in France, Italy, Prussia, Spain, and Russia. The large number of Polish insurgents, who helped form the Polish section of the league under the leadership of General Józef Hauke-Bosak (a former officer in the tsar's army and 1863 conspirator), must have alarmed Dostoevsky, especially since earlier that year at a celebration of the fourth anniversary of the uprising, Marx had encouraged Polish exiles by calling for the liberation of Poland and emphasizing the importance of its restoration for the international proletariat.[22] Several of them, such as legendary commanders Walery Wróblewski and Dąbrowski, then fought on the barricades in Paris in 1871 for the commune that Dostoevsky characterizes as a union of Catholic idealism and socialist utopianism.[23] Bakunin's friend Jan Zagórski, who played a leading role in the Polish section of the league, was in Vevey in May 1868 while the Dostoevskys briefly resided there, so Dostoevsky may have him or his infamous comrade, the 1863 insurgent Walery Mroczkowski, in mind when complaining to Maikov from Vevey: "But really they must know that the nihilists and liberals of *The Contemporary* since the year −3 have been flinging filth at me, because I broke with them, I hate little Polacks, and I love my fatherland. Oh the scoundrels!" (*Pss*, 28.2:310).[24]

Consequently, the presence of revolutionaries who had promoted rebellion in the Catholic nations of Italy, Poland, and France fueled Dostoevsky's growing concerns about a transnational Catholic revolutionary conspiracy against Russia. Famous conference participants from such nations had demonstrated their opposition to the Russian Empire through their support of Poland. For example, Victor Hugo implores Russian officers in the pages of *The Bell* to refuse to fight the Poles by choosing Warsaw over Petersburg, or "freedom" not "autocracy."[25] Garibaldi's presence in Geneva bolstered critics of Russian imperialism, since his supporters fought for Poland, thereby alienating those Russians who had once celebrated his successful expulsion of foreign troops from Italian lands, as Pogodin's letter to the Italian revolutionary indicates:

> We love and respect you, we wished you every success in the liberation of the Italian people from the yoke of those from another tribe, and now, hearing about the part you took in the Polish affair, we are extremely distressed. . . . Today's Polish war is not about the liberation of the Poles from the Russian yoke, but about the submission of the Russian population in the Western provinces under the power of a future Poland.[26]

Although Garibaldi alarmed Catholics at the congress by calling for "la déchéance de la papauté comme la plus nuisible des sectes" and embracing "la religion de Dieu, c'est-à-dire, la religion de la vérité et de la raison," anti-Garibaldi proclamations protesting his comments, for Anna Grigorevna, attested to the significant Catholic community in the city willing to challenge the charismatic general in defense of the Roman pontiff.[27] The debate raged on at the congress, as James Fazy's *Journal de Genève* indicates with its descriptions of various speeches, such as one in which a delegate declares: "Que dans ce qu'on appelle la morale du Christ, il y avait deux morales, une *païenne* qui est la bonne, la sienne et celle de ses amis, avec une autre qui est chrétienne, et qui apporte la *guerre* et *non la paix* aux familles et aux peuples, selon les paroles mêmes du Christ."[28] Such a merging of Christ's words with warfare advanced a militant image of the Western church, which often appears in Dostoevsky's notes and published writings after his return to Russia.

Dostoevsky was fascinated by the revolutionaries gathered before him "for the first time not in books but in real life" because he concludes that in viewing them from Russia "we . . . see it all wrong" (*Pss*, 28.2:224, 217). As an eyewitness, he realized that the viewpoint of these experienced conspirators "was learned by heart already twenty years ago" and that "socialists and revolutionaries . . . lied from the podium before 5,000 listeners": "The comicality, the weak argumentation, the obtuseness, the lack of consensus, the self-contradictions—you can't imagine!" (*Pss*, 28.2:224). Herzen's cousin and collaborator on *The Bell*, Ogarev, who encouraged Dostoevsky to attend the congress, agreed with Dostoevsky that it was governed by infighting and trite political thought.[29] In his correspondence, Ogarev notes the heated disagreements among the participants with remarks on the German scientist Carl Vogt (mentioned in *Demons*, *Pss*, 10:269) who "shouted furiously à l'ordre and did not let the orator finish his speech," Bakunin who "constantly scolded Molinari," and James Fazy (a Genevan politician with widespread Catholic support) who "furiously objected to Gambuzzi, saying, that to reject the papacy means to destroy religious freedom."[30] Although Dostoevsky criticizes the crowds of revolutionaries left behind after Garibaldi's brief visit to the city, he nevertheless finds in their "four days of shouting and swearing" and rhetoric of "disorder" and destruction by "fire and sword" source material for the young conspirators in *Demons* (*Pss,* 28.2:217, 224).

For instance, the league's arguments over revolution and religion are present not only in Myshkin's observation that lapsed-Catholics-turned-socialists employ "sword and the blood" but also in Petr's willingness to employ fire and Fedka's knife to motivate his circle of conspirators (*Pss,* 8:451). As Ogarev recognizes, the role of religion in society remained a contentious issue at the conference with Fazy's aforementioned protest, Gambuzzi's call for "the destruction of the papacy," and the presence of such anti-papal speakers as Edgar Quinet and Garibaldi.[31] Dostoevsky expresses his fear that this abolition of religion is only a point of departure for the destruction of empires (Bakunin's contribution) and private capital (a point supported by the Marxists): "It was immediately decided that in order to attain peace it is necessary to exterminate the Pope and the entire Christian religion by fire and sword. Next, since great powers showed that they cannot exist without having large armies and waging wars; it is necessary to destroy them and replace them with small republics. Next, it is necessary to destroy capital by fire and sword" (*Pss,* 28.2:354). With the repetition of the phrase "fire and sword" which is often attributed to forced conversions by armed Catholics such as Charlemagne or crusading knights, Dostoevsky underscores a link between Catholicism and socialism while asserting his belief in the coercive nature of their statecraft. Dostoevsky appropriates from the congress in "la patrie de ce grand citoyen, de ce J.-J. Rousseau, qui retrouva le premier les droits de l'homme enterrés par le despotisme" the vision of a destructive Catholic force with a priestly army: "M. Dupont . . . a demandé hautement que l'on détruisit toutes les religions avec leurs armées permanentes de prêtres, et que l'on fit table rase des églises aussi bien que des casernes."[32] Hence, in Geneva he encounters in the flesh the Rousseauian link between socialism and Catholicism about which he wrote in the aftermath of the 1863 uprising, but in Dostoevsky's conception, such socialists do not abandon the priestly armies but join with the Jesuits, the knights of Christ, whose rapid and forcible expansion throughout Europe and the Americas earned them widespread recognition as the papal army (*Pss,* 20:190).

In 1868 plans for his unrealized novel *Atheism* (*Ateizm*), Dostoevsky infuses this socialist/atheist-Catholic model with national essentialism when his Russian atheist "catches the hook of a Jesuit, a propagator, and a Pole" but ultimately finds "Christ and the Russian God" by returning to "the Russian land, the Russian Christ" (*Pss* 28.2:329).[33] In some respects, Dostoevsky's discussion of atheism, Poland, and a Russian Christ echoes phrases employed by Bakunin in his article "The People's Affair: Romanov, Pugachev, or Pestel?" ("Narodnoe delo: Romanov, Pugachev, ili Pestel'?"). Bakunin demands that Alexander II, viewed by the Russian people as "a kin of the Russian Christ, father, and benefactor," liberate the Polish nation that Nicholas I "suppressed."[34] However, Dostoevsky uses this terminology to underscore the importance of nationhood, whereas Bakunin, according to the September 11 issue of *Journal de Genève,* insists that Russian patriots supporting liberty may not endorse the tsar's government: "Il n'y avait aucune solidarité même de patriotisme national entre les Russes dévoués à la cause de la liberté et leur gouvernement."[35] Although Dostoevsky prefers to limit himself to the more ambiguous concepts of the Russian land and the Russian Christ, he does challenge a vision emerging from the league's congress that resembles Bakunin's demand for the dissolution of empires in favor of a united states of Europe: "And our little liberals preach the dissolution of Russia into united states! Oh, the little shits!" (*Pss,* 28.2:260).[36] As Bakunin explains further in an 1869 article, "Quelques paroles à mes jeunes frères en Russie," the end of the Russian Empire would serve the aims of both Russian populists and Polish patriots by destroying a Russocentric state governed by tsarist and aristocratic privilege.[37] Thus, his vision of a European federation of states presents an effective response to the very political questions that concerned the close circle of Polish émigrés who surrounded him in Florence and Switzerland.[38]

Dostoevsky clearly distinguishes his own political leanings from this group in the aftermath of the congress in an October 1867 letter to Maikov, which celebrates the submission of a former Herzen collaborator, Vasily Kelsiev, to the tsar and, in an apparent allusion to the Herzen circle, anticipates how the Poles and "all our little liberals . . . will rail like beasts" at the rapprochement (*Pss,* 28.2:227). Although Dostoevsky does not specifically name Bakunin, he repeatedly refers to his political circles in correspondence. For example, he notes the "aged exiles and socialists" at the congress, of whom Garibaldi and Bakunin were prominent examples, as is evident from the general excitement aroused by their appearance and speeches at the league's meeting (*Pss,* 28.2:354).[39] Then, in March 1868, Dostoevsky writes to Maikov of the "many Russian aristocrats" choosing to winter in Geneva, the "rotten little Polacks" in Genevan coffee houses, and the "Russian traitors abroad" (*Pss,* 28.2:259, 260). After his move to Vevey, where Bakunin was living amidst young Russian and Polish radicals (including Utin and Mroczkowski), Dostoevsky complains to Maikov about being under surveillance because of suspected "treason to the Fatherland" and "dealings with the little Polacks" (*Pss,* 28.2:310).[40] Maikov's questioning of Dostoevsky about potential Genevan rivals to *The Bell,* one of which was Bakunin's *The People's*

Affair (*Narodnoe delo*), shows that the two Russian writers were following the political debates between the Herzen circle and the younger generation.[41]

Such frequent encounters with the Herzen circle during his residence abroad likely encouraged Dostoevsky to abandon his plan for the novel *Atheism* in favor of a political novel censuring Russian liberals and nihilists with links to Geneva and Jesuitism that began to resemble the final shape of *Demons* as early as February 1870. Even before Dostoevsky had departed Russia for Europe in 1867 such connections were discovered in the official investigations into the underground group Land and Will (Zemlia i volia), whose network of revolutionaries included Russians and Poles collaborating with Kelsiev, Herzen, Bakunin, and Ogarev. Kelsiev's desire to agitate among the Old Believers drew him in 1862 to St. Petersburg where he lived with members of Land and Will, Alexander and Nikolai Serno-Solovevich, the latter of whom was arrested along with Nikolai Chernyshevsky after correspondence with the Herzen circle was seized from a messenger at the Russian border.[42] The tragic death of Nikolai Serno-Solovevich in Siberia as he was organizing the 1866 Krasnoyarsk Rebellion of Polish exiles and the subsequent suicide of his brother Alexander in Swiss exile advanced the perception that their radical causes spelled the destruction of Russian youth.[43] In citing the surname Serno-Solovevich alongside Nechaev's to represent the younger generation possessed by the demons from Luke's gospel (the passage, located in chapter 8 of the Gospel, is cited as an epigraph to *Demons*), Dostoevsky alludes to the immediate relevance for *Demons* of radicals agitating for Polish independence: "The Demons went out of the Russian man and entered into the herd of swine, i.e. into the Nechaevs, into the Serno-Soloveviches, etc. . ." (*Pss*, 29.1:145). As the writings of Herzen, Nechaev, and Bakunin demonstrate, the Genevan exiles were willing to embrace the Catholicism, Jesuitism, and Roman mysticism of Polish liberationists in order to create trouble in Russia sufficient enough to unseat the Romanov tsar.

POLISH CATHOLIC LINKS TO THE HERZEN CIRCLE IN *DEMONS*

A potential indication that episodes in Russo-Polish history weighed on Dostoevsky's mind while he was outlining *Demons* may be found in an 1869 letter to Maikov in which Dostoevsky outlines a Russian historical epic in which "Poles would have to take up a lot of space" (*Pss*, 29.1:41). His plan to include historical accounts "up to the liberation of the serfs and up to the boyars, who have scattered their last little paper rubles around Europe" in the cycle of legends, therefore connects Polish history to the Russian émigré experience that he observed while living abroad. Dostoevsky, himself, shared

Herzen's Polish misfortunes, since they both suffered the demise of their respective journals *Time* and *The Bell* owing to their publications on the 1863 Polish uprising. While abroad in the late 1860s, Dostoevsky was still suffering from the debts incurred as a result of the closing of *Time* over Strakhov's article, and Herzen, owing in part to his journal's drop in circulation, decided in the summer of 1867 to suspend publication of *The Bell* after breaking with the younger generation over his objection to Berezowski's terrorist tactics.[44] An 1870 posthumous collection of Herzen's work, which included the article "M. Bakunin and the Polish Affair" ("M. Bakunin i pol'skoe delo"), likely clarified for Dostoevsky Herzen's active collusion with Polish Catholic revolutionaries in fomenting the 1863 uprising, about which he wrote in *Diary of a Writer*.[45] Furthermore, articles on Bakunin and Nechaev in the Russian and foreign press as well as Herzen's death in January 1870 encouraged Dostoevsky to pursue in *Demons* the timely subject of Herzen's impact upon multiple generations of Russia's intellectuals who had witnessed Polish Catholic unrest in the 1830s, 1840s, and 1860s.[46]

Katkov used his articles on the Nechaev affair to renew his opposition to the Herzen circle's support of Polish independence, with which he continues to identify his old friend Bakunin who "married a young Polish girl from an exiled family, associated with many of his wife's fellow tribesmen and, when the Polish affair went down, fled Siberia and took part in 1863, together with some terrors from the Polish emigration, in a naval expedition against Russia."[47] Because Bakunin's political leaflet "Quelques paroles à mes jeunes frères en Russie" reminds Katkov of the previous dangers posed by his (and Herzen's) 1862–63 endorsement of Polish patriotism, Katkov concludes that Russia should not remain indifferent to Bakunin's support of Nechaev's political agitation.[48] Bakunin defends Herzen's stance on the Polish Question in his necrology of Herzen in *La Marseillaise* (a mouthpiece for the IWA) in March 1870. In the article, Bakunin challenges other published retrospectives which suggest (as Alexander Serno-Solovevich had once maintained) that his colleague, after the liberation of the serfs, no longer opposed the tsar or the birth of a new (i.e., Russified) Poland.[49] Also, Pogodin's more unforgiving remembrance of Herzen, "Friend of Mazzini, Garibaldi," which ran in the 1870 February issue of *Dawn* (*Zaria*) along with Dostoevsky's *Eternal Husband* (*Vechnyi muzh*), focuses on Pogodin's objection to Herzen's support of the Polish cause, thereby demonstrating its importance for the émigré's reputation.[50] A few years later, when writing his reflections on Herzen in an 1873 *Diary of a Writer* entry entitled "Old People" ("Starye liudi"), Dostoevsky cites Pogodin's "most outstanding and curious article" before offering his own mixed review of the gentleman poet's political activities (*Pss*, 21:8).[51]

The entry, published in *The Citizen* (*Grazhdanin*) on the tenth anniversary of the Polish uprising, addresses Herzen's part in the Polish uprising and refuses to allow Herzen to escape culpability in the deaths of Russian officers, who fought for a free Poland, by simply chronicling Bakunin's part in the affair:

> Whether he sent his appeal to the Russian revolutionaries to Russia in '63, to please the Poles, while at that time not believing the Poles and knowing that they deceived him, knowing that with his appeal he would destroy hundreds of these unfortunate young people; whether out of unprecedented naïveté he himself admitted it in one of his latest articles, not even suspecting in what light he presented himself with such an admission, he was above all, always, everywhere, and throughout his life *gentilhomme russe et citoyen du monde.* (*Pss*, 21:9)[52]

Bakunin's numerous appeals to the Slavs on behalf of the Poles (which he continued to publish after Herzen's death) serve to implicate him more directly in the loss of Russian life during the 1863 uprising, but Dostoevsky still holds Herzen in *Demons* more directly accountable for the subversive activities of the Russian youth. For instance, Petr invokes Herzen's name to convince conspirators of his radical credentials, Alexei Kirillov contemplates signing his suicide note with the signature "gentilhomme russe et citoyen du monde" or "gentilhomme-séminariste russe et citoyen du monde civilisé," and Stavrogin's self-fashioning includes an imitation of Herzen as he, "like Herzen, registered as a citizen of the canton of Uri" not long before his demise (*Pss*, 10:423, 473, 513). However, the presence of Herzen's name in the novel and absence of direct references to Bakunin do not necessarily signify that Dostoevsky dismisses the latter as merely an "old rotten sack of ravings" (as is written in his notebooks to *Demons*), because in his notes from 1877, he identifies Bakunin, Herzen, and Proudhon as "obsolete" liberals with "slavish worship of authority" (*Pss*, 11:116; 25:231).

Although the debate over the nature and extent of Bakunin's and Herzen's separate influences on *Demons* remains divisive, the novel nonetheless attests to their mutual contribution to Dostoevsky's understanding of the Polish Question.[53] The importance of the Polish Question for the novel is suggested in the notebooks by Ivan Shatov, when he opposes a commonly proposed resolution to the Polish unrest—the severance of the Congress Kingdom from the Empire: "Entire newspapers, journals, serious people, even some professors and department heads insist on the idea of dismembering Russia and alienating our border areas" (*Pss*, 11:108). Early in the novel's narrative, the demand by Polish patriots for "the restoration of Poland up to the Dniepr" and the Bakuninist Russian federation of nationalities appear amidst a long list of causes supported by student radicals in St. Petersburg (*Pss*, 10:22).[54] This unremarkable introduction to an issue discussed widely

in the Russian press for decades diminishes the Polish independence movement by reducing its advocates to naive disciples or to the "swindlers" who
exploit them (*Pss*, 10:22). The first Polish Catholic presence, in the form of
the exiled priest Slontsevsky, briefly enters the chronicler's provincial circle
along with several other guests, such as "the little yid Lyamshin" who represents Dostoevsky's "little yids" caught up in the chaos during "the times
of troubles" owing to the leadership of Petr, who includes the sixteenth-
century Polish Catholic astronomer Copernicus among his men of "higher
abilities" (*Pss*, 10:30, 322).[55] This ethnic grouping and the novel's references
to the Internationale and the Peace Congress, in addition to the allusions to
Genevan conspiratorial networks, trace the troubles in *Demons* to Western
circles similar to those of Bakunin and Utin, who vied for influence over the
Russian members of the Internationale in Switzerland (*Pss*, 10:180, 77).[56]

Bakunin further enters the novel's narrative through a reference to
Raphael's *Sistine Madonna*, which Dostoevsky admired in the Zwinger gallery while in Dresden. As Herzen mentions in "M. Bakunin and the Polish
Affair," Saxony inculpated Bakunin in the seizure of the *Sistine Madonna*
for his Dresden barricades during the May 1849 Dresden uprising when
he fought alongside Polish comrades: "Bakunin is the commander of
Dresden; the former artillery officer teaches army affairs to the professors,
musicians, and pharmacists who have taken up arms; he advises them to
put Raphael's 'Madonna' and Murillo's paintings on the municipal walls to
protect themselves from the Prussians, who, *zu klassisch gebildet* [overedu-
cated in the classics], would not dare to shoot at Raphael" (*Ss*, 11:356).[57]
When Dostoevsky, underscoring its Dresden location, transposes this image
to *Demons*, he maintains it as a romantic ideal of the men of the 1840s by
replacing Stepan Trofimovich's preference for Pushkin: "with this queen of
queens, with this ideal of humankind, with the Sistine Madonna" (*Pss*, 10:235,
23, 265). Stepan Trofimovich juxtaposes this ideal not with the "boots" of the
1860s generation but with Herzen's materialist rendering of the "daily bread"
in the Lord's Prayer (which Dostoevsky's Lebedev dismissed in *The Idiot*):
"Those carts, or how is it there: 'the rumble of the carts transporting bread to
humankind' is more beneficial than the Sistine Madonna" (*Pss*, 10:23, 172).[58]
Therefore, when Stepan Trofimovich then refers to anyone who would seek
to destroy "the divine countenance of a great ideal in the name of equality"
as a lackey, he metatextually implicates Bakunin in the lackeyish destruction
of an 1840s ideal (*Pss*, 10:266).[59]

Dostoevsky's notes to *Demons* also attest to his conviction that the influence of Polish Catholicism on Herzen's circle evinces a weakened sense of
Russian national pride. Although Shatov, when discussing marriage to foreign
women in the notes to the novel, refers to Herzen's old friend Granovsky,
the contamination by marriage to a Pole may also apply to Bakunin, whose

name Granovsky utters several pages before the following observations: "The impact of Polish Catholic women on our bureaucrats and generals. Their own women always must please them more. It is a sign of a strong nationality, if citizens love and respect their own women most of all. . . . The first wife of Granovsky was a German and the second—a Pole" (*Pss*, 11:120). As Świderska notes, this passage demonstrates Dostoevsky's negative association of Poland with Catholicism in opposition to a Russian Orthodox national identity.[60] In this manner, the threat to nationhood that Dostoevsky perceives emerging from the league's gathering is associated with the Polonization and Catholicization of a Russian Westernizer from the 1840s, whose friends, for example, Herzen, Bakunin, Turgenev, and Belinsky, appear in the drafts and the text of *Demons*.

This aesthetic sense that appreciates non-Russian beauty also encourages a love of Shakespeare, which Granovsky shares with a Polish Catholic priest in the notebooks. Although Yury Levin notes that William Shakespeare's plays participated in the development of this circle's "formulation of a new realistic aesthetic," Dostoevsky imparts to Granovsky a belief in Shakespeare as "the chosen one, whom the creator annointed a prophet in order to expose before the world the secret of man" (*Pss*, 11:157).[61] Granovsky along with the priest is linked to "betrayal of the fatherland" before the citation from *Othello*, but Granovsky's line signifying Othello's recognition of Desdemona's infidelity (act 4, scene 1) underscores the priest's association with this betrayal (*Pss*, 11:139, 142). In the final version of *Demons*, the Granovsky type, Stepan Verkhovensky, follows a tradition of the Herzen circle in attaching a Shakespearean persona to a friend (Stavrogin), thereby enhancing the friend's conspiratorial reputation. In this respect, Stepan fulfills in *Demons* the role of a narrating Horatio in relating "fixed shadows forgotten by a departed world on the soil of the new" which Herzen ascribes to Granovsky, in a biography that Dostoevsky requested from Strakhov in 1870 (*Pss*, 29.1:111):[62] "Many times when I listened to Granovsky, I vividly imagined Horatio, with a constricted heart, narrating the tale of Hamlet next to the platform on which reposes his body" (*Ss*, 2:123).[63] The Shakespearean dimension to Stepan seems a consciously ironic allusion to the "famous pleiad" of "our past generation" such as Belinsky, Granovsky, and Herzen, especially given Herzen's use of the aforementioned quote to demonstrate Granovsky's interest in the chivalric past at the expense of the present—an accusation that may be launched at Stepan, as Derek Offord demonstrates (*Pss*, 10:8).[64]

Despite Stepan's recognized literary authority, however, his reported characterization of Stavrogin as Prince Harry is dismissed by Mme Stavrogina, who likens her son to the favorite Shakespearean prince of 1840s Russia— Prince Hamlet. Their debate over his Shakespearean dimension provides Stavrogin with a legendary literary reputation before his appearance in the novel.[65] Stepan relies on his comparison of Stavrogin to a young Prince Harry in order to allay his mother's concerns about the scandalous rumors regarding her son's behavior. Stavrogin shares with Princes Harry and Hamlet an apparent initial aversion to political affairs as he acts the part of the wayward youth with his "wild licentiousness" and his public insults launched at prominent people (*Pss*, 10:36). Yet, like the young Harry, Stavrogin appears as a privileged prodigal son whose dramatic "purposed reformation" is awaited by multiple generations, so Stepan's comparison suggests that Stavrogin's actions may portend future noble deeds worthy of a Henry V.[66] Although the repetitions of the image by the narrator, Liza Tushina, and Captain Lebyadkin reinforce this persona (*Pss*, 10:36, 37, 102, 208), Mme Stavrogina's preference for the Prince Hamlet prototype allows her to confirm the "loftiness of his soul and his calling" (*Pss*, 10:151). Her statement that Stavrogin's failure to realize her ambitions for him may be attributed to the absence of "a quiet Horatio, great in humility" betrays a familiarity with Turgenev's praise for Horatio as a "type of follower" whose greatness lies in a recognition of his "deficiency" vis-à-vis Hamlet as a result of which he "submits to him not as to a prince but as to a leader" (*Pss*, 10:151).[67] Her reading of Hamlet-Stavrogin as tormented by "melancholy" and a "sudden demon of irony" reflects the brooding Russian Hamlet of the 1840s romantics, which Dostoevsky identifies with "our contemporary Russian Hamlets and Hamletiks" already in *Epoch* (*Pss*, 20:136). From such internal demons, which make Hamlet appear mad and Stavrogin imbalanced, arise Hamlet's suicidal thought, evident in his most famous soliloquy, which Dostoevsky links to an early prototype of Stavrogin in his notebooks—the Prince: "Prince—morose, passionate, demonic and disordered character without any measure, with the highest question reaching 'To be or not to be?'" (*Pss*, 11:204). Such an emphasis on Hamlet's "evil demon" suggests Belinsky's influence on the formation of the demonic Stavrogin owing to Belinsky's frequent references to Hamlet's "rage [*beshenstvo*]" or "raging madness [*beshenoe sumasshestvie*]."[68]

Stavrogin's association with *Hamlet* enhances his link to Poland, which is introduced with his 1863 military service and further attested in a variant of his confession to Tikhon that refers to Poles in his "Sodom" of an apartment building (*Pss*, 12:109).[69] Hamlet's observations on the futility of a war with Poland encouraged those who supported the uprisings of 1831 and 1863 to draw on his literary image, which appears in *My Past and Thoughts*. For example, the Hamlet imagery that Herzen attaches to Garibaldi, Mazzini, and Stanisław Worcell connects these revolutionaries to the Polish Question, especially when the dying Worcell, like the ghost of Hamlet's father, extracts an oath ("Swear!") from his surviving friend Mazzini that "Poland would not be forgotten during the awakening of nations" (*Ss*, 12:442).[70] Such passages reflect a similarity to Bakunin's politicization of the tragedy with the discussion of Poland, which is evident in his manuscript on *Hamlet*.[71] For Bakunin, Hamlet's witnessing of Fortinbras's march to Poland with 20,000 troops to seize "a small little piece of land" compelled the heretofore vacillating Danish prince to undertake decisive action.[72] According to Bakunin, the passages surrounding Hamlet's criticism of Fortinbras's military mission as men going to their graves "out of empty glory" or "for land" (act 4, scene 4) serve to highlight how a mission forces Hamlet to realize his own idleness, a sentiment with which the 1840s romantics and Stavrogin can empathize:[73]

> Truly to be great, means
> Not to rise up without important motive
> But not to respect great idleness [*bezdelka*]
> When it is about honor. What am I?
> Neither the death of Father, nor Mother's dishonor
> Exciting my blood and reason,
> Nothing, Nothing roused me! (*Hamlet,* act 4, scene 4)[74]

These images of Hamlet in Bakunin's article and Herzen's remembrances as well as the biographical detail that Bakunin shares with Stavrogin—that is, being involuntarily dispatched to military service as a means of distraction for wayward youth—suggest that the Hamlet references in *Demons* serve as additional links to the Polish Question and the Herzen circle (*Pss,* 10:36).[75] All the same, Bakunin's frequent discussion of the fate of Polish exiles and Hamlet's interest in Poland's battle with Fortinbras "for a plot / Whereon the numbers cannot try the cause" (act 4, scene 4) contrast strikingly with Stavrogin's indifferent service during Poland's most recent uprising against Russia.[76]

Dostoevsky's knowledge of Granovsky's lectures on medieval Catholic Europe, the prominent place he intended for Luther and the Poles in his aforementioned book of legends, and his interest in the Time of Troubles intimate that he appreciated Hamlet's reference to the battle over Livonia between Protestant Sweden and Catholic Poland during Zygmunt III Waza's expansionist wars that engulfed Russia at the beginning of the seventeenth century.[77] The presence of *Hamlet* and *Don Quixote* in the drafts and final narrative of *Demons* points to Dostoevsky's dialogue with Turgenev's comparative speech that locates the two texts within this violent legacy of St. Bartholomew's night.[78] Turgenev's notation on the curious coincidence of the publications of *Hamlet* (1601) and the first part of *Don Quixote* (1605) in the same year further indicates the study's importance for *Demons,* particularly since the novel's reference to Otrepev connects its narrative to the First False Dimitry's historic seizure of the Moscow throne in 1605. The association of Prince Myshkin with quixoticism and the Prince of the notebooks with Hamlet identify two mentally imbalanced princes in Dostoevsky with Turgenev's productive model. Whereas Herzen links former Catholic revolutionaries to the tragic figure of Don Quixote for their unrealized "fantastical beliefs in the feasibility of harmonious order and common bliss," Dostoevsky's quixotic figure in *Demons*, Stepan Verkhovensky, appears pathetic as he perishes soon after he takes the initiative to abandon years of inactivity by going to the people (*Ss*, 16:153).[79]

TROUBLED TIMES IN DOSTOEVSKY'S PROVINCIAL RUSSIA

Since the comparison of the "era of the Great Reforms with the Time of Troubles" was common during this period, Dostoevsky's use of seventeenth-century historical references to highlight imposture in *Demons* is not unique to his chronicle of Russian history.[80] Indeed, Alexander II's use of the phrase "Polish troubles [*po'lskie smuty*]" in his April 1863 manifesto, which attempted to strengthen the Russians' resolve in their fight against Polish insurgents, appears to encourage the cultural identification of the 1863 instability with a seventeenth-century precedent.[81] Dostoevsky, as well, links the two historic eras in 1873 as a way of highlighting the significance of the 1870s for the development of Russia's history: "We are living through possibly the most troubled [*smutnyi*], the most awkward, the most transitional, and the most fateful [*rokovoi*] moment of all Russian history" (*Pss*, 21:58). This reinterpretation of the *smuta* for the 1860s places him within the more patriotic tradition of Katkov, Pogodin, and Kostomarov, who characterized the unrest in the Congress Kingdom as "troubles [*smuty*]" arising from the competing national loyalties of Westernized Catholic Poles and the Russian (and Ukrainian) Orthodox supporters of the tsar. Thus, Dostoevsky's reference to his own time as both troubled [*smutnyi*] and fateful [*rokovoi*] not only links the 1860s to the seventeenth century but specifically to its Russo-Polish dimension, since his terminology recalls not only the tsar's manifesto but also his personal tragedy ensuing from Strakhov's publication of "The Fateful [*Rokovoi*] Question." In addition, Dostoevsky more directly connects the two historical periods in an October 1876 entry to *Diary of a Writer*, when he refers to the year 1863 as "our most 'troubled' time [*samoe 'smutnoe' vremia nashe*]" (*Pss*, 23:141). Therefore, the repeated use of the word "smutnoe" and its related forms in *Demons* allows Dostoevsky to underscore further the outsidedness of his *Nechaevy* to Russian society by associating their political movement with a historic Catholic Polish invasion.

In reading these troubles as a conflict between two Slavic peoples, Dostoevsky rejects the political stance of Herzen and *The Bell*, which

Bakunin and Nechaev continued to disseminate, that the events of 1863 represent more a mass protest against tsarist tyranny arising from imperial abuse of civil rights rather than an uprising against Russian rule by patriotic Poles seeking nationhood. The Time of Troubles remained a significant historic precedent for these revolutionaries, because it was after the *smuta* that the Russian tsar was replaced not with a Polish-sponsored Catholic on the throne but with "newly Orthodox Protestant Germans" owing to a successful anti-Polish campaign (*Ss*, 16:113). In political pamphlets published during Dostoevsky's residence abroad, Bakunin outlines the significance of the Time of Troubles for Russia's history of dissent by choosing to divide people only by social class rather than adopting the usual Russian division by ethnic group that results in the *smuta* being attributed to a foreign invasion.[82] He thus challenges historian Kostomarov's recent criticism of the Poles for their past and present oppression of Russian peoples in his *The Time of Troubles of the Moscow State* (*Smutnoe vremia Moskovskogo Gosudarstva*) which was collected in three volumes in 1868: "Our troubled epoch was training for capriciousness, discord, anarchy, political nonsense, duplicity, deceit, frivolity, and dissipation of petty egoism, not appreciating the common need—in a word, all of that, which subsequently was absorbed into the flesh and blood of Polish society and led it into disintegration."[83]

Ironically, in one of his early historical debates with Pogodin, Kostomarov advances Bakunin's underlying assumption that Boris Godunov tied peasants to the land in the late sixteenth century, thereby laying the foundation for serfdom, against which Bakunin maintains the populace was rebelling in the early seventeenth century:[84] "Les communes s'étaient soulevées en masse contre la tyrannie du tzar, du clergé, de la noblesse et de la bureaucratie moscovites, dans les premières années du XVIIe siècle, et cette révolution mémorable avait manqué de détruire l'Empire."[85] In Herzen's *Du développement des idées révolutionnaires en Russie,* which is dedicated to Bakunin and mentions Dostoevsky in connection with the Petrashevsky Circle, the first False Dimitry is an "Homme instruit, civilisé, chevaleresque" who obtained the throne with the help of the Poles and Cossacks in a civil war over the tsar's legitimacy (*Ss*, 7:34).[86] Bakunin concludes that despite the failure of the first False Dimitry, the Russian people continued to search for their "liberation" in "revolt" so that three times "they arose in mass nationwide revolt": "At the time of the interregnum, then with Stepan Timofeevich Razin, then under the leadership of Pugachev."[87] Since *Time* had published Shchapov's article linking the schism to later popular uprisings led by Pugachev, Razin, and other pretenders, Bakunin's article must have seemed like hackneyed political theory to Dostoevsky.[88] Still, Bakunin consistently dates Russian rebellions to "the time of the False Dimitry" when the Russian peasant became "an immutable rebel against the state" and so demands that, for their benefit, "the tsar, and his dynasty" along with the state "go to the devil."[89]

For Dostoevsky, on the other hand, the Time of Troubles was a time of national unity when the people came together to expel foreign invaders, so his demons are the Westernized aristocratic Russians whose historic associations with Catholic Poles, dating from the Time of Troubles and continuing to the present, pose a destabilizing threat to Russia and its people. Several Time of Troubles dramas, stories, and historical writings were published or reviewed in the thick journals, for example, *The Voice* (*Golos*) or *The Herald of Europe* (*Vestnik Evropy*), that Dostoevsky read regularly in the 1860s and 1870s and mentions in his Dresden correspondence (*Pss*, 29.1:89, 107). Dostoevsky specifically discusses Kostomarov's association with *The Herald of Europe* at a time when the historian was in the midst of publishing extensively in the journal on the Time of Troubles as well as on the history of Poland.[90] In 1867, *The Herald of Europe* also published "Dimitry the Impostor and Vasily Shuisky" ("Dimitrii Samozvanets i Vasilii Shuiskii") by the dramatist Alexander Ostrovsky, while Kostomarov's article on the performance of the first play in Alexei Tolstoy's trilogy *The Death of Ivan the Terrible* (*Smert' Ivana Groznogo*), *Tsar Fedor Ioannovich,* and *Tsar Boris* (1863–69) appeared in *The Voice*.[91]

The historical chronicles relating the *smuta,* as Harriet Murav discusses, share with Dostoevsky's *Demons* a "fragmentary" quality that demands the reader seek "connectedness" from a divine framework, owing to the "incompleteness" of the narrator's presentation.[92] Nonetheless, Murav joins Lyudmila Saraskina in recognizing the chronicler's attempt to prepare the reader for the impending "time of troubles [*smutnoe vremia*]": "In what lay our time of troubles and in what direction our transition was to be—I do not know" (*Pss,* 10:354).[93] Although the chronicler professes ignorance as to the origin of the trouble, the aforementioned political and literary allusions to Poland and the Herzenist liberalism of Stepan Trofimovich, which informs the activities of various conspirators, anticipate Petr's introduction of the pretender Stavrogin.[94] Carol Apollonio finds that since "Stavrogin the pretender is Peter Verkhovensky's creature," the "Polish base of operations of the impostor in the Time of Troubles is surely relevant."[95] This Polonized Russian reflects his Polish parentage by playing the role of what Świderska characterizes as Dostoevsky's "negative stereotype of the 'Polish seducer.' "[96] Petr does not seek to satisfy his libido but a lust for power and therefore recognizes that he must persuade a capable aristocrat to play convincingly the part of Ivan-Tsarevich in the midst of Petr's artificially created *smuta.* Petr discloses to Stavrogin the importance of his chosen pretender, when the former states that without Stavrogin he is, as Herzen once unflatteringly called Bakunin, "a Columbus without an America" (*Pss,* 10:324; *Ss,* 10:316).[97] In order to seize this future, Petr, like the Jesuits who "enslave and equalize everybody in order for them to rule over everyone and live in luxury," intends to exploit the popular Russian tradition of *samozvantsvo* by disseminating tsar-in-hiding legends to recruit support among the peasants for his aristocratic populist leader (*Pss*, 11:272).[98] In the drafts to *Demons*, the Nechaev figure shares additional papal-inspired visions of a privileged despot who controls his slaves by encouraging them to spy and inform on each other (*Pss*, 11:273). Thus, at the center of Petr's plan lies a jesuitical populist approach more cynical than Bakunin's proposal, which concludes the Russian people's search for an ideal tsar may organically lead to the appearance of "a samozvanets-tsar, Pugachev, or a new Pestel-dictator."[99] Stavrogin, himself, expresses surprise at Petr's surreptitious plans for mass manipulation with his disbelief signified by the utterance of the word "impostor [*samozvanets*]," but by this point in the narrative, his character has been effectively associated with pretendership by other personages in the novel who recognize this potential in him, as Petr keenly understands (*Pss*, 10:325).

In a parallel to Pushkin's Otrepev, who experiences the initial premonition of his rise to fame in "Night: A Cell in Chudovy Monastery" ("Noch'. Kel'ia v Chudovom monastyre"), Stavrogin, in the chapter "Night" ("Noch'"), first realizes Petr's and Shatov's expectations that he "raise their banner" by playing for them "the role of Stenka Razin 'on account of an unusual capacity for crime'" (*Pss*, 10:201).[100] This association of Razin's celebrated pretendership with criminal activity denigrates Stavrogin's future imposture even before its inception. At the same time, it provides Stavrogin with a further link to the marginalized in Russia's western borderlands, since Razin's leadership of a Cossack rebellion was a point of national pride for Ukrainians, as is evident from Kostomarov's popular study *The Rebellion of Stenka Razin* (*Bunt Sten'ki Razina*) which was reprinted in 1863 and 1872. Therefore, the connection of Razin with a "capacity for crime" resembles a conservative Russian reading of history in contrast to Kostomarov's account of the Razin revolt, which agrees with Bakunin's theory of popular unrest insofar as Razin's rebellion is traced to Boris Godunov's imposition of serfdom.[101] In a further debasement of Otrepev's *samozvanstvo*, his prophetic dream of rising to Moscow's heights only to plunge downward becomes Stavrogin's metaphoric fall prosaically revealed to him by Shatov: "Oh you don't wander along the edge but boldly fly over it headlong" (*Pss*, 10:202). In the subsequent chapter "Night (A Continuation)" ("Noch' (prodolzhenie)") Stavrogin's wife taints his pretendership by slowly demoting him from a "prince [*kniaz'*]" or "falcon [*sokol*]" to the anathematized impostor Otrepev (*Pss*, 10:219). Saraskina finds in this demotion formal similarities between Maria Timofeevna's naming Stavrogin an impostor and the holy fool Nikolka's identification of Boris Godunov as a "tsar-Herod" for his order to kill the tsarevich Dimitry.[102] Thus,

Maria Timofeevna's unmasking scene, which, as Murav maintains, "alerts us to the broader drama of recognition that the novel as a whole contains," diminishes Stavrogin's pretendership, since Maria Timofeevna "is not tempted by Stavrogin the way everyone else in the novel is" but "calls him a pretender (*samozvanets*)."[103] Her ability to demonize Stavrogin's imposture contrasts strikingly with the failure of her Pushkinian counterpart, Marina, to shame her pretender after exposing his lack of royal lineage.

In Pushkin's tragedy, Marina's unmasking of Otrepev in "Night. Garden. Fountain" ("Noch'. Sad. Fontan") ultimately bolsters his Catholic-sponsored imposture by encouraging him to assert: "I am the Tsarevich" (*PssP*, 7:64). Otrepev, recognizing that his lineage matters little to the Poles and Catholics seeking to exploit his claim to profit from a war with Moscow, repulses the attempt of this "Polish maiden" to challenge his pretendership (*PssP*, 7:64). After Marina attempts to soothe his ego with the appellations "Tsarevich," "prince," and "Dimitry," he concludes that intrigue with Jesuits is preferable to contact with such a "snake" as she and so decides to embrace "ruin or the crown" in Russia (*PssP*, 7:65). Stavrogin, on the other hand, is associated with a "serpent [*zmii*]" starting with his appearance in the chapter "The Most Wise Serpent" ("Premudryi zmii"), which offers a contrast to the preceding chapter "The Lame One" ("Khromonozhka") introducing Maria Timofeevna.[104] The juxtaposition between a woman steeped in Marian imagery (virgin birth, prophecy, and discussions of Mariology) and a serpent recalls the twelfth chapter of Revelations, in which the Serpent (*zmii*) attacks the woman clothed in the sun to devour her man-child (*Pss*, 10:116–17).[105] Such an allusion not only anticipates the tragedy that awaits Stavrogin's Marias (Maria Timofeevna and Maria Shatova) but also furthers the demonic image of Stavrogin, which is suggested already by his associations with Catholicism for in his understanding "Catholicism . . . proclaimed the Antichrist" (*Pss*, 10:197).[106]

Dostoevsky's pretender encounters a Russian prophetess with what Murav characterizes as the wisdom of a holy fool rather than the cunning Polish maiden of Pushkin's tragedy.[107] Because of her divine connection, Maria's pronouncement "Grishka Ot-rep-ev a-na-the-ma"—which echoes the anathematization of the pretender by the Russian Orthodox Church in Pushkin's tragedy—curses Stavrogin's pretendership (*Pss*, 10:219). Maria's clear denunciation of Stavrogin does not allow him to maintain the ambiguous persona of Pushkin's pretender, who is labeled alternately Impostor (*Samozvanets*), Dimitry, and False Dimitry (*Lzhedimitrii*) in recognition of the difficulty in establishing the identity of the pretender. Dostoevsky knowingly destroys this ambiguity, because he was familiar with the historical debates over the identity of the pretender. In *Time*, he had criticized Prosper Mérimée's 1852 depiction of the False Dimitry as a Cossack pretender from

Ukraine, who was defending historic freedoms against Boris's tyranny in his *Le Faux Démétrius, scènes dramatiques* (*Pss*, 18:48). Dostoevsky was also familiar with Kostomarov's 1864 study "Who Was the First False Dimitrii" ("Kto byl pervyi Lzhedimitrii?"), which explored "various hypotheses about Dimitry's identity" with expressions of "doubts, sophisticated arguments, and different psychological insights."[108] Finally, Kostomarov's history of the *smuta* and the 1870 premiere of Pushkin's historic drama on the Russian stage more recently contributed to the public debate on the question of the historical identity of the first False Dimitry. Therefore, Dostoevsky's decision to use Otrepev's name and the label pretender (*samozvanets*) to refer to Stavrogin signals a conscious association of his conspirator with the pretender anathematized in Pushkin's tragedy.

Dostoevsky further simplifies the complex relationship between temporal and divine authority explored in Pushkin's scene "The Square in Front of the Cathedral in Moscow" ("Ploshchad' pered soborom v Moskve") by juxtaposing in a binary apposition his representative of Russian Orthodoxy—Maria—and his Polish-sponsored impostor—Stavrogin. In Pushkin's scene, competing viewpoints on the political intriguers Boris and Otrepev are entertained by various representatives of Russian Orthodoxy, for example, church officials, a congregant, and the holy fool Nikolka. The official anathematization declared by a deacon at the cathedral after a service attended by Boris Godunov appears to be politically motivated, particularly since it directly follows a scene in which Dimitry and his multinational troops celebrate a victory over the Russians. Then, a common congregant on the parvis—whose location in the space reserved for catechumens marks him as a liminal believer—responds by endorsing the anathematization for "the tsarevich has no business with Otrepev" (*PssP*, 7:76). Nevertheless, he believes the tsarevich to be alive and therefore condemns the officials as "Godless ones" for singing eternal remembrance to a living person (*PssP*, 7:76). Nikolka then more directly challenges Boris's legitimacy by depicting him as a murderous usurper: "The little children are offending Nikolka . . . order their throats cut, like you cut the throat of the little tsarevich" (*PssP*, 7:78). The voices of the congregant and Nikolka thereby serve to underscore the politicization of Otrepev's anathematization and mitigate its significance for believers.

Using this image of Boris's knife, Dostoevsky's Maria motivates her anathematization with an allusion to the murderous pretendership of the infanticide Boris: "'Away, impostor!' she screamed imperiously, "I am the wife of my prince; I am not afraid of your knife" (*Pss*, 10:219). Stavrogin obsesses over the knife ("A knife, a knife!") until he encounters his co-conspirator Fedka, in whose hands appears "a short, broad cobbler's knife" which he used to slit the throat of a watchman who helped him steal an icon (*Pss*, 10:221). Maria's accusation, thus, not only attributes to Stavrogin the violence of a usurper's rise to power but also debases his pretendership by associating his subversive activities with the iconoclasm, or icon smashing, attributed to Western Christendom owing to papal objections to the veneration of the holy images. The Eastern Church established the doctrinal significance of this veneration at the seventh Ecumenical Council of Nicea in 787 A.D. (not recognized by Rome), so Maria's linking of Stavrogin to Otrepev, who "was cursed at the Seven Councils," further alienates Stavrogin from Russian Orthodox traditions (*Pss*, 10:217). The criminal activities of the bandit Fedka, therefore, indicate that the common application of Petr's ethics leads to a "dangerous . . . moralizing" that justifies the destruction of icons and "a death, in the jesuitical manner" (*Pss*, 10:427; 11:240).[109] Maria's vision of the knife appears prophetic, since she ultimately shares the fate of the "little tsarevich" in that she is murdered with a knife by those conspiring to make her false prince a tsar. As she foretold, she did not fear the knife that cut the throat of her brother but "beat and struggled with the murderer" sent to kill her, because she impeded Petr's ambitious plans for her prince (*Pss*, 10:396–97).

The curse and murder of the innocent advance Stavrogin's link to the demonic, which Murav finds common to the "nineteenth-century nihilist impostor" and "his seventeenth-century predecessor."[110] Although W. J. Leatherbarrow traces "demonic resonances" to both Stavrogin and his "demon" Petr, Stavrogin's demonic dimension is enhanced by Dostoevsky's dialogue with Pushkin's tragedy, in which the Patriarch associates the lure of the defrocked monk, Otrepev, with the powers of the devil.[111] Upon his learning of Otrepev's imposture, the Patriarch describes him as a "vessel of the devil" but fails to appreciate Otrepev's popular appeal, driven in part by the support he receives from the early endorsement of his pretendership by the Polish nobleman Vishnevetsky and the Catholic priest Pater Chernikovsky (*PssP*, 7:24). Later in the tragedy, the Patriarch realizes the way in which the impostor exploits rumor to manipulate the "true believer" and so intends to counteract the tactics of this "son of the Devil" by placing the tsarevich's remains in the Kremlin. Such a ceremony will allow the dispersal of demons haunting Moscow: "the people will clearly see / Then the deceit of this godless villain. / And the power of the demons will disappear like dust" (*PssP*, 7:71). Yet, as Maria Timofeevna's scene with Stavrogin suggests, the demonic pretender Stavrogin requires more aggressive confrontation if Russia is to be cleansed of the demons and their swinish vessels, as Stepan Trofimovich reveals in his reading of the epigraph—a reading that echoes the aforementioned reference in Dostoevsky's correspondence to demons entering the Nechaevs and Serno-Soloveviches (*Pss*, 29.1:145). Stepan concludes that the strength of "the demons" who have been accumulating in Russia "for centuries" requires that "a great idea and a great will [*volia*]" (as opposed to the progressives' Land and Will) descend "from on high" to drive out the demons so that they "ask to enter the swine. . . . It is we, we and those such as Petrushka . . . et les autres avec lui [and the others with him], and I perhaps first, at the head, and we, mad and rabid, will throw ourselves from the cliff into the sea and drown" (*Pss*, 10:499).

The use throughout the novel's narrative of words related to demons (*besy*) and troubles (*smuty*) merge past and present diabolical conflicts with predictions of future troubles, because the demonic Nechaevs experience history as a materialist process, not as Stepan's Russocentric revelation of the sacred in historical time. Dostoevsky's 1873 series "Foreign Events" ("Inostrannye sobytiia") for *The Citizen* identifies a similar clash between Christianity (here, Roman Catholicism) and atheist movements that he observed in Geneva: "The Pope, discalced and on foot, poor and naked, can go to the people with an army of 20,000 Jesuit fighters who have become experts at catching the souls of men. Will Karl Marx and Bakunin stand their ground against this army? Hardly" (*Pss*, 21:202–3). In *Demons*, however, these similar papal and communist images appear in Petr's vision for the future for which he intends to persuade the Internationale to return the world to the Holy Pontiff so that he can rule over all Russia where citizens will enjoy "complete equality" in their slavery (*Pss*, 10:323). Petr and Otrepev, hence, share a model of pretendership and *smuta* that exploits the worldly ambitions of the pope and his Jesuit army for the pragmatic political goal of seizing the Russian throne. Their links with the Jesuits leave them vulnerable to their diabolical characterization by their compatriots, since the conspirators join with spiritual forces historically opposed to the church that legitimates the Russian throne.

Their Polish connections cause further concern for Dostoevsky, not only because of the historic association with Catholicism but also because of Poland's political history being tied in the Russian consciousness to a representative government that placed power in the hands of the nobility serving in Poland's General Assembly (Sejm). Dostoevsky's article "Exhibition at the Academy of Art for 1860–61" ("Vystavka v Akademii khudozhestv za 1860–1861 god") expresses skepticism about the ability of the General Assembly to represent the interests of the people as he comments on the painting *The State Sejm at Which Jan Zamoyski Brings the Complaints of the People to King Zygmunt III* (*Gosudarstvennyi seim, na kotorom Ivan Zamoiskii prinosit zhaloby naroda koroliu Zigmundu III*): "Here about a hundred choristers, dressed in purple kaftans with long lapels, sit and stand, and one sits on a special chair. The faces are all serious, animated by passionate movement, and everyone is troubled about the benefit of the people, that is, about themselves" (*Pss*, 19:160). This portrait of the empty rhetoric of Polish participatory governance helps elucidate Maikov's disdainful equating of Polish nihilists with the "republican and socialist Herzenists" because he uses, as a historic parallel, a meeting in Tushino during the *smuta* between Russian boyars and Polish nobility, who were trying to convince the boyars to support the claim of Władisław (son of Polish King Zygmunt III Waza) to the throne of Moscow.[112] Maikov juxtaposes the Russian and Polish systems of governance with the boyars in maintaining that Polish freedom "means that inasmuch as you are a big man, you can trample every little man" and concluding that in Russia "the little man will always find justice from the great sovereign."[113]

Maikov's comparison of the Herzenists and Tushino boyars is a potential source for Liza Tushina's surname, since it recalls the nickname of the second False Dimitry, that is, the Tushinsky rogue (*Tushinskii vor*).[114] Liza also figures in Petr's plans for imposture, since he believes that the privileged willful Liza, like Raskolnikov's Napoleon, "will step over these little corpses" necessary for the rise to power (*Pss*, 10:405). Her part in the Polish Petr's plan for "trouble," like the boyars' support of Władisław in Tushino, encourages the conspirators (*Pss*, 10:324). As a result, the narrative of *Demons* suggests that a cultural ethnic bias informs its author's skepticism of democratizing reforms proposed by the aristocratic Genevan liberals. Their support of representational government in Russia (leading to the 1863 uprising) repeats a familiar historical pattern of privileged Russian boyars conspiring with their Polish counterparts to govern Russia but ending with the destabilization of their country by their Catholic Slavic brethren. Dostoevsky's *Demons*, therefore, represents a challenge to Herzen's reading of the historical precedent of the Time of Troubles as a warning to Russia regarding her domination of Poland: "If Russia were to conquer, say, Poland, there would be a struggle. The Polish nation would bring in its traditions of aristocratic [*szlachta*] liberty and would send forth into Little Russia, as in the times of the impostors, Lyapunovs, Minins, Pozharskys, and Khmelnitskys, from the insulted nationality" (*Ss*, 16:59).

Their historical analyses, for example, in Herzen's "Le premier pas vers l'émancipation des paysans serfs en Russie" ("The First Step Toward the Emancipation of Rural Serfs in Russia"), Bakunin's "Quelques paroles à mes jeunes frères en Russie," and Nechaev's "A Look at the Former and Present Understanding of the Affair" ("Vzgliad na prezhnee i nyneshnee ponimanie dela"), trace popular support to the advent of a populist pretender—the first False Dimitry—whose ability to represent the vox populi the revolutionaries hoped to imitate.[115] The juxtaposition in the drafts to *Demons* of spontaneous popular revolt with Petr's revolution led by the "ax" after the example of Karakozov (who is also equated here with spies) reveals a divide between Dostoevsky and Herzen, who mocked such "police mania for spies-impostors, journalists-informers, and literary executioners" in *The Bell* in the aftermath of Karakozov's failed attempt on the tsar's life (*Pss*, 11:103; *Ss*, 19:61).[116] Nevertheless, both Russian writers foresee a violent outcome to the growing tensions between Russia and Poland and predict, as the suicide of Dostoevsky's Hamlet in the aftermath of a failed Polish-sponsored conspiracy intimates, that the "latest events in Poland" will, "like the shadow of Hamlet's Father, call for vengeance, not sparing Hamlet himself" (*Ss*, 11:124).[117] Yet, with the end of Stavrogin's line ensured by the deaths of his wife, his mistress, and his son, and with no provision for a successor, Dostoevsky quashes Herzen's hope that in the future a "Northern Fortinbras" may be inspired by Horatio's tale or the feats of the aged Don Quixotes (e.g., Garibaldi) to set out for "his homeland—for the Volga, for his own zemstvo affair" (*Ss*, 16:167).[118]

TRANSNATIONAL CATHOLICISM

Rather, in the world of Dostoevsky's *Demons*, apocalyptic predictions do not come to pass, the false tsarevich does not seize the throne, the vast conspiratorial network in Russia does not exist, and its connections abroad remain tenuous. Drawing on Nechaev's fictional conspiracies for the phantom nature of Petr's secret society, Dostoevsky exploits the gap between co-conspirators' expectations fed by revolutionary rhetoric and the disappointing banality of Petr's secret activities. Such societies physically destroy ideologists like Kirillov and Shatov, while the opportunists like Petr escape abroad where they write "fantastical things" recalled in biographies "of all the present émigrés abroad," which resemble "an unbridled kingdom of specters and nothing more" (*Pss*, 10:430).[119] The references to the pope, to Jesuitism, to Polish independence movements, and to Polish-sponsored revolutionaries serve to undermine further the reputation of Russians living in the West by illustrating that the roots of their rebellion may be traced to the historic transnational appeal of Catholicism and its contemporary manifestation—socialism. For example, Dostoevsky's Nechaevists believe that the legendary Russian Westernizer, Peter the Great—a likely namesake for Dostoevsky's most jesuitical socialist Petr Verkhovensky—fell under Catholic influence, since under his guidance Russia gave herself up "to the Jesuits and to Catholicism" (*Pss*, 11:272).[120] Dostoevsky's commentary on *Demons* in *Diary of a Writer* shows his agreement with Herzen on the power of the "idée fixe" as he maintains that "*great ideas*" inspire the potential Nechaevists of the new generation much as the universal revitalization of the world through (Christian) socialism once inspired the Petrashevtsy of the 1840s (*Pss*, 21:135). Yet, his presentation of Catholic Europe in the 1870s and his novels *The Idiot*, *Demons*, and *The Brothers Karamazov* reveal his fears concerning the vibrant appeal of "the Catholic idea" not only for the West but also for Westernized Russians.

References to the art of Shakespeare and Raphael in *Demons* remind the reader that idealism can impact history through artistic forms, since these aesthetic accomplishments of the turbulent Reformation period transcend time and space to inform a Russian narrative exploring troubles arising from a history of political and religious conflict. Using these Western artistic forms—representative of Dostoevsky's striving "for an ideal unrealizable in earthly existence"—Stepan Trofimovich universalizes their aesthetic by proclaiming the superiority of this Reformation dramatist and a Renaissance Vatican painter over "nationality" and "almost all humankind, for they are already the fruit, the real fruit of all humankind" (*Pss*, 10:372).[121] Dostoevsky's identification with the aesthetics of his Stepan Trofimovich, as described by Robert Jackson in *Dostoevsky's Quest for Form*, therefore attests to the Russian author's valuation of these Protestant and Catholic images as ideals with universal appeal, despite their origins in theologies that Dostoevsky finds alterior to Russian culture.[122] In addition, Stavrogin's recasting of Claude Lorrain's seventeenth-century painting *Acis and Galatea* as *The Golden Age* enhances the spiritual significance of this mythological painting, since its paradisiacal landscape and "beautiful people" evoke tears of happiness from this aesthete who believes that it represents the dream "for which all humanity its entire life devoted all its strength, for which it sacrificed everything, for which prophets were killed and died on crosses, without which people do not want to live and cannot even die" (*Pss*, 11:21). Such appreciation for these art forms from Western Christendom reveals their ability to speak to humankind's search for the ideal, which Ivan Karamazov characterizes as a believer's universal desire for harmony "when everyone suddenly realizes what it was all for," because "on this desire all the religions on earth are based" (*Pss*, 14:222).

Yet, as the Latin iconoclasts argued, images can lead to idolatry, and Leatherbarrow implicates Petr in this sin owing to his love of beauty, particularly in the form of Stavrogin, his "idol" (*Pss*, 10:323).[123] Dostoevsky fears such fanatical devotion to "the Catholic idea," because he believes that Catholicism does not represent merely a metaphysical ideal but an international conspiracy armed with the papal Jesuit troops and with a political program of "the Roman idea of worldwide domination" (*Pss*, 21:191).[124] The allusions to personages connected to Europe's Reformations, that is, Otrepev, Don Quixote, Hamlet, and the Jesuits, in the novels he conceived abroad—*The Idiot* and *Demons*—remind the reader that such religious movements historically engendered devastating social conflict that the West had yet to resolve. Dostoevsky's temporary residence in lands that had witnessed one of the most destructive wars in Europe's history—the Thirty Years War—served as a frequent reminder of the worldly ambitions of Catholic Europe.[125] The Sonderbund War in the Swiss cantons (in which Dostoevsky's co-conspirator Speshnev participated), the religious debates sparked by the Peace Congress, the rise of Old Catholicism, the papal battle for Rome, and Bismarck's *Kulturkampf* demonstrated that Reformation history continued to haunt nineteenth-century Europe. In fact, Bakunin speaks of the coming revolution in terms of the seventeenth century in an 1871 pamphlet found among Dostoevsky's papers:[126] "C'est une révolution mille fois plus formidable que celle qui, à partir de la Renaissance et du XVIIe siècle surtout, avait renversé les doctrines scolastiques, ces remparts de l'Église, de la monarchie absolue et de la noblesse féodale, pour les remplacer par le dogmatisme métaphysique de la raison soi-disant pure."[127] The physical destruction of Prince Myshkin and Stepan Trofimovich—Dostoevsky's quixotic figures representative of a bygone age—attests to the author's agreement with Bakunin that the chivalric age had come to an end.[128] Dostoevsky understood in his present transitional age the limited appeal of chivalry's dedication to the ideal of beauty, which Ivanits effectively links to Dostoevsky's princes rooted in the feudal era—Stavrogin and Myshkin.[129] Like their mentally impaired counterparts in *Hamlet* and *Don Quixote*, they fail to transition successfully to a new epoch in their nations' histories.

However, out of the same Reformation era emerged the Society of Jesus, which flourished in the post-feudal era with its own response to the age of chivalry. Ignatius of Loyola's vision of establishing a "new supranational apostolic order" *ad maiorem dei gloriam* embraces rigorous asceticism in contradistinction to the morally lax chivalric code that he adopted before his conversion.[130] Both Bakunin and Dostoevsky share fears regarding the power of their Jesuit contemporaries owing to the rise of the "ultramontanist" party "of Catholic-Jesuits" in the West.[131] Bakunin links this concern to Italian politics, since he describes Mazzini's political shift from Italian freedom fighter to "le dernier grand prêtre de l'idéalisme religieux, métaphysique et politique" with "la foi dans la prédestination messianique de l'Italie, reine des nations, avec Rome, capitale du monde."[132] Bakunin further identifies a Russian target for the Roman church's agitation, because it views the tsar as "the Antichrist, the Anti-pope" and therefore is prepared to see in populist movements "the finger of God" which can ensure the resurrection of "aristocratic Poland" to secure the dissemination of "Roman Catholic propaganda" throughout Russia.[133] Likewise, Dostoevsky complains in articles published in *The Citizen* (soon after the completion of *Demons*) about the ability of the clericals, the pope, the Jesuits, and the "clever" socialists to convince "the ignorant and destitute people" of Christ's support for their respective movements—movements that Dostoevsky associates with the Antichrist (*Pss*, 21:203).

Yet, despite Bakunin's care in differentiating himself politically from revolutionaries, like Mazzini, who act in concert with Catholic movements, Dostoevsky frequently merges the ideologies of Christian revolutionaries and atheists like Bakunin. Dostoevsky's aligning of the radical conspirators with the pope and the Jesuits (specifically Gagarin) in *Demons* and its drafts intimates that, for him, the Herzen circle is connected to the ascendant power of the papacy. Dostoevsky remains convinced of this papal power in spite of Pius IX's loss of papal territory and the recent defeat of France—the pope's historic protector—by Germany. Even though Bakunin self-identifies with Don Quixote, for Dostoevsky he represents the Jesuit legacy of the Reformation owing to the jesuitical tactics that he employs and because of his aquaintance with various Catholic revolutionaries, who had fought recently for regime change in Italy, France, and Russia.[134] Perhaps Dostoevsky draws here on Katkov's blend of "quixoticism and Jesuitism [*donkikhotstvo i iezuitstvo*]" that he finds at the heart of the intrigue in Warsaw in 1863.[135] Whereas Bakunin divides Catholic aristocratic revolutionaries from the atheistic socialists, Dostoevsky clearly places them on a continuum, as evidenced by the comparisons of Catholicism, atheism, and socialism by Prince Myshkin and Shatov (*Pss*, 8:450–53; 10:197–201). Although his visionaries Shatov and Prince Myshkin betray a conviction that a national idea can save Russia from Catholicism and its derivatives, Dostoevsky's tragic novels *The Idiot* and *Demons* express skepticism about the ability of the Russian idea to enact social change in a way similar to that of the Roman idea propagated by the Catholic Church. Instead, the physical destruction of many central characters associated with Russianness—the murders of Shatov and Nastasya Filippovna, Prince Myshkin's descent into idiocy, and the conversion of Aglaya Yepanchina to Catholicism—demonstrates the limited power of Russian idealism to address immediate concerns. This ideal image that Dostoevsky finds incarnated in Nikolai the Wonderworker—"the Russian spirit and Russian unity"—is literally destroyed in *Demons* when the materialist Fedka steals his icon to sell the casing for profit (*Pss*, 29.1:144–45).[136]

Dostoevsky continues to follow these Catholic and atheist forces in Spain, France, Italy, Germany, and Austria after his return to Russia, because he feels that the Western "struggle of faith with atheism, struggle of Christian origin with a new coming origin" will, as it had historically, reach Russia (*Pss*, 21:192). His study of the "Roman idea" in history—a continuation of *Crime and Punishment*'s dialogue with Hegel's conception of Roman law—leads him to conclude that the Franco-Prussian War pitted the traditional defender of Rome (France) against "the German idea, which in the end stood for the Reformation with all its consequences" (*Pss*, 21:184). Despite Bismarck's victory, Dostoevsky continues to view the strength of clerical parties in Europe as evidence of "militant Catholicism" and fears that Bismarck does not comprehend the magnitude of the Catholic, socialist, and atheist forces that threaten his empire. For this reason, Dostoevsky explores in *Diary of a Writer* and *The Brothers Karamazov* the centuries-old conspiratorial history of Roman Catholicism in an effort to understand the cultural impact of this dominant religious and political force on the future of Russia.

PART III

The Catholic Reformation in *The Brothers Karamazov*

Une armée poussait des profondeurs des
fosses, une moisson de citoyens dont la
semence germait et ferait éclater la terre, un
jour de grand soleil. Et l'on saurait alors si,
après quarante années de service, on oserait
offrir cent cinquante francs de pension à un
vieillard de soixante ans, crachant de la houille,
les jambes enflées par l'eau des tailles. Oui!
le travail demanderait des comptes au capital,
à ce dieu impersonnel, inconnu de l'ouvrier,
accroupi quelque part, dans le mystère de son
tabernacle, d'où il suçait la vie des meurt-de-
faim qui le nourrissaient!

(An army pushed from the depths of the
pits, a harvest of citizens in which the seed
germinated and would burst from the earth,
a day of great sunshine. And one would know
then if, after forty years of service, one would
dare to offer 150 francs of pension to an old
man of sixty, coughing up coal and legs swollen
from the water of the tunnels. Yes! Labor
would ask for an accounting of the capital, from
this impersonal god, unknown to the worker,
who crouched somewhere in the mystery of his
tabernacle, from where he sucked the life from
the hungry paupers who fed him!)
—Émile Zola, *Germinal* (1885)

Chapter Five

Old Catholicism and the Revolutionary Inquisitor

"Dieu aura égard à l'état, et ne donnera pas
à l'enfer le méchant plaisir de lui envoyer un
prêtre."
—Alexandre Dumas, *père*, *Le Comte de Monte-
Cristo*

IN SELECTING AN INQUISITOR for the main char-
acter of Ivan Karamazov's poem (*poèma*), Dostoevsky was well aware of its
political association with the tsarist government owing to its inquisitional
legal system, linked by Herzen to the Petrine reforms: "Everything increasing power, everything suppressing man was taken; everything protecting the
person is left to the side; the casuistry of the inquisitorial process was en-
riched by Tatar torture and the German order by Byzantine servility" (*Ss*,
16:58).[1, 2] As a frequent critic of Peter's reforms, Dostoevsky likely knew that
after the introduction of Peter's spiritual regulations, inquisitors assigned to
every diocese in Orthodox Russia maintained surveillance over bishops' activities, ensured their adherence to regulations, and reported back to the
Synod's arch-inquisitor (*protoinkvisitor*).[3] Therefore, his Grand Inquisitor's
unification of church and state has historical roots in the Petrine era, when
the influence of Roman law and the Roman church reshaped Russian society.
Still, Dostoevsky underscores the Inquisitor's Catholic heritage when Alesha
Karamazov links Ivan's creation to the Jesuits and then recalls: "We know the
Jesuits; about them nasty things are said" (*Pss*, 14:237). Alesha thereby attributes the historic trials of the Dominicans in sixteenth-century Spain to the
Society of Jesus, whose origins in the religious warfare of the Reformation
were frequently invoked in the press after the 1870 decree supporting
papal infallibility. Those opposed to the decree, such as the Old Catholics
in Germany, felt the Jesuits' hand in this latest move to promote papal sovereignty. For this reason, the protocols to the Society of Lovers of Spiritual
Enlightenment (Obshchestvo liubitelei dukhovnogo prosveshcheniia, hereafter OLDP), to which Dostoevsky belonged, returned to Samarin's criticism
of the Jesuits, i.e. that "to the Jesuit is permitted [*dozvoleny*] all *unchristian*
means" for the Order is convinced of "the internal sanctification of every evil
deed":[4]

The Jesuits systematically prepared this already before 1870: in many works, especially in *Civiltà Cattolica* [*Catholic civilization*], they preached that to defend freedom of conscience is heresy and rather clearly expressed the thought that the proclamation of infallibility has, by the way, as its object—to maintain this position of theirs and to turn into dogma the teaching about the permissibility [*dozvolitel'nost'*] or the obligatoriness of using violence against those of another creed.[5]

Precisely this issue of acceptable violence, an idea of Ivan's upon which the jesuitical Smerdyakov seizes, informs the poem about the Grand Inquisitor, as Alesha recognizes with the meaningful repetition of Ivan's slogan "All is permitted" in the closing pages of the chapter (*Pss*, 14:240).[6] In contrast to other Christian witnesses to capital punishment in Dostoevsky, such as the priest at the Lyons execution observed by Prince Myshkin or the Christian brethren at Richard's guillotining, the Grand Inquisitor acts for the state as investigator, prosecutor, and judge to produce victims for the auto-da-fé in Ivan's Seville of the Reformation period (*Pss*, 8:55–56; 14:219). The author does not, however, form this executioner in the tradition of his sadistic, indifferent, or sensualistic types from his *House of the Dead,* for the Grand Inquisitor outlines a calculated theological motivation for his legal system of tyranny by employing "miracle, mystery, and authority" to remake society under the "banner of earthly bread" (*Pss*, 14:234, 232). His eloquent defense of this social justice system also precludes the reader from assuming that the Grand Inquisitor fatalistically accepts the limitations of an imperfect legal system after the example of Dostoevsky's Siberian acquaintance Baron Wrangel, who consoles himself with "the Roman proverb 'Dura lex sed lex'" before the fatal lashing of a devout Old Believer.[7] Rather, the Grand Inquisitor represents one of Dostoevsky's idealistic reformers, who in shrouding himself in ecclesiastical vestments and biblical rhetoric appears as a false prophet manipulating disciples with the mirage of a harmonious "worldwide union [*vsemirnoe soedinenie*]," which Dostoevsky consistently associates with the Catholic tradition and its socialist manifestations (*Pss*, 14:235).

THE OLDP AND THE TEMPTATION OF HARMONY

Dostoevsky witnessed the impact of the Roman church on Russian intellectuals when members of the St. Petersburg intelligentsia attempted a rapprochement with the Old Catholics through the OLDP. Although F. Evnin and Dirscherl document well Dostoevsky's growing interest in Roman Catholicism and ultramontanist agitation in the wake of the papal decree on infallibility, they overlook the impact of the OLDP on Dostoevsky's understanding of Roman Catholic–Russian Orthodox relations.[8] Vladimir Viktorovich, in outlining Dostoevsky's contact with the Society, emphasizes his interest in its discussion of *edinoverie* on which Terty Filippov, a friend of Prince Vladimir Meshchersky and a regular contributor to *The Citizen*, presented at multiple meetings in 1873.[9] When Dostoevsky briefly served as editor of Meshchersky's journal *The Citizen* in 1873–74, the substance of Filippov's research presentations before the OLDP appeared in its pages. The journal, therefore, displays Dostoevsky's familiarity with the OLDP at a time when it was examining closely the issue of a union of the Anglican, Old Catholic, and Russian Orthodox churches (*Pss*, 21:139–42). During this period, Dostoevsky regularly met or corresponded not only with Filippov but also with fellow society members Maikov, Konstantin Pobedonostsev (the future procurator of the Holy Synod), and Vsevolod Solovev.[10] Furthermore, Dostoevsky edited several articles for *The Citizen* written by Pobedonostsev that address the issue of a potential union by studying Protestantism, the nature of the (Old) Catholic Church in Germany, and their potential for dialogue with the Russian Orthodox Church.[11] Dostoevsky's own articles in the series "Foreign Events," in their strong objection to Catholicism in all its forms, represent a challenge to the OLDP's attempts to return to the one, undivided church through communion with the Anglican and Old Catholic churches. These articles as well as the discussions of Anglican, Orthodox, and Catholic Church history in the OLDP's protocols provide source background to the Grand Inquisitor's Reformation history.[12]

In September 1871, a group of Catholics in Germany, who had refused to recognize the new papal decree and had rejected papal infallibility as an innovation in Catholic doctrine, held the first in a succession of congresses in an effort to define the Old Catholic movement. Believers from various Christian traditions met at the congress, because they were united in their opposition to the papal decree that, according to the Old Catholic leader Ignaz von Döllinger, declared both the Eastern and the Protestant churches heretical owing to their opposition to papal infallibility.[13] A professor of the Saint Petersburg Spiritual Academy, I. T. Osinin,[14] after representing the Eastern church at the congress, returned to St. Petersburg where he read and published a series of public lectures on Old Catholicism.[15] The following year, a St. Petersburg branch of the OLDP was formed to open "a semiofficial branch of communication" with the Old Catholics.[16] The protocols further establish that in addition to contact "with significant religious movements in the West," the OLDP was to advocate a theological exchange between clerical and secular segments of society as well as to disseminate the Russian Orthodox faith both at home and abroad.[17] Such a broad focus encouraged members such as Filippov and Dostoevsky to discuss spiritual topics that sparked considerable public debate and, at times, official displeasure.

Pobedonostsev, mindful of his prominent social position, avoided specific mentions of the OLDP in his articles and distanced himself from them with the use of pseudonyms, but both Filippov and Dostoevsky drew the censure of the OLDP's secretary and aide-de-camp to Grand Duke Konstantin Nikolaevich, General Alexander Kireev, for their direct commentary on the *edinoverie* debate before the Society. In a letter to Filippov, General Kireev specifically objects to Dostoevsky's personal attacks on a specialist on the Schism, Ivan Nilsky, during an overzealous defense of Filippov's appeal for a church council to define the relationship between the Old Believers and the Russian Orthodox Church: "And you and D-sky, being members of the S-ty, of course are not obligated to conceal that which is said in the S-ty; but the articles of *Gr-n* prove very palpably that our poor S-ty—tsarstvo, has divided itself and that it will be short-lived."[18] *The Citizen* continued to report regularly on the Society's meetings, to publish Filippov's research, and to discuss the issues before the Society but adopted a less confrontational approach as suggested by General Kireev.[19]

For instance, in the summer and autumn of 1873, Pobedonostsev's articles on religious movements in England, France, Spain, and Germany brought to *The Citizen* the controversial issue of interfaith dialogue. An earlier series entitled "Church and State" ("'Tserkov' i gosudarstvo") in April and May 1873 had provided a foundation for the subsequent interfaith discussion with a comparative analysis of American and western European political responses to ecclesiastical concerns.[20] The timely focus in "Church and State" on the development of Protestantism and Catholicism in the West—the main subject of Professor Ilarion Chistovich's report on Old Catholicism at the April 30 OLDP meeting—likely encouraged Pobedonostsev (a member of the Society's Council) to analyze various creeds during his travels abroad.[21] After having discussed different denominations in western Europe, Pobedonostsev decides in the August 1873 article "Toward the Question of the Unification of Churches" ("K voprosu o vossoedinenii tserkvei"): "The more clearly distinct tribal characteristics of each denomination become apparent in one's mind, the more one is convinced of what an unattainable and dreamlike business is the unification of denominations into one artificial, forced agreement on dogma and on the beginning of a mutual compromise in immaterial parts."[22] Largely dismissing the Old Catholics as a splinter group supported in Germany as part of Bismarck's political challenge to the Vatican, Pobedonostsev devotes considerable space to the alterity of Protestantism, especially Anglicanism, to Russian Orthodoxy in order to account for his doubts about the potential for union.[23] Maintaining Russia's national predisposition toward "tolerance for every confession," Pobedonostsev concludes that Protestantism begins "with a preaching on tolerance, on freedom of thought and creed" but ends in "fanaticism of proud reason and a self-assured righteousness before all other forms of belief."[24]

Nevertheless, the OLDP's renewed commitment to define the relationship of the Eastern church to the Old Catholics through a formal commission and the presentation by the dean of Westminster Abbey, Arthur Stanley, at the January Society meeting (with an introduction by Pobedonostsev) attest to a growing official interest in advancing the cause for union.[25] Kireev's 1873–74 report on the OLDP's activities, in which he addresses the Society's relations with the West, reflects this sentiment: "In the concluding words of last year's report the hope for a successful path to our relations with the Old Catholics was expressed. Having looked at the results, attained by us, it is possible, it seems, to say with conviction that we were not mistaken in our suppositions and hopes."[26] A presentation from the previous year's protocols by Alexander Katansky, a professor at the St. Petersburg Spiritual Academy, underscores the historic significance of such hopes, by dividing attempts at church union into three separate periods. Katansky concludes that since his present marks the end of the Reformation period, that is, "the period of Jesuit propaganda of the Uniate idea," the church is entering a third period—"a period of awakening . . . aspirations for religious reunification, aspirations created not artificially and not forcibly imposed but naturally, voluntarily taking root in the heart of the religious feeling of the East."[27] While Dostoevsky's series "Foreign Events" and his later commentary in the *Diary* suggest that he agreed with the religious awakening in the East, he still seemed to number among those Society members who wished to promote Russian Orthodoxy but feared that its dialogue with the Old Catholics might harm the dignity of the Russian church.[28]

His articles, in conscious dialogue with Pobedonostsev's publications, depict the "struggle of Roman Catholicism and the Roman idea of universal sovereignty [*vsemirnoe vladychestvo*]" in a battle between faith and atheism playing out in contemporary Germany, France, and Spain (*Pss*, 21:191–92).[29] Whereas Pobedonostsev ascribes to Protestants the pedantic application of reason to faith, Dostoevsky associates "la Raison" with the French Revolution and its manipulation of the Catholic Church (*Pss*, 21:152). Pobedonostsev theologically objects to the Protestant doctrine of election that, at the expense of the weak and unfortunate, celebrates: "Blessed are the robust and strong in their work: to them belong the kingdom."[30] Dostoevsky anticipates his Grand Inquisitor's argument in finding that the "strong brethren, proud minds, representatives of power, and intelligentsia" will drive into the arms of Rome those "weak" and "pure of heart throughout all Protestant Europe" who tire of the burden of their freedom of conscience—a proud legacy of the Reformation—and seek the mediation of Rome in their relationship with the Christian God (*Pss*, 21:207). Because of their quest for peace of mind secured by the "'mediation' of the pope," Dostoevsky predicts a second Catholic Reformation for the West, which he realizes poetically in "The Grand Inquisitor" (*Pss* 21:207). The Catholic agitation in Germany, the strength of the Clericals in France, and the election of Don Carlos to the Spanish throne encourage Dostoevsky to believe in the international political muscle of the Catholic Church, which Nikita Gilyarov-Platonov identifies in his journal *Contemporary News* (*Sovremennye izvestiia*) as "militant ultramontanism [*voinstvuiushchee ul'tramontantstvo*]."[31] Dostoevsky reevaluates his discussion of the pretenders to the French and Spanish thrones (Henri, Count de Chambord and Don Carlos, respectively) in an 1876 *Diary* entry in order to place them within the context of Reformation history. Here, he describes the Count de Chambord as a knight following in the footsteps of Don Quixote for his rejection of power but concludes that Don Carlos may be viewed as a knight in whom "is visible the Grand Inquisitor" for his shedding of "rivers of blood *ad majorem gloriam Dei* and in the name of the Mother of God" (*Pss*, 22:93). This association of the contemporary Don Carlos with the Grand Inquisitor thus further motivates Dostoevsky's dialogue with Schiller's play, *Don Carlos*, in Ivan's poem.[32]

In agreement with Pobedonostsev, Dostoevsky predicts that the Old Catholics, born out of Berlin's "crusade 'with blood and iron'" against the "Roman idea," will not withstand the overwhelming strength of those ultramontanists and Jesuits remaining loyal to Pius IX (*Pss*, 21:184). Nevertheless, a record of his encounter with a priest in Wiesbaden with Old Catholic sympathies demonstrates his anger at the dialogue between Orthodoxy and Old Catholicism. When Dostoevsky arrived in June 1874 at the resort town of Ems in the Duchy of Baden, he came to a center of Old Catholicism, whose disciples had won a major political victory in June when a government commission had recognized them as an entity separate from the Roman Catholic Church.[33] In *Diary of a Writer,* Dostoevsky alludes to a similar triumph in Germany in 1875, when the Old Catholics gained the right to church properties, which were divided subsequently among the Old Catholics and those Catholics who remained loyal to Rome (*Pss,* 22:35).[34] Therefore, in his meeting with the Wiesbaden priest, Arseny Tachalov, who maintained correspondence with the Old Catholics, participated in several Old Catholic congresses, and served as a delegate of the OLDP at the second Old Catholic Congress (1872) in Cologne, Old Catholicism was a likely topic of conversation.[35] Indeed his comments about the encounter in a letter to his wife indicate as much. Characterizing the priest as an "intriguer [*intrigan*]" and a "scoundrel [*merzavets*]," Dostoevsky maintains that he "will sell Christ and everything" and that he "shames our church by his ignorance in front of foreigners" (*Pss*, 29.1:340).[36]

Dostoevsky's strong reaction to this Orthodox priest suggests his opposition to a potential union with the Old Catholics and thus also provides a motivation for his anti-Catholic rhetoric in "Foreign Events," *Diary of a Writer, The Adolescent,* and *The Brothers Karamazov.* Dostoevsky's discussion of the chimerical allure of Catholics' appeal for universal harmony echoes Pobedonostsev's sentiments about the "dreamlike" unification of different creeds (*Pss,* 25:7). Both writers indicate that such a union requires coercion, which Dostoevsky finds at the heart of the "Roman idea" of *"forced* unity of humanity" that had inspired the French Terror's demand for "Liberté, Egalité, Fraternité—ou la mort" (*Pss,* 25:7).[37] Because of the violent history of Roman Catholicism (particularly during the Reformation), several members of the OLDP recognized the need for caution in approaching the issue of an Old Catholic-Orthodox union. Filippov and Professor Katansky speak to these concerns as they believe that the Eastern church holds a responsibility to explore union as part of its mission to support "the one, holy, conciliar and apostolic Church."[38] Filippov, addressing directly those concerned about the negotiations between the Orthodox and Old Catholics at the Bonn conference of 1874, contends:

> From the time that the Old Catholic Society announced that for its teachings and church organization, it intended to search for its foundation in the teaching and decrees of the ancient undivided Church, the followers of the Eastern Church, as the only successors and custodians in the world of the sacred heritage of this undivided Church, could not, that is, did not have the right to look indifferently on the efforts of a portion of Western Christians to return to the truth they had lost.[39]

While Dostoevsky remained immune to this appeal for a return to the Golden Age, such a harmony attracted one young philosopher, Vladimir Solovev (brother of Vsevolod), with whom he met while working on his final novel. Before the OLDP, Solovev presented both "The Three Forces" ("Tri sily," 1877),[40] on the relationship of Islam, Catholicism, and Orthodoxy, as well as his first lecture in the series "On Godmanhood" ("O Bogochelovechestvo," 1878), which explores religion as the "reunification of man and the world with its absolute and complete beginning."[41] These lectures, in addition to his 1883 articles discussing the Orthodox Church's attempt to unify with the Old Catholics, show that a return to the undivided church was on the mind of Solovev when he shared a pilgrimage with Dostoevsky to Optina Pustyn in 1878.[42]

Dostoevsky, however, maintains until his death, as is evident in his 1880 Pushkin speech, that the "all-unifying spirit [*vseediniashchii dukh*]" comes from the Russian national spirit rather than from an ecumenical communion

(*Pss,* 26:132). Dostoevsky continues to juxtapose the Eastern and Western churches, even while Old Catholics, Anglicans, and Orthodox worked at reconciling the greatest discrepancies, for example, *filioque* and the Immaculate Conception, in their doctrines at conferences in Bonn in 1874 and 1875.[43] His apposition of the young hero's natural father, Andrei Versilov, and legal father, Makar Dolgoruky, in *The Adolescent* reflects this religious divide. The spiritual wanderer Makar Dolgoruky embodies the Russian religious tradition with his compassion for peasants, with his Old Believer icon, as well as with references to a holy fool, cenobitic monasticism, and the gift of tears. The Catholic-leaning Versilov, on the other hand, shares the Grand Inquisitor's disdain for humanity and dream of an earthly paradise while displaying the violence attributed to historic Catholic Iconoclasts by destroying Makar's heirloom Old Believer icon, the legacy he left Versilov. The allusion to the Seventh Ecumenical Council in Nicea (787), a century to which the Grand Inquisitor also refers as the moment when he started siding with the devil, highlights for both novels a similar point of separation between East and West (*Pss,* 14:234). This council represents the final ecumenical gathering guiding the Orthodox "Church of the Seven Councils" and the point in the history of church doctrine to which the Old Catholics wished to return.[44] Such references to the historical development of Roman Catholicism within "Pro and Contra" ("Pro i contra") attest to Dostoevsky's dialogue with the Old Catholic movement in this book of *The Brothers Karamazov.*

THE GRAND EXECUTIONER

Through his creation of Ivan's poem, "The Grand Inquisitor," Dostoevsky participated in his contemporaries' (e.g., Bakunin's and Katansky's) association of modern conflict with the bloodshed of the Reformation period. In an 1877 *Diary* entry, Dostoevsky criticizes a historian for not believing in the existence of the Crusades and Crusaders "'in our century of affirmative goals and progress,'" since Dostoevsky affirms the contemporaneity of historic medieval types and movements (*Pss,* 25:14).[45] Thus, Dostoevsky's historiography embraces an earlier historical concept espoused by Granovsky that "an internal connection—the religious connection" links the Middle Ages to the present.[46] However, he does not accept Granovsky's thesis that "the idea of universal monarchy [*ideia vsemirnoi monarkhii*]" founded by Rome had come to an end in the Middle Ages, since Dostoevsky maintains that the Roman idea survived in both state and religious institutions influenced by the Catholic Church.[47] His friendship with Pobedonostsev in the 1870s reminded Dostoevsky that the Russian legal system as well as the Russian church felt pressure from a Latinizing influence, since Pobedonostsev's 1876 study of capital punishment ascribes torture to Roman law and capital punishment to medieval necessity:

> The need to discover truth [*istina*] in the criminal process, to find the criminal, to prove his guilt, and to subject him to punishment was as natural, as lawful, and as powerful in the epoch of the Middle Ages as it is in our time; it appeared doubly urgent in those cases when the crime committed belonged to the number of the particularly important for religious, state, and social relations.[48]

In his introduction of this universal legal issue into a sixteenth-century context, Dostoevsky links a contemporary debate about death by flogging to the historical controversy surrounding capital punishment for heretics (often linked to the Inquisition) and so reinforces for those seeking universal harmony through ecclesiastical union the moral divide between Roman Catholicism and Russian Orthodoxy.

The correspondence between Dostoevsky and Pobedonostsev during the summer of 1879 discloses their mutual interest in the Russian penal system at a period when Dostoevsky was working on his books "Pro and Contra" and "The Russian Monk" ("Russkii inok"). Responding to Pobedonostsev's discussion of the many accommodations (books, freedom from their chains, and religious services) that he arranged for 600 prisoners in a dispatch from Odessa to Sakhalin, Dostoevsky belatedly replies: "Your prisoners (Sakhalin and that which you wrote me about them) rattled all my soul; this business is too near to me, despite the distance of 25 years" (*Pss*, 30.1:105).[49] Thus, Dostoevsky's decision to depict the interaction between a prisoner and the official sentencing him to death, between the silent Christ before Pontius Pilate in the Synoptic Gospels[50] and the Inquisitor made infamous by Reformation and Enlightenment literature, is motivated by political events in Russia.[51] For Dostoevsky, the image of the Inquisitor may date from his own interrogation, for his co-conspirator, Petrashevsky, had invoked the image in his testimony: "Be not inquisitors but friends of humanity . . . And on completion of the affair, the cry of the condemned man dying in the smoke of the auto-da-fé will not be united with your names, but the words of sincere gratitude will rise to heaven from our hearts."[52] This background accounts for why in the encounter between Ivan's Christ and his Grand Inquisitor, the ecclesiastical representative remains true to the Roman idea by responding to the needs of his citizens less as a priest than as a statesman and therefore depends on all lawful means at his disposal, including capital punishment, to ensure social stability rather than eternal salvation.[53]

In his creation of the Grand Inquisitor, Dostoevsky draws on priestly types associated with the French Revolution that he discusses in his series

"Foreign Events." The Grand Inquisitor shares the trappings of office with a cowardly member of France's first estate, who appears in the form of a Parisian archbishop, garbed "in vestments, with a cross in his hand and accompanied by numerous clergy" as he emerges out onto the public square after the first French revolution "to lay aside publicly his power and all its signs" (*Pss*, 21:152). This Archbishop, out of terror, tries to pander to public opinion by revealing that while holding his privileged ecclesiastical position he believed "Très peu" in God, for which he is beheaded because of his exploitation of the faithful to retain power (*Pss*, 21:152).[54] On this type of priest, Dostoevsky blames the ensuing liquidation of the Christian faith in the name of reason, which represents the violence that the Grand Inquisitor seeks to avoid by maintaining order with a combination of spiritual manipulation and the corrective measure of inquisitional torture—the auto-da-fé—which may be added to the five categories of Roman torture that Pobedonostsev maintains Russia borrowed.[55] In his response to Reformation conflict, the Grand Inquisitor combines the brutality of Dostoevsky's warrior priest, who acts as a revolutionary by shooting enemy captives for his political cause, and the self-sacrificial impulse of the martyr-priest, who relinquishes his own life (or, in the case of the Grand Inquisitor, his "ticket" to heaven) for a death that cleanses "the shame" of religious history by "honest blood" (*Pss*, 21:152). Yet, Dostoevsky does not directly link his Grand Inquisitor to the type of common Jesuit-intriguer who appears in the Devil's narrative in book 11 as a French priest abusing the office of confession, an image that Dostoevsky had already explored in an 1864–65 notebook.

Instead, the Grand Inquisitor's abuse of the confessions or "secrets [*tainy*]" entrusted to him by the penitent constitutes a cornerstone of his theocracy, since he expects from his flock an obedience born of gratitude in return for absolution. As Deborah Martinsen highlights, the Grand Inquisitor's invocation of "miracle, mystery [*taina*] and authority" when coupled with Fedor Karamazov's discussion of the sacrament (*tainstvo*) of confession underscores the importance of the sacrament for the novel.[56] Locating her analysis within Rousseau's confessional legacy identified by Robin Feuer Miller, Martinsen remarks upon Dostoevsky's juxtaposition of Catholicism and Orthodoxy with an analysis of Fedor's public confession in the monk's cell and the Devil's account of the marquis's private session with a Jesuit in the confessional booth.[57] Even within Ivan's "Rebellion" ("*Bunt*") confession is extracted by Protestant Christian philanthropists who "exhorted, convinced, pressed, pestered, and suffocated" the prisoner Richard, condemned to death, as if to legitimize theologically the decision of a secular authority, in a theocratic parallel to the Grand Inquisitor's auto-da-fé (*Pss*, 14:218).[58] These philanthropists, armed with Richard's confession, endorse Richard's state-sanctioned death as the triumph of justice and send him off to the guillotine in good conscience "covered with his brothers' kisses" (*Pss*, 14:219). Orthodoxy does not escape an association with the exploitation of confession, which is linked repetitively by the narrator to the elders. First, the narrator defends the tradition of confession to the elders by both "the commoners and the most distinguished people" while recognizing that the enemies of the elders protest that the practice "autocratically and thought-lessly debases the sacrament of confession" (*Pss*, 14:27). Then, the narrator records the rumor that "the elders abuse the sacrament of confession," even though Fedor Pavlovich discusses its significance as "a great sacrament" in the tradition of the "whispered confession" by "the holy fathers" (*Pss*, 14:82). Such specific references in *The Brothers Karamazov* to the abuse of the sacrament of confession, which was also a point of doctrinal controversy during the Reformation, attest to the significance of the sacrament for Dostoevsky's artistic representation of theological figures.

Since the time of Peter the Great's ecclesiastical reform of "the mystery of confession [*taina ispovedi*],"[59] priests as the "spiritual arm of the state" were required to "violate the confidence of confession" particularly for crimes against the state or the propagation of false miracles.[60] Such a retreat from unconditional absolution discouraged those guilty of state crimes from confessing to an Orthodox priest and, consequently, could also prevent them from receiving the sacred bread and wine central to the Orthodox tradition. The importance of the Eucharist to prisoners is evident from Goryanchikov's description of the convicts at a service: "When the priest with the chalice in his hands read the words '. . . but like the brigand take me,' almost everyone fell to the ground, their fetters ringing, having taken these words as literally referring to themselves, it seems" (*Pss*, 4:177). Dostoevsky, as a former prisoner, encountered the politicization of this sacrament during his interrogation, since the Petrashevtsy were required to account for when they attended confession and received communion at the beginning of their interrogations.[61] Dostoevsky's concern over the clerical ties to the state is evident from both his hostility toward priests during Siberian exile and his accusation that while in Vevey his missing correspondence may be related to the priest who "is serving in the secret police" (*Pss*, 28.2:309).[62] Herzen also refers to police-priest collaboration in Russia: "Le 'pope' a perdu toute influence à force de cupidité, d'ivrognerie et de relations intimes avec la police" (*Ss*, 7:284–85).[63] Ivan alludes to church-state collusion when he notes that if the church turns into the state then excommunication will eventually replace capital punishment: "If everything became the church, then the church would excommunicate the criminal and the disobedient and would not then cut off their heads" (*Pss*, 14:59). Yet, the Grand Inquisitor, who repeatedly assures his Christ (guilty even by Petrine standards of performing a miracle) that he will burn as a heretic, employs both excommunication and capital punishment in a tradition emblematic of the Inquisition, which also may be considered indicative of Russian Orthodoxy after its reformation by Peter's regulations (*Pss*, 14:228).[64]

In this respect, the Grand Inquisitor falsely juxtaposes "earthly" and "heavenly" bread before Christ, since through his ecclesiastical and state duties, he provides both the daily and sacramental bread to his flock as a means of ensuring not only their happiness but also their obedience, for they represent his power base (*Pss*, 14:232). Granovsky highlights a similar state-church collusion in his study of the Spanish Inquisition, when he records that since those receiving a sentence of capital punishment from the Inquisition forfeited their property to the state, the state treasuries benefited financially from the ecclesiastical judgment of its citizenry.[65] Fedor's stock criticism of the elders' luxuries reinforces the Eucharistic imagery by reminding the "holy fathers" that they live "in the monastery on ready bread" and drink "old port" provided with the hard-earned "pittance" of the Russian peasants (*Pss*, 14:83).[66] The Grand Inquisitor's common usage of bread's materialist image, defined by the French Revolution with its Republican Lord's Prayer, attests to what Nina Perlina identifies as the significant presence of Herzen in Ivan's logic.[67] However, before Herzen's interpretation of the Lord's Prayer appears in Dostoevsky's oeuvre, in *House of the Dead*, Goryanchikov recalls its frequent employment by Lieutenant Smekalov, who relishes his biblically based torture, because "he himself created it out of literary pride" (*Pss*, 4:151).[68] Depending upon his victim's memorized knowledge of the prayer, Smekalov tells him to recite it so that he can rhyme the end of the second line, "in heaven [*na nebesi*]," with his order to begin the flogging, "Give it to him [*podnesi*]," which he, the soldier-witnesses, and even the inmates enjoy for its creativity (*Pss*, 4:151). Throughout his description of the spectacle, Goryanchikov exposes the theatricality of the flogging, since each player knows his role: "And already the prisoner knows what to read and knows beforehand what will be during this reading, because this thing has been repeated already thirty times before with others. Indeed, Smekalov himself knows that the prisoner knows and knows that even the soldiers . . . also already long ago heard enough of this same thing" (*Pss*, 4:151).

The Grand Inquisitor displays a similar preoccupation with the "art" of execution and "the theatricality" of his prescribed ritual on the public square, which signifies "a symbol of the communal performance" (*Pss*, 4:148, 156).[69] A popular prison song from Dostoevsky's era identifies the square as a place of execution, to which "the executioners [*palachi*]" lead "the brigand [*razboinik*]" to die.[70] Ivan's discussion of capital punishment in "Rebellion" with the guillotining of Richard and the Tatar instruction in use of the "knout"— an international symbol of Russian barbarism—prepares the reader for the appearance of the auto-da-fé on the square of Seville (*Pss*, 14:219).

Furthermore, the background provided by Pobedonostsev's discussion of eighteenth-century criminal processes in Russia had informed already the nineteenth-century reader of Dostoevsky's novel about ecclesiastical punishments of convicts and, more specifically, about the burning of those guilty of crimes "offensive to God."[71] The Grand Inquisitor, "in his splendid cardinal's clothing" reserved for his attendance at the "splendid" auto-da-fé "in the presence of the king, court, knights, cardinal, and the most charming court ladies," displays a conscious intent to enhance the spectacle of his ceremony (*Pss*, 14:227, 226). Ivan's attention to such aesthetics of ritual may be anticipated by his theatrical commentary at the beginning of "Rebellion" which recommends that beggars, in order to maximize contributions, present themselves "on stage, in a ballet, where beggars . . . arrive in silken rags and torn lace and ask for alms, gracefully dancing" (*Pss*, 14:216). In the tradition of the Menippean satire, the Grand Inquisitor "profanely unmasks a holy thing" when he describes to his prisoner the next day's ceremony with predictions that reveal its pro forma nature.[72] With an indifference toward the fate of his victim, characteristic of Dostoevsky's previous executioners, the Grand Inquisitor informs the prisoner of his certain future: "I will condemn and burn you on the bonfire as the most evil of heretics, and those same people who today kissed your feet, tomorrow with a lone nod from me will throw themselves into raking coals around your bonfire" (*Pss*, 14:228). The prisoner seems to recognize the Grand Inquisitor's right to direct when he follows the command: "Don't respond; be silent" (*Pss*, 14:228).

The Grand Inquisitor's assured demeanor thus confirms Goryanchikov's conclusion that "tyranny is a habit" which may be learned by the executioner, who wields unlimited power "over the body, blood, and spirit" of one created as "his brother according to the law of Christ" (*Pss*, 4:154). Even when confronted with the image of Christ, the Grand Inquisitor follows Lieutenant Smekalov's example of exploiting his prisoner's biblically based utterances, which are attributed to Seville's newest arrival despite professed doubts about his identity. The Grand Inquisitor's sophisticated biblical exegesis, with little concern for precise Gospel citations and much space reserved for argumentative interpretation, artistically represents Myshkin's point that Catholicism "preaches a distorted Christ" (*Pss*, 8:450). Unlike Sonya Marmeladova's "performative reading" of the Gospel account relating Christ's resurrection of Lazarus, or Alesha Karamazov's "commentary" on Father Paissy's reading of Christ's miracle at Cana, the Grand Inquisitor's analysis overwhelms the Holy Writ which he paraphrases, misquotes, and challenges in his theological exposition.[73] Indeed, he casts doubt on the historical veracity of the Bible itself when asking Christ to confirm the temptation in the desert: "It has been passed down to us in books that he apparently 'tempted' you. Was this so?" (*Pss*, 14:229). Because, as he discloses later, the Grand Inquisitor sides with the "terrible and intelligent spirit" who created the *miraculous* three questions "in which are united all the irreconcilable historical contradictions of human nature throughout the earth," the Grand Inquisitor draws on the experience of fifteen centuries of human history to analyze the response of a historically distant Christ presented to him "in books" (*Pss*, 14:229, 230).

The Grand Inquisitor's identification with the "spirit of self-destruction and non-being" in the text encourages him to suppress the voice of the biblical Christ, as Malcolm Jones finds: "In the first act of suppression he had rewritten the Gospel narrative to suppress God" (*Pss*, 14:229).[74] The Grand Inquisitor's reading of the passage to demonstrate the human demand for bread also presents a challenge to church history, since it contradicts directly the passage's traditional ecclesiastical usage by multiple Christian denominations to provide a theological justification for the Lenten fast. The depiction of Goryanchikov's participation in the fast and in Easter services in *House of the Dead*, Raskolnikov's Lenten preparations, as well as the discussion of peasant hostility toward the Lenten fast in *Diary of a Writer* testify to Dostoevsky's knowledge of the passage's theological significance (*Pss*, 4:176–77; 6:419; 21:58–59). In offering his own exegesis, the Grand Inquisitor simultaneously acknowledges its doctrinal import and aggressively contradicts an ecclesiastical tradition, which identifies with the biblical Christ's response to the temptation: "It is written, 'One does not live by bread alone'"—an allusion to the Old Testament discussion of manna sent from heaven that adds "but by every word that comes from the mouth of the Lord" (Luke 4:4; Deuteronomy 8:3). Since he silences the voice of the living Christ, the Grand Inquisitor must depend on bread and "some fragments of the 'sacred testament'" that still retain "a potential for discovery and renewal" to inform his theological vision.[75] Thompson, in discussing the distance between "the memory of Christ's voice" and the characters' citation of the sacred text, recognizes the violence perpetrated on the scripture by Fedor, Ivan, and Smerdyakov.[76] In this respect, the Grand Inquisitor's analysis unites him with other characters' struggle against Orthodox traditions, for example, Fedor's criticism of monasticism, Ivan's attempt to lure Alesha away from Father Zosima, and Smerdyakov's propagation of jesuitic casuistry.

The private denunciation of Christ by this prominent ecclesiastical Roman authority attests to a moral laxity that Dostoevsky frequently attributes to Catholic political figures. In one of his notebooks Dostoevsky distinguishes between the Grand Inquisitor's ethics, that is, following the dictates of one's own conscience, and the moral certitude found by remaining true to his image of Christ.[77] Christ represents the "moral example" that does not burn heretics whereas the Inquisitor, like the title character of Adam Mickiewicz's 1828 poem "Konrad Wallenrod," has a conscience that permits the exploitation of fellow believers: "The Inquisitor is already by this alone immoral, so that the idea about the necessity of burning people could go along with his heart and his conscience. Orsini also. Konrad Wallenrod also" (*Pss*, 27:56).[78] The three personages mentioned here represent three different Catholic nations—Spain, Italy, and Polish-Lithuania—during historic periods of transition, when the Inquisitor, von Wallenrode, and Orsini acted surreptitiously with the goal of increasing their political power. The Grand Inquisitor here becomes linked to European Catholic nationalist liberation movements that Dostoevsky witnessed in his lifetime. Felice Orsini was an active Italian revolutionary in the 1840s and 1850s who plotted to assassinate Napoleon III, and Wallenrod was a rallying cry for nineteenth-century Polish nationalists willing to employ Machiavellian tactics like their hero Wallenrod, who betrayed his Order of the Teutonic Knights because of their destruction of his Lithuanian homeland. Gogel's study of Jozafat Ohryzko finds Mickiewicz's image of Wallenrod foundational for Ohryzko's Polish network, which jesuitically embraced deceit (false oaths, fake identities, and falsified decrees) in service to the cause of liberation.[79] Dostoevsky criticizes Orsini for concealing himself rather than, like Kirillov in *Demons*, openly sacrificing himself for the truth, and his labeling of Polish émigrés seeking to return to Russia with the appellations "Konrad Wallenrods, traitors" establishes that his previous encounters with Polish revolutionaries inform his depiction of the Grand Inquisitor (*Pss*, 11:303; 26:58). At the same time, such associations reinforce the Grand Inquisitor's executioner persona, for Orsini and Wallenrod were not, for Dostoevsky, self-sacrificial but murderous and even treasonous.[80]

Thus, the execution imagery surrounding the Grand Inquisitor weakens his claim to martyrdom for the sake of his children, which parallels the father-son relationship in the executioner-victim discourse in *House of the Dead*: "'Of course, your honor, it is a known deal; you are the father and we are the children. Be my own father!' cries the prisoner, already beginning to hope" (*Pss*, 4:148). Such language and imagery undermines the Grand Inquisitor's self-characterization as the suffering servant of humanity and exposes the coercive nature of the measures he adopts in order to impose, in the name of Christ, political solutions on moral issues. The Grand Inquisitor's use of the auto-da-fé on his flock connects him to a tradition of armed idealism that Dostoevsky considers foundational for Catholicism, since its history of chivalry defines for Europe "chivalric understandings of honor" which impart a "narrowness of view" and a tendency toward "too much punishment" to a nineteenth-century legal system (*Pss*, 24:183). Ivan, himself, links a historic age which saw the decline of chivalry, that is, the Reformation, with his contemporary period when placing his Grand Inquisitor within the context of "all this Catholic movement of the last centuries" (*Pss*, 14:237). The novel's exploration of the chivalric tradition in the modern age demonstrates further Dostoevsky's dialogue with Herzen, whose *Endings and*

Beginnings asserts the revival of the age of chivalry with the Polish rebellion against Russian authority in the 1860s: "Everything that had long ago withered in the old world, from the miter and the knight's sword to the Phrygian cap, appeared again in all its poetic luster in a Poland having risen in rebellion" (*Ss*, 16:129).[81]

THE INQUISITOR AND THE AGE OF CHIVALRY

Perlina presents examples of Dostoevsky's "bastardized form" of Herzen's "philosophical dialogue" in *From the Other Shore* in Ivan's poems "The Grand Inquisitor" and "Geological Cataclysm" ("Geologicheskii perevorot").[82] Herzen's return to this image of the "geological cataclysm" in *Ends and Beginnings* underscores the literariness of his revolutionaries or "Holy Don Quixotes" as he maintains that "every geological cataclysm has its novel, its own poem of the mountains" (*Ss*, 16:153). The austere Grand Inquisitor in Seville, being "an old man, tall and erect, with a withered face and sunken eyes," shares commonalities with the "thin, severe, Lenten type of Spaniard" that Herzen characterizes as the aged Don Quixote of the revolution in his *Ends and Beginnings* (*Pss*, 14:227; *Ss*, 16:157). Dostoevsky previously engages Herzen's text when entitling the aforementioned entry to his *Diary of a Writer*, highlighting the Count de Chambord as a modern Don Quixote, with the phrase "Again Signs 'of the Beginning of the End'" ("Opiat' priznaki 'nachala kontsa'"; *Pss*, 22:91). Herzen's Quixotes, like the Grand Inquisitor, are "fanatics of earthly religion, visionaries not of the Kingdom of God but of the Kingdom of Man; they remain the last sentinels of the ideal" (*Ss*, 16:151). Yet, while Herzen's aged Quixotes appear tragic for having perished without having reached their unattainable ideals, the "tragedy" of Ivan's elderly Inquisitor lies in his having realized, in the tradition of Dostoevsky's Quixote, his "ideal" of harmony only by means of "a deception" which leads his people "to death and destruction" (*Pss*, 26:25; 14:238). The Grand Inquisitor thereby demonstrates his kinship to Dostoevsky's Quixote, who lacks the "genius" to translate his ideal vision into a "truthful, and not fantastical or mad, path of action for the benefit of humanity" and so must engage in deception with his children as he struggles with a "fruitless superiority" over feeble youth that plagues Herzen's quixotic revolutionaries (*Pss*, 26:25; *Ss*, 16:154).

Through Ivan's poem, Dostoevsky responds to Herzen's regret that a revolutionary type—"the old man of '89 who is living out his days on the bread of his grandchildren"—is disappearing without having had his image embodied in literature for posterity: "This artist, which here scrutinizes grandfathers and grandsons, fathers and children and fearlessly, mercilessly, embodies them in a black terrifying poem, he will be the graveside laureate of that world" (*Ss*, 16:149). Assuming the Grand Inquisitor's contemporaneity to Ivan, he is of the approximate age of this grandfather revolutionary but does not retain the idealism of the aging revolutionary. Rather, because the poem is written by the "grandson" of the Grand Inquisitor, the latter resembles one of Ivan's "old men [*stariki*]" who have abandoned the "eternal questions" that preoccupy "young Russia [*molodaia Rossia*]" in favor of studying "the practical questions" such as providing bread for humanity (*Pss*, 14:212–13).[83] This characterization emerges, in part, from Ivan's discomfort with aging, which is apparent throughout his conversation with Alesha, in which he expresses disgust at his father's aged sensuality ("until seventy is foul") and mocks Alesha's belief in his Father Zosima, of whose dying Ivan reminds his brother at the conclusion of "The Grand Inquisitor" (*Pss*, 14:210). In his rebellion against God, Ivan rejects a future harmony manured by children's suffering but refuses to defend adults who "ate the apple and came to know good and evil and became 'like gods'" (*Pss*, 14:216). Indicting parents in the abuse of their own children, Turkish soldiers in the murder of infants, and a Russian landowner in the public dismemberment of a young serf, Ivan repeatedly equates adult authority figures with cruelty.

All the same, this grandson remains attached to his aged Catholic creation, which he defends against the critical analysis of his brother and against the mockery of the Devil (*Pss*, 14:237–39; 15:83). Ivan argues for the potential existence of many living examples of dedicated men like "my old man Inquisitor, who himself ate roots in the desert and raved like one possessed, conquering his flesh in order to make himself free and perfect" (*Pss*, 14:238). Thus, Ivan's argument for the sincere sacrifice of his Inquisitor follows the pattern of Herzen's idealistic Quixotes who follow the example of "the stoics of the first centuries" or "anchorites, who fled to the steppe from Christianity vulgarized into the official religion" (*Ss*, 16:151). Like Ivan, Herzen emphasizes the tragic end of his Reformation hero's "role-playing" which is formative for Don Quixote's "identity of profound moral integrity."[84] Herzen details the fate of these Quixotes who never fully abandoned their Catholic roots, which were embedded in the ideals of the French Revolution: "The Revolution secularized what it could from the catechism, but the Revolution thus, like the Reformation, stood on the Church's graveyard" (*Ss*, 16:177). Fellow revolutionary Bakunin also caustically evaluates their religiously inspired idealism, as is evident from his aforementioned characterization of Mazzini as "le dernier grand prêtre de l'idéalisme religieux."[85] The expression of Herzen's sympathy for these historical revolutionaries, who steadfastly retained their ideals, mitigates in *Ends and Beginnings* their responsibility for encouraging and then abandoning the hopefuls who cried out "from Golgotha" as the Don Quixotes "one after another disappear into the haze of winter twilight" (*Ss*, 16:179).

In keeping with *Diary of a Writer's* censure of Herzen for his appeal to Russian youth to support the Poles in the 1863 uprising, Dostoevsky reveals no empathy for Herzen or Catholic revolutionaries in his final novel.[86] Dostoevsky's choice of the surname Herzenstube (*Gertsenshtube*) for the German physician, who is described by the narrator as an "elderly and most venerable old man," allows the émigré author a presence in the closing chapter of "Pro and Contra" (*Pss*, 14:256).[87] The aged doctor's diagnosis of Smerdyakov's sham fit, sandwiched between the poetry of the Grand Inquisitor and the Elder Zosima's parting words, underscores the sterility of his medical science as signaled by his confiding to various patients that he does not understand anything (*Pss*, 14:165, 191). Although he, like the elderly Inquisitor and Zosima, offers a solution to innocent suffering, on which parents like Marfa Ignatevna, Captain Snegirev, and Mme Khokhlokova depend to alleviate their children's illnesses, the facetious presentation of his medical knowledge intimates that his expertise will achieve no results (*Pss*, 14:191). Nevertheless, his generosity toward the poor, sentimental recollections of the neglected child Mitya, and association with a fifteenth-century sect of "Moravian Brothers" opposing the hierarchical feudal class structure recall the positive attributes of the *citoyen du monde* whom Dostoevsky describes in his *Diary of a Writer* (*Pss*, 21:9). Furthermore, the description of Doctor Herzenstube acting "out of the goodness of his heart" suggests that the physician's name plays on the German word for "heart [*Herz*]" to highlight the sentimentality of the doctor and his namesake (*Pss*, 14:191).

Dostoevsky's novels demonstrate that he does not identify with this sentimentality, which once inspired in Herzen feelings of solidarity with the Poles, owing to their shared experience of imprisonment and exile, as described in *My Past and Thoughts:* "In the stockade's darkness of Nicholas's reign, sitting locked up with prison comrades, we felt for, rather than knew, each other. . . . But a second time the government united us with them. Before the shots at priests and children, at crucifixes and children, before the shots at hymns and prayers all questions fell silent and all differences were effaced" (*Ss*, 11:367). Since Dostoevsky felt that the Russian convicts rather than the Poles were his comrades in misfortune, he could not relate to Herzen's vocal defense of the Poles whom the exile regarded as Polish martyrs to the Russian "iron claw" (*Ss*, 12:437). Instead, in his 1880–81 notebook, Dostoevsky concludes that Poles seeking an "ethnographic Poland" are guilty of Pius IX's sinful quest to establish an earthly domain and therefore, like the Grand Inquisitor, seek the kingdom offered by the devil: "It is like when Italy knocked at Rome, and the Holy Father before the evident and inevitable loss of his tiny earthly state—precisely there proclaimed the Roman idea that the High Priest is the master of all the earth and that without the earthly kingdom (without the third temptation of the Devil) Christ cannot stand" (*Pss*, 27:66). For this reason, he does not accept Herzen's idealistic characterization of his contemporary Catholic revolutionaries—such as close friends Stanisław Worcell and Mazzini—as tragic aged Quixotes whose fanatical dedication to a righteous cause one often encountered "at the time of the Renaissance or Reformation" (*Ss*, 12:438). While Dostoevsky appreciates the attachment of such revolutionaries to their ideals, his break with Bogusławski in *Notes from the House of the Dead* indicates that even estrangement from a rare friendly face in Omsk did not prevent him from challenging the convictions of Polish political prisoners. In addition, his *Diary of a Writer* credits Catholicism with contemporary fanaticism and the Vatican with the revival of Polish nationalism.

Both Herzen's image of the tragic idealistic revolutionary and Dostoevsky's concept of the Catholic revolutionary defined by a (self-) deception in service to liberation are applied to the Grand Inquisitor by Ivan and Alesha, respectively. While Ivan, like Herzen, defends his aging "great idealist," the hero and "the realist" Alesha deflates the tragic poetic image crafted by his brother with critical observations, such as "Your suffering Inquisitor is only a fantasy" or "they do not have any such mysteries and ennobled sufferings" (*Pss*, 14:238, 24, 237). Whereas Ivan maintains that the Inquisitor is a leader "who so stubbornly" in his own way loves humanity, Alesha simply categorizes the Grand Inquisitor as an atheist and characterizes his fellow members of the Roman army as landowners in the new age of serfdom (*Pss*, 14:239). Dostoevsky, as well, refers to a link between serfdom and Catholicism in his notebook (1876–77) when he credits the Polish gentry with understanding "the faith of the Russian people" as "slave faith [*khlop'ska vera*]" while Dostoevsky understands the "Master's faith [*barskaia vera*]" as "atheism" and "indifference" (*Pss*, 24:191). This Russian aristocracy produced intellectuals like Herzen, whom Dostoevsky describes as "a product of the former system of serfdom, which he hated and from which he came, not only by way of his father, but precisely through a break with his native land and with her ideals" (*Pss*, 21:9). Ivan's character reveals a similar paradox in that his incomplete break with serfdom becomes apparent not only through his attachment to his father, who enjoys the privileges of this old order, but also through the image of his Devil, a now impoverished "gentleman who belongs to the class of former manicured landowners, who flourished during serfdom" (*Pss*, 15:70). Ivan also maintains a connection with the theocratic feudal order described by Alesha by defending the hierarchical ecclesiology of the Grand Inquisitor. Alesha's characterization of Ivan's protagonist, therefore, underscores the Grand Inquisitor's alienation from the masses, whereas his biography of the Elder Zosima demonstrates the Elder's ability to transcend social divisions during Russia's transition to the modern industrial age. Such varying responses by these two aging ecclesiastical witnesses to the breakdown of the feudal age in their respective countries reflect Dostoevsky's longstanding thesis that the West continues to suffer from conflict between "les boyards" and "les serfs," while Russia long ago found "a neutral ground on which all merged into one unanimous harmonious whole" (*Pss*, 18:49).[88]

Dostoevsky's "Grand Inquisitor," therefore, validates Granovsky's observation that medieval feudalism "in diverse forms" survived in the West into the sixteenth and seventeenth centuries, when the hierarchical chivalric order, supported by the Catholic Church to ensure the success of the Crusades, began to deteriorate owing to Columbus's discovery of America, Niccolò Machiavelli's political theory, the figures of the Reformation, and the scientific discoveries of the humanists, such as Desiderius Erasmus and Johann Reuchlin.[89] Knighthood, the "noble" vestige of the "feudal world," rests on a paradoxical chivalric tradition, as Granovsky outlines, because the privileged position of the knight, who vowed to protect and serve the powerless, represented a feudal order that required the exploitation of serf labor.[90] This placed the knights and the Catholic Church, which endorsed the chivalric order and defined its requirements regarding fasts, prayers, and oaths, in the position of both self-proclaimed protector and de facto oppressor of the peasantry. Dostoevsky appears to sense this paradox of chivalry, in his aforementioned description of the discrepancies between Don Quixote's imagined ideal and the actions that he undertakes for the common good. The Grand Inquisitor's theological justification for the use of the auto-da-fé on his flock for their own protection continues this paradoxical tradition. At the same time, the Grand Inquisitor's manipulation of the sacred "mysteries" to maintain control over his flock parallels the measures of political repression and ecclesiological discipline adopted by a Catholic Church attempting to protect its magisterium during the breakdown of secular and sacred authority during the Reformations. Thus, Dostoevsky's conscious choice to represent Catholicism with "one of the most important high priests of the Catholic Church" reinforces its image as a feudal institution, which Alesha Karamazov's comments confirm as its present status and not a historically remote reality (*Pss*, 15:198).[91]

Yet, in creating his "answer" to the Grand Inquisitor with the Orthodox Elder Zosima, Dostoevsky selects a simple monk with no worldly possessions who resides some distance from any center of political power (*Pss*, 30.1:122). Still, both the Grand Inquisitor and Zosima emerge from a revolutionary tradition, which is evident in Zosima's biography both from his brother's having fallen under the influence of a political exile and from the oblique reference to the young Zosima's duel over a political statement about the Decembrists (*Pss*, 14:269). Also, Zosima's life as an officer intimates that he once displayed some chivalric tendencies typical of his class, such as a heightened sense of honor as signified by the duel and "the shine of civility and refined manners acquired together with the French language" that characterized his experience in the cadet corps (*Pss,* 14:268). The landowner Maximov further implicates Zosima in the chivalric tradition, when describing him as "un chevalier parfait" to Fedor Pavlovich and Miusov before they meet him at the monastery (*Pss,* 14:33). As a monk, Zosima is not completely free from Catholic influence, since in his cell "the ivory Catholic cross, embraced by the *Mater dolorosa,* and several foreign engravings from the great Italian artists of the last centuries" lie next to "pages of the most common Russian lithographs of saints, martyrs, hierarchs, etc. . ." (*Pss,* 14:37). Here, the *Mater dolorosa* suggests a Polish connection owing to the politicization of Marian imagery during the period, which is evident in Herzen's article "Mater dolorosa" in which he appropriates the image for Poland in reference to the Warsaw Massacre of 1861 (*Ss,* 15:81). Also, the association of Catholicism with ivory crucifixes and Italian masters advances the elitist image of Western Christendom, which is similarly evident from the Catholic art in Versilov's drawing room: "On the wall hung a large magnificent engraving of the Dresden Madonna and opposite there, on the other wall, an expensive photograph, of an enormous size, of the cast bronze doors of the Florentine cathedral" (*Pss,* 13:82).

However, in contrast to the raiments of the Grand Inquisitor, Zosima's robes freed the Elder from a lasting legacy of feudalism by depriving him of rank and monetary possessions obtained with the help of serf labor. Zosima's memory of his family's exploitation of the serfs, whom they purchased from a landowner, is linked to his recollections of his brother's ultimately fatal illness: "I still remember how of these four Mama sold one cook Anfimya, who was lame and elderly, for sixty paper roubles and hired a free one in her place. And there during the sixth week of Lent my brother suddenly became worse" (*Pss,* 14:261). Zosima's decision to renounce his privileged social position, in response to his own abuse of his servant Afanasy, prepares the Elder for an authentic reunion with Afanasy as depicted in the section of his teachings entitled, "*Something About Lords and Servants and About Whether or Not It Is Possible for Lords and Their Servants to Become Reciprocally Brothers in Spirit*" ("*Nechto o gospodakh i slugakh i o tom, vozmozhno li gospodam i slugam stat' vzaimno po dukhu brat'iami*"; *Pss,* 14:285). In acting as an advocate for a society forged through brotherly union, Zosima finds a middle ground between the two opposing examples of monasticism presented in Pushkin's *Boris Godunov,* that is, the seclusion of Dostoevsky's beloved Pimen and the spiritually sanctioned imposture of Otrepev in the chivalric tradition.[92] In this respect, Dostoevsky's Russian monk represents an idealized image of the monastery, presented in the article "Our Monasteries" ("Nashi monastyri"), as a place of peaceable social reform in contrast to the "violence" or despotism that consistently accompanies "the renewal of society" (*Pss,* 21:139).

In distancing Zosima from the hierarchy of the Holy Synod and in showing his ability to transcend class distinctions defined by the legacy of serfdom, Dostoevsky isolates him from "the blasphemy . . . of the upper social stratum" that informs Ivan's conversation with his brother (*Pss,* 30.1:66). Unlike the monastic types of Otrepev and the Inquisitor, Zosima's desire to help others leads him to join the people, since he asserts that "from the people is the salvation of Rus. The Russian monastery has been with the people from time immemorable" (*Pss,* 14:285). Such a populist conception of Russian monasticism contradicts its common elitist image, which had been widespread in the Russian press since the exposé *Description of the Rural Clergy (Opisanie sel'skogo dukhovenstva)* by parish priest Ioann S. Bellyustin had appeared in a foreign press in 1858.[93] Dostoevsky's series "Foreign Events" suggests that he was familiar with Bellyustin's accusations against Catholic and Orthodox clergy in the 1870s, when the priest criticized their use of miracles (particularly those connected to the Madonna) and relics as a means of indoctrinating the faithful.[94] Zosima's posthumous corruption and the absence of "the relics of holy saints" and "wonder-working icons" in the monastery exculpate the Elder from such charges (*Pss,* 14:26). However, Bellyustin's reproofs remain applicable to the Grand Inquisitor owing to his slogan "miracle, mystery, and authority" in opposition to its liberative, yet deceptive, counterpart "Liberté, Egalité, Fraternité" which Dostoevsky characterizes in his *Diary of a Writer* as "only loud phrases and nothing more" (*Pss,* 23:34). The Grand Inquisitor, thus, consistently appears guilty of elitist coercive religious practices "ad majorem gloriam Dei" that empower monks with political pretensions, like Otrepev, to take up arms in the chivalric tradition of defending righteous causes through violent means (*Pss,* 14:226).

THE REFORMATION AND PERMISSIBLE VIOLENCE IN *THE BROTHERS KARAMAZOV*

With the Grand Inquisitor Dostoevsky continues to demonstrate the appeal of Catholic types for educated Russians, like Ivan, who are aesthetically drawn to literary images linked to Western Christendom. Ivan does not identify with the Catholic visual arts, for example, Raphael's *Sistine Madonna* or Lorrain's *Acis and Galatea* like personages in *Demons* and *The Adolescent.* Ivan also does not admire those linked "with the great technical discoveries" of the Renaissance and Reformation periods, such as Nicolaus Copernicus or Galileo Galilei whose names, along with those of Charlemagne, Pushkin, Shakespeare, and Napoleon, signify greatness for the Adolescent (*Pss,* 21:268; 13:76).[95] Although the notebooks to *Demons* conclude that Raphael and Galileo attest to the ability of a single man to *regenerate* the world, Ivan places this power in the hands of the Grand Inquisitor, who represents the Catholic institution that condemned Galileo for defending Copernicanism, which Galileo was forced to abjure (*Pss*, 11:168).[96] Since the middle of the nineteenth century, Galileo's trial had become a cause célèbre owing to the debate over the use of torture during the Inquisition's proceedings, so the Grand Inquisitor's defense of capital punishment touches upon a prominent public issue in Dostoevsky's Europe.[97] Ivan's preference for a Reformation authority figure advances Ellis Sandoz's conclusion that the Grand Inquisitor emerges, in part, from Belinsky's tradition of promoting the destructive power of historical heroes like Luther and Voltaire.[98] Dostoevsky's opposition to such violence and to its proponents whom he observed in the West encourage his increased antipathy toward those advocating armed conflict, which finds its artistic expression in the Grand Inquisitor, who evokes both the Catholic legacies of benevolent chivalry and principled rebellion as well as the Catholic reputation for coercion and false martrydom.

In Dostoevsky's correspondence, the Grand Inquisitor serves as a participant in that blasphemy uttered in the book "Pro and Contra," in which he appears to be a creation-in-progress as a consequence of the poetic analysis of Ivan and Alesha. He does not follow Napoleon's role in *Crime and Punishment* as an inspirational source for rebellion within the novel but rather remains significant primarily for highlighting Ivan's connection to a violent Catholic tradition. Ivan's interest in a Reformation figure continues in the tradition of another unbalanced hero in Dostoevsky, that is, Golyadkin, because their attachment to the literary types of the Inquisitor and Otrepev, respectively, exposes them to ridicule and causes them to appear quixotic as they fall victim to their own "fiction, fable, and falsehood, and dreams."[99] In their idealism, they share Herzen's romantic predilection for viewing life through a literary lens and reading the present age in dialogue with feudalism. Ivan's devil, linked to Otrepev through Ivan's label of "impostor," reinforces both of these traits about his interlocutor's personality by referring to him as "a great lover of literature" and characterizing his defense of his brother Mitya with the French adjective *"chevaleresque"* (*Pss*, 15:86, 83).[100] Yet, Dostoevsky's portrayal of the chivalric tradition conflicts with Herzen's admiration of the Middle Ages for its social cohesion arising from "the common sacred objects, before which, as before gifts, all bowed" and "the ideals, creeds, and words, for which beat both the simple heart of the poor citizen and the heart of the arrogant knight" (*Ss*, 16:141).

Dostoevsky's discussions of Spanish and French instability in the 1870s in terms of medieval and Reformation turmoil necessarily contradict Herzen's conclusion in *Endings and Beginnings* that the violence of the Renaissance and Reformation culminated in 1848 (*Ss*, 16:176). Since this revolution in his youth, Dostoevsky had witnessed in Siberia Catholic hostility to the Crimean War, and in Europe the aftermath of the 1863 Polish uprising, the Italian struggle for unification, and the Franco-Prussian War. These experiences inform the comments of his own witness to history, Ivan's devil, who, calling himself "a specter of life, who lost all endings and beginnings," refuses to bring about the end of human history by joining the chorus of hosannas (*Pss*, 15:77).[101] For the Devil, conflict is normative, so he does not search, like Herzen, for "that psalm which can be sung in our time with faith and enthusiasm on all floors of the house, from the basement to the garret" (*Ss*, 16:141). His reference to Luther suggests that, like Ivan, the Devil is drawn to the turmoil of the sixteenth century, in spite of his attachment to the legend "of our Middle Ages—not yours but ours" (*Pss*, 15:78). The Devil delights not so much in the fallen ideologues like the Grand Inquisitor but in the Jesuits' confessional, where he can enjoy their casuistry and witness a priest succumbing to the banal temptation of sexual desire. In his enjoyment of casuistry and status as a "lackey" the Devil resembles "the lackey Smerdyakov" who sits in Ivan's soul while the Devil torments his mind (*Pss*, 14:242; 15:73).[102] While Ivan's devil and disciple find his moral reasoning liberating, Ivan remains preoccupied with darker thoughts of execution: "Just as thousands of things are remembered unconsciously, even when they cart one away for execution" (*Pss*, 15:79). His identification with a victim to be executed undermines his earlier defense of the poetic Inquisitor-executioner so that he comes to represent one of the "decent people who still have a conscience and honor" whom the Devil may torment with "pangs of conscience" (*Pss*, 15:78).

Ivan's earlier association of his Christ figure with "enlightenment [*prosveshchenie*]" intimates that he does not follow the example of those post-Enlightenment "unscrupulous" types whose lack of conscience renders them immune to these pangs (*Pss*, 14:227; 15:78).[103] However, his lackey Smerdyakov, Fedor's "fine Jesuit," describes a more flexible ethical system that allows for even renunciation of Christianity in the face of torture for the faith at the hands of Tatars with the conviction that this is only "a little sin, a highly ordinary one" (i.e., venial sin) and sin for which one may compensate by good deeds (as Svidrigailov has already established): "To my mind, there would not have been any sin in it—if one were to renounce . . . one's own baptism in order to save by it one's life for good deeds, which over the course of years would expiate faintheartedness" (*Pss*, 14:120, 117; 6:379). The Catholic emphasis on works (instead of faith alone), so divisive during the Catholic-Protestant debates of the Reformation, thereby serves to alleviate potential pangs of conscience for Smerdyakov, which seem largely absent from his moral reasoning. His display of lackey casuistry calculated to impress Ivan does not later dissuade the intellectual from sharing his poem, "The Grand Inquisitor," which exhibits far greater genius in its dialogue with

Jesuit theologians, whose influence Ivan discloses: "'Everything, they say, has been given over to the pope and has now become the pope's'. . . . In this sense they not only speak but write—the Jesuits at least. I myself have read their theologians" (*Pss*, 14:228). The Latin root *contrā*—meaning against or opposite—present in the title of the chapter "Controversy" ("Kontroverza") with Smerdyakov's casuistic display further binds it to the book "Pro i contra" containing Ivan's poem. Here, the presence of the Jesuits' moral reasoning in the novel's multiple discussions of torture and execution further implicates the Order in the temporal suffering of humankind in both Reformation and modern Europe.

Chapter Six

Roman vs. Russian Justice in *The Brothers Karamazov* and the *Diary*

> "Yes, gentlemen, you see before you, in blue
> jeans and misery, the wanderin',
> exiled, trampled-on, and sufferin' rightful King
> of France."
> —Mark Twain, *Adventures of Huckleberry Finn*
> (1884)

REFERENCES TO the Jesuits, *Hamlet,* and *Boris Godunov* in *The Brothers Karamazov* suggest that the Reformation continues to haunt Dostoevsky's narrative in which the Karamazovs, an embodiment of Russianness, repeatedly come into conflict with Western values. Whereas Ivan and Smerdyakov openly betray their Jesuit influences, Mitya and Grushenka encounter a more muted form of Catholicism in the Polish gentlemen, who in several respects resemble Dostoevsky's elitist Catholic comrades in Omsk. The drafts to the novel reveal Dostoevsky's conception of the scene at Mokroe as a confrontation between Catholic Poles, invoking the Marian cult of the "Holy mother of Częstochowa," and the Russians Mitya and Grushenka (*Pss,* 15:279). Dostoevsky likely encountered this veneration in Omsk, since Tokarzewski mentions a medallion "with the image of the Częstochowa Virgin," which he clutched during his 2,000 lashes while praying: "This is for Your honor, Queen [*Królowo*] of Royal Poland—this is for Your redemption beloved Fatherland!"[1] The papal bull *Ineffabilis Deus* on the Immaculate Conception (1854), which some viewed as evidence of Pius IX's de facto infallibility, reinvigorated devotions to Mary, including the worship of the Jasna Góra "icon" of Częstochowa.[2] In Dostoevsky's drafts, familiar Polish references in the notes to the Poles' Catholic priest and "a slave's faith" identify the nationality with Dostoevsky's stereotypical depictions of Polish Christianity (*Pss,* 15:286; 24:191). In their aristocratic exclusivity, their disdain for the uncivilized Russians ("The Russian people cannot be good, because they are not civilized"), and in Pan Mussyalovich's chivalric displays ("I am a knight [*rytsar*'],"), the gentlemen at Mokroe represent the Polish nobility who have an automatic association with Rome in Dostoevsky's understanding: "The faith of the Polish nobility [*pan'ska vera*] was all the same Catholicism" (*Pss*, 15:285; 14:388; 24:191). This faith informs their national pride, which contributes to the religiously and ethnically divisive scene at Mokroe. Hence, in Dostoevsky whereas the French Catholics continue to flirt with socialism/communism and Italy has become a nation of Catholic bourgeoisie, the Polish Catholics remain dedicated to the cause of national liberation, as Dostoevsky maintains in *Diary of a Writer* (*Pss*, 24:149, 160).

Mitya's citation of *Boris Godunov* on the way to Mokroe in anticipation of his confrontation with Grushenka and her former Polish lover imparts a dramatic and historical significance to the impending scene, since Mitya utters the first words of the chronicler-monk Pimen in Pushkin's historical tragedy: "Still a final narrative" (*Pss*, 14:367).[3] Linking this Russo-Polish encounter to the chronicle of the Orthodox monk also enhances Mitya's spiritual dimension, while reminding the reader of the historic animosity, embedded in the tragedy, between Orthodox Russia and Catholic Poland. Mitya thereby establishes a bond between his own experience with Poles and Pimen's narrative relating the murder of the tsarevich Dimitry (Mitya's namesake), whose premature death provides a pretext for the pretendership of the Catholic-sponsored False Dimitry. Although Pimen believes in the instructional potential of his "truthful narratives" for "descendants of the Orthodox," his recitation of the account creates a new chapter in Polish Catholic history, since "Pimen's chronicle is midwife" to the pretendership of the Orthodox novice Otrepev who conspires with the Catholics to seize the Moscow throne (*PssP*, 7:17).[4] With his reference to Pimen's narrative, Mitya places the culture clash at Mokroe between Russians (himself and Grushenka) and Poles (Pan Vrublevsky and Pan Mussyalovich) within a historic tradition of interreligious conflict. While the epical religious conflict in books 5, "Pro and Contra," and 6, "The Russian Monk," brings the brothers' story into dialogue with the expanse of church history, the Russo-Polish divide at Mokroe localizes or "humanizes" the conflict by introducing it into a Rabelaisian "joyful hell."[5] Ivan's references to Dante, to Hugo's presentation of "Le bon jugement de la très sainte et gracieuse Vierge Marie" ("The Good Judgment of the Very Holy and Gracious Virgin Mary"), and to "The Wandering of the Mother of God Through Torments" ("Khozhdenie bogoroditsy po mukam") link "The Grand Inquisitor" to the "Sodom" at Mokroe through Mitya's celebration of the "the ideal of Sodom" and his own torments in "The Wandering of the Soul Through Trials" ("Khozhdenie dushi po mytarstvam"; *Pss*, 14:225, 388, 100, 412). Mitya's ties to the Greek goddess Demeter, highlighted by his citation from Schiller's "Eleusinian Festival" ("Das Eleusische Fest"), further connect him to the underworld, since in Greek mythology Demeter wanders in search of her daughter Persephone, whom Hades kidnapped and made his queen.[6] Mitya, like Persephone, therefore remains a liminal character on the threshold of hell, for he also is destined to live "under the earth" but in chains in the Siberian mines (*Pss*, 15:31).

The other Siberian, Pan Mussyalovich, and his companion Pan Vrublevsky do not empathize with Mitya but rather prey upon him by cheating him out of money while playing cards with a marked deck and by offering selective testimony that implicates him in parricide. They embody the spirit of Ivan's theory "All is permitted," since behind their deception lies not the lying (*vran'e*) celebrated by Dostoevsky in his foolish Russians but the purposeful deceit of the Devil's "unscrupulous [*bessovestnye*]" who have profited in the modern age owing to an absence of conscience (*Pss*, 15:78).[7] In their lack of honesty, they resemble their fellow native son, Uladzimir Spasovich, whom Dostoevsky liberally critiques in his notes and *Diary of a Writer*, for he is a lawyer, that is, "'a hired conscience,' that is bought by not only money but liberalism, glory, poetry" (*Pss*, 24:135). He repeatedly attributes Roman imagery to Spasovich by likening him to Vibulenus and accuses him of censuring the Orthodox as well: "And in Russia none of our sacred objects fears free investigation, did you know this Mr. Spasovich. . . . We Russians even take pride in our particularities. Our Orthodoxy itself translates the Bible" (*Pss*, 24:154).[8] Such Polish personages, hostile to Russia's way of life, find the judicial system accommodating, since it favors these Westernizers owing to a Roman influence on the reformed court. Thus, Dostoevsky's final novel suggests that Russia continues to absorb Roman and Polish tendencies into its culture but remains inconclusive about whether Russia will succeed in assimilating these forces without affecting the dominant culture of the Great Russians within the empire.

POLISH CATHOLIC CONSPIRATORS IN DOSTOEVSKY'S *DIARY*

An examination of Dostoevsky's *Diary of a Writer* reveals a building anti-Polonism in his writing as he becomes alarmed at potential Catholic agitation during the Russo-Turkish War and expresses concerns over the return of exiled Polish aristocrats to Russia. This connection of Catholic Poles to political unrest constitutes part of his focus on the resilience of the "Catholic idea" in the modern era, particularly in France, "the representative of Catholicism," which accepts Catholicism as "the general banner of unification of the old order of things—for all nineteen centuries—the unification against something new and imminent, vital and fateful" (*Pss*, 25:6, 145).[9] This understanding of French Catholicism seems derivative of a summary of its history in a report on a Bonn Conference (1874) recorded in the 1875–76 Protocols of the OLDP, which was in Dostoevsky's library. The summary recalls Louis XIV's support for the Jesuits, his suppression of Jansenism at Port-Royal, and the restoration of the Catholic Church by Napoleon to demonstrate France's continuous relationship with Rome dating from the Middle Ages. Its contention that Catholics in contemporary France consist of "only ultramontanes and non-believers" parallels Dostoevsky's association of France with atheistic socialism and papal loyalists.[10] This same summary discusses the history of papal influence in Poland, whose history is one of a Catholic nation trapped between Protestant Germany and Orthodox Russia. A Polish reputation for political intrigue is linked to the presence of papal nuncios and Jesuits, the Order that educated the nobility to which most of Poland's bishops belong.[11] Dostoevsky's image of Poland in *Diary of a Writer* similarly understands the nation as uniformly Catholic, largely ultramontanist, and perpetually engaged in political intrigue, particularly against Russia.

Although Dostoevsky's commentary on Russo-Polish relations is located primarily in the 1877 entries, earlier entries reveal his support for Bismarck's *Kulturkampf*, which was part of the German leader's campaign to suppress Polish ultramontanism within his nation's borders. As Richard Blanke demonstrates in his study *Prussian Poland in the German Empire*, the *Kulturkampf* represented only one in a series of anti-Polonist policies implemented by Bismarck, since Polish participation in the 1848 unrest had threatened the monarchy.[12] Blanke's observation that Bismarck sometimes "described the Polish nobles as the most reactionary figures in creation" and "at others he imagined them in collusion with the revolutionary Left all over Europe" may also be applied to Dostoevsky, who depicts both revolutionary and reactionary Poles in *House of the Dead* and *The Brothers Karamazov*.[13] Both Bismarck and Dostoevsky believe that the Roman Catholic Church helped Polish nobility sustain a distinct national identity, and therefore they implicate the Vatican directly in political turmoil in historically Polish lands, as the latter maintains: "The Vatican never betrayed Old Poland, but on the contrary, supported all of her fantasies with all its strength when other states no longer even wanted to listen to them!" (*Pss*, 26:58). Praising Bismarck for perceiving a threat to German unification "in Roman Catholicism and in socialism, the monster born of Catholicism," Dostoevsky advocates for "the power of a renewed Germany, her Protestant and protesting spirit, against the ancient and new Rome," because the "fate of Poland awaits France, and politically she will not live—or Germany will not exist" (*Pss*, 26:88, 91, 89).

Dostoevsky's passing reference to the archbishop of the Poznanian Church, Cardinal Mieczysław Ledóchowski, in *Diary of a Writer* further attests to his familiarity with the Polish dimension to Bismarck's *Kulturkampf*. Owing to Pobedonostsev's 1873 article in *The Citizen*, "The Ledóchowski Affair" ("Delo Ledokhovskogo"), Dostoevsky was acquainted with Ledóchowski's refusal to vacate his episcopal seat at the request of German officials: "The Episcopal title, with all its rights and responsibilities, I accepted from God through his deputy on earth . . . And so no kind of secular authority has the power to take this calling from me."[14] Such ultramontane sentiments encouraged him to disregard governmental policies, including one that restricted the language of instruction to German, so he was arrested and imprisoned in 1874. Dostoevsky's criticism of Ledóchowski's civil disobedience may be implied from his comments in the October 1877 entry "Roman Clericals in Our Russia" ("Rimskie klerikaly u nas v Rossii"), in which Dostoevsky dismisses news of Ledóchowski's potential candidacy for the papal throne as a rumor "of Polish origin, since only the head of a thoughtless Polish émigré agitator could seriously believe that the Roman Conclave . . . would stoop to elect Ledóchowski" (*Pss*, 26:56). However, his view of Ledóchowski appears temperate when compared with the language found in a lead article of *Saint Petersburg News* (*Sankt-Peterburgskie vedomosti*), which likens the archbishop to a "Jesuit-fanatic" but all the same dismisses concerns that his selection as head of the church could result in a "cultural battle" or "a more threatening revolution."[15]

When Dostoevsky follows this discussion of Cardinal Ledóchowski with a rejection of what he characterizes as attempts by "agitator-clerics" to promote a false reconciliation with Russia, he links Cardinal Ledóchowski to a larger clerical conspiracy gaining strength in Europe (*Pss*, 26:59). Convinced that Polish Catholic priests promote simultaneously ardent nationalism and Catholic universalism, Dostoevsky maintains that the advocacy for permitting Polish émigrés to return from abroad is a clerical act and part of "a pan-European clerical conspiracy" (*Pss*, 26:58). A report on "a spiteful Polish priest" denouncing a Russian scholar traveling in Austrian Galicia as a "Russian Panslavist, propagandist, and agitator" advances Dostoevsky's thesis on the subversive activities of Catholic clerics (*Pss*, 26:59). Such images of Polish and Catholic priests demonstrate the transborder nature of the Polish Question for Dostoevsky, who consistently connects it to a larger religious network aiming to expand the influence of the Roman church in Russia.

In the midst of the Russo-Turkish War, Dostoevsky fears a potential Anglo-Hungarian-Polish conspiracy in addition to Hungarian and French support for the Turks, because such alliances would expose Russia to a sustained conflict on its southern and western borders. For this reason, Dostoevsky foresees the possible dissemination of Catholicism within the empire: "We find in our outlying areas, and even in our interior, our own Roman clerics. . . . But it would be strange if the Vatican conspiracy passed over our Roman clerics and did not use them in their affairs. Trouble [*Smuta*] at the rear of the Russian armies would be especially advantageous to the Vatican, particularly at the present moment" (*Pss*, 26:55). Although he does not provide details in this entry, an article published in a May 1877 issue of the *Saint Petersburg News* confirms that Polish émigrés were fighting with the Turkish legions against Russia and concludes that Hungarian magnates, Pius IX, and Polish natives were collaborating against Russia's interests in Turkey.[16] An 1877 report on the war by the *Daily News* clarifies that the Polish legion formed within the Turkish army was composed of displaced Poles: "The men, principally residents in Constantinople, volunteered for the Army of the Danube. Among them was a considerable sprinkling of ex-Austrian and Russian officers, who undertook, by the distribution of Polish revolutionary proclamations, to cause the wholesale desertion of the Polish element in the regiments opposed to them and subsequently to organize these deserters into a Turko-Polish legion."[17] The article in the *Saint Petersburg News* stimulated a series of discussions about the Polish Question, its exploitation by Western powers, and the role of Polish émigrés in the future of Russia.[18] Similar articles in *The Voice* in March and October also examine Polish-Turkish relations and the *Morning Post*'s critical evaluation of Tsar Alexander II's policies in Russian Poland.[19] These frequent articles dedicated to the Polish Question encourage Dostoevsky to attempt to account for Poland's place in the promising future that he envisions for Slavdom while Russia was enjoying victories over the Turks.

By dividing Poland into "Old Poland" and "New Poland" Dostoevsky avoids the language of class warfare common to studies of the Polish Question, evident in Vladimir Solovev's writings: "Russian authority, saving the Polish nobility from the fury of rebelling serfs . . . secured the future of a real, not only a noble and not a serf, but Polish Poland."[20] Instead, Dostoevsky's "Old Poland" translates into a select group of Polish agitators abroad who instinctively hate Russia and will never be reconciled to a Russian Poland. Because Dostoevsky firmly believes that only "by the great centralized strength" of Russia "will the Slavs live on earth," "Old Poland" threatens Russia's future: "Her ideal is to stand in place of Russia in the Slavic world" (*Pss*, 26:84, 59). He therefore concludes that "Old Poland will never exist, because she cannot get along with Russia" but finds that "a New Poland" under the power of the tsar can "expect a fate equal to that of every Slavic tribe when Slavdom is liberated and resurrected in Europe" (*Pss*, 26:58–59). In his notebooks, Dostoevsky characterizes Russia as the "alma mater" of the Slavic nations while judging Poland to be "the example of the political inability to live among the Slavic tribes" (*Pss*, 24:120). In his understanding, Russia acted out of self-defense in seizing Poland, whose influence continues to infiltrate Russian culture. Nevertheless, he adopts a conciliatory tone when he promises not to turn a Pole into a Russian and paternalistically approaches the Poles and Czechs by offering to give them autonomy at some future point, when they "will reach out to us, as to a friend, an older brother, and a great center" (*Pss*, 24:194).[21]

While understanding that the "Great Russian *great* tribe" constitutes only half the population of Russia, Dostoevsky still remains convinced of the power of Russia to create an Orthodox federation with a Russian Constantinople at its center (*Pss*, 21:267). In his discussion of Constantinople, religion takes precedence over ethnicity in his worldview, since he defends Russia's potential occupation of the city with a reference to its role as the "leader of Orthodoxy, as its protector and guardian" (*Pss*, 23:49). Furthermore, Dostoevsky's support of the Greek church canons over Bulgarian Orthodox nationalism in the dispute over phyletism shows that the author prioritizes Orthodoxy over ethnicity. The issue of phyletism presented the danger of schism within the Eastern church in the 1870s, when the Bulgarian Orthodox Church, trying to establish its own diaspora in Constantinople, clashed with the Greek Patriarchate. At a local council in 1872, the patriarch of Constantinople declared phyletism to be in violation of the canons, and rejected "the parallel existence of 'nationally defined' churches."[22] Despite his pan-Slavist sympathies, Dostoevsky supports the Greek church: "In the canonical, or better yet, in the religious respect I acquit the Greeks. For the most noble goals and aspirations one should not *distort* Christianity, i.e., look at Orthodoxy at least like a secondary thing, like the Bulgars in the present case" (*Pss*, 29.1:263). This also exhibits the importance of Orthodoxy for Dostoevsky's vision of a future Slavic Empire, which Scanlan discovers "extends beyond the unification of the Slavic peoples alone."[23] Dostoevsky's opposition to various Protestant, Catholic, and Jewish groups already residing within the territories of the Russian Empire suggests that a plurality of religious traditions would not be welcomed in this future nation, especially since Dostoevsky frequently implicates them in politically subversive activities.

Dostoevsky's story "The Peasant Marei" in an 1876 entry exemplifies this marginalization of Catholic ethnicities in what Robin Feuer Miller describes as a "two-tiered memory interlocking childhood and young adulthood" that recalls a Siberian memory about the author's childhood encounter with a peasant.[24] Whereas Mirecki stands in the foreground of the Siberian remembrance, the Orthodox Marei's comforting and blessing of the nine-year-old Dostoevsky remains the focus of the childhood memory. Miller highlights Dostoevsky's reshaping of memory in the passage as he reinvents "that self from the past who himself had invented his own present and past."[25] Jackson identifies "The Peasant Marei" as the *House of the Dead*'s "fitting prologue" when remarking upon Dostoevsky's own allusion to this novel in the entry, which reminds the reader of the distance between his prison experience and that of his "invented" narrator by gently mocking the reader who assigns Goryanchikov's background as a murderer to the author (*Pss*, 22:47).[26] Dostoevsky's self-referential opening phrase that "all these *profes-*

sions de foi I think are very boring to read" signals the audience to proceed with caution to the "anecdote" about Marei (*Pss*, 22:46).[27] A revelation by Dostoevsky's fellow Petrashevets, Fedor Lvov, that a lead investigator—the "serpent" Pavel Gagarin—"demanded from many a *profession de foi* about various political and social questions" in order to torment the imprisoned Petrashevtsy demonstrates the practical necessity of preventing full disclosure in such professions.[28] A bemused Ivan Karamazov also signals the form's potential for misreadings when he tells his naive younger brother: "I terribly love such *professions de foi* from such . . . novices" (*Pss*, 14:210).

The 1876 reinvention in "The Peasant Marei" follows soon after the 1875 edition of *House of the Dead* appears without the chapter "Comrades" about his fellow Catholic Polish inmates (*Pss*, 4:278). The similar presentation of Polish political prisoners' hatred of the "serfs [*khlopy*]" in *House of the Dead* and at the end of *Crime and Punishment* places Mirecki, with his limited utterance about the peasants, within the Dostoevskian tradition of Polish-peasant conflict (*Pss*, 6:418).[29] In naming Mirecki to this role, the author Dostoevsky acts disingenuously when failing to disclose that in the eyes of the abusive commandant of the prison, Major Krivtsov, Mirecki shared the status of a muzhik with the "brigands." Tokarzewski records how the Major translated Mirecki's lack of noble status into an excuse for flogging him in a threat to his comrade: "You are a peasant [*mužik, chłop*], one may beat you [*ciebie*]!"[30] The Major's threat indicates that an instinct for self-preservation likely contributed to Mirecki's attempt to distance himself from a category of prisoners that primarily bore the burden of corporal punishment in Omsk. The final sentence of the account, "No, these Poles endured then more than ours," is reminiscent of Goryanchikov's general observation, "it was very difficult for them, much more difficult than for us," that follows his description of the tensions among the "morally sick" and "irritable" Catholic Poles in the prison (*Pss*, 22:50; 4:210). Marei's blessing of the child Dostoevsky additionally separates the Orthodox Russians in the earlier narrative from the later appearance of Mirecki, particularly since the childhood events, as the author shapes them, coincide approximately with the 1830–31 Polish uprising.[31] Dostoevsky's labeling Mirecki as "The Unfortunate One!," a name by which Russians call criminals, further identifies the author of *Diary of a Writer* with the peasant and necessarily distances him from Mirecki, who has no "Mareis" and instead in Omsk enjoyed a Polish Christmas feast with the Catholics and non-Orthodox prisoners (*Pss*, 4:46; 22:49). Such an apposition, based on religious and ethnic differences, prepares the reader thematically for the chapter on the famous Kronenberg case that follows, in which the defendant is a father who once resided in Warsaw and who is implicated in child abuse, in contradistinction to the portrait of the child-loving Marei. Therefore, "The Peasant Marei," whose "double encoding" points to the generic confusion of

House of the Dead, may "transform his [Dostoevsky's] real experiences into a collective myth of the Russian people," but it sacrifices the personhood of Mirecki to achieve this effect.[32]

As Murav demonstrates in *Russia's Legal Fictions,* Dostoevsky views the trial as a cultural clash between Russian and European mores with the "youth and innocence of the girl . . . tied to a self-definition of Russia" and the "rage" and beatings of S. L. Kronenberg revealing him to be "more European than Russian."[33] When briefly presenting Kronenberg's biography, Dostoevsky carefully connects his sympathies to the French and Poles by recording, selectively, the defense presented by Spasovich: "Mr. Kronenberg, you see, finished his course of study; he studied first in Warsaw at the university, then in Brussels where he fell in love with the French, and then again in Warsaw where he finished his studies at the Main School in 1867 with a Master's Degree in Law" (*Pss,* 22:59). Kronenberg's studies at the Main School particularly emphasize his Western leanings, since the opening of the University of Warsaw as the Main School (Szkoła Główna) in 1862 was a concession granted by Alexander II to Polish nationalists. In 1869 the Main School was shut down and then replaced by a new University of Warsaw as part of the Russification process in the wake of the 1863 unrest. Kronenberg, who left Warsaw to fight on the side of his fellow Catholic nation in the Franco-Prussian War, lost track of his daughter when his mistress left her in Geneva. Dostoevsky criticizes Spasovich's appreciation for the liberal adoption laws in "the Kingdom of Poland," since the former holds them partially responsible for placing the abused child with Kronenberg (*Pss,* 22:59).

Dostoevsky's response is motivated by Spasovich's favorable comparison of the Polish legal system with its Russian counterpart on the issue of torture, which had a more narrow definition in the Congress Kingdom; Murav observes that "this point about the superiority of Polish over Russian law could hardly have struck a responsive chord in Spasovich's broader public audience beyond the courtroom."[34] Dostoevsky was familiar with Spasovich's work, which included a defense of the Nechaev conspirators, so he would have been familiar with the pro-Polish sympathies of this liberal lawyer, who came from a "mixed" marriage between a Uniate father and Catholic mother.[35] According to Spasovich, he was Orthodox because an official decree (1832) under Nicholas I forced such families to convert to Orthodoxy but his sisters still remained Catholic, attesting to the strength of his mother's religious devotion.[36] The biographies of Spasovich and Dostoevsky overlap starting in St. Petersburg of the 1840s, when they both attended school in the capital and were linked to charismatic conspirators—Jakób Gieysztor and Petrashevsky, respectively. Spasovich clarifies that, owing to the mutual exclusion of Polish and Russian student circles, his acquaintances in Saint Petersburg drew inspiration from Polish intellectuals portending a European cataclysm and the 1846 uprising in Galicia rather than from the French utopianists like Fourier and Saint-Simon. While Dostoevsky was arrested and sent to Omsk, Spasovich maintained his connections with Polish literati, established contact with Herzen's circle (particularly Konstantin Kavelin), worked on translating a work on Polish history from the Reformation period, and pursued his interest in early Polish law by investigating the history of marital law in various parts of the Congress Kingdom.[37] Spasovich's friendship with "my school and university comrade" the editor Ohryzko, in whose Polish journal he published an 1859 article criticizing the Slavophile movement, and with others implicated in the Polish unrest gave Russian officials sufficient cause to search his residence.[38] Spasovich's acquaintance with Turgenev, whose connection to Ohryzko's affairs was exposed in Nikolai Berg's 1873 publication *N. V. Berg's Notes About Polish Conspiracies and Uprisings* (*Zapiski N. V. Berga o pol'skikh zagovorakh i vozstaniiakh, 1831–1862*), also identifies the lawyer with the progressive and émigré circles that Dostoevsky found so damaging to Russian Orthodox identity.[39] Spasovich's criticism of Pobedonostsev's presentation of family law reveals the contrast between himself and Dostoevsky, since Spasovich, seeking to protect the rights of Polish Catholics, opposes Pobedonostsev's support for unified governance by church and state as a historic Byzantine tradition as well as his promotion of the Russian Orthodox Church's jurisdiction over marital law.[40] Dostoevsky's friendship with Pobedonostsev and his paraphrasing of the future procurator in the account of Spasovich's handling of the Kronenberg defense intimate that Dostoevsky was acquainted with the ideological debates between the two legal minds (*Pss*, 22:51, 347–48; 24:130). Pobedonostsev's presence in Tokarzewski's *By a Thorny Path* further attests to his reputation, among Poles, for promoting Orthodox autocracy, as the Polish exile observes: "It is said that Pobedonostsev became the strongest opposition of complete amnesty for Chernyshevsky."[41]

In a reversal of *House of the Dead*'s ethnic roles, Dostoevsky's narrating voice in the Kronenberg entry educates a Pole with a Warsaw-educated client about the Siberian practice of flogging prisoners. The reference to the floggings further links "The Peasant Marei" to the Kronenberg account, because *House of the Dead* suggests that the author's knowledge of flogging is derived partially from the experience of Mirecki, who tells Goryanchikov: "It burns like fire, as if the back is roasting in the hottest fire" (*Pss*, 4:154). Goryanchikov's juxtaposition of Mirecki's angry embarrassment over the flogging with the "unusual good-naturedness" of the Russian convicts, who "tell tales and laugh like children" over the beatings, attests to Dostoevsky's expression of nationalist essentialism through the motif of flogging (*Pss*, 4:146). Ironically, the pro-Polish liberal Spasovich, whose oratorical finesse encourages Dostoevsky to recall Alphonse de Lamartine and the revolutionaries of

1848, represents the tormentor rather than the flogging victim in the entry. In this manner, Dostoevsky effectively joins contemporary liberalism, French revolutionary history, and the torture of innocents in a legal narrative with allusions to Warsaw and Siberia. Dostoevsky underscores Spasovich's re-victimization of the seven-year-old by recalling his sexualized image of her ("a bright girl with a rosy face, laughing, crafty, and spoiled by secret vices") in a description that resembles the laughing five-year-old with the flushed and "insolent face of a Camélia for sale" from Svidrigailov's erotic dream (*Pss*, 22:57; 6:393). Such imagery recalls the "erotic excess" of the Marquis de Sade, to which Goryanchikov refers in a discussion of flogging (*Pss*, 4:154). Since Jackson demonstrates that Sade in Dostoevsky's understanding signifies both decadence and "the breakdown of society," Spasovich's defense of Kronenberg contributes to the social decline evident in *The Brothers Karamazov* with the disintegration of the family Karamazov.[42] This presentation of Polish, Catholic, and liberal influences on the crown's judicial system suggests that Dostoevsky concurs with Pobedonostsev regarding the jurisdiction of the ecclesiastical courts over marital law. His decision to highlight in the title of his final novel the familial relations among the Russian male protagonists necessarily marginalizes the rootless Poles of unknown origin, who make trouble for Mitya by exploiting a judicial system that identifies with them.

SIBERIAN TENSIONS AT MOKROE

Dostoevsky highlights the presence of Westernizing proclivities among intellectuals with Ivan's poem, in the church with the seminarian Rakitin, in the courts in the speech of the judge, prosecutor, and defense attorney, and in the army with Grushenka's Polish officer. The reader meets the officer as the scoundrel who seduced and abandoned a teenaged Grushenka, whose "family was honest and came somehow from a religious rank; she was the daughter of some provincial deacon or something of that sort" (*Pss*, 14:311). Her cousin-seminarian Mikhail Rakitin enhances Grushenka's ecclesiastic connection, which is further attested by her spiritual legend about the little onion that resurrects Alesha's faith. Grushenka interprets her officer's desire to meet her after five years as a chance at a "new life," but Rakitin cynically discloses to Alesha: "He is a Pole, this officer of hers . . . and he is not even an officer now; he served as a customs agent in Siberia, near the Chinese border—he must be some sort of brainless Polack. He lost his place, they say. Now he heard that Grushenka had acquired some capital and so he returned—there's the whole miracle" (*Pss*, 14:324). Rakitin's portrait of the officer is reinforced by the Poles' repeated attempts to obtain money from Mitya and Grushenka, even if it requires cheating with a marked deck. The officer's chivalry, Siberian connections, and frequent deception place him within the tradition of Dostoevsky's Polish exiles, who share in their nation's contamination by Jesuitism that renders them hostile toward the Russian Orthodox. His companion Pan Vrublevsky reflects similar "Jesuit" values and a familiar Siberian animosity toward the Russians at Mokroe so that both Polish gentlemen continue in the tradition of Dostoevsky's Catholic Poles, such as Aglaya Ivanovna's false count or Mirecki in "The Peasant Marei," who represents Dostoevsky's Pole from Omsk acting as a foil to Russian believers.

The presence of Dostoevsky's Siberian experience in the writer's final novel is evident from the central importance of the Ilinsky story for Mitya Karamazov's character development.[43] A sublieutenant of a Tobolsk line battalion, D. N. Ilinsky shared Dostoevsky's prison in Omsk, because he was falsely implicated in his father's death, so Ilinsky's story signifies the imprisonment of an innocent nobleman, as is revealed in passages in *House of the Dead* and in the notes to *The Brothers Karamazov* (*Pss*, 4:195; 17:5).[44] Although Dostoevsky's Siberian experience touches Mitya's story in several respects, this connection is particularly apparent in Mitya's encounter with the Poles at Mokroe. Pan Mussyalovich is connected to Siberia before his appearance at Mokroe when Grushenka speaks of a "message from Siberia" from "the officer," whose significance Fenya later clarifies for Mitya with the disclosure that the officer "is taking Agrafena Alexandrovna now in marriage, for which he returned from Siberia" (*Pss*, 14:330, 368). The description of Pan Mussyalovich's letter as "vague" yet "grandiloquent" and "filled with sentimentality" resembles the secretive but noble patriotic strivings of Aglaya's count (*Pss*, 14:330). The epistolary form heightens the Pole's connection to subversive activities, since the exchange of letters allowed exiles to communicate surreptitiously with contacts within the empire and abroad.[45] Furthermore, Victor Terras proposes when discussing this parody of Pushkin's "famous missive" to the exiled Decembrists, "In the Depths of Siberian Mines" ("Vo glubine sibirskikh rud," 1827), that this "side-thrust of Dostoevsky's may be aimed at a familiar target: the Polish patriots."[46]

Yet, Pan Mussyalovich is not merely a Polish nationalist but a former officer of the tsar's army who does not respect Russia's occupation of the Congress Kingdom. Many prominent 1863 insurgents share this conspiratorial history, including General Józef Hauke-Bosak and Jarosław Dąbrowski, and were linked to organized networks of officers extending from the St. Petersburg Engineering Academy to the garrisons in Warsaw. In his study of the Russian and Polish liberation movements in the tsar's army (1856–65), Dyakov detects a strong Catholic presence among the conspirators (57.5%), even though only 25 percent were born in the Kingdom of Poland.[47] Famous opponents of the tsar in St. Petersburg, particularly those with links to Land

and Will, helped radicalize army units struggling with serious dissension within the ranks.[48] The Herzen circle even directed their propaganda at the Russian army in Poland, as evidenced by Hugo's and Bakunin's appeals, Herzen's friendship with the famous martyred officer Andrei Potebnya, and the statement in *My Past and Thoughts* that "in the officer's world after the Crimean War the serious movement began; it was proven both by the executed Slivitsky and Arngoldt . . . and by the murdered, like Potebnya" (*Ss*, 11:304).[49] Therefore, Pan Mussyalovich's status as a Polish patriot who served as an officer in the tsar's army but lost his commission suggests some past history of intrigue. His Siberian residence, his refusal to drink a toast to Russia, and his demotion from an officer to an impoverished veterinarian further contribute to this conspiratorial image. Although he comes to Mokroe to claim Grushenka, Pan Mussyalovich there encounters Russian army officers Mitya and Maximov who defend Russia and deride Polish culture, thereby re-creating the Russo-Polish tensions familiar to Dostoevsky from the military fortress at Omsk.

Mitya's celebration of the abyss and his repetition of words from a Russian type admired by Dostoevsky in his 1880 Pushkin speech further accentuate his Russianness. In the speech, Dostoevsky insists upon the historic significance of the "majestic Russian image" of the Orthodox chronicler-monk Pimen that Pushkin found "in the Russian land" and "now placed before us forever in its indisputable, humble, and majestic spiritual beauty as a testimony of the powerful spirit of the nation's life" (*Pss*, 26:144). Mitya's brief utterance thereby unites him with this expression of the Russian spirit, which is also apparent from his attraction to risk and to "the abyss," like *The Gambler*'s Alexei, as "tomorrow I fly from the clouds, because tomorrow life will end and begin" (*Pss*, 14:97).[50] Russianness also informs the character of Grushenka, because her beauty "is often encountered in precisely a Russian woman" (*Pss*, 14:137). This image of a Russian woman constitutes an integral part of Dostoevsky's vision for Russia's future, as he depends on her for the "moral elevation of our society" and believes that "our Russian woman has proven herself so loftily, so radiantly, and so sacredly, it is impossible to doubt that lofty fate that certainly awaits her among us" (*Pss*, 26:33). The discussion at Mokroe in which Grushenka agrees to live with Mitya in Siberia ("Why Siberia? What of it, in Siberia if you want. It's all the same to me . . . we will work . . . in Siberia there is snow . . .") also unites her to a beloved symbol of Russian womanhood—the Decembrist wives—since it foreshadows her fate as a convict's companion, a fate that she shares with Sonya Marmeladova (*Pss*, 14: 399). Her compassionate care for the Poles with provisions of money and pirozhki advances this connection to the maternal imagery surrounding Sonya in Siberia.

The Russified Polish that Dostoevsky selectively includes in the scene, especially various titles, labels, and names that the Poles and Russians apply to one another, highlights the distinct cultural encoding of personal address that concerns several narrators of Dostoevsky's Siberian life. Martyanov notes this formality of military life in Siberia in the words of a director: "I call my wife Sashenka, my subordinate says Your Excellency to her, a lady and close friend addresses her as Alexandra Rodyonovna."[51] The variations of address in Tokarzewski show that the Polish Catholic political prisoners frequently used nicknames within their close circle of Polish friends (e.g., Szymek, Józik, and Olech) while with their Russian acquaintances from town the more formal combination of name and patronymic constituted the norm.[52] However, in exchanges with Russian officials, Tokarzewski often preserves the Russian in transliteration, for example, "Your Honor [*wasze błagorodie*]" or "Your Excellency [*prewoschoditielstwo*]" to impart the sense of Russian hierarchy with the address.[53] On the other hand, in *The Brothers Karamazov* Dostoevsky reverses this tendency when the formal Polish titles "Pan" and "Pani" are repeatedly used even among friends in the Mokroe scene—a practice that appears even more ridiculous when Mitya applies the illustrious title "My Lord [*iasnevel'mozhni*]"—a Cyrillic rendering of *Jaśnie wielmożny*—to the dentist Vrublevsky, perhaps because he has yet to learn Vrublevsky's name (*Pss*, 14:383).[54] When Mitya extends these Polonisms to Grushenka by calling her his "queen [*kruleva*]"—a hybrid of the Russian *koroleva* and Polish *królowa*—Grushenka exposes Dostoevsky's linguistic play with the exclamation: "What's this *kruleva*, a queen or something? It seems strange to me . . . the way you're all talking" (*Pss*, 14:377). This ethnic struggle manifested in forms of address continues what Tokarzewski identifies as an ongoing argument between the Poles and Dostoevsky:

> "Nobility . . . Gentleman . . . Nobility, I am a gentleman . . . We noblemen," he constantly repeated. Every time that he addressed us Poles saying "we noblemen," I always interrupted him.
>
> Excuse me sir, I think that in this jail there are no noblemen; there are only people deprived of their rights, there are convicts.[55]

However, in accordance with his discussions of the self-isolation of aristocratic Catholic Poles, Dostoevsky attributes the concern over proper personal address to his Poles at Mokroe.

The elitism of Pan Mussyalovich is demonstrated not only in his proud behavior (mocked by Grushenka) but by his comment, in reaction to an offensive anecdote related by Maximov: "Pani Agrippina, the pan saw peasants in the Polish territory and not noble panis" (*Pss*, 14:380). Since the Polish political prisoners in Goryanchikov's Omsk and in Raskolnikov's Siberia as a group expressed disdain for the peasantry, Pan Mussyalovich here reflects the bias of Dostoevsky's Siberian Poles, including that of his namesake, Jan Musiałowicz. Dostoevsky, knowing that Musiałowicz's status was defined as "illegitimate aristocracy," nevertheless provides Pan Mussyalovich with noble pretensions (mocked by the narrator in *The Brothers Karamazov*) that, in light of his namesake's parentage, must appear as mere posturing.[56] Even Goryanchikov's description of Musiałowicz and Korczyński suggests a lack of noble lineage, for these political prisoners from *House of the Dead* are "still very young men, sentenced to short terms, little educated but honest, simple, and straightforward" (*Pss*, 4:217). At the same time, Dostoevsky contributes to his officer's reputation for intrigue by assigning him the name of an insurgent who participated in the 1846 Krakow uprising and who arrived along with three other Polish political prisoners in Omsk in July 1850.[57] Still, the gap between the political backgrounds of Musiałowicz and Grushenka's "former one"—an officer-turned-veterinarian with aristocratic pretensions—renders Pan Mussyalovich exceedingly ridiculous. The narrator's synecdochal references to Pan Mussyalovich as "the pan with the pipe" or "the pan with the wig" articulate an exclusionary discourse independent from Mitya's and Grushenka's critical voices, since the narrator discloses that Pan Mussyalovich's little nose, aristocratic pencil mustache, and "somewhat flaccid" face "did not arouse in Mitya even the least questions for now" (*Pss*, 14:378).

In the naming of Pan Mussyalovich's Polish companion, Dostoevsky selects a surname associated with both socialists and Catholics and with anti-authoritarian uprisings in Siberia as well as the Congress Kingdom. Dostoevsky would have encountered the surname in Siberia, since Bogusławski records its physical presence on the grave of those linked to the Omsk conspiracy (led by the Uniate monk Jan Sierociński) who did not survive the execution of their flogging sentences. Indeed, Bogusławski cites his frequent visits to the grave, residence in Omsk, and access to knowledge about the affair as motivating factors in his decision to relate the details of this failed attempt by Polish exiles to return to Europe by fleeing Russia through the Kirghiz steppe, Bukhara, and Persia. Bogusławski's memory of the grave site (where "wormwood and wild asparagus grow"), the infamous nature of the conspiracy, and Dostoevsky's intellectual curiosity about the effects of corporal punishment suggest that the Russian writer knew of this connection to the Wróblewski name when he wrote *The Brothers Karamazov*.[58] In addition, the Polish surname Wróblewski was famous in the 1870s not only owing to Walery Wróblewski's aforementioned leading role in the defense of the Left Bank (during the Paris Commune) but also because of his alliance with the circle of Marx and Engels. Wróblewski had acquaintances among those who attended the 1867 meeting of the League of Peace and Freedom and had a Siberian connection through his uncle Eustachy Wróblewski, who was arrested while he was still a university student in 1849 in connection with the conspiratorial Cyril and Methodius Brotherhood.[59] Following his return from Siberian exile in 1856, Eustachy introduced to subversive circles in Vilnius his nephew Walery, who may have witnessed in 1848 the "execution" and departure of conspirators Bogusławski and Apolin Hofmeister to Siberia.[60] Also, Walery had established contacts with Polish secret societies linked to Zygmunt Sierakowski and Jarosław Dąbrowski in St. Petersburg, where he studied at the Institute of Forestry and Land Surveying in the 1850s.[61] Owing to the collaboration between Sierakowski and Chernyshevsky, as well as to the secret connections between the St. Petersburg Polish community (including the army) and well-known conspirators in the West (e.g., Herzen, Bakunin, and Mierosławski), Dostoevsky likely encountered Wróblewski's name in the Russian capital in the 1860s.

By providing these Siberian Poles, rooted in an illustrious Polish revolutionary history through their surnames, with the professions of dentistry and veterinary science, Dostoevsky plays with the stereotype of the long-suffering patriotic Polish exile by denying them the gravitas necessary for impressing their audience with their deep-rooted Polish nationalism. Mitya takes Pan Vrublevsky, a Siberian dentist, for Mussyalovich's bodyguard, since Grushenka's "former one" seems cowardly in his reluctance to confront Mitya without the strikingly tall Pan Vrublevsky (*Pss*, 14:386). Pan Vrublevsky's demeanor appears more caustic than Pan Mussyalovich's, since the former calls Mokroe a "Sodom" and Grushenka a "common cheat" (*Pss*, 14:388–89). His profession and elitism link him to the Underground Man's "civilized man" suffering from a toothache, who, unlike "a coarse peasant," takes pleasure in groaning and performs "a more nasty trill" out of spite for his audience (*Pss*, 5:107). Mitya and Grushenka mock the Poles' emulation of chivalry when they apply to the Poles labels reminiscent of the cock imagery in *The Gambler*, such as Mitya's calling the Poles capons for hoping to live off of Grushenka or an enraged, disillusioned Grushenka referring to them as "turkey cocks" (*Pss*, 14:387, 386). Then, in a parallel to Maria Timofeevna's invocation of fowl imagery during Stavrogin's unmasking, Grushenka discloses that her vision of the affected Mussyalovich as a "falcon" was delusional, because he is only a "drake" (*Pss*, 10:219; 14:388).[62] Grushenka recognizes the Polish aristocratic manners as a false charade, because this officer who seduced and abandoned her now greets her with reserved disdain, magnanimously offers to forgive her, and storms off "blazing with arrogance and indignation" (*Pss*, 14:389).

This connection to Polish chivalry is advanced by the novel's dialogue with Zagoskin's historical novel about the Time of Troubles, *Yury Miloslavsky.*

Świderska demonstrates that Zagoskin's Polish types and Mussyalovich share a common heritage in seventeenth-century Polish nobility known as "the Old Polish Sarmatian nobility."[63] Zagoskin's and Dostoevsky's similar use of toasts at a feast to expose patriotic loyalties (of Yury Miloslavsky, Grushenka, and Mussyalovich) during Russo-Polish conflict furthers the parallels between *Yury Miloslavsky* and Dostoevsky's final novel. In Zagoskin's novel, when the Russian Yury refuses to toast the victory over the Russian inhabitants of Smolensk (his native town) and the health of "His Highness the Most Sovereign King Zygmunt of Poland and Tsar of Russia," he enrages the Poles and Russians who empathize with them, including his host Timofei Kruchina.[64] Yury then requires the protection of the holy fool Mitya, when he proposes the alternative noncommittal toast: "Long live the lawful Russian tsar and may the enemies and traitors to the fatherland perish!"[65] Dostoevsky, on the contrary, begins with a toast to Poland, in which Grushenka does not participate, when Mitya attempts to appease the Poles by drinking "to your Poland, to the Polish territory [*pol'skii krai*]!" (*Pss*, 14:382). Then, when Mitya offers a second toast "For Russia, *hurray!*" Grushenka, Kalganov, and Maximov decide to join the drinking, but the Poles raise their glasses only for Vrublevsky's modified toast that reflects a common slogan of the 1863 rebels, who insisted that Poland return to pre-partition borders: "To Russia within her borders before 1772!" (*Pss*, 14:383).[66] Because Dostoevsky finds in his 1880–81 notebook that this Polish insistence on an "ethnographic Poland" is motivated by a desire "for dominion over (all) the Slavs in the name of Latindom and Western civilization," his toasts more definitively than Zagoskin's marginalize the Poles, while celebrating the diverse Russianness in the scene (*Pss*, 27:66). For both Zagoskin and Dostoevsky, these toasts represent oaths of loyalty that force their Russians to reconsider their collaborations with the (Catholic) Poles. As a result, Grushenka becomes so annoyed by clichés of Polish patriotism that she interrupts a proposal by her Polish suitor with a demand that he speak in Russian: "'In Russian, speak in Russian, so that there isn't a single word in Polish!' she screamed at him. 'You used to speak in Russian; have you already forgotten it in five years!'" (*Pss*, 14:387–88).

Even before this tumultuous encounter, Grushenka encourages Maximov's abuse of the Poles through his anecdotes that reinforce negative stereotypes, such as the account of the little Polish woman who danced the mazurka "with our uhlan" and "like a little kitten . . . a little white one" jumped onto his lap, with the approval of her parents, to seduce him into marriage (*Pss*, 14:380). This comparison of a Polish woman to a white kitten alludes to Pushkin's rewriting of the Lithuanian ballad by Mickiewicz of the "The Three Budryses" ("Trzech Budrysów," 1827) in the poem "Budrys and His Sons" ("Budrys i ego synov'ia," 1833) in which Pushkin uses the feline to describe a Polish maiden: "Merry like a kitten on a stove / And a blush like a rose, / but white as sour cream" (*PssP*: 3.1:311–12).[67] Maximov's reshaping of Pushkin and Mickiewicz to project a sexualized image of a desperate Polish "kitten" discloses his misogynistic hostility toward Polish women, a hostility shared by Dostoevsky, according to his comment on Polish Catholic women in the notes to *Demons* (*Pss*, 11:120).[68] Maximov's dancing anecdote resembles in some respects the Prince's "vaudeville" in *Uncle's Dream* about a dancing Lord Byron (really a Polish cook posing as a count) who breaks his leg performing the Krakoviana at the Congress of Vienna; Maximov's description of his marriage to a lame Polish woman reinforces this connection to the Siberian novella (*Pss*, 2:313). In both anecdotes, the storyteller's politicized gaze places Poles in the midst of their military occupiers, but the Prince's verse more closely reflects the orality and semi-literate world of Siberian prison theatricals.[69]

Texts that were politicized by Dostoevsky's exile experience, including Gogol's *Dead Souls* (*Mertvye dushi*, 1842) and Pushkin's "Egyptian Nights" ("Egipetskie nochi," 1835), are present in Maximov's self-identification with Maximov in Gogol's novel and Mitya's use of the title "tsaritsa" for Grushenka in the midst of their feast (*Pss*, 14:377).[70] By linking the thrashing in Gogol to his own beating for "Piron," Maximov participates in the bravado of the prison world that translates the Russian experience of torture into song, sayings ("The more birch bites—they say—the more the pangs"), and anecdotes (*Pss*, 4:154).[71] When the Poles try to counter with their own Warsaw anecdote about Pan Podvysotsky's honor, Mitya not only derides the concept of "Polish honor" but then labels Vrublevsky and Mussyalovich with the plural version of the name ("Hey you . . . Podvysotskys"), thereby attributing to Mitya Dostoevsky's tendency to strip Poles of their individual identities (*Pss*, 14:385, 398).[72] Kalganov's objection to the drunken insults that Mitya launches at the Poles ("If you would stop mocking Poland . . .") allows Dostoevsky the author to distance himself from charges of chauvinism even while his hero effectively defends himself: "Shut up, boy! If I called him a scoundrel, it does not mean that I called all of Poland a scoundrel" (*Pss*, 14:398). Yet, given the precedent of Yankel in *House of the Dead*, the enjoyment of the Ukrainian Gogol by the fool Maximov, who tells amusing anecdotes in the tradition of Pushkin's (not Mickiewicz's) Poland, effectively denigrates "all of Poland" without requiring any input from Vrublevsky or Mussyalovich.[73] Thus, Dostoevsky re-creates the abusive world of the Omsk fortress that forced his Polish comrades to seek isolation rather than accommodation with the other prisoners.

Mokroe, therefore, represents a way station where Poles returning from Siberia cross paths with the new prisoner Mitya on his way there. The experience of exile is apparent in the living conditions of the haughty yet impoverished Poles, who have no food, cigarettes, or firewood but, like the Underground Man's French revolutionaries, sentimentally embrace revolutionary rhetoric all the same (*Pss*, 5:126). Dostoevsky's notes to the novel present a more complex presentation of Polish Catholic culture with more significant speech acts for the Poles as well as the Polish surname Bem, whose presence advances the importance of Siberia for the scene and for Mitya's story. Bem's name appears in place of Mussyalovich in a draft of the interrogation scene, when Mitya is asked by the investigator: "Why did you bribe Bem with three thousand?" (*Pss*, 15:296, 299). Here, Mitya's answer links Bem to the entrepreneurial class (identified with opportunism), to which his fellow inmate and successful painter Karol Bem belonged:

> "Did you think that he would take it?"
>
> "Forgive me, he could take not only three thousand here but four or six thousand there. These Poles are masters at it. He would assemble lawyers—little Polacks and little Yids—and would gain Chermashnya for himself through litigation." (*Pss*, 15:297)

This passage on Polish and Jewish lawyers unites the Polish issues with those of judicial reform, but in the final version, the Siberian Poles align themselves with the Russian system of justice in a cruel "side-thrust" at Wróblewski and Musiałowicz, whose counterparts in the novel cooperate with the Russian authorities responsible for arresting, imprisoning, convicting, flogging, and exiling generations of their compatriots.

Dostoevsky's inclusion of these Siberian Poles with such conspiratorial and Catholic connections suggests that he tried to find a middle ground between alluding to their political intrigue without directly implicating them in specific plots against the tsar. His readership would recognize the familiar slogan with the reference to the first partition of Poland, as well as the exile history of the Poles that included Siberian epistles, expulsion from the army, and the impoverishment of those having been stripped of their rank. However, Dostoevsky could not overlook how such plots resulted in tragedy for the young Russian officers, so Pan Mussyalovich participates in Mitya's destruction by giving testimony about Mitya's offering him 3,000 rubles, which "was inserted into the report in the fullest detail," while "the fact about the cheating at cards was hardly mentioned; Nikolai Parfenovich was too thankful to them without any of that and did not want to bother them with trifles" (*Pss*, 14:453). In this manner, the Poles directly profit from the testimony, because they retain the 200 rubles that they won from Mitya and escape their own potential journey to Siberia with which the innkeeper threatens them: "Brute? And with which cards have you been playing? I gave you a deck, and you hid it! You were playing with marked cards! I can hide you away in Siberia for marked cards" (*Pss,* 14:389). In the account of the trial, the narrator continues to regard them with a hostile gaze as he selectively cites their testimony: "They loudly testified that, first, they 'served the crown' and that 'Pan Mitya' offered them three thousand in order to buy their honor and that they themselves saw more money in his hands" (*Pss,* 15:102). He then mocks Pan Mussyalovich while discrediting the judge and the prosecutor by recalling how "Pan Mussyalovich interjected an awful lot of Polish words into his sentences and, seeing that it only raised him in the esteem of the judge and prosecutor, finally let his spirit rise completely and began to speak entirely in Polish" (*Pss,* 15:102). Even though the defense attorney Fetyukovich discredits the Poles by revealing their card-sharping, the narrator's commentary still exposes the Western-leaning bias of the Russian judicial system.

THE WHEELS OF RUSSIAN JUSTICE

The purchase of honor and reference to loyalty to the crown links Fetyukovich to the history of these Polish personages, since he must defend himself against similar accusations. Fetyukovich's complaint that the prosecuting attorney made insinuations "dangerous to my person as a citizen and a loyal subject" echoes the Poles' opening statement that they "served the crown" (*Pss,* 15:175). Although Fetyukovich's repetition of the word "kara" for punishment in the closing paragraph of the argument may simply link the surname Karamazov with punishment, it also introduces a potential Polonism into the defense attorney's speech. In addition, Fetyukovich's reference to Jupiter links him to Rome and suggests his potential similarities to another defense lawyer with a Roman connection—Spasovich.[74] Although Fetyukovich's connections to Roman Catholicism remain tenuous, his allusion to the crucifixion in the depiction of Christ as "a crucified lover of humanity" (a rare image of Christ in Dostoevsky) is suggestive of the Roman church, particularly given the pointed mention of the "Catholic cross" in Zosima's cell (*Pss,* 14:37; 15:175).[75] In an argument with the atheist Belinsky, Dostoevsky presents visions of Christ emerging from the Orthodox tradition—"the radiant personhood of Christ himself"—and socialist movement—one of the "movers of humanity"—that do not correspond with the abovementioned crucifixion imagery (*Pss,* 21:10, 11). The image of the crucified Christ and the reference to "Sodom" at Mokroe unites Fetyukovich to Vrublevsky through a passage in Revelations, in which John foretells that the city in which the Lord was crucified will bear the symbolic name of Sodom or Egypt (11:8). Fetyukovich's Roman leanings are displayed in his image of Russian nationalism when he invokes "not a mad troika but a great Russian chariot" in an appeal to the Russian peasants to "leave other nations the letter of the law and punishment [*kara*]; we have the spirit and meaning, the saving and rebirth of the lost" (*Pss*, 15:173). Although Fetyukovich here employs both his knowledge of the West and rhetoric embracing Russian populism to ensure his client's release, in this contrast between (Roman) Western law and Russian mercy he also introduces an apposition that remains a focus of the novel during Mitya's trial.

Lednicki's comparison highlighting the similarities in Fetyukovich's legal defense and Dostoevsky's critique of Spasovich's Kronenberg case mentions Dostoevsky's anti-Polonist and anti-Catholic motivation for creating Fetyukovich.[76] Although Dostoevsky's writings clearly attribute Polish and French bourgeois tendencies to Spasovich, Dostoevsky does not directly group him with Catholics even in his notes, where Spasovich's name appears only in proximity to some observations about Catholicism, for example, "Really did Jesuitism not sell the body of Christ" (*Pss*, 24:150). Still, the comments on the swindling of Polish and Jewish lawyers, Jesuits selling Christ, and Poles selling their honor do not appreciably differ ethically or economically from Dostoevsky's notes on Spasovich's eloquent defense being inspired by the money he receives from his clients (*Pss*, 24:82, 149, 150). Furthermore, the salvation through exoneration that Fetyukovich attempts to procure for Mitya remains the moral equivalent of escape from punishment that may be equated with flight from Siberia—a Polish solution advanced by Porfiry and a Jesuit's response according to Mitya. The realization of this salvation requires equivocation, or what Rosenshield recognizes as Fetyukovich's "appropriation and usurpation of the Word," for which he resembles a "contemporary Grand Inquisitor" who exploits "psychology and artistic talent."[77]

Because Spasovich published both literary criticism and legal writings from trials of famous conspirators, Dostoevsky conducts both poetic and political arguments with him. Whereas Dostoevsky attributes expansiveness and potential for universality to the Russian character in his 1880 speech on Pushkin, Spasovich believes that tolerance and inclusion belong to the Polish tradition, as he indicates during the defense of the Nechaev co-conspirators: "I will cite for you, MM. Judges, for a historical comparison the words of one of the greatest sovereigns, Zygmunt I, who said when they offered to exterminate the Protestants for him: 'I want to be king over both the goats and the sheep.' And this was that same king who said that he could peacefully bunk down at the home of every one of his subjects" (*Pss*, 26:145).[78] Spasovich distances himself from the religious extremes of Polish and Russian society as he attacks Jesuits for promoting a "spirit of aristocratism" in Polish schools and the Slavophiles for their idealization of the "Old Muscovite past" and the "true faith" of Orthodoxy to the exclusion of Roman Catholicism and

Protestantism.[79] Dostoevsky, on the other hand, emphasizes the need for unity in Russia, defines Moscow and St. Petersburg as the *"two centers* of Russian life," and announces the era of the "Great Russian who is only now beginning to live" (*Pss*, 23:7). Invoking the image of Moscow the Third Rome, he wishes long life to Moscow, the capital of the Great Russians, in a manner that marginalizes many citizens of the empire. Therefore, the similar appeal to Russianness that betrays a Roman influence, that is, the transformation of Gogol's "mad troika" into "a great Russian chariot," appears ridiculous in the speech of the liberal Fetyukovich and may account for his failure to convince peasants (*muzhichki*) on the jury of his client's innocence (*Pss*, 15:173).

Moreover, Fetyukovich's troika imagery would seem derivative to the jury, since he borrowed it from the prosecutor Ippolit Kirillovich, who also betrays some Westernizing influences.[80] For example, the presence of Belinsky's "Letter to N. V. Gogol" is evident in the prosecutor's dismissal of the very Chichikovs and Nozdrevs as drivers for his troika whom Belinsky numbers among Gogol's critics.[81] This link brings the prosecutor into dialogue with Belinsky's image of Russian justice under Nicholas I as the caprice of feudal authority: "And your concept of national Russian justice and violence, whose ideal you found in the words of the stupid granny in Pushkin's story, that according to reason one must flog the just and the guilty."[82] Fedor Karamazov's maltreatment of his family and its retainers advances Belinsky's image of the abusive nobility, but Dostoevsky also believed that Alexander II's reforms addressed this concern to some extent, so the cruelest violence by authority figures has the Roman face of the Grand Inquisitor in his final novel. Therefore, Ippolit Kirillovich's confidence in the troika of the future, his "liberalism in the portrait of the Russian troika," reveals a literary analysis distinct from Dostoevsky's more conservative readings (*Pss*, 15:125). The liberalism of the troika becomes evident in the conclusion of Ippolit Kirillovich's speech, when in the name of "our fateful troika," he calls upon the jury to find Mitya guilty of parricide so that "the agitated voices of Europe" will not decide for themselves to halt "the insane galloping of our licentiousness with a view of saving themselves, enlightenment, and civilization" (*Pss*, 15:150). This characterization of Europe as civilized and enlightened further signals the presence of Belinsky's thought in Ippolit's speech, since Belinsky contends that "Russia sees her salvation not in mysticism, not in asceticism, not in pietism, but in the successes of civilization, enlightenment, and humanity."[83] Therefore, for all his enthusiastic civic desire to participate in the salvation of Russia through his summation, Ippolit Kirillovich still betrays a Roman preference for civilization in his resolution to the "accursed questions."

For the reader of classical French drama, however, Ippolit's presentation of civilized Europe objecting to a galloping Russian troika appears ironic owing to his namesake's tragic end in Jean Baptiste Racine's *Phèdre* (1677), which draws on Greek and Roman precedents.[84] Like the consumptive Ippolit Terentev in *The Idiot* and Racine's Hippolyte, Ippolit Kirillovich is destined to die soon after the presentation of "the chef d'oeuvre of his whole life, his swan song" (*Pss*, 15:123). Hippolyte suffers the most bestial end when, fated to be executed by the gods at the request of his father Thésée, his mad horses drag his chariot until he is mangled in the reins:

> L'essieu crie et se rompt. L'intrépide Hippolyte
> Voit voler en éclats tout son char fracassé;
> Dans les rênes lui-même il tombe embarrassé. . . .
> Ils s'arrêtent, non loin de ces tombeaux antiques
> Où des rois ses aïeux sont les froides reliques.
> J'y cours en soupirant, et sa garde me suit.
> De son généreux sang la trace nous conduit:
> Les rochers en sont teints; les ronces dégoûtantes
> Portent de ses cheveux les dépouilles sanglantes. (act 5, scene 6)[85]

Here, the innocent Hippolyte perishes on his chariot owing to the jealousy of his powerful father Thésée, who believes a rumor that Hippolyte forced himself on his stepmother Phèdre. Because of his relationship with Neptune, the Roman god of the sea, Thésée knows that he can commit the filicide by divine proxy. The murder of a son by a jealous father competing for the love of his wife Phèdre offers an inverse parallel to the intergenerational conflict related by Ippolit Kirillovich, who concludes that Mitya's parricide is motivated by the father-son competition for Grushenka. Ippolit Kirillovich imparts a royal French flair to Fedor's indifferent care of his sons by uttering the phrase famously attributed to Louis XV in anticipation of the French Revolution of 1789: "All the moral principles of the old man are: 'après moi le déluge'" (*Pss*, 15:126). Louis XV's historical quotation and the savage death of Hippolyte in his chariot reinforce the bond between European civilization and Catholic violence, since *Phèdre*'s tragedy unites both "Greek fatality" and "Jansenist grace" on the seventeenth-century French stage.[86]

Ippolit Kirillovich draws on another seventeenth-century tragedy— *Hamlet*—to account for his theory that a Karamazov lives always in the present moment, with repeated references to the title character's concern over the hereafter, or "What will be *there*?" (*Pss*, 15:124). Again disclosing a bias toward the West, Ippolit Kirillovich denies a Karamazov the ability to reflect "like Hamlet" and then juxtaposes the two types—Hamlets and Karamazovs: "No, gentlemen of the jury, they have their Hamlets, and so far we still have Karamazovs" (*Pss*, 15:145). Yet, the citation from Shakespeare's popular drama within the context of the lawyer's speech allows room for Dostoevsky's irony, since by the time that the reader arrives at Ippolit Kirillovich's oration, Mitya's connection to *Hamlet* has already been established. The presence of *Hamlet* in the novel begins in the first chapter when his mother, à la Ophelia and "under the echo of foreign tendencies," throws herself away on Fedor Karamazov (*Pss*, 14:8). Although Mitya does not resemble a typical brooding Russian Hamlet and instead self-identifies with the jester Yorick, his citation of Shakespeare indicates that he does contemplate the beyond: "This is me, perhaps; Yorick is me. Just now I am Yorick but a skull afterwards" (*Pss*, 14:367). Ivan's allusion to Polonius's ability to "twist words" attests to a Karamazov-Hamlet connection through poetic wordplay (*Pss*, 14:217). Thus, Shakespeare's Reformation tragedy exposes the simplicity of Ippolit Kirillovich's literary and psychological analysis, since he fails to comprehend the complexity of Mitya's "broad" personality, which can contemplate Schiller, Shakespeare, and even Raphael (in his appeal to "the ideal of the Madonna") while remaining quintessentially Russian in his pursuit of "the two extreme abysses" (*Pss*, 15:159; 14:100). Instead, Ippolit Kirillovich displays a Western preference for a more civilized Hamlet from Europe while discovering only the depraved sensualist Karamazovs in Russia.

Dostoevsky thereby expresses his irritation at the Western liberalism of the courts through the literary analysis, rhetoric, testimony, and gestures of multiple representatives of the modern judicial system. Since some of his fellow Petrashevtsy had been educated at the School of Jurisprudence, as he recognizes in *Diary of a Writer*, he had long understood the ability of those linked to the legal professions to enact social change (*Pss*, 25:25). His additional acknowledgment that some of the former Petrashevtsy succeeded as professors suggests that he was familiar with the legal career of Boris Utin, who was a professor of legislative history at St. Petersburg University. Utin and Spasovich quit the university together in 1861 in response to the government's handling of the student unrest, but Utin continued to work as a member of the St. Petersburg Chamber of Justice and published several articles on judicial and peasant reforms. In a discussion of the Kairova case, Dostoevsky criticizes his younger brother, the famous lawyer Evgeny Utin, who had spent time abroad in France and Italy, where he had observed legal elocution. Dostoevsky objected to his defense, which did not follow a factual progression of events but instead read like "a panegyric to crime" (*Pss*, 23:8). Because Evgeny Utin was celebrated for his carefully prepared defense speeches with passionate oratorical flourishes, he is another potential prototype for Fetyukovich. For Dostoevsky, the Utin family—Boris, Nikolai, and Evgeny—along with the Herzens and Turgenevs represented those (former) subversives seeking progressive reforms that would Westernize Russian society. Dostoevsky also comprehended that through the legal process those from Jewish heritage (Utins) and historically Catholic regions (Spasovich) were incrementally advancing the rights of the marginalized within the empire at the political expense of Orthodox Russians.

The year 1880 marked not only the year of the famous Pushkin celebration but also the fiftieth anniversary of the 1830 Polish uprising. While Dostoevsky read his speech in honor of Pushkin at the unveiling of his statue in Moscow that summer, socialists in Geneva prepared to celebrate the Polish contribution to the worldwide emancipation of the working classes. Turgenev, primarily residing in exile, returned to Russia to give his speech alongside Dostoevsky at the Pushkin celebration. Still, Turgenev's 1879 celebration of Józef Kraszewski's fifty-year literary career and Spasovich's praise for Turgenev at a dinner in the progressive novelist's honor provided Dostoevsky with two reminders of the close connection between the liberal reformers and the Polish Question.[87] Some members of this 1840s generation had suffered in exile for their youthful political indiscretions, but Turgenev, Spasovich, and Boris Utin were spared the harsh punishments that Nicholas I ordered for the most dedicated conspirators. Dostoevsky recognizes the distinction between his sentence and those of other Petrashevtsy—"those sent to Siberia, those punished in Russia with exile to fortresses in Russia and the Caucasus or sent into service in remote cities, or finally simply those having remained under surveillance" (*Pss*, 25:25). Under questioning in connection with the Petrashevsky affair, Utin had been able to persuade the commission that he was not engaged in any politically subversive activities.[88] Turgenev managed to avoid returning to Russia to be questioned about his links to Herzen, while Spasovich cooperated well with the authorities when he was under suspicion after the 1863 uprising and was refused only the right to teach and to publish his legal textbook.[89] This ability to explain one's actions in a way that exonerates oneself in the eyes of the political authorities translated well to a successful career in legal defense in the reformed judicial system. Dostoevsky's critical assessment of the elaborate justifications, equivocations, and theatrical performances of the new legal profession implicates liberal lawyers who empathized with Western and Roman Catholic movements in both Nicholas I's and Alexander II's Russia in deception worthy of a Jesuit.

Mitya, on the contrary, represents the Russian youth, who when faced with the trials of "transitional times [*vremena perekhodnye*]" remains one of the "most simple-hearted people with the purest of hearts" (*Pss*, 21:131). In a parallel to Ivan's conflict with his Inquisitor and impostor Devil, Mitya must grapple with his own period of personal reformation in the midst of Polish Catholic opportunists who disparage the "Sodom" that Mitya holds as one of his ideals. Mitya's strife is rooted in the seventeenth century through his citations of *Boris Godunov* and *Hamlet,* the latter of which played a role in Dostoevsky's encounter with the Petrashevsky Circle, as evidenced by

Boris Utin's marginalia in Friedrich Feuerbach's *The Religion of the Future* (*Die Religion der Zukunft*): "Religion of the future. Man or Christ? To be or not to be?"[90] Mitya's connection to Othello's jealousy and a namesake, the young lover Demetrius, in *Midsummer Night's Dream* (in which Theseus and Hippolyta are to be wed!) enhance his Shakespearean dimension. During his time of transition, Mitya indulges his violent impulses arising from jealousy but the purity of his heart, embodied in the dream of "the wee'un," remains unnoticed by investigators. Mitya's sincerity is displayed in the three consecutive chapters beginning with the phrase "Confession of a Burning Heart" ("Ispoved' goriachego serdtsa") in which he bares his soul to Alesha. Confessions to the investigating officers ("the old man and his blood! . . . I understand") and to the court ("But of the death of the old man, my enemy and father—I am not guilty") additionally attest to his artless nature (*Pss*, 14:400; 15:94). Mitya wishes to establish his innocence rather than adopt Ivan's jesuitical plan of escape, but when faced with exile in Siberia Mitya does not rule out the romantic vision of living among the Mohicans in the American West, a vision with which Dostoevsky identifies, since he views himself and Pobedonostsev as "the last Mohicans" (*Pss*, 30.1:122).

Mitya's conviction that he will be with God underground in solidarity with those hundreds in chains forms the genesis of a moral idea upon which a civic nationality may be constructed. For Dostoevsky, the moral idea, grounded in religious belief, forms a nation as the Mosaic law led to a Jewish nation and "Muslim nationalities" followed the appearance of the Koran (*Pss*, 26:165). Despite the masses of Catholic Poles exiled to Siberia in the wake of the 1863 uprising, Mitya seems to expect to be underground with his fellow Russians, since he describes a common vision of God and then emphasizes the national particularity of virtue by affirming that "I have one virtue and a Chinese man has another" (*Pss*, 15:32). This suggests that Dostoevsky imagines the concept of brotherhood, underscored in the title of the novel with the word "Brothers," in an exclusionary manner, just as his Polish Catholic fellow inmates employed the term *towarzystwo*. He appears to leave behind Catholic cultures when planning for "our civilizing mission in Asia": "In Europe we were spongers and slaves, but in Asia we will appear as masters. In Europe we were Tatars, but in Asia we will be Europeans" (*Pss*, 27:36–37). Thus, Mitya can participate in an Asian renaissance that will allow Russia to shed its image among European civilizations as a barbaric and heretical nation.

Conclusion

> "The play's the thing
> Wherein I'll catch the conscience of the King."
> —William Shakespeare, *Hamlet*

DOSTOEVSKY SHARED with former political prisoners throughout nineteenth-century Europe the difficulties of reestablishing his career and personal reputation after imprisonment and exile. His reading of literature about prison (Dumas's *Le Comte de Monte-Cristo* or Dickens's *The Posthumous Papers of the Pickwick Club*), his own encounters with Polish and Russian subversives, and his extensive familiarity with Russian émigré writings exposed Dostoevsky to the transnational experience of political exile. Yet, to distinguish himself from this crowd of conspirators and to distance himself from his progressive past, he asserted a strong sense of self to break the automatic perception of him as a Petrashevets, a lesser scion of the famous Decembrists. Thus identified in the annals of Russian revolutionary history with Peter the Great's legacy through *Petra*shevsky, Dostoevsky realized in Siberia that he had been labeled a Westernizer by those opposed to tsarist autocracy. Herzen's 1851 study *Du développement des idées révolutionnaires en Russie,* naming Dostoevsky among those Petrashevtsy whose death sentences were commuted, furthered the impression that the novelist belonged to a contemporary revolutionary movement uniting Russia to Europe, particularly through the cause of Polish liberation. Herzen's published letter to Jules Michelet, "Le peuple russe et le socialisme" (1851), describes shared Polish and Russian animus for the tsar with references to the Petrashevtsy, who conspired "à deux pas du Palais d'hiver," and to Bakunin, the victim of an international criminal conspiracy of governments that transferred him from Saxony through Habsburg Austria into the hands of Nicholas I (*Ss,* 7:304, 305).[1] Yet, Polish and Russian remembrances from his Siberian period depict Dostoevsky's resistance to this progressive label, as he challenged attempts to Polonize him and maintained a degree of separation from his fellow Petrashevtsy.[2]

Having been reduced to a political type himself, Dostoevsky does not hesitate to discuss his opponents in terms of similar types, for example, "Hamletiks," "Utins," and "Nechaevs." At the same time, he identifies increasingly in his writings with native literary types such as the "Russian chronicler in *Boris Godunov*" who is indicative "of the independent monks-chroniclers" who sought "truth" rather than courtly privileges under the Muscovite tsars (*Pss*, 19:9). Dostoevsky admires such an "invented" personage, because he believes in Pimen's potential to embody a popular national spirit through which "poetic truth" may be revealed (*Pss*, 19:9). Since Dostoevsky similarly numbers Achilles (whose helmet makes its way into *Crime and Punishment*) among the "invented" Greek types in the "national ancient Greek poem," *The Iliad,* he does not appropriate for Russia alone the expression of a collective national spirit through prominent literary works (*Pss*, 19:9). However, as his Polish fellow prisoners perceived, Dostoevsky imparts to Russia the ability to integrate foreign literary manifestations of nationhood into a Russian consciousness. Hence, a saint from Rome during the patristic era, Saint Alexis (Alexei, the Man of God), whose popular vita is extant in such languages as Greek, Latin, Old French, and Russian, can nevertheless represent "the ideal of the people [*narod*]" and inspire them with "hope" (*Pss*, 27:55; 24:285).[3] In Pushkin, Dostoevsky can discern the presence of the "spirit of the Koran" and "the soul of Northern Protestantism" so that Pushkin in his Russianness reflects a world soul rather than a strictly Russian worldview (*Pss*, 26:146). Still, that which Dostoevsky praises as an attribute of Russian expansiveness those opposed to its imperialism may understand as Russian expansionism under the guise of literary analysis.

THE RUSSIAN IDEA IN A POST-FEUDAL AGE

Since his nationalism is motivated by the Russian *idea,* Dostoevsky does not recognize the adverse political consequences of such Russocentrism, from which subjected peoples in the eastern and western edges of the empire had already suffered owing to Russification policies enforced by Nicholas I and Alexander II with the cooperation of the Russian Orthodox Church.[4] This suggests that, in a certain respect, Dostoevsky agrees with Raskolnikov that great men with foundational ideas drive history, but Dostoevsky discounts Napoleon's idea, the Jesuits' "one idea," as well as the coercive "Roman idea" (*Pss*, 24:311; 25:162; 21:184). Apposed to these ideas of Western and Catholic origin is the Russian idea, which Dostoevsky presents at a conceptual level that allows him to deceptively avoid scrutinizing from multiple perspectives the conflict arising from competing national ideas on the same soil. He advances Russian exceptionalism while insisting that he does not wish to fortify the Russian national character at the expense of Europe. Also, by demanding substantial religious (Orthodox, Catholic, Protestant) and historical (Byzantine, Roman, medieval) significance of nations capable of bearing such powerful ideas, he often views the world's past as a history of empires. In his Russocentrism, he reduces Poland to a papal vassalage and often over-looks the importance of the celebrated British Empire, a major Protestant presence on the European, African, North American, and Asian continents that seriously threatened Russia's immediate strategic interests in the East. By contrast, Granovsky's translation of W. F. Edwards's letter to the French historian Amédée Thierry employs the modern language of cultural assimila-tion in an outline of ethnic and racial categories according to physical char-acteristics. In a more holistic examination of the history of geopolitics, the inhabitants of conquered nations are portrayed as having to choose between assimilation to the dominant culture or flight from their native land in order to maintain desired independence.[5]

For Dostoevsky, since nationhood is rooted in soil, flight from one's native land can result in a dilution of ethnicity. Consequently, Russian aristocrats living abroad have voluntarily severed their connections to the Russian people and have become increasingly removed from the concerns of their fellow countrymen residing within the borders of the empire. The St. Petersburg Westernizer and the "Jesuit Gagarin" so idolize the West that they abandon Russia by converting to Catholicism or by promoting a narrow Russian Europeanism that contributes to Russia's nineteenth-century foreign policy disasters, including the war with Napoleon that ultimately benefited Europe, and Alexander's freeing the Poles who revolted in 1863 (*Pss,* 24:204, 208; 21:268–69). In this respect, in an age of social Darwinism, Dostoevsky avoids a reliance on physiognomy in his discussions of ethnicity and national character. Instead, his fictional characters shape their own ethnicities as they employ French, Polish, or Russian, according to their own preferences. Through their choices in dress, behavior, and political loyalties, they par-ticipate in the formation of national identity, which can accommodate other traditions over the course of time. At the same time, he recognizes that resis-tance to assimilation by certain religious groups—clericals and Jews—each of which sought to form "status in statu"—threatens the existence of the Russian land and the well-being of its peasantry (*Pss,* 21:201; 23:42).

The determined separateness that he regularly attributes to the Poles, particularly in their conflicts with Russians, indicates that this ethnic group signifies for him a potentially lethal challenge to his concept of the all-encompassing Russian spirit, since the Poles bring a Western civilizing force defined by a Roman/Latin tradition. Although at the end of his life he does not believe that these Poles have enough immediate political strength to realize their goal of independence, he nevertheless fears the power "of this Polish idea" of dominion over the Slavs in the name of the Latin world (*Pss,* 27:66). Spasovich's 1872 publication, "The Politics of Suicide" ("Polityka samobójstwa"), demonstrates the nature of this threat, since he understands accommodation with Russia as a way of preserving Polishness for the future: "The reconstruction of Poland will not occur either tomorrow or in ten years, and so it is necessary to resign oneself to patience, legality, and modest, silent, organized activity."[6] Spasovich's friend Ohryzko had advocated a similar model (borrowed by Nechaev), even encouraging conspirators to reach the upper levels of state service, so that a network could strike at officialdom from within simultaneously with a revolutionary uprising in the streets.[7] Whereas Spasovich likens the Poles practicing such disciplined politics to Christians patiently awaiting the arrival of Christ, Dostoevsky characterizes this activity on the part of Poles as duplicitous and jesuitical in his depictions of Mirecki and the Poles of "Old Poland."

Dostoevsky's understanding of Germany's Protestant spirit, the French center of Christendom, and the Polish Latinizing idea suggests that his weltanschauung remains Christocentric as he fears the growing strength of atheist and Jewish movements along with the development of international socialism. In his 1880–81 notebook Dostoevsky reveals his concerns over Catholics and Poles joining with the Jews as well as Catholic France yielding to socialism: "Jewry as a fact of the whole world. Catholicism, yielding to Jewry. *Reconciliation with the Poles.* France, finally destroying itself in Catholicism, or if not Catholicism, they immediately must accept socialism" (*Pss*, 27:48).[8] Prince Myshkin's infamous discussion of Catholicism's descent into atheism or violent socialism, Petr Verkhovensky's intent to cooperate with the pope in forming his *egalitarian* society, and the Inquisitor's ability to burn Christians in good conscience attest to Dostoevsky's conviction that Catholicism remains a potent political force in nineteenth-century Europe. Although he observed disparate dissident groups gathering at the league's conference in Geneva—socialists and anarchists, Catholics and Jews, pacifists and insurrectionists—the decree of papal infallibility and its Jesuit supporters encouraged Dostoevsky to attribute contemporary European violence to a resurgence in Catholic devotion (in spite of the Prussian victory over France), especially since the decree roughly coincided with a crisis in the Eastern church resulting from the divisive controversy over phyletism.

The Jesuits remain a focus of his concern, because he views them as a *status in statu* loyal only to the pope and therefore morally empowered to act as a supranational order of priests, whose religious vocation allows them to act extralegally as Raskolnikov envisions for his extraordinary man. A playful passage (recalling Ivan Karamazov's ethics) in his 1880–81 notebook indicates that even in the final year of his life the Order continues to fascinate him:

O, the Jesuit is the thing, and everything else is rot. The Jesuit is an important man.

All is permitted [*pozvoleno*] and all is hidden—there it is. (*Pss*, 27:77)[9]

Even though the Society of Jesus had been suppressed in 1773, Dostoevsky associates the Jesuits' moral reasoning with the despotism of the French Terror: "The Jesuits—war. That is be my brother or be a brother to everyone or off with his head *(ou la mort)*" *(Pss,* 24:119). His accusations against contemporary Jesuit revolutionaries reveal that, for Dostoevsky, this Order is not content with lurking in the shadows like Sue's Rodin or in the confessional of Tolstoy's Hélène but actively encourages subversive movements in Europe and Russia. For this reason, Dostoevsky senses Jesuitism behind the Polish liberation movement and modern socialist movements, whether Catholic or atheist in origin, because: "A Jesuit lies, convinced that lying is useful for a good goal" *(Pss,* 27:85). As a result, Dostoevsky implicates the Jesuits directly in the European bloodshed of the eighteenth and nineteenth centuries, when the Terror's guillotine replaced the Inquisition's auto-da-fé as an international symbol of "Roman" torture. Consequently, for Dostoevsky, the Jesuits' vision of a Catholic brotherhood signifies fraternal union by coercion, which necessarily precludes any spiritual union between the Polish Catholic aristocracy and Orthodox Russia, despite Herzen's and Bakunin's testimony to the contrary.

Instead, Dostoevsky relies on the Russian idea to gather the Slavic nations in reconciliation rather than through coercion, even though he recognizes that such Slavophilism has "an egotistical side" for it proclaims "Russians will save the world" *(Pss,* 24:206). Dostoevsky accepts this egoism, because he prefers an Orthodoxy that "preserves all personalities" in its union to a Catholicism, "developed by the Jesuits," that consumes the faithful: "The Orthodox Christ is better than that which was agreed to by the Inquisition in Spain" *(Pss,* 24:222, 184, 205). For the ultimate success of his Russian idea, he turns to the endorsement of history and at times depends upon a providential reading of world history, as is evident from his citation relating the prophecy that Moscow is the Third Rome and "a fourth Rome there will not be" *(Pss,* 23:7). Nevertheless, his historiography still betrays a belief in the power of human agency, since he culls Russia's past for crisis moments that are celebrated for individual displays of the national spirit. He then places their activities within the geopolitical context of his nation's current requirements so that even the loss of the Crimean War serves the national interest, because a weakened Russia posed no threat to a Europe entertaining the idea of "a crusade" against Russia in 1863 *(Pss,* 22:121). In this respect, he engages in what Hayden White describes as "Organicist" historical writing, which is "governed by the desire to see individual entities as components of processes which aggregate into wholes that are greater than, or qualitatively different from, the sum of their parts."[10] The teleological nature of his portrayal of the Russian idea and his focus on national development as an end goal to history place him within the tradition of nineteenth-century romantic historiography. Like Hegel, Dostoevsky identifies the West with the epic failure of great men—Alexander the Great, Julius Caesar, and Napoleon Bonaparte—who draw their nations into their tragedies.[11] White finds that in Hegel such tragic heroes may transform nations "who are at once beneficiaries and captives of the spiritual forms in which their exertions against the world and for the world manifest themselves."[12]

In differentiating between Russian and Western historical processes, Dostoevsky finds that the Russian nation receives the benefits from its native sons (Minin, Foma Danilov, and Pushkin) but suffers from captivity by foreign spiritual forms (Polish Catholics, Jesuits, and Napoleons). The liberation of the serfs encourages Dostoevsky to join with the progressives in heralding an end to the feudal age, but he fears the feudal vestiges of the Westernizing atheist *barin* and the Catholic Polish aristocrat who play at revolution financed by the Russian land and its people. His travels to Napoleon III's France reveal his disdain for the emerging dominance of the Catholic bourgeoisie, which, to Dostoevsky's dismay, was making inroads into Russia owing to modernizations such as the reform of the legal system and the promotion of industry within the empire. All the same, he believed that the bourgeoisie in Russia would be counterbalanced by the force of its Orthodox peasantry, since the latter was freed with land and would therefore escape the extreme poverty that plagued the industrial working classes of Europe and motivated the international socialist and workers' movements (*Pss*, 24:87, 184). Furthermore, to forestall the tragedy of post-feudal conflict portended by Marx, Dostoevsky recommends that Russia isolate itself from Catholic, Jewish, and Westernizing trends by controlling eastward migration, especially since Orthodoxy represents the means by which the Russian idea will be disseminated to the peasantry (*Pss*, 24:192–93).

ARTISTIC GENIUS VS. THE MARKETPLACE OF IDEAS

At the same time, Dostoevsky understands the movement of ideas, whose pace was accelerated by the advent of the railroad, which promotes the mobility of the petty bourgeoisie whose expertise was required by the demands of industry. His troublemakers with Catholic connections (Petr Verkhovensky, Pavel Smerdyakov, and Pan Mussyalovich) frequently hail from a similarly displaced stratum of Russian society, but they are decisively unliterary when compared to the educated Russians (Stavrogin, Ivan, and Mitya) in their novels. Since the displaced have few ties to the land, they can follow Petr's example and flee by railroad in the wake of destruction, commit a murder in Smerdyakov's fashion, or simply disappear after causing irreparable harm like Pan Mussyalovich. Marx identifies such representatives of a growing bourgeoisie with a "world literature [*Weltliteratur*]" in *The Manifesto of the Communist Party* (*Manifest der Kommunistischen Partei*, 1848): "The intellectual production of an individual nation becomes common property. The national one-sidedness and narrowness become more and more impossible, and from the many national and local literatures is formed a world literature [*Weltliteratur*]."[13] For Marx, Raphael's success is determined not by national character or even his own talent but "entirely on demand, which in turn depends on the division of labor and human cultural conditions having emerged from it."[14] Dostoevsky, who in his youth admires Raphael ("the gods were created under his hand") alongside Pushkin and Gogol, retains a belief in artistic "genius" throughout his lifetime and in his "Explanatory Word" on the Pushkin speech recognizes it in Shakespeare, Cervantes, Schiller, and Pushkin (*Pss*, 28.1:107; 26:130–31). This genius is linked not only to the author's talent in forming types reflecting the "national character" but also to the ability of a writer to embody the spirit of his time in a way that speaks to the ages, so Dostoevsky does not limit such genius to a particular nationality or religious creed (*Pss*, 26:131).

Apollon Grigorev in a discussion of literature of the 1830s outlines a transcultural trend, that is, "the parallelism of events in various spheres of world life—the strange, mysterious coincidence of the creation of Don Quixote and Hamlet" that attests to "the solidarity of well-known ideas, their worldwide continuous connection."[15] Mochalov's Hamlet and Marius Petipa's ballet *Don Quixote* provided the Reformations with a living presence on the nineteenth-century Russian stage. Shakespeare's and Cervantes's creations, linked to St. Bartholomew's night by Turgenev, are part of the fascination of Grigorev's generation with the Middle Ages, chivalry, and "the mysteries from the world beyond the grave" as a protest against the Age of Reason that engendered the revolution of Robespierre and Rousseau (*Pss*, 24:133).[16] Shakespeare, the gothic novels of Ann Radcliffe, Scott's historical novels, and Schiller's *The Robbers* (*Die Räuber*)—all admired by Dostoevsky—participate in this international medieval spirit of the age.[17] Grigorev's discussion of this literary international solidarity in medievalism accounts for the chivalric imagery common to Marx, Herzen, Dostoevsky, and their contemporaries. For Dostoevsky, this age witnesses "the broadening of human thought (the discovery of America, the Reformation, and astronomical discoveries, etc . . .)" when many Catholic historical figures, for example, Copernicus, Galileo, and Cervantes, contributed to the advancement of civilization during an age of Christian faith, which was to reconcile the "despair" that he sensed in Shakespeare's Hamlet (*Pss*, 21:268; 24:162). For this reason, Don Quixote, who steadily preserves his "faith in something eternal" despite repeated challenges to his chivalric ideal, remains a positive literary type for Dostoevsky even while his contemporaries value Cervantes's satire for its "ideal conceptions of a past epoch, and of a class which has lost its functions."[18]

For example, Marx identifies Don Quixote with feudal landowners, the adversary of capitalists with movable property, but recounts how the proponent of movable property "muffles his reminiscences, poetry, and visions by a historical and sarcastic enumeration of the baseness, cruelty, degradation, prostitution, infamy, anarchy, and rebellion, of which Romantic castles were the workshops."[19] Turgenev and Dostoevsky, not identifying with such proponents of movable property, appreciate in Don Quixote his steadfast dedication, requiring heroic self-sacrifice, to a fantastical truth that exists independent of his reason. For Dostoevsky, he lives in real time as a dreamer seeking an idea, even as a jaded Herzen applies the image of the errant knight to his idealistic friends and Marx analyzes political contemporaries with the Don Quixote–Sancho Panza dynamic.[20] While Dostoevsky recognizes the tragedy that emerges from Don Quixote's encounter with the chivalric tradition, which inspires the sublime but does not impart the genius necessary to translate it into action, the author nevertheless maintains the universal value of Cervantes's novel for present and future generations, since he claims: "Man will not forget to take with him this *saddest* of books to God's last judgment" (*Pss,* 26:25). His analysis of the novel, therefore, underscores the transcendent nature of literary genius, even when it emerges from a noble image of chivalry, which not only provided a Catholic cultural model for Dostoevsky's nineteenth-century Poles and Westernized Russians but also gave rise to the Society of Jesus, whose founder Saint Ignatius is likened in his origins to "Don Quichotte, le célèbre chevalier de la Manche!" by Zaccone.[21] Thus, Dostoevsky's identification with a quixotic dedication to an absurd ideal, even one inspired by the Catholic knight errant, dominates his reading of Cervantes's satire of the chivalric romance.

Part of Shakespeare's attraction for Dostoevsky, likewise, lies in his ability to embody the spirit of his Christian age: "Shakespeare is still during Christ. Then it was permitted. Now it is not permitted and once again came forward. Hamlet. Don Quixote. The accursed questions" (*Pss,* 24:167). Dostoevsky proposes a despairing Shakespeare, based on his seventeenth-century tragedies, in which Desdemona's beauty brings about her own death, Othello's "trusting" nature allows *honest* Iago to manipulate him into murdering Desdemona, and Hamlet, haunted by suicidal thoughts, remains earthbound out of fear of "what will be there . . ." (*Pss,* 24:160; 14:344; 22:6). Dostoevsky's identification of Othello as English rather than Venetian emphasizes the significance of the Bard's English nationality, in agreement with Grigorev's discussion of the author in an 1862 issue of *Time:* "Shakespeare, Byron, Dickens and Thackeray, Goethe, Schiller, Hoffmann, Heine, Dante and Mickiewicz, Hugo and Sand—are worthy of common human interest but together with this they are in the highest degree Englishmen, Germans, Italians, Poles, and Frenchmen."[22] For Dostoevsky genius is far more exclusive than the solidarity of ideas proposed by Grigorev, and even Shakespeare's genius is limited further by his Englishness, unlike Pushkin's universal genius. Therefore, in a certain respect, Dostoevsky's 1880 discussion of this Russian genius represents the maturation of his early juxtaposition "of the Slavic genius with European civilization" that he mentions in his 1863–64 notebook as a corollary to a future conflict between Russian Orthodoxy and Catholicism (*Pss*, 20:170).

Corneille, who ranks as "almost" Shakespeare "for his titanic characters and spirit of Romanticism," and Racine, who "was not a genius," both remain significant for their historic century: "Corneille and Racine would respond with their influence at such strange and decisive moments for the entire nation's historical life that it would seem, and was at first, inconceivable to make such old fools' caps as Corneille and Racine in such epochs" (*Pss*, 28.1:70; 18:78). Since it was appropriate for France's national development in the seventeenth century, Dostoevsky thus expresses an appreciation for French classicism, outdated in a romantic age that favored Shakespeare and certainly unpopular with the utilitarians whom he was addressing.[23] The monumental historicism of *Le Cid* is evident in the final scene when Don Fernand speaks both to the upheaval of the sixteenth century and Raskolnikov's Napoleonic thesis by maintaining that "le temps assez souvent a rendu légitime / Ce qui semblait d'abord ne se pouvoir sans crime" (act 5, scene 7).[24] In his maturity, Dostoevsky recalls the public quarrel over *Le Cid,* when Cardinal Richelieu demanded that the French Academy critique Corneille's popular play, by citing from Nicolas Boileau-Despréaux's "Satire IX" (1667):

> En vain contre le Cid un ministre se ligue,
> Tout Paris pour Chimène a les yeux de Rodrigue:
> L'Académie en corps a beau le censurer,
> Le public révolté s'obstine à l'admirer.[25]

The young Dostoevsky likewise values the political relevance of the French stage when praising Emperor Augustus's forgiveness for Cinna's treason in *Cinna ou la Clémence d'Auguste* (1640), which Corneille wrote in response to Cardinal Richelieu's ruthless suppression of a popular protest against burdensome taxation in Rouen.[26] The citation of Boileau's satirical verse on Cardinal Richelieu's censorship, the admiration of Corneille's surreptitious commentary on the cardinal, and the national historical significance imparted to Corneille and Racine suggest that Dostoevsky celebrated the political satire of these Catholic dramatists, whose classical plays contained veiled critiques of the French political and ecclesiastical hierarchies.[27]

The consequences of the Reformations reverberated throughout seventeenth-century Europe, which saw the appearance of pretenders, schismatics, and rebels in Russia, the Thirty Years War ravaging central Europe, the (attempted) assassination of English and French kings, and the rise of French Catholic authoritarianism under Cardinals Richelieu and Mazarin. The century remains important for Dostoevsky's literary development owing to French theater (Molière, Racine, Corneille, and Boileau), French philosophy (René Descartes and Pascal), Cervantes's satirical novel, and Shakespeare's innovative plays that address controversial spiritual concepts (predestination, divine grace, and human will) central to Reformation conflict. Dostoevsky appreciates this spiritual dimension to the century's literature in his discussion of Hamlet on the afterlife, Shakespeare's depiction of the Moor Othello, Racine's Greek plays portraying human-divine encounters, and the resolution of love and duty in medieval Spain in Corneille's *Le Cid*. The literary (especially theatrical) response to ecclesiastical and monarchical authorities in England, Spain, and France yielded fecund creations that caught the imagination of European literati for centuries, as Dostoevsky realizes in his discussion of European genius and in his identification of Corneille as the worthy predecessor of the popular eighteenth-century satirist Voltaire, whom he admires for "a passionate faith" (*Pss*, 5:89; 22:6–7).

In Dostoevsky's estimation, the seventeenth century was a time of discovery as well as a troubled time for Western Christendom, and he finds that the Roman church's demand for obedience when faced with the challenge of scientific discoveries encouraged the Encyclopedists to rebel against the Catholic Church and Christ in the name of science (*Pss*, 24:164). The presence of great historical personages like Galileo, Columbus, and Copernicus in *Demons* and *The Adolescent* as well as the references to seventeenth-century literature in his writings allow Western Catholic culture to enter his poetics. For example, Dostoevsky notes the false prudery (in the tradition of his pious yet lecherous priests) and roguish deception (shared by Dostoevsky's "Polacks") displayed by the title character of Molière's *Tartuffe, ou l'imposteur* (1667), who serves as a likely model for his mischievous hero Foma Opiskin, in the Siberian novella *The Village of Stepanchikovo and Its Inhabitants* (*Selo Stepanchikovo i ego obitateli*, 1859; *Pss*, 19:104, 2:276).[28] Stepan Trofimovich uses Pascal's anticlerical comment to express his thoughts, since "I am all the same no Pascal, *et puis* [and besides] . . . second, we Russians are unable to say anything in our own language" (*Pss*, 10:51). At Mokroe, Dostoevsky ridicules the merging of Russian and French cultures with Maximov's humorous citation of a verse from Ivan Krylov's: "Epigram on the Translation of the Poem 'The Art of Poetry' " ("Epigramma na perevod poèmy 'L'art poétique' "): "Is it you Boileau . . . what funny attire" (*Pss*, 14:382).[29] Then, Ivan's devil cites Descartes's famous aphorism "Je pense donc je suis," to demonstrate that he meditates like a learned philosopher on the universe but also to mock a fundamental contribution to the century's study of human consciousness (*Pss*, 15:77).

For representations of this period in Russian literature, Dostoevsky turns to Pushkin, whose poem "The Wanderer" he praises as an "almost literal transposition of the first three pages from a strange mystical book [*Pilgrim's Progress*] written in prose by an ancient English religious sectarian," because Pushkin poetically re-creates the spirit of the Protestant Reformation:

> Reading these strange verses . . . you understand the militant fire of an emergent Protestantism, finally you come to understand the history itself, and not only through thought, but as if you yourself were there, passed by the armed camp of the sectarians, sang their hymns with them, cried with them in their mystic ecstasy, and believed together with them in that, which they believed. (*Pss*, 26:146, 501)[30]

Thus, Dostoevsky extends the Reformation to the late seventeenth century by establishing an emotional connection with Pushkin's pious reformers, who exhibit a religious fervor similar to that of the Russian Orthodox Old Believers, who rebelled against the established church during the same period. Despite his note that Protestantism borders on "pure atheism" with little to differentiate it from Catholicism (hence the reference to "Protestant Catholicism") and that "the English religion is without Christ and God, according to Pobedonostsev," Pushkin's portrayal of genuine worship by the Protestant faithful appeals to Dostoevsky's imagination (*Pss*, 24:128, 75, 156).

For Dostoevsky, Pushkin's most poetic expression of the seventeenth century remains his Time of Troubles tragedy, *Boris Godunov*, not only because of its image of "a true ancient Russian character" in the person of the chronicler seeking a truth independent of the Moscow tsar but also for its portrayal of Russianness in the personages of Otrepev, the Patriarch, and various monks, for example, Misail and Varlaam (*Pss*, 19:9, 15). *Boris Godunov* combines elements from Shakespearean historical dramas and Molière's satire on imposture with popular seventeenth-century Russian traditions of pretenders and holy fools acting on the public square for his innovative tragedy confronting dramatic norms of the Reformation stage.[31] Emerson suggests that Pushkin's own admiration of *Le Cid*, controversial for its deviations from the classical unities, inspires Pushkin to create a "tragicomedy of history," *Boris Godunov*.[32] Pushkin's comparison of Dimitry to the French King Henri IV (reigned 1594–1610), who during this period successfully challenged the Catholic League that had assassinated his predecessor Henri III (also Henri de Valois, first elected king of the Polish-Lithuanian Commonwealth), heightens the historic reforming spirit evident in the False Dimitry's pretendership in the tragedy.[33] However, Dostoevsky focuses on *Boris Godunov*'s contribution of "common [*bytovye*] types" to the stage, "types of the positive beauty of the Russian man and his soul taken exclusively from the national spirit" (*Pss*, 26:130). Dostoevsky finds this national spirit in the very language of Pushkin's tragedy: "Russian speech is imbued with this meek, humble . . . love in Pushkin in Godunov" so that as he prepares for his public reading of Pimen's monologue at a June 1880 gathering of the Society for the Lovers of Russian Literature (Obshchestvo liubitelei rossiiskoi slovesnosti) he emphasizes the need for "calm" as well as "mastery of the subject" (*Pss*, 20:229; 30.1:180). Owing to Pushkin's imparting "poetic truth" to these positive Russian characters, Dostoevsky discerns in him a fellow servant to the tsar and nation: "I, just as Pushkin, am a servant to the tsar, because his children, his people, do not disdain the tsar's servant" (*Pss*, 27:86). For Dostoevsky, therefore, Pushkin combines the populist tradition of the Russian provincial theater (unrecorded peasants' and soldiers' productions) observed by Dostoevsky in Siberia and the French classical and romantic dramas from Dostoevsky's youth in a historical tragedy situated amidst the chaos of the Reformation.

Although *Diary of a Writer* encourages the young to learn from Cervantes and praises the works of Shakespeare, Dostoevsky also maintains that only Pushkin, and similar Russian geniuses, can integrate literary forms of other nations into their writings in such a way that these forms preserve their distinctive national character. Therefore, for Dostoevsky, types from other nations retain their outsidedness to Russian culture even as they enter the works of Russian writers, so that a certain hierarchy based on nationality is embedded in Dostoevsky's poetics. For this reason, Dostoevsky prefers Gogol's laughter to Molière's satire and Pushkin's tragedy to Shakespeare's as he searches for a new Russian word that reflects his ideal of universality in Russian nationality. With Shakespeare he can introduce despair and with Cervantes a sadness emerging from satirical tragedy for "tragedy and satire are two sisters and walk side by side and the name for both of them, taken together: *truth*" (*Pss*, 24:305). He finds tragic satire in the modern Russian drama of Ostrovsky, Gogol, and Griboedov as well, but in his search for positive role models for the Russian people, he requires a native genius like Pushkin who can create positive Russian characters that appeal to a broad audience, which having lost its faith, demands from literature "the final positive word—happiness" (*Pss*, 24:160–61).

Viewing tragedy as an ancient form of worship and literature as a medium that can shape faith, Dostoevsky does not endorse a transnational romantic literary solidarity or a Marxist world literature without borders (*Pss*, 24:160). Instead, the Russian realism of Pushkin can inspire faith in the nation through an encounter with his literary types such as his monk: "The monk is not an ideal—all is clear and palpable; he is and cannot not be" (*Pss*, 26:210). If literature can thus interact with life, artistic forms can penetrate the imaginations of not only one's own people but also of foreign peoples, for art freely transcends the national barriers of the physical world. Although Dostoevsky focuses on Pushkin's potential for international appeal, the masterpieces by Gogol, Turgenev, and Tolstoy also encourage him to believe in Russia's growing literary prominence that may allow the Russian spirit to infiltrate the West (*Pss*, 24:133). Dostoevsky senses that the decline of the West has translated into an abatement of French literary dominance, so that instead of reading the novels of Hugo or Sand, the bourgeoisie in Napoleonic France stage the vulgar art of sentimental melodrama, and a new generation enjoys the "filth" of Émile Zola (*Pss*, 29.2:100). Consequently, Dostoevsky reserves for a Russian consciousness the artistic legacies of the Renaissance and Reformations, since the European revolutionaries contaminated by the Catholic legacies of socialism and atheism have no appreciation for such antiquated forms of Roman art. In his Pushkin speech, Dostoevsky concludes that the absorption of such traditions into the Russian consciousness allows other nations to contribute to Russia's genius, which will realize an international brotherhood without the use of the sword so that he can speak for "the enlightened Russian European people" (*Pss*, 26:147; 27:193).

At the same time, Dostoevsky recognizes that in his age Catholics continue to brandish the sword, so, ever mindful of the tragic dimension to his satire, Dostoevsky exploits the Catholic tradition in order to subvert the ideal that it represents. His satire represents a fleeting solace that assuages the human tragedy—the wretched consciousness of createdness coexisting with an elusive vision of the expanse of eternity in space, as per Ivan Karamazov's rebellion.[34] Although the references to Copernicus, Galileo, Newton, and Kepler disclose a fascination with the stars, not unique to this former Siberian, Dostoevsky remains earthbound in his criticism of Catholicism's poor substitutions for the infinite, for example, materialism (gambling), illicit sensual pleasures (Madame Bovary and the Marquis de Sade), and pursuit of Roman power with the deceptive appeals to chivalry and honor. In his satirical engagement with Catholicism, Dostoevsky resorts at times to typage, such as with his depictions of French and Polish seducers, lackeys, and gamblers who inherit the deceit, libido, and flattery of Tartuffe, the honor of Boileau's *honnête homme,* the patriotism of Fortinbras's Polish foes, and the attractive duplicity of Otrepev's Polish sponsors. Thus, Dostoevsky's art appears to seek comfort in the familiar forms created by literary geniuses during turbulent times that attest to the ability of nations to survive the violence accompanying social reformation.

Notes

INTRODUCTION

1. Ralph Gibson, *A Social History of French Catholicism 1789–1914* (New York: Routledge, 1989), 48. Gibson concludes that "the Concordat of 1801 was to be the basic document governing Church-State relations in France until the Separation of Church and State of 1905" (49).

2. Nigel Aston, *Religion and Revolution in France, 1780–1804* (Washington, D.C.: Catholic University of America Press, 2000), 347. Aston discusses the attraction of ultramontanism and links it to the Congress of Vienna, after which the papacy was identified as "an essential bastion of order."

3. For an account of Russian policies toward the Catholic Church in the Congress Kingdom after the uprisings, see chapter 7 of Jerzy Kloczowski's *A History of Polish Christianity* (Cambridge: Cambridge University Press, 2000).

4. Georg Wilhelm Friedrich Hegel, *The Philosophy of History*, trans. J. Sibree (New York: Dover, 1956), 429, 425, 421.

5. Hegel, *Philosophy of History*, 415–18; Karl Marx, "Zur Kritik der Hegelschen Rechtsphilosophie: Einleitung," in *Werke* by Karl Marx and Friedrich Engels, 43 vols. (Berlin: Dietz Verlag, 1958–90), 1:386.

6. N. I. Kostomarov, "Dolzhno li schitat' Borisa Godunova osnovatelem krepostnago prava," in *Istoricheskiia monografii i izsledovaniia Nikolaia Kostomarova*, vol.1 (St. Petersburg: Tipografiia Tovarshchestva "Obshchestvennaia pol'za," 1863), 1:393–428. Prosper Mérimée, who was fascinated by the Time of Troubles pretender—the False Dimitri—recognizes the importance of Boris Godunov's suspension of the St. George's Day privilege, which allowed peasants to change their terms of labor, in Pushkin's tragedy. For his discussion of Pushkin, see Prosper Mérimée, *Correspondance générale: 1847–1849*, ed. Maurice Parturier (Paris: Le Divan, 1946), 5:497.

7. Hegel, *Philosophy of History*, 420.

8. I. S. Turgenev, "Gamlet i Don-Kikhot," in *Polnoe sobranie sochinenii i pisem v dvadtsati vos'mi tomakh*, 28 vols. (Moscow: Izdatel'stvo Akademii Nauk SSSR, 1960–68), 8:186. Dostoevsky was also familiar with the polemic between

Herzen and Turgenev on these types from his knowledge of Turgenev's writings and readings of Alexander Herzen's *Ends and Beginnings* (*Kontsy i nachala*).

9. D. H. Lawrence, *Reflections on the Death of a Porcupine and Other Essays,* ed. Michael Herbert (Cambridge: Cambridge University Press, 1988), 379.

10. Ibid., 379, 381.

11. V. G. Belinskii, "Stat'ia desiataia: 'Boris Godunov,'" in *Polnoe sobranie sochinenii,* 13 vols. (Moscow: Izdatel'stvo Akademii Nauk SSSR, 1953–59), 7:508.

12. Ibid., 527–28.

13. See chapter 4 for further discussion of Bakunin's political philosophy.

14. A. N. Pleshcheev, "Pokazanie A. N. Pleshcheeva," in *Delo Petrashevtsev,* ed. V. A. Desnitskii, 3 vols. (Moscow: Izdatel'stvo Akademii Nauk SSSR, 1937–51), 3:305. Pleshcheev admits to having visited Granovsky in his testimony and writes to Dostoevsky about both Granovsky and the lectures (3:305, 294).

15. A. V. Stankevich, *Timofei Nikolaevich Granovskii* (Moscow: Tipografiia Gracheva i K., 1869), 161.

16. T. N. Granovskii, *Lektsii po istorii srednevekov'ia* (Moscow: Izdatel'stvo "Nauka," 1986), 132.

17. Caryl Emerson, *Boris Godunov: Transpositions of a Russian Theme* (Bloomington: Indiana University Press, 1986), 9, 2. Emerson discusses these "transpositions" further in "Pretenders to History: Four Plays for Undoing Pushkin's *Boris Godunov*," *Slavic Review* 44, no. 2 (Summer 1985): 257–79 and along with Robert William Oldani in *Modest Musorgsky and Boris Godunov: Myths, Realities, Reconsiderations* (Cambridge: Cambridge University Press, 1994).

18. Harriet Murav, *Holy Foolishness: Dostoevsky's Novels and the Poetics of Cultural Critique* (Stanford, Calif.: Stanford University Press, 1992); Liudmila Saraskina, *Besy: Roman-Preduprezhdenie* (Moscow: Sovetskii pisatel', 1990). See chapter 4 for further engagement of these studies.

19. During 1872–73, Pogodin published in *The Citizen* (*Grazhdanin*) a series of articles on Russian patriots, including Kuzma Minin, Dmitry Pozharsky, Mikhail Skopin-Shuisky, and Ivan Susanin, who helped defeat the seventeenth-century invaders. Since the final article "For Susanin" ("Za Susanina") was published under Dostoevsky's editorship, the article is mentioned in Dostoevsky's correspondence with the historian (*Pss*, 29.1:307–8).

20. Kostomarov published his analysis in "Lichnosti smutnogo vremeni: Mikhail Skopin-Shuiskii.—Pozharskii.—Minin.—Susanin," *Vestnik Evropy* 6 (1871): 497–527. Although Dostoevsky could agree with Kostomarov's critical assessment of Polish nationalism, he nevertheless found him too academic as a historian and therefore unequal to Pushkin's expression of the popular, even vulgar, Russian spirit (*Pss*, 20:178).

21. In his "Dostoevskii i voinstvuiushchii katolitsizm 1860—1870kh godov (K genezisu 'Legendy o velikom inkvizitore')," *Russkaia literatura* 10, no. 1, F.

Evnin thus characterizes Dostoevsky's depiction of Catholic politics and ideology in his *Diary of a Writer* and in his final novel (39).

22. Joseph Frank, *Dostoevsky: The Seeds of Revolt 1821–1849* (Princeton, N.J.: Princeton University Press, 1976), 8, 12.

23. Chester S. L. Dunning, *Russia's First Civil War: The Time of Troubles and the Founding of the Romanov Dynasty* (University Park: Pennsylvania State University Press, 2001), 5.

24. Andrei Dostoevskii, *Vospominaniia* (Moscow: Agraf, 1999), 69.

25. Frank, *Dostoevsky: The Seeds of Revolt*, 45.

26. After their initial interrogation by the commission, the Petrashevsky conspirators were required to provide a written explanation of their involvement with the subversive group.

27. Alexander Herzen in *Du développement des idées révolutionnaires en Russie* (*The Development of Revolutionary Ideas in Russia*) describes the Petersburg youth's "amour de liberté" (love for freedom) expressed in the social philosophy of Charles Fourier during this period (*Ss*, 7:123), and Dostoevsky himself admits in his testimony that the Petrashevsky Circle discussed Fourier (*Pss*, 18:180).

28. Alfonso Scirocco, *Garibaldi: Citizen of the World*, trans. Allan Cameron (Princeton, N.J.: Princeton University Press, 2007), 132.

29. A. P. Miliukov, "Fedor Mikhailovich Dostoevskii," in *F. M. Dostoevskii v vospominaniiakh sovremennikov: V dvukh tomakh*, ed. K. Tiun'kin and M. Tiun'kina, 2 vols. (Moscow: "Khudozhestvennaia literatura," 1990), 1:259.

30. "the miserable Byzantium"; "the lofty thought of religion"; Pierre Tchaadaev, *Lettres philosophiques: Adressées à une dame* (Paris: Librairie des Cinq Continents, 1970), 56.

31. Tchaadaev, *Lettres philosophiques*, 62–63.

32. Jean-Jacques Rousseau, *Du contrat social ou principes du droit politique*, in *Oeuvres complètes de Jean-Jacques Rousseau*, vol. 3 (Paris: Éditions Gallimard, 1964), 3:460–69.

33. "You shall never be free so long as there remains a single Russian soldier in Poland"; Jean-Jacques Rousseau, *Considérations sur le gouvernement de Pologne et sur sa réformation projettée*, in *Oeuvres complètes de Jean-Jacques Rousseau*, 3:1037. In *La Pologne, Lamennais et ses amis (1830–34)* (Paris: Éditions du dialogue, 1985), Gaston Bordet describes *l'Avenir's* discussion of the Polish insurrection (37–68).

34. For a discussion of Mickiewicz's influence on Lamennais, see Bordet, *La Pologne, Lamennais et ses amis*, 104–18; Manfred Kridl, "Two Champions of a New Christianity: Lamennais and Mickiewicz," *Comparative Literature* 4, no. 3 (Summer, 1952): 239–67; Manfred Kridl, *Mickiewicz i Lamennais: Studyum porównawcze* (Warsaw: Księgarnia E. Wende i S-ka, 1909).

35. Bordet, *La Pologne, Lamennais et ses amis*, 117, 126.

36. F. G. Nikitina, in "Petrashevtsy i Lamenne," *Dostoevsky: Materialy i issledovaniia* 3 (1978), concludes that Dostoevsky knew about the planned publication of a translation of Lamennais's text for propaganda purposes by members of the Petrashevsky Circle (257–58). Parts of the translation were read at an evening at Sergei Durov's.

37. Włodzimierz Djakow, *Piotr Ściegienny i jego spuścizna* (Warsaw: Państwowe Wydawnictwo Naukowe, 1972), 67, 161.

38. F. G. Nikitina, "Idei Lamenne v Rossii," *Dostoevskii i mirovaia kul'tura* 8 (1997): 209. For more on these connections, see Frank, *Dostoevsky: The Seeds of Revolt* (184–86) or Nikitina, "Petrashevtsy i Lamenne" (206–11).

39. "the brothers of Christ have not been condemned to slavery by their Father."

40. Lamennais, *Paroles d'un croyant* (Paris: Flammarion, 1973), 67.

41. V. G. Belinskii, "Pis'mo k N. V. Gogoliu," in *Polnoe sobranie sochinenii,* 10:214.

42. Ibid., "Pis'mo k N. V. Gogoliu," 214–15.

43. This phrase is recalled by Fedor Lvov in V. R. Leikina-Svirskaia, ed., "Zapiska o dele Petrashevtsev: Rukopis' F. N. L'vova s pometkami M. V. Butashevicha-Petrashevskogo," *Literaturnoe nasledstvo* 63, no. 1 (1956): 182; and by Jan Jastrzębski in "Memuar Petrashevtsa," *Minuvshie gody* 1 (January 1908): 30.

44. Jan Jastrzębski, in "Memuar Petrashevtsa," recalls being interrogated about his knowledge of Warsaw and Vilnius and about some statements that he made concerning Polish nationalism (25; 29–30). In "Zapiska o dele Petrashevtsev," Lvov remembers Grigorev being questioned about his Polish Jesuit connections (184). For agent P. D. Antonelli's testimony regarding the discussion by the Petrashevtsy of potential rebellions among the schismatics in the Caucasus, Poland, and Siberia, see Desnitskii, *Delo Petrashevtsev,* 3:386.

45. N. F. Bel'chikov, *Dostoevskii v protsesse Petrashevtsev* (Moscow: Izdatel'stvo "Nauka," 1971), 151.

46. This was likely an attempt to establish a connection between the Petrashevtsy and the Cyril and Methodius Brotherhood (Kyrylo-mefodiïvs'ke tovarystvo), linked to the historian Mykola Kostomarov. In P. S. Sokhan', ed., *Kyrylo-mefodiïvs'ke tovarystvo u tr'okh tomakh* (Kiev: Naukova dumka, 1990), it is reported that Nikolai Mombelli had ties to Ukrainian poet Taras Shevchenko (2:6).

47. "the Hungarian campaign," "the proportions of a vast conspiracy"; Herzen's connection to the TDP, to which at least two of Dostoevsky's prison inmates had ties, likely contributes to Dostoevsky's animosity toward the exiled writer.

48. A. E. Vrangel', *Vospominaniia o F. M. Dostoevskom v Sibiri 1854–56 gg.* (St. Petersburg: Tipografiia A. S. Suvorina, 1912), 5. Baron Wrangel recalls that

his father, nervous about being overheard, whispered the news about revolution in France and unrest in Germany.

49. J. H. Sheddon, *The Petrashevtsy: A Study of the Russian Revolutionaries of 1848* (Manchester: Manchester University Press, 1985), 206, 237.

50. V. I. Semevskii, "Petrashevtsy: Kruzhok N. S. Kashkina I. Kashkin. Khanykov. Debu," *Golos minuvshago* 2 (February 1916): 56; Desnitskii, *Delo Petrashevtsev*, 2:217; 3:52, 77.

51. V. I. Semevskii, "M. V. Butashevich-Petrashevskii," *Golos minuvshago* 8 (August 1913): 79.

52. *Moskal* is used frequently by Poles during this period to refer pejoratively to Russians, but its intensity varies according to the writer or speaker and is therefore difficult to translate.

53. V. I. Semevskii, *M. V. Butashevich-Petrashevskii i Petrashevtsy*, vol. 2, *Sobranie sochinenii* (Moscow: Zadruga, 1922), 193, 44. See Sheddon's *The Petrashevtsy* for an evaluation of Speshnev's Polish connections (206). Also, Jastrzębski's discussion may be found in the second volume of Desnitskii's *Delo Petrashevtsev* (220).

54. Lvov describes being under the influence of Sue's novel (Leikina-Svirskaia, "Zapiska o dele Petrashevtsev," 176), while Sheddon in *The Petrashevtsy* records Petrashevsky's, Speshnev's, and Mombelli's contact with M. l'abbé Barruel's study (209, 216). Sheddon notes that Dézamy's study was among the books found in Speshnev's possession when he was arrested (71).

55. Leikina-Svirskaia, "Zapiska o dele Petrashevtsev," 176.

56. Eugène Sue, *Le Juif errant* (Verviers, Belgium: Gerard, n.d.), 1:72.

57. Sheddon, *The Petrashevtsy*, 217. This aspect of *The Double* is discussed at greater length in chapter 3.

58. Golyadkin's description of the Jesuit principle resembles the maxim that the end justifies the means—a maxim that was attributed to the order by its opponents, as observed by René Fülöp-Miller in *The Power and the Secret of the Jesuits* (New York: Viking, 1930), 153. The Catholic dimension to casuistry will be explored in greater detail in chapter 3.

59. N. A. Speshnev, "Pis'ma k K. É. Khoetskomu," in *Filosofskie i obshchestvenno-politicheskie proizvedeniia petrashevtsev*, ed. V. E. Evgrafov (Moscow: Gosudarstvennoe izdatel'stvo politicheskoi literatury, 1953), 500.

60. Leikina-Svirskaia, ed., "Zapiska o dele Petrashevtsev," 174.

61. Frank, *Dostoevsky: The Seeds of Revolt*, 8.

62. Kniaz' Meshcherskii, *Vospominaniia* (Moscow: Zakharov, 2001), 307.

63. Edward W. Said, *Reflections on Exile and Other Essays* (Cambridge, Mass.: Harvard University Press, 2000), 177. Said finds an "essential association" between nationalism and exile, since nationalism "affirms the home created by a community of language, culture, and customs; and, by so doing, it fends off exile, fights to prevent its ravages" (176).

64. In "Repositioning Pushkin and the Poems of the Polish Uprising," in *Polish Encounters, Russian Identity,* ed. David L. Ransel and Bożena Shallcross (Bloomington: Indiana University Press, 2005), Megan Dixon convincingly argues that Pushkin desires with his "poems of the Polish uprising" to "pull the cultural center of gravity eastward closer to Russia and away from exclusive location in Europe" (64). For a more extensive comparison of the two poems see Bogusław Mucha, "Syberyjskie wiersze Dostojewskiego," *Zeszyty naukowe Uniwersytetu Jagiellońskiego: Prace historycznoliterackie* 36 (1977): 94–95; or the commentary on Dostoevsky's ode in the second volume of his collected works (*Pss,* 2:521–23).

65. In *The Jesuits in Poland* (New York: Haskell House, 1971), A. F. Pollard describes the unique nature of the Jesuit Order which "reject[ed] the monastic habit" in favor of its evangelical and educational mission (20).

66. Austin Gough, *Paris and Rome: The Gallican Church and the Ultramontane Campaign 1848–1853* (Oxford: Clarendon, 1986), 181.

67. In *Dostoevsky the Thinker* (Ithaca, N.Y.: Cornell University Press, 2002), James P. Scanlan, citing this passage, discusses Rousseau's significance for Dostoevsky's vision of moral beauty (155). Also, Rousseau's repeated presence in his discussion of the Polish revolutionary movements suggests that Dostoevsky knew of the philosophe's support for Poland's independence, possibly through his literary discussions with fellow inmate Józef Bogusławski.

68. For further information, see T. I. Ornatskaia's commentary in Dostoevsky's collected works (*Pss,* 20:378).

69. See Iu. M. Steklov, ed., *Sobranie sochinenii i pisem.* 4 vols. (Moscow: Izdatel'stvo Vsesoiuznogo obshchestva politkatorzhan i ssyl'no-poselentsev, 1934–35) for Mikhail Bakunin's letter to Mikhail Katkov from Tomsk, in which Bakunin attributes the following citation to Rousseau: "Si vous ne pouvez empêcher la Russie d'avaler la Pologne, faites de sorte que jamais elle ne parvienne à la digérer" (4:294; "If you can not prevent Russia from devouring Poland, make it so that she does not manage to digest her").

70. "have accomplished great things"; "have divested the throne and altar of their prestige without achieving freedom."

71. Diane Oenning Thompson, *"The Brothers Karamazov" and the Poetics of Memory* (Cambridge: Cambridge University Press, 1991), 282. Also, see Ellis Sandoz, *Political Apocalypse: A Study of Dostoevsky's Grand Inquisitor* (Wilmington, Del.: ISI Books, 2000), 89.

72. Denis Dirscherl, S.J., *Dostoevsky and the Catholic Church* (Chicago: Loyola University Press, 1986), 97.

73. The fact that conversion to Jesuitism was grounds for a Russian's expulsion from the empire may account for Dostoevsky's creating this Europeanized Russian type in an 1876 entry to *Diary of a Writer.*

74. Catherine Gallagher and Stephan Greenblatt, *Practicing New Historicism* (Chicago: University of Chicago Press, 2000), 30.

75. For a discussion of Ivan's views on Dante, see Ivan A. Esaulov, "The Categories of Law and Grace in Dostoevsky's Poetics," in *Dostoevsky and the Christian Tradition,* ed. George Pattison and Diane Oenning Thompson (Cambridge: Cambridge University Press, 2001), 117.

76. Scanlan, *Dostoevsky the Thinker,* 216–17.

77. Dostoevsky describes Russians' hatred of such "formulae," since "our people will not follow after forms, especially after prepared foreign ones" (*Pss,* 27:21).

78. "The soul of a conspirator and the soul of a lackey." This citation found in the notes to *The Brothers Karamazov,* in addition to a similar quotation about Victor Hugo's police inspector Javert from *Les misérables* (1862) that equates spies and priests through a common religious fanaticism, attests to Dostoevsky's association of Catholics with conspiracy (*Pss,* 24:83).

79. Mikhail Bakhtin, *Rabelais and His World,* trans. Hélène Iswolsky (Bloomington: Indiana University Press, 1984), 188. Caryl Emerson discusses Bakhtin's participation in this tradition in *The First Hundred Years of Mikhail Bakhtin* (Princeton, N.J.: Princeton University Press, 1997), 8–9.

CHAPTER ONE

1. For a discussion of his contemporaries' reception, see Joseph Frank, *Dostoevsky: The Stir of Liberation, 1860–1865* (Princeton, N.J.: Princeton University Press, 1986), 224–26. Also, although Dostoevsky refers to six of the Poles by their initials (Zh—kii, B—kii, T—kii, M—kii, B—m, and A—chukovskii) their identities are well established in Dostoevsky scholarship, and therefore they will be addressed by their Polish names for the sake of clarity.

2. For the Catholic identity of this generation, see Jerzy Borejsza, *Emigracja polska po powstaniu styczniowym* (Warsaw: Państwowe Wydawnictwo Naukowe, 1966), 119. For statistics on the overwhelmingly Catholic population in Poland, see R. F. Leslie, *Reform and Insurrection in Russian Poland 1856–1865* (London: Athlone, 1963), 50.

3. A. P. Miliukov, "Fedor Mikhailovich Dostoevskii," *Russkaia Starina* 31, no. 5 (May 1881): 36.

4. For a discussion of the critical controversy surrounding these texts, see Elizabeth Blake's introduction to her partial translation of the remembrances in "Portraits of the Siberian Dostoevsky by Poles in the *House of the Dead,*" *Dostoevsky Studies,* n.s., 10 (2006): 58–63; or the concerns regarding authorship raised by Wiktoria Śliwowska in *Ucieczki z Sybiru* (Warsaw: Wydawnictwo Iskry, 2005), 350–56.

5. Although Śliwowska raises good reasons for caution in *Ucieczki z Sybiru,* the attribution of the editing of this text to the Siberian exile Józef Tokarzewski rather than Szymon appears to be a copying error (350–51).

6. Vrangel', *Vospominaniia o F. M. Dostoevskom*, 52.

7. Jacques Catteau provides this structural contrast between the first and second parts in "De la structure de *La maison des morts* de F. M. Dostoevskij," *Revue des études slaves* 54, nos. 1–2 (1982): 66.

8. Józef Bogusławski, "Wspomnienia Sybiraka: Pamiętniki Józefa Bogusławskiego," *Nowa reforma* 264 (1896): 1; Szymon Tokarzewski, *Siedem lat katorgi: Pamiętniki Szymona Tokarzewskiego 1846–1857 g.*, 2nd ed. (Warsaw: Gebethner i Wolff, 1918), 134–35.

9. Gary Saul Morson, "Paradoxical Dostoevsky," *Slavic and East European Journal*, 43, no. 3 (Fall 1999): 492.

10. For a more detailed description of the Konarski conspiracy, see Michał Janik, *Dzieje polaków na Syberji* (Krakow: Krakowska Spółka Wydawnicza, 1928), 123–33.

11. Wiktoria Śliwowska, *Zesłańcy polscy w Imperium Rosyjskim w pierwszej połowie XIX wieku* (Warsaw: Wydawnictwo DiG, 1998), 69, 504. Mierosławski's role in the conspiracy is discussed in Leslie, *Reform and Insurrection*, 18; 24–25. Iu. A. Borisenok lists Röhr among Bakunin's Berlin University acquaintances in *Mikhail Bakunin i "pol'skaia intriga": 1840–e gody* (Moscow: Rosspén, 2001), 166.

12. Śliwowska, *Zesłańcy polscy*, 391, 522.

13. Janik, *Dzieje polaków*, 133.

14. Sheddon, *The Petrashevtsy*, 99. For Kamieński's links to the TDP, see Djakow, *Piotr Ściegienny*, 67.

15. Leslie, *Reform and Insurrection*, 66.

16. For Raciborski's organizational role in the conspiracy, see Djakow, *Piotr Ściegienny*, 107. For his encounter with Tokarzewski in Siberia, see Tokarzewski, *Siedem lat*, 104–5.

17. Bogusławski, "Wspomnienia Sybiraka," 255:1; 261:1.

18. Śliwowska, *Zesłańcy polscy*, 284; Włodzimierz Djakow, "Polscy zesłańcy w Syberii Zachodniej i północnym Kazachstanie (1830–1862)," in *Polacy w Kazachstanie: Historia i współczesność*, ed. Stanisław Ciesielski and Antoni Kuczyński (Wrocław: Wydawnictwo Uniwersytetu Wrocławskiego, 1996), 56.

19. For their meeting with former Omsk inmate, Jan Woźniakowski, see Tokarzewski, *Siedem lat*, 140; Bogusławski "Wspomnienia Sybiraka," 275:1. Goryanchikov refers to Mirecki's meeting with the inmates after his release as well (*Pss*, 4:217).

20. Tokarzewski, *Siedem lat*, 187.

21. Śliwowska, *Zesłańcy polscy*, 728.

22. Ibid., 727–28.

23. Bogusławski, "Wspomnienia Sybiraka," 261:1.

24. P. K. Mart'ianov, "V perelome veka. (Otryvki iz staroi zapisnoi knizhki)," *Istoricheskii vestnik* 62 (November 1895): 456.

25. Śliwowska, *Zesłańcy polscy*, 35.

26. Tokarzewski observes the difference in the treatment of the latter four ("With them Waśka [Major Krivtsov] got on entirely different than with us") and attributes it to Major Krivtsov's newfound sobriety or guilt over the punishment of Żochowski (*Siedem lat,* 176).

27. The Bem reference is noted in N. F. Budanova and G. M. Fridlender, eds., *Letopis' zhizni i tvorchestva F. M. Dostoevskogo v trekh tomakh 1821–1881,* 3 vols. (St. Petersburg: Gumanitarnoe agentstvo "Akademicheskii proekt," 1995), 1:184.

28. Jerzy Stempowski, "Polacy w powieściach Dostojewskiego," *Przegląd Współczesny* 109 (1931): 182. Stempowski bases this assertion both on textual evidence from Dostoevsky's novels as well as on the fact that Dostoevsky never observed Poles in their own country.

29. Stanislaw Eile, *Literature and Nationalism in Partitioned Poland, 1795–1918* (New York: St. Martin's, 2000), 76–77.

30. Mart'ianov, "V perelome veka," 456. Although Martyanov calls this person by the name of Zhukovsky, D. D. Akhsharumova concludes that his description resembles that of Żochowski in the notes to an excerpt of Martyanov's text in Tiun'kin and Tiun'kina, *Dostoevskii v vospominaniiakh sovremennikov,* 1:592.

31. Tokarzewski, *Siedem lat,* 158–59.

32. Józef Żochowski, *Życie Jezusa Chrystusa, ozdobione rycinami, według obrazów pierwszych mistrzów przedstawiającymi główne zdarzenia z życia Zbawiciela* (Warsaw: Nakład Gustawa Leona Glücksberga, 1847), 3–4. *Polska Biblioteka Internetowa,* http://www.pbi.edu.pl/book_reader.php?p=54617.

33. Nina Perlina provides a description of this file in "Dostoevsky and His Polish Fellow Prisoners from the *House of the Dead,*" in *Polish Encounters, Russian Identity,* ed. David L. Ransel and Bozena Shallcross (Bloomington: Indiana University Press, 2005), 107.

34. Joseph Frank notes Dostoevsky's withdrawal of Strauss's study in *Dostoevsky: The Years of Ordeal, 1850–1859* (Princeton, N.J.: Princeton University Press, n.d.), 25.

35. Bogusławski, "Wspomnienia Sybiraka," 275:1. Tokarzewski has a similar passage in *Siedem lat* (139).

36. Bogusławski, "Wspomnienia Sybiraka," 275:1.

37. Tokarzewski, *Siedem lat,* 170, 102, 70.

38. This is an approximate quotation of verses from Mickiewicz's "To the Polish Mother" as recorded in *Siedem lat* (170).

39. Tokarzewski, *Siedem lat,* 151, 137, 147.

40. "Dante's hell"; A. Dumas, *Le Comte de Monte-Cristo,* vol. 1 (Paris: Nelson Éditeurs, n.d.), 1:235. For a history of Krasiński's poem, see Eile, *Literature and Nationalism in Partitioned Poland,* 64–65.

41. Aside from *Seven Years,* the works attributed to him include *Without a Passport (Bez paszportu,* 1910), *By a Thorny Path (Ciernistym szlakiem,* n. d.),

Hard Labor Convicts: Siberian Images (*Katorżnicy: Obrazki syberyjskie*, n. d.), *From the Year 1863 and the Years Afterwards* (*Z roku 1863 i lat następnych,* 1912), *Fugitive: Recollections from Siberia* (*Zbieg. Wspomnienia z Sybiru,* 1913), *Among the Civilian Dead* (*Pośród cywilnie umarłych, n. d.*), *Into Flight* (*W Ucieczce,* n. d.), and *In the Wandering* (*Na tułactwie,* n. d.).

42. Nina Perlina, "Dostoevsky and His Polish Fellow Prisoners," 105.

43. Szymon Tokarzewski, *Ciernistym szlakiem: Pamiętniki Szymona Tokarzewskiego z więzień, robót ciężkich i wygnania* (Warsaw: Druk L. Bilińskiego i W. Maślankiewicza, 1901), 118–19.

44. Ibid., 115.

45. Jerzy Kloczowski, *A History of Polish Christianity,* 130–31.

46. Tokarzewski, *Siedem lat,* 168.

47. Ibid., 169.

48. John Meyendorff, *Byzantine Theology: Historical Trends and Doctrines* (New York: Fordham University Press, 1979), 214.

49. Bogusławski, "Wspomnienia Sybiraka," 286:1. Tokarzewski includes a similar passage in *Siedem lat* (168–69).

50. Kloczowski, *A History of Polish Christianity,* 219.

51. Tokarzewski, *Siedem lat,* 119.

52. Bogusławski, "Wspomnienia Sybiraka," 261:1.

53. Tokarzewski, *Siedem lat,* 119.

54. Stempowski, "Polacy w powieściach Dostojewskiego," 195.

55. Bogusławski, "Wspomnienia Sybiraka," 297:1.

56. Tokarzewski, *Siedem lat,* 116.

57. Bogusławski, "Wspomnienia Sybiraka," 297:1; 294:1.

58. Tokarzewski, *Siedem lat,* 194.

59. Bogusławski, "Wspomnienia Sybiraka," 297:1.

60. Ibid., 294:1.

61. Ibid., 286:1.

62. Ibid., 286:1.

63. Bogusławski, "Wspomnienia Sybiraka," 286:1. Although Bogusławski likely remembers Dostoevsky's emotional state at the successes and defeats of the Russian army in the Crimea, the Polish prisoner refers to a historical event—the retreat of Mikhail Gorchakov (the brother of Petr) from beyond the Danube—that takes place after Dostoevsky's release from prison.

64. Tokarzewski, *Siedem lat,* 167.

65. Since this comment follows the discussion of the Polish war as a conflict between two Christianities, Dostoevsky's assessment of the Polish situation informs the comment.

66. In his notes about this investigation, Martyanov in "V perelome veka." quotes Malczewski, whom Tokarzewski remembers for his notes about previous military campaigns under Napoleon and in 1830, as informing the officials: "May

Jesus Christ be praised! How not to write! We write, sirs, we write our complaints and consolations, only we write them, sirs, not on papyrus but in our hearts with blood . . . so we write nothing" (456). See also Tokarzewski, *Katorżnicy* (184). Tokarzewski dates Malczewski's arrival to 1851, but Martyanov notes his part in the investigation. Since Martyanov does not remember Żochowski's name accurately, it is possible that he is referring to one of the Polish inmates, rather than Tokarzewski's Malczewski who was living in the Omsk settlement. Janik discusses a more famous Franciszek Malczewski, a Polish major who settled in Siberia after having been sent there for his role in the 1830 uprising (*Dzieje polaków,* 159, 190).

67. Tokarzewski, *Katorżnicy,* 107.

68. Tokarzewski, *Siedem lat,* 169–70. Tokarzewski here refers to Sue's novel, *Le Juif errant,* which in Polish is rendered *Żyd wieczny tułacz.*

69. "On the Siberian cape, a man on his knees extends arms toward America with an expression of indefinable despair. On the American promontory, a young and beautiful woman responds to the despairing gesture of this man by showing him the heavens"; Sue, *Le Juif errant,* 1:12.

70. Bogusławski, "Wspomnienia Sybiraka," 286:1.

71. Ibid., 286:1.

72. Harold B. Segel, *Stranger in Our Midst: Images of the Jew in Polish Literature* (Ithaca, N.Y.: Cornell University Press, 1996), 71.

73. As Edyta Bojanowska recognizes in *Nikolai Gogol: Between Ukrainian and Russian Nationalism* (Cambridge, Mass.: Harvard University Press, 2007), the narrative takes place close to the period of the Union of Brest (1596), which saw the formation of an Eastern rite Catholic Church and the subsequent expansion of Catholicism in Ukraine and Lithuania (280).

74. Mart'ianov, "V perelome veka.," 451.

75. In *The Art of Dostoevsky: Deliriums and Nocturnes* (Princeton, N.J.: Princeton University Press, 1981), Robert Louis Jackson links Dostoevsky's discussion of Hugo and Dante in this introduction to *House of the Dead* but does not note its connection to Aristov (37). Instead, he links it to the author's "idea of resurrection" and his conception of the Russian convict as expressing "the vast untested creative potential of the Russian people" (39).

76. "The ugly, it is the beautiful."

77. Wacław Lednicki, *Russia, Poland, and the West: Essays in Literary and Cultural History* (Port Washington, N.Y.: Kennikat, 1966), 278.

78. Morson, "Paradoxical Dostoevsky," 492.

79. For a discussion of Goryanchikov's ontological status and its effects on the novel, see Nancy Ruttenburg, *Dostoevsky's Democracy* (Princeton, N.J.: Princeton University Press, 2008), 85–86.

80. G. I. Chulkov, *Kak rabotal Dostoevskii* (Moscow: Sovetskii pisatel', 1939), 76.

81. Rusin, "Zametka na odnu gazetnuiu stat'iu: Po povodu pol'sko-rusinskogo voprosa" *Vremia* 9 (1862): 43, 45.

82. Borisenok, *Mikhail Bakunin i "pol'skaia intriga,"* 225–71. See note 11 above.

83. E. H. Carr, *Michael Bakunin* (London: Macmillan, 1937), 226–27.

84. V. A. D'iakov, *Deiateli russkogo i pol'skogo osvoboditel'nogo dvizheniia v tsarskoi armii 1856–1865 godov: Biobibliograficheskii slovar'* (Moscow: Izdatel'stvo "Nauka," 1967), 221; Bogusławski, "Wspomnienia Sybiraka," 255:1.

85. The sudden recollection by Wrangel of an 1858 meeting with Bakunin in Amur and his account of Bakunin's history in Saxony amidst his remembrances of Dostoevsky in Semipalatinsk further intimate that Bakunin had a connection to the town (Vrangel', *Vospominaniia o F. M. Dostoevskom,* 33–34).

86. A. V. Dulov, *Petrashevtsy v Sibiri* (Irkutsk: Izdatel'stvo Irkutskogo universiteta, 1996), 111–13.

87. Vrangel', *Vospominaniia o F. M. Dostoevskom,* 28–29. This is the group that conspired with Ściegienny.

88. Tokarzewski, *Siedem lat,* 130; Bogusławski, "Wspomnienia Sybiraka," 263:2.

89. Vrangel', *Vospominaniia o F. M. Dostoevskom,* 65.

90. Ibid., 115.

91. Lednicki, *Russia, Poland, and the West,* 277.

92. Tokarzewski, *Siedem lat,* 183.

93. For Krzyżanowska's 1861 letter to Dostoevsky, which shows her acquaintance with both of the Petrashevtsy in Omsk, see V. G. Bazanov and G. M. Fridlender, eds., *Dostoevskii i ego vremia* (Leningrad: Izdatel'stvo "Nauka," 1971), 251–54.

94. Tokarzewski, *Siedem lat,* 136, 156.

95. Tokarzewski, *Katorżnicy,* 181.

96. Budanova and Fridlender, *Letopis',* 1:187–88.

97. Mart'ianov, "V perelome veka.," 451.

98. Karla Oeler, "The Dead Wives in the Dead House: Narrative Inconsistency and Genre Confusion in Dostoevskii's Autobiographical Prison Novel," *Slavic Review* 61, no. 3 (Fall 2002): 527.

99. Ruttenburg, *Dostoevsky's Democracy,* 64. For a discussion of the arguments between Dostoevsky and Tokarzewski on class identity, see Jackson, *The Art of Dostoevsky,* 42–43.

100. Bogusławski, "Wspomnienia Sybiraka," 260:1.

101. Ibid., 297:1; 294:1.

102. Lednicki's criticism of Dostoevsky's impressions of the Poles seems harsh in consideration of this attempt to understand the severe sentences faced by the Poles. For his assessment, see Lednicki, *Russia, Poland, and the West,* 278.

103. Rufin Piotrowski, "Souvenirs d'un Sibérien," trans. Julian Klaczko, *Revue des deux mondes* 38 (1862): 853.

104. Śliwowska records and describes the memoirs *Muscovite Cruelties Performed on Poles in Siberia* (*Okrucieństwa moskiewskie dokonane na Polakach w Syberyi*) published in 1846 in *Dziennik narodowy* (*Zesłańcy polscy*, 463, 549).

105. Perlina, "Dostoevsky and His Polish Fellow Prisoners," 105.

106. Tokarzewski, *Siedem lat*, 161.

107. Ibid., 163.

108. Mart'ianov, "V perelome veka," 448.

109. Mart'ianov, "V perelome veka," 452; Frank, *Dostoevsky: The Years of Ordeal*, 81–82.

110. Mart'ianov, "V perelome veka," 456.

111. Małgorzata Świderska, *Studien zur literaturwissenschaftlichen Imagologie: Das literarische Werk F. M. Dostoevskijs aus imagologischer Sicht mit besonderer Berücksichtigung der Darstellung Polens* (Munich: Verlag Otto Sagner, 2001), 177.

112. Tokarzewski, *Siedem lat*, 160.

113. Elizabeth Wormeley Latimer, *Russia and Turkey in the Nineteenth Century* (Chicago, Ill.: A. C. McClurg, 1897), 103.

114. Ibid., 103.

115. A. N. Maikov, *Polnoe sobranie sochinenii*, 4 vols. (St. Petersburg: Izdanie T-va A. F. Marks, 1914), 2:19.

116. Ibid.

CHAPTER TWO

1. This point is reiterated in *The Gambler* (*Pss*, 5:225).

2. Jacques Bonhomme has both populist and feudal connotations, since he was the traditional representative of the common man.

3. Edward Wasiolek, introduction to *The Gambler, with Polina Suslova's Diary*, by Fyodor Dostoevsky (Chicago: University of Chicago Press, 1972), vii–xxxix.

4. I. S. Aksakov identifies the ambiguous reference to the year –12 with "those bells" rung by Moscow's patriotic literati in "Pis'ma Kas'ianova," in *Otchego tak nelegko zhivetsia v Rossii?* (Moscow: Rosspén, 2002), 210.

5. V. S. Nechaeva, *Zhurnal M. M. i F. M. Dostoevskikh "Vremia," 1861–1863* (Moscow: "Nauka," 1972), 171. Nechaeva demonstrates effectively that Dostoevsky's experience editing Razin's political articles as well as his contact with a well-traveled circle of friends gave him "not only rich information about what awaited him in Europe but even a definite viewpoint into its life."

6. Dostoevsky writes to his younger brother Andrei on the eve of his journey that "I am a sick man, constantly sick" and that "I am going abroad until September to undergo treatment" (*Pss*, 28.2:24). In A. S. Dolinin, ed., *F. M. Dostoevskii: Materialy i issledovaniia* (Leningrad: Akademiia Nauk SSSR, 1935), a letter from his older brother Mikhail reveals his concern over the younger

Dostoevsky's illness, as Mikhail writes: "I would not advise you to go out at night. It is fatiguing and, with your illness, not safe" (535).

7. Wayne Dowler, *Dostoevsky, Grigor'ev, and Native Soil Conservatism* (Toronto: University of Toronto Press, 1982), 125.

8. F. Shcheglov, "Semeistvo v rabochem klasse vo Frantsii," *Vremia* 11 (November 1861): 287. In *Dostoevskii v shestidesiatye gody* (Moscow: "Khudozhestvennaia literatura," 1966), Valery Kirpotin writes of Engels's and Proudhon's influence on this article that warns against Russia adopting this Western model of industrialization (42–43).

9. Dostoevsky's linking of these two names in a commentary on Mérimée's drama is perceptive, since in his reminiscences Dumas does cite Mérimée's *Le Faux Démétrius* when telling the story of Dimitry the Pretender, as V. S. Dorovatovskaia-Liubimova points out in "Frantsuzskii burzhua: Dostoevskii i Aleksandr Diuma," *Literaturnyi Kritik* 9 (September 1936): 204.

10. Starting in late 1862 in the series "Our Domestic Affairs" ("Nashi domashnie dela") Razin begins discussing the need for Russia to dedicate resources to the building of railroads and modern infrastructure to reduce her economic dependence on the industrialized West. For a more extensive discussion, see Nechaeva, *Zhurnal M. M. i F. M. Dostoevskikh "Vremia,"* 99–105. As Razin descended from serfs in the Vladimir region, he was liberal on issues relating to serfdom and so staunchly supported peasant causes that his fellow contributor to *Time*, Apollon Grigorev, called him Stenka Razin (Nechaeva, *Zhurnal M. M. i F. M. Dostoevskikh "Vremia,"* 61).

11. [A. E. Razin], "Politicheskoe obozrenie," *Vremia* 2 (February 1863): 189, 192. In *Zhurnal M. M. i F. M. Dostoevskikh "Vremia,"* Nechaeva discusses Razin's responsibility for the series of articles in *Time* (155–74).

12. [Razin], "Politicheskoe obozrenie," *Vremia* 3 (March 1863): 2:129.

13. In "Dostoevsky: The Encounter with Europe," *Russian Review* 22, no. 3 (July 1963), Joseph Frank shows that the presence of these Russian letters may be felt most strongly in the first three chapters of Dostoevsky's impressions, in which he compares Russia's past and present relations with Europe (240). In *Dostoevskii i drugie: Stat'i i issledovaniia o russkoi klassicheskoi literature* (Leningrad: "Khudozhestvennaia literatura," 1989), Arkady Dolinin finds the presence of Herzen particularly strong in Dostoevsky's chapter "Bribri i ma biche" (149–54).

14. [Razin], "Politicheskoe obozrenie," *Vremia* 4 (April 1863): 2:216.

15. Anne Dwyer, "Of Hats and Trains: Cultural Traffic in Leskov's and Dostoevskii's Westward Journeys," *Slavic Review* 70, no. 1 (Spring 2011): 67–73. Dwyer discusses the significance of the new railway for the two authors.

16. Dwyer, "Of Hats and Trains," 86.

17. "To the great men, the grateful homeland"

18. "he drove a stud into the wall in the Pantheon and hitched his coup d'état to this stud"; Victor Hugo, *Napoléon le Petit* (Paris: J. Hetzel, n.d.), 51.

19. *Le Panthéon: Symbole des révolutions* ([Paris]: Picard Éditeur, 1989), 224.

20. Ibid.

21. [A. E. Razin], "Politicheskoe obozrenie," *Vremia* 3, no. 4 (March 1861): 10–12. In *Time*, Razin records the eloquent defense of free speech by Jules Favre before a tribunal investigating the publication of a brochure critical of Napoleon III. Favre was a longtime critic of Napoleon's political activities in Italy and was famous for having represented an Italian nationalist, Felice Orsini, who tried to assassinate Napoleon on January 14, 1858. At his execution, Orsini had Favre read a letter appealing to the emperor for Italian freedom.

22. Heine in *Deutschland* satirizes Rousseau's *Confessions,* as discussed in the notes to *Winter Notes* in the academic collection of Dostoevsky's collected works (*Pss,* 5:373). For additional background on Heine in Dostoevsky's works, see V. Komarovich's "Dostoevskii i Geine," *Sovremennyi mir* 10 (1916): 97–107.

23. Herzen had visited Pecherin at a Catholic monastery at Clapham near London in 1853 about which he writes in the seventh chapter of *My Past and Thoughts.* Pecherin's work is a source for a poem by Stepan Verkhovensky in *Demons* (*Pss,* 10:10; 12:278). *The Idiot* also contains a reference to his published correspondence with Herzen (*Pss,* 8:312; 9:393).

24. N. N. Strakhov, "Vospominaniia o Fedore Mikhailoviche Dostoevskom," in *Biografiia, pis'ma i zametki iz zapisnoi knizhki F. M. Dostoevskogo* (St. Petersburg: Tipografiia A. S. Suvorina, 1883), 240. Here, Strakhov differentiates Dostoevsky's early admiration of Herzen from his later animosity toward this editor of *The Bell.* Strakhov's memoirs are the first to discuss Herzen's influence on Dostoevsky's *Winter Notes.*

25. A. S. Dolinin, *Poslednie romany Dostoevskogo: Kak sozdavalis' "Podrostok" i "Brat'ia Karamazovy"* (Moscow: Sovetskii Pisatel', 1963), 217–18; Dolinin, *Dostoevskii i drugie,* 146–55.

26. Dolinin, *Poslednie romany Dostoevskogo,* 222–24.

27. Ibid., 224. *Endings and Beginnings* appeared in *The Bell* from July 1862 to February 1863 so that only its final installment came out after the first four chapters of *Winter Notes* were published in February 1863.

28. G. R. Derzhavin, *Stikhotvoreniia,* ed. G. R. Gukovskii (Leningrad: Izdatel'stvo pisatelei, 1933), 190. Dostoevsky slightly misquotes these lines, which should read: "He steps on the mountains, the mountains crumble" and "The Towers he hurls beyond the clouds" (*Pss,* 5:365).

29. Świderska, *Studien zur literaturwissenschaftlichen Imagologie,* 239–40. In "Of Hats and Trains," Dwyer makes some similar observations about *Winter Notes* (87).

30. Świderska, *Studien zur literaturwissenschaftlichen Imagologie,* 240.

31. Karl Marx, "Der achtzehnte Brumaire des Louis Bonaparte," in *Werke* by Marx and Engels, 8:203.

32. Dwyer, "Of Hats and Trains," 87.

33. [Razin], "Politicheskoe obozrenie" (1863): 2:185.

34. See note 63 of chapter 1 for further information on Gorchakov's importance for Dostoevsky's Siberian period.

35. Leslie, *Reform and Insurrection in Russian Poland,* 128–29.

36. Strakhov, "Vospominaniia o Fedore Mikhailoviche Dostoevskom," 230.

37. V. S. Nechaeva, *Zhurnal M. M. i F. M. Dostoevskikh "Ėpokha," 1864–1865* (Moscow: Izdatel'stvo "Nauka," 1975), 92.

38. Desnitskii, *Delo Petrashevtsev,* 2:220. The interrogation of Jastrzębski reveals that this subject was under dispute at the meetings.

39. M. N. Katkov, *1863 god. Sobranie statei po pol'skomu voprosu* (Moscow: V Universitetskoi tipografii, 1887), 26.

40. [A. E. Razin], "Nashi domashnie dela," *Vremia* 4 (1863): 194. In the index to Dostoevsky's journals in *Zhurnal M. M. i F. M. Dostoevskikh "Ėpokha,"* Nechaeva identifies Razin as the author of the article (254).

41. Dowler, *Dostoevsky, Grigor'ev, and Native Soil Conservatism,* 80.

42. A. S. Khomiakov, *Zapiski o vsemirnoi istorii,* vol. 7, *Polnoe sobranie sochinenii* (Moscow: Tipolitografiia T-va I. N. Kushnerev, 1906), 443.

43. Aksakov, *Otchego tak nelegko zhivetsia v Rossii?,* 188. Here, Aksakov draws on Ivan Kireevsky's analysis of Poland's foreign civilization.

44. N. N. Strakhov, "Rokovoi vopros," *Vremia* 4 (April 1863): 2:158.

45. For an alternative reading of Dostoevsky's understanding of the Polish Question, based on the articles in *Time,* see Edyta M. Bojanowska, "Empire by Consent: Strakhov, Dostoevskii, and the Polish Uprising of 1863," *Slavic Review* 71, no. 1 (Spring 2012): 18–23.

46. Strakhov, "Vospominaniia o Fedore Mikhailoviche Dostoevskom," 246.

47. See note 52 of the introduction for an explanation of *Moskali.*

48. [A. E. Razin], "Chto takoe pol'skie vosstaniia," *Ėpokha* 1–2 (January/February 1864): 393–420.

49. In 1866, Ogarev supported this position in an article published in issue 224 of *The Bell,* and the young radical Alexander Serno-Solovevich wanted to publish his protest in the journal as well, but Herzen refused. For a copy of the protest, see F. Freidenfel'd, "Listovka A. A. Serno-Solov'evicha protiv N. P. Ogareva," *Literaturnoe nasledstvo* 41–42 (1963): 111–15. For more on their disputes, see B. P. Koz'min, "Aleksandr Serno-Solov'evich: Materialy dlia biografii," *Literaturnoe nasledstvo* 67 (1959): 698–733.

50. Budanova and Fridlender, *Letopis',* 1:236–37. In 1857, Dostoevsky's rights were restored but not his former property.

51. Lednicki, *Russia, Poland, and the West,* 263.

52. A. G. Dostoevskaia, *Dnevnik 1867 goda* (Moscow: Izdatel'stvo "Nauka," 1993), 68, 111.

53. "Pis'ma A. E. Vrangelia k Dostoevskomu," *Dostoevskii: Materialy i issledovaniia* 3 (1978): 281.

54. In "Vospominaniia o Fedore Mikhailoviche Dostoevskom," Strakhov

recalls that a Frenchman drove Dostoevsky to abandon a common dining room during coffee (245).

55. In *Vospominaniia o F. M. Dostoevskom*, Wrangel recalls that the locals enjoyed describing popular legends about the size of the snakes, which populated Zmeinogorsk, from which the mine had received its name (87–88).

56. Vrangel', *Vospominaniia o F. M. Dostoevskom*, 89.

57. Charles Herbert Cottrell, *Recollections of Siberia in the Years 1840 and 1841* (London: John W. Parker, 1842), 191–93.

58. Bogusławski, "Wspomnienia Sybiraka," 259:1.

59. Cottrell, *Recollections of Siberia*, 232.

60. Jackson, *The Art of Dostoevsky*, 212.

61. William Makepeace Thackeray, *The Kickleburys on the Rhine*, vol. 17, *The Complete Works of William Makepeace Thackeray* (New York: Harper & Brothers, 1903), 193. Based on similarities between Thackeray's story and *The Gambler*, Evgeniia Kiiko finds that Dostoevsky was familiar with *English Tourists* (*Angliiskie turisty*), an 1851 Russian translation of *The Kickleburys on the Rhine* (*Pss*, 5:401).

62. Jackson, *The Art of Dostoevsky*, 212.

63. Ibid., 214.

64. The quotation is taken from Chatsky's final farewell speech, given after he discovers his beloved Sofia has enjoyed the favors of another suitor.

65. Apollinariia Suslova, *Gody blizosti s Dostoevskim*, ed. A. S. Dolinin (New York: Serebrianyi vek, 1982), 76, 82, 95–96, 103.

66. Here the title "pan" links the man to the Polish nobility, which Dostoevsky has identified with the Catholic faith.

67. Świderska, *Studien zur literaturwissenschaftlichen Imagologie*, 250–52.

68. Katkov, *1863 god*, 389.

69. Ibid., 392.

70. Vrangel', *Vospominaniia o F. M. Dostoevskom*, 217. Suslova alludes to a similar episode involving Dostoevsky's attempt to obtain a visa at the papal embassy in Paris in *Gody blizosti s Dostoevskim* (58).

71. A. G. Dostoevskaia, *Vospominaniia*, ed. S. V. Belov and V. A. Tunimanov (Moscow: Izdatel'stvo "Khudozhestvennaia literatura," 1971), 65. She provides an account of her first acquaintance with her future husband during October 1866 when she worked as his stenographer on *The Gambler* so that he could meet a deadline set by the publisher.

72. Joseph Frank, "*The Gambler*: A Study in Ethnopsychology," in *Freedom and Responsibility in Russian Literature: Essays in Honor of Robert Louis Jackson*, ed. Elizabeth Cheresh Allen and Gary Saul Morson (Evanston, Ill.: Northwestern University Press; New Haven, Conn.: The Yale Center for International and Area Studies, 1995), 70.

73. For Racine's presence in the story of Manon and des Grieux, see Abbé Prévost, *Histoire du Chevalier des Grieux et de Manon Lescaut* (Paris: Éditions

Garnier Frères, 1957), 154. When des Grieux soberly admits his lack of control to his friend Tiberge, the latter attributes Jansenist tendencies to des Grieux, who does not deny them (106).

74. "My son do you have heart?"; This is taken from act 1, scene 5 of Corneille's tragedy.

75. See the depiction of summertime in *House of the Dead* for imagery of freedom connected to the Kirghiz tent and the simple life of a Kirghiz woman (*Pss*, 4:178).

76. "A real Russian, a Kalmyk!"

77. Dostoevskaia, *Dnevnik 1867 goda*, 137–38.

78. Bogusławski, "Wspomnienia Sybiraka," 286:1.

79. Desnitskii, *Delo Petrashevtsev*, 3:404.

80. Vrangel', *Vospominaniia o F. M. Dostoevskom*, 26.

81. Ibid., 26, 215.

82. Suslova, *Gody blizosti*, 60.

83. See the discussion of Svidrigailov and casuistry in chapter 3 for a more detailed discussion of his Polish connection.

84. Dulov, *Petrashevtsy v Sibiri*, 46.

85. "an old Russian countess, having lapsed into childhood."

86. Zbigniew Żakiewicz, "Polacy u Dostojewskiego," *Twórczość* 24, no. 6 (June 1968): 84.

87. Świderska, *Studien zur literaturwissenschaftlichen Imagologie*, 256.

88. Nicolas Boileau-Despréaux, *L'art poétique*, in *Oeuvres de Boileau, à l'usage de la jeunesse* (Brussels: La Société Nationale, 1837), 260; Jean-Paul Sartre, *Qu'est-ce que la littérature?* (Paris: Gallimard, 1948), 158.

89. V. S. Vainerman, "Omskoe okruzhenie Dostoevskogo," *Dostoevskii: Materialy i issledovaniia* 6 (1985): 187–88. Vainerman also discusses Dostoevsky's acquaintance with the family.

90. "just another moment." In *Surprised by Shame: Dostoevsky's Liars and Narrative Exposure* (Columbus: Ohio State University Press, 2003), Deborah Martinsen discusses Lebedev's calculation in depicting the fate of this "poor sinner" who is sacrificed "to the bloodlust of the Parisian mob" (157).

91. In *The Petrashevtsy*, Sheddon recalls that Petrashevsky wrote an introduction to *Don Quixote* (37). For a discussion of Herzen's use of the type in *Ends and Beginnings*, see chapter 5.

92. Sir Walter Scott, *Waverly* (London: Thomas Nelson and Sons, n.d.), 35. In an 1880 letter, Dostoevsky discloses that "in my twelfth year, I read all of Walter Scott during my vacation in the country, and although it developed my imagination and impressionability, I then aimed it in a good direction" (*Pss*, 30.1:212).

93. See Robin Feuer Miller, *Dostoevsky and "The Idiot": Author, Narrator, and Reader* (Cambridge, Mass.: Harvard University Press, 1981) for further dis-

cussion of Aglaya's "double-edged" reading of this poem and its quixotic intertext (189–91).

94. Ibid., 9–10. Miller also provides a summary of comparative studies of Don Quixote and Madame Bovary (258).

95. Gustave Flaubert, *Madame Bovary: Mœurs de province,* vol. 8, *Oeuvres complètes de Gustave Flaubert* (Paris: Louis Conard, Libraire-Éditeur, 1921), 50–51.

96. Soledad Fox, *Flaubert and Don Quijote: The Influence of Cervantes on Madame Bovary* (Brighton: Sussex Academic, 2008), 110.

97. Ibid., 119.

98. Linda Ivanits, *Dostoevsky and the Russian People* (Cambridge: Cambridge University Press, 2009), 128–29. Ivanits also provides a summary of the scholarship on the theme of Stepan Verkhovensky's chivalry (222).

99. M. N. Katkov, "Moskva, 5go ianvaria," *Moskovskie vedomosti* 4 (January 6, 1870): 2.

CHAPTER THREE

1. For further discussion of casuistry's Aristotelian roots and pre-Reformation Catholic heritage, see Fülöp-Miller, *The Power and the Secret of the Jesuits,* 142–43, 156–62, 165–66; or Albert R. Jonsen and Stephen Toulmin, *The Abuse of Casuistry: A History of Moral Reasoning* (Berkeley: University of California Press, 1988), 69–70, 126–36.

2. For a summary of early Protestant engagement with casuistry, see M. W. F. Stone's "The Adoption and Rejection of Aristotelian Moral Philosophy in Reformed 'Casuistry,'" *Humanism and Early Modern Philosophy,* ed. Jill Kraye and M. W. F. Stone, 59–90 (London: Routledge, 2000). In "The 'New Art of Lying' Equivocation, Mental Reservation, and Casuistry," in *Conscience and Casuistry in Early Modern Europe,* ed. Edmund Leites (Cambridge: Cambridge University Press, 1988), Johann P. Sommerville separates the definition of casuistry into two meanings to differentiate between (1) the application of "general moral principles" to "particular cases" and (2) "sophisticated, equivocal, or specious reasoning" in the Catholic (Jesuit) tradition (159).

3. In *The Power and the Secret of the Jesuits,* Fülöp-Miller holds Protestants, Old Catholics, and Pascal responsible for the attribution of this maxim to the Jesuits (153). I am indebted to Gary Saul Morson for recommending Pascal's discussion of casuistry for this chapter.

4. "Iezuity," in *Spravochnyi èntsiklopedicheskii slovar',* ed. A. V. Starchevskii, vol. 5 (St. Petersburg: Tip. Voenno-Uchebnykh Zavedenii, 1847), 262. The motto is rendered in English as "For the greater glory of God."

5. Father Ivan Martynov wrote a letter, published in issues no. 45–46 of *Day* in 1865, in response to anti-Jesuit sentiments expressed in a March

1864 issue of *Day*. Samarin's five letters to Martynov were collected and published the following year as *Iezuity i ikh otnoshenie k Rossii: Pis'ma k Iezuitu Martynovu* (Moscow: Tip. Lazarevskago Inst., 1866). Herzen, observing Samarin's lengthy response to Martynov's brief letter, complained in *The Bell* that "Jesuits are always lucky" (*Ss*, 18:477). Dostoevsky wrote of his admiration for Samarin in an 1876 entry to *Diary of a Writer* (*Pss*, 22:102). For references in Samarin's history to the Jesuits in Russia, see *Iezuity i ikh otnoshenie*, 224, 235, 265, 270.

6. Dmitrii A. Tolstoi, *Rimskii katolitsizm v Rossii: Istoricheskoe issledovanie*, 2 vols. (St. Petersburg: Izdanie i tipografiia V. F. Demakova, 1876).

7. In *Dostoevsky the Thinker*, Scanlan maintains that Dostoevsky rejects casuistry in favor of "deontological ethics, according to which . . . the morality of any action is determined not by its future consequences but by its present inherent character" (176). In "Dvoinichestvo i samozvanstvo," *Dostoevskii: Materialy i issledovaniia* 11 (1994), R. N. Poddubnaya notes the common theme of pretendership in Dostoevsky's two novels but contrasts Golyadkin's "petty everyday" role-playing in the tradition of Gogol's Khlestakov with Raskolnikov's pretendership, which maintains the "spiritual-moral ties" of imposture indicative of Pushkin's Otrepev (36–37). Also, general parallels between Pushkin's tragedy and Dostoevsky's *Crime and Punishment*, especially between Otrepev's and Raskolnikov's self-congratulatory and self-appointed roles as benefactors of humanity, may be found in Ia. S. Bilinkis, "Romany Dostoevskogo i tragediia Pushkina 'Boris Godunov': K probleme edinstva puti russkoi literatury XIX stoletiia," *Dostoevskii: Materialy i issledovaniia* 2 (1976): 168; M. P. Alekseev, "O dramaticheskikh opytakh Dostoevskogo," *Tvorchestvo Dostoevskogo, 1821–1881–1921: Sbornik statei i materialov*, ed. L. P. Grossman (Odessa: Vseukrainskoe gosudarstvennoe izdatel'stvo, 1921), 52.

8. Scanlan, *Dostoevsky the Thinker*, 90.

9. In *Studien zur literaturwissenschaftlichen Imagologie*, Świderska notes the resemblance between the two works (283). Robin Feuer Miller also analyzes similarities between the conclusion of the novel and Goryanchikov's depiction of the arrival of spring in *Dostoevsky's Unfinished Journey* (New Haven, Conn.: Yale University Press, 2007), 40–43.

10. Stephen T. Cochrane, *The Collaboration of Nečaev, Ogarev and Bakunin in 1869: Nečaev's Early Years* (Giessen, W. Ger.: Wilhelm Schmitz, 1977), 24.

11. This quotation from Emmanuel Sa's *Aphorismi confessariorum ex doctorum sententiis collecti . . .* (Cologne: Joannes Crithius, 1610), 611, is cited from Harro Höpfl, *Jesuit Political Thought: The Society of Jesus and the State, c. 1540–1630* (Cambridge: Cambridge University Press, 2004), 315.

12. Desnitskii, *Delo Petrashevtsev*, 1:571; Pierre Zaccone, *Histoire des sociétés secrètes, politiques et religieuses* (Paris: Arthême Fayard, Editeur, n.d.), 27–29. *Google books*, https://play.google.com/books/reader?id=GyAVAAAAQAAJ&printsec

=frontcover&output =reader&authuser=0&hl=en_US&pg=GBS.PP1. This Jesuit connection to assassination is also traced in the aforementioned encyclopedia entry "Iezuity" in note 4 above (263).

13. J. Michelet, *Le prêtre, la femme, et la famille* (Paris: Ernest Flammarion, Éditeur, n.d.), 49.

14. In *The Demetrius Legend and Its Literary Treatment in the Age of the Baroque* (Rutherford, N.J.: Fairleigh Dickinson, 1972), Ervin C. Brody finds that de Vega positively portrays Dimitry's Catholic connections by showing the pretender as a devout Christian whose "heroic and popular" rule is predestined by divine providence (83).

15. It is very likely that these writers saw Sumarokov's drama on stage, since, as Harold B. Segel reports in the second volume of *The Literature of Eighteenth-Century Russia* (New York: E. P. Dutton, 1967), the drama was "immensely popular" when staged at the St. Petersburg Imperial theater in 1771 and so became standard in the Russian theatrical repertoire into the 1820s (394).

16. This dialogue with Pushkin's drama is characteristic of the period, as Caryl Emerson observes in her study of its transpositions in *Boris Godunov* (9).

17. A. E. Rizenkampf, "Vospominaniia o Fedore Mikhailoviche Dostoevskom: 'Vospominaniia o F. M. Dostoevskom v zapisiakh i pereskaze O. F. Millera,'" in *Dostoevskii v vospominaniiakh sovremennikov*, ed. Tiun'kin and Tiun'kina, 1:185. In "O dramaticheskikh opytakh Dostoevskogo," Alekseev identifies a common link to the Time of Troubles for these dramas, since Schiller also depicts the first False Dimitry in an 1804 dramatic fragment *Demetrius*, a scene of which was translated by K. Pavlova for the November 1840 issue of *The Muscovite* (*Moskvitianin*, 51).

18. See Dostoevsky's 1840 letter to his brother Mikhail for the author's further discussion of Shidlovsky as a romantic type as well as his general appreciation of writers in the romantic tradition (*Pss*, 28.1:66–71).

19. Other than Risenkampf, Andrei Dostoevsky is the only person to note the existence of this early play, which he recalls having seen in a letter to A. S. Suvorin, editor of *Novoe vremia* (*New Time*). For further discussion of the play see, L. R. Lanskii, ed., "Dostoevskii v neizdannoi perepiske sovremennikov (1837–1881)," *Literaturnoe nasledstvo* 86 (1973): 366.

20. Samarin, *Iezuity i ikh otnoshenie*, 234.

21. Alekseev, "O dramaticheskikh opytakh Dostoevskogo," 49–50.

22. Charles E. Passage, *Character Names in Dostoevsky's Fiction* (Ann Arbor, Mich.: Ardis, 1982), 58.

23. Richard Peace, "Motive and Symbol: 'Crime and Punishment,'" in *Bloom's Major Literary Characters: Raskolnikov and Svidrigailov*, ed. Harold Bloom (Philadelphia, Pa.: Chelsea House, 2004), 161–62. Previously published in Richard Peace, *Dostoyevsky: An Examination of the Major Novels* (Cambridge: Cambridge University Press, 1971).

24. Michael Cherniavsky, "The Old Believers and the New Religion," in *The Structure of Russian History*, ed. Michael Cherniavsky, 158–69 (New York: Random House, 1970).

25. In her *Zhurnal M. M. i F. M. Dostoevskikh "Vremia,"* Nechaeva isolates in Shchapov's article two democratic trends within the Russian populace: (1) a movement of "rebellious outburst" like those of "Pugachevs, Razins, or self-proclaimed tsars" owing to centuries of oppression; and (2) a "quiet spiritual-moral, mystic-idealistic" movement aligned with "Christ, the prophets, and teachers" (197). Dostoevsky's depiction of an Old Believer in *House of the Dead* suggests that he links the schismatics with ties to religious sects, like Mikolka, to the latter movement, since the sympathetic description of a "quiet and gentle" Old Believer with "clear bright eyes" is followed by the narrator's question: "How could this humble person, meek like a child, be a rebel?" (*Pss*, 4:33).

26. As Sheddon discusses in *The Petrashevtsy*, Petrashevsky had once intended to disseminate revolutionary ideas with the help of such schismatics in Siberia (205). The Old Believers' anti-authoritarian sentiments did not escape the notice of the Herzen circle, which followed Shchapov's articles, as attested by Turgenev's and Herzen's correspondence as well as Bakunin's article: "The People's Business: Romanov, Pugachev, or Pestel?" ("Narodnoe delo: Romanov, Pugachev, ili Pestel'?"). For more discussion of Shchapov, see I. S. Turgenev, *Polnoe sobranie sochinenii i pisem v dvadtsati vos'mi tomakh*, 5.2:517–18. See also Herzen's 1862 letter to Turgenev, in which Herzen refers to an article written by Shchapov (*Ss*, 27.1:213).

27. Molly W. Wesling, *Napoleon in Russian Cultural Mythology*, The Age of Revolution and Romanticism: Interdisciplinary Studies 29 (New York: Peter Lang, 2001), 38.

28. In "Wspomnienia Sybiraka," his fellow inmate Bogusławski recalls a meeting with Old Believers in southwest Siberia, where he encountered an insular community of Old Believers who, although initially hesitant to communicate with an outsider, warm to him once he divulges that "I am not from the type of people who must repay good with evil" (259:1).

29. V. D'iakov et al., eds., *Vosstanie 1863 goda: Materialy i dokumenty*, 2 vols. (Moscow: I-d Akademii Nauk SSSR, 1963), 2:567.

30. In a potential revision for *The Double* from 1861–62, Dostoevsky gives Golyadkin dreams of becoming another Napoleon or a leader of a Russian uprising (*Pss*, 1:434). For a discussion of Prince K., see Robert. L. Jackson, "Napoleon in Russian Literature," *Yale French Studies* 26 (1960): 111–12, 114.

31. L. N. Tolstoi, *Voina i mir*, in *Sobranie sochinenii v dvadtsati dvukh tomakh*, 22 vols. (Moscow: Khudozhestvennaia literatura, 1979), 4:28.

32. For a discussion of *Hamlet*'s influence on the young Herzen, Bakunin, and Dostoevsky, see Iu. D. Levin, *Shekspir i russkaia literatura XIX veka*, ed. M. P. Alekseev, 137–41; 152, 167; 120–21 (Leningrad: Nauka, 1988). Here,

Dostoevsky has in mind Apollon Grigorev in this 1864 introduction to Strakhov's remembrances of the author.

33. S. F. Udartsev, "Rukopis' M. A. Bakunina 'Gamlet,'" in *Pamiatniki kul'tury: Novye otkrytiia* (Leningrad: Nauka, 1986), 55–57. The tragedy's popularity in the 1840s—owing to the 1837 performance of Pavel Mochalov in the title role and its famous review by Belinsky—encourages Udartsev to date Bakunin's "Hamlet" to the period of his friendship with Belinsky (1837).

34. The circle's interest in Hamlet may be further attested by the publications of fellow member Ivan Turgenev, who published the 1849 short story "Hamlet of Shchigrovsky District" ("Gamlet Shchigrovskogo uezda") as well as the famous 1860 speech "Hamlet and Don Quixote" discussed at the beginning of the introduction.

35. Udartsev, "Rukopis' M. A. Bakunina 'Gamlet,'" 57.

36. Ibid., 60.

37. In *The Casuistical Tradition in Shakespeare, Donne, Herbert and Milton* (Princeton, N.J.: Princeton University Press, 1981), Camille Wells Slight confirms the casuistic nature of Hamlet's "decision-making process," since he carefully applies moral values "to a particular set of circumstances" in order to identify an ethical response (105).

38. In Herzen's 1860 article announcing the end of the Hamlet period, the famous émigré denies the assertion by an anonymous radical that Russia has no recourse but to turn to the ax (*Ss,* 14:239, 541).

39. Samarin, *Iezuity i ikh otnoshenie,* 136.

40. This type of providentialist argument was common to Jesuit political thought, as Höpfl's *Jesuit Political Thought* indicates (109–10).

41. Höpfl, *Jesuit Political Thought,* 189.

42. Joseph Frank, *Dostoevsky: The Miraculous Years, 1865–1871* (Princeton, N.J.: Princeton University Press, 1995), 109.

43. Samarin, *Iezuity i ikh otnoshenie,* 8.

44. "Trifles console us because trifles distress us"; "one always finds more monks than reason"; Blaise Pascal, *Pensées,* in *Oeuvres complètes,* ed. Michel le Guern, 2 vols. (Paris: Gallimard, 1998–2000), 2:986; in "Les provinciales," Pascal writes about the Jesuits' judgment of their theological critics, the Jansenists: "De sorte qu'après tant d'épreuves de leur faiblesse, ils ont jugé plus à propos et plus facile de censurer que de repartir, parce qu'il leur est bien plus aisé de trouver des moines que des raisons" ("In such a way that after so many proofs of their weakness, they judged it more appropriate and easier to censure than to start over again, because it is much easier to find monks than reasons") (*Oeuvres complètes,* 1:611).

45. This reading of the Scientific Revolution is summarized from an entry on Pascal in A. V. Grube, *Biograficheskie kartinki* (Moscow: Izdanie knigoprodavtsa A. L. Vasil'eva, 1877), 58. N. F. Budanova includes this book in her

catalogue of Dostoevsky's library: *Biblioteka F. M. Dostoevskogo: Opyt rekon-struktsii: Nauchnoe opisanie* (St. Petersburg: Nauka, 2005), 163. For the young Dostoevsky's complaints to his father about the "strange science" of Pascal's mathematics (as opposed to "military sciences") whose benefits he compares to "a soap bubble," see an 1839 letter to his father (*Pss*, 28.1:59–60).

46. "The extremes touch [and reunite by force of having moved away and find themselves in God, and in God alone]"; Pascal, *Pensées*, 2:1042. See Dostoevsky's 1880–81 notebook for his geometric understanding of eternity (*Pss*, 27:43).

47. In *Dimitry's Shade: A Reading of Alexander Pushkin's "Boris Godunov"* (Evanston, Ill.: Northwestern University Press, 2004), J. Douglas Clayton finds that "the Pater who wrings from the pretender a promise to promote the Catholic Church in Russia" attests to a Jesuit presence in Pushkin's tragedy (105–6).

48. Samarin, *Iezuity i ikh otnoshenie*, 270.

49. Although his extant correspondence does not speak specifically of the drama, Chaev's epistolary responses about the publication and editing of his drama in early 1865 attest to Dostoevsky's work on the drama. For summaries of Chaev's responses, see the listing of Dostoevsky's business papers and letters in his complete works (*Pss*, 28.2:522–23).

50. In Mikhail Bakhtin, *Problems of Dostoevsky's Poetics*, ed. and trans. Caryl Emerson, Theory and History of Literature 8 (Minneapolis: University of Minnesota Press, 1984), Bakhtin first notes this reference (169).

51. N. A. Chaev, "Dimitrii Samozvanets. (Drama v piati deistviiakh)," *Ėpokha* (January 1865): 73.

52. In "Pretenders to History," Emerson discovers Otrepev's connection to Renaissance Poland and finds that he plays the role of a "Polish nobleman while courting Marina" (266, 262).

53. In "Paradoxes of the Popular Mind in Pushkin's *Boris Godunov*," *Slavonic and East European Review* 64, no. 1 (January 1986), Ilya Serman characterizes Otrepev as "the first Russian European" for his orientation toward the West (38).

54. Bakhtin, *Problems of Dostoevsky's Poetics*, 167–69.

55. Martinsen, *Surprised by Shame*, 20, 21.

56. Bakhtin, *Problems of Dostoevsky's Poetics*, 169.

57. For observations about the similar Napoleonic pretensions shared by Raskolnikov and Pushkin's Germann, see Jackson in "Napoleon in Russian Literature" (106); W. J. Leatherbarrow, *A Devil's Vaudeville: The Demonic in Dostoevsky's Major Fiction* (Evanston, Ill.: Northwestern University Press, 2005), 81; F. I. Evnin, "Roman 'Prestuplenie i nakazanie,'" in *Tvorchestvo F. M. Dostoevskogo* (Moscow: Izdatel'stvo Akademii Nauk SSSR, 1959), 132.

58. Caryl Emerson and Chester Dunning, "Introduction: Reconsidering History and Expanding the Canon," in *The Uncensored Boris Godunov: The Case for Pushkin's Original Comedy, with Annotated Text and Translation* (Madison: University of Wisconsin Press, 2006), 7.

59. "the egalitarian type"; "Oh! Madame, at least they have something that replaces all of that: it's fanaticism. Napoleon is the Muhammad of the West; it's for all these coarse men, with supreme ambitions, not only a legislator and a master but even more it is a type, the egalitarian type"; Dumas, *Le Comte de Monte-Cristo*, 1:91. For Dostoevsky's interest in Dumas from his Siberian period, see the third section of the first chapter.

60. In "K voprosu o 'prototipakh obraza idei' v romanakh Dostoevskogo," *Dostoevskii: Materialy i issledovaniia* 10 (1992), B. N. Tikhomirov finds that Raskolnikov's reference to Muhammad links his theory to the concept of the historical hero as prophet whereby a prophet such as Muhammad disseminates religious thought by force, much in the way that Raskolnikov's benefactor Napoleon spreads his humanitarianism (53).

61. Georg Wilhelm Friedrich Hegel, *The Philosophy of History*, trans. J. Sibree (New York: Dover, 1956), 251, 253, 262–63, 451. Although Hegel's lectures were originally delivered in the winter of 1822–23, this translation is based on the 1830–31 readings of his course on the philosophy of history. For a more detailed consideration of Hegel and Dostoevsky, see Malcolm V. Jones, "Some Echoes of Hegel in Dostoevsky," *Slavonic and East European Review* 49 (October 1971): 500–520.

62. "Politics is fate"; Hegel, *Philosophy of History*, 278.

63. Hegel, *Philosophy of History*, 278.

64. Hegel, *Philosophy of History*, 312–13. In his first letter to Mikhail after his release from prison, Dostoevsky includes Hegel's *History of Philosophy* on a list of books that he would like his brother to send him (*Pss*, 28.1:173). Citing from a letter about Dostoevsky that he wrote to a relative from Semipalatinsk, Wrangel records that "with him I study daily and now we are going to translate Hegel's *Philosophy*" (*Vospominaniia o F. M. Dostoevskom*, 34).

65. Hegel, *Philosophy of History*, 452–53.

66. T. N. Granovskii, "Lektsii iz srednei istorii T. N. Granovskogo," *Vremia* 9 (September 1862): 15.

67. Evnin, "Roman 'Prestuplenie i nakazanie,'" 152.

68. *History of Julius Caesar;* In *Napoléon dans la littérature russe* (Paris: L'Association Langues et Civilisations, 1974), Dmitri Sorokine finds that the history's influence on Dostoevsky's novel is suggested both by the appearance of the names of Napoleon and Julius Caesar in his notebooks to *Crime and Punishment* and by the fact that in 1862 the thick journals were full of articles on the 1812 campaign (237, 240).

69. Tolstoi, *Voina i mir*, 6:271.

70. "to accomplish in a few years the work of several centuries"; Leonid Grossman and Boris Tikhomirov identify a greater role for providence in Napoleon III's historical perspective. In *Dostoevskii* (Moscow: Molodaia Gvardiia, 1965), Grossman finds that with the help of such instruments as "banishments, executions, triumvirates, coups d'état . . . historical heroes executed the

deed assigned to them by providence" (348). In "K voprosu o 'prototipakh obraza idei' v romanakh Dostoevskogo," *Dostoevskii: Materialy i issledovaniia* 10 (1992), Tikhomirov further outlines the "providential interpretation of historical progress" presented by Napoleon III in the preface that allows the reader "to better see the providential character of Raskolnikov's philosophy of history" (44, 45).

71. "The historical truth must be no less sacred than religion"; Napoleon III, *Histoire de Jules César*, 5.

72. "If the precepts of faith raise our soul above the interests of the world, the teachings of history, for their part, inspire in us a love of the beautiful and just, a hatred of that which becomes an obstacle to the progress of humanity"; Napoleon III, *Histoire de Jules César*, 5, 6.

73. "a Jesuit in a short robe"; "director of conscience"; "abbot in a long robe"; Tolstoi, *Voina i mir*, 6:293–95. I am grateful to the second reader at Northwestern University Press for pointing out this Jesuit image in Tolstoy's novel.

74. Tolstoi, *Voina i mir*, 4:28, 27.

75. "It's not only the general interest that concerns them, but also they themselves, since your casuists, cited in my letters, extend their permission to kill even them"; Pascal, "Les provinciales," 1:742.

76. "one theory or another"; see chapter 5 for further discussion of the Grand Inquisitor.

77. Hegel, *Philosophy of History*, 254.

78. Emerson, "Pretenders to History," 258. See note 7 above for an overview of the scholarship (specifically the articles by Poddubnaia, Bilinkis, and Alekseev) linking *Crime and Punishment* to *Boris Godunov*. L. D. Opulskaya, in the notes to Dostoevsky's collected works, also posits a link between his novel and *Boris Godunov* based on their shared discussion of Napoleonic ambitions and crises of conscience (*Pss*, 7:343–45).

79. Clayton, *Dimitry's Shade*, 93.

80. Gary Rosenshield, *Western Law, Russian Justice: Dostoevsky, the Jury Trial, and the Law* (Madison: University of Wisconsin Press, 2005), 226.

81. Iaroslav Dombrovskii, "Dva pis'ma Iaroslava Dombrovskago," *Kolokol* 200 (July 15, 1865): 1640.

82. Ibid., 1640.

83. "this gives him so much pleasure and causes me so little trouble"; a likely source for this confessional scene is Michelet's *Le prêtre, la femme, et la famille*, in which the Jesuits exploit their roles as confessors to gain influence over women and children (49–50).

84. Gerald Fiderer, "Raskolnikov's Confession," *Bloom's Major Literary Characters: Raskolnikov and Svidrigailov*, ed. Harold Bloom, 91. Previously published in *Literature and Psychology* 30, no. 2 (1980): 62–71.

85. Although in *Dostoevsky's Secrets: Reading Against the Grain* (Evanston, Ill.: Northwestern University Press, 2009), Carol Apollonio finds valid traces of

Dunya's desire for Svidrigailov in this scene, she frequently relies on Svidrigailov's testimony, which seems unreliable given his obsession with Dunya and his similarities to the attractively seductive spy Aristov "with an insatiable thirst" for "the most bestial bodily delights" (*Pss*, 4:63; *Dostoevsky's Secrets*, 84–86). In "Svidrigailov and the 'Performing Self,'" in Bloom's *Major Literary Characters: Raskolnikov and Svidrigailov*, R. E. Richardson recognizes the mysterious attraction of Svidrigailov and attributes it to his theatricality (102). Richardson's article is reprinted from *Slavic Review* 46, nos. 3–4 (1987): 540–52.

86. In "Motive and Symbol: 'Crime and Punishment,'" Peace finds this connection significant because it marks him as "the barbarian *par excellence*, the perpetrator of cynical sacrilege for the goal of self-interest" (161–62).

87. Saulius Sužiedėlis, *Historical Dictionary of Lithuania*, European Historical Dictionaries 21 (Lanham, Md.: Scarecrow, 1997), 289. In *The Livonian Crusade* (Washington, D.C.: University Press of America, 1981), William Urban records that Švitrigaila and his followers were referred to as schismatics at the Council of Basel (280–81). Also, in Simas Sužiedėlis and Antanas Kučas, eds., *Encyclopedia Lituanica*, vol. 5 (Boston, Mass.: Juozas Kapočius, 1976), it is recorded that the politically ambitious Bishop Zbigniew Oleśnicki (chancellor of Poland), who sought to advance Polish interests throughout Lithuania, declared Švitrigaila a Russian and a schismatic (350).

88. N. M. Karamzin, *Istoriia gosudarstva Rossiiskago*, vol. 5 (St. Petersburg: Voennaia Tipografiia Glavnago Shtaba Ego Imperatorskago Velichestva, 1817), 183.

89. Ibid., 184.

90. Frank, *Dostoevsky: The Seeds of Revolt*, 8. In *Dostoyevsky: An Examination of the Major Novels*, Peace offers an interesting observation on this common Lithuanian link between Svidrigailov and Dostoevsky: "The Dostoyevskys themselves were conscious of being descended from noble Lithuanian stock, and in choosing this name perhaps the author is indulging in a device typical of his writing—self-identification with his worst characters" (315).

91. Bogusławski, "Wspomnienia Sybiraka," 286:1.

92. See note 25 for information on the article.

93. This is another potential allusion to Bakunin in Dostoevsky, since the former had just celebrated his flight to freedom from Siberia to America.

94. Wesling, *Napoleon in Russian Cultural Mythology*, 125.

95. In *Napoleon in Russian Cultural Mythology*, Wesling finds that following the Decembrist uprising, "in the Russian literary tradition, the close identification of a character with Napoleon was ever afterward a harbinger of failure—a reference to Napoleon's own tragic fall, but even more so to the social tragedy of the westward-looking, Siberian-bound Decembrists, whose story of exile fueled the nineteenth-century Russian literary imagination" (43).

96. For more on self-sanctification, see Dietrich Bonhoeffer's *Discipleship*,

vol. 4, *Dietrich Bonhoeffer Works,* trans. Barbara Green and Reinhard Krauss and ed. Geffrey B. Kelly and John D. Godsey (Minneapolis, Minn.: Fortress, 2001), 148.

97. Wesling, *Napoleon in Russian Cultural Mythology,* 15.

98. Sorokine, *Napoléon dans la littérature russe,* 78.

99. Ibid., 163–66.

100. Jackson, "Napoleon in Russian Literature," 107. Jackson attributes this image to the Russian romantics of the 1820s and 1830s with a particular focus on Mikhail Lermontov.

101. Hegel, *Philosophy of History,* 254.

CHAPTER FOUR

1. Gagarin, who wrote *La Russie sera-t-elle catholique?* (1856), was a cousin of the outspoken critic of the Jesuits, Yury Samarin.

2. For a discussion of this quotation in *The Double,* see the first section of chapter 3.

3. N. T. Ashimbaeva, "A. N. Maikov: Pis'ma k F. M. Dostoevskomu 1867–1878," *Pamiatniki kul'tury. Novye otkrytiia* 8 (1982): 81.

4. K. Marx and F. Engels, *L'Alliance de la démocratie socialiste et l'Association internationale des travailleurs,* in *Sochineniia,* 2nd ed., vol. 18 (Moscow: Gosudarstvennoe izdatel'stvo politicheskoi literatury, 1961), 424.

5. For a more extensive discussion of the "Geneva Idea" in Dostoevsky, see Bruce K. Ward, *Dostoevsky's Critique of the West: The Quest for the Earthly Paradise* (Waterloo, Canada: Wilfrid Laurier University Press, 1986), 46–51.

6. Anna Grigorevna notes that Ogarev gave Dostoevsky four books of *My Past and Thoughts* in 1867 (*Dnevnik 1867 goda,* 336).

7. In *Pamiętniki z lat 1857–1865,* ed. Tadeusz Korzon, 2 vols. (Vilnius: Księgarnia Stowarz. Nauczycielstwa Polskiego, 1921), Jakób Gieysztor mentions being with both Giller and Tokarzewski on the same evening (1:197).

8. Michel Bakounine, "K ofitseram russkoi armii," in *Michel Bakounine et ses relations avec Sergej Nečaev 1870–1872,* ed. Arthur Lehning (Leiden: E. J. Brill, 1974), 33.

9. Ibid., 32.

10. D'iakov, *Deiateli russkogo i pol'skogo osvoboditel'nogo dvizheniia,* 126; Cochrane, *The Collaboration of Nečaev, Ogarev and Bakunin in 1869,* 37, 45. Cochrane clarifies that much of the information concerning Berezowski's interests in the Jesuits was widely known (24, 37).

11. In "Ot russkogo revoliutsionnogo komiteta," *Narodnaia rasprava* 1 (Summer 1869; reprint, *Novyi Zhurnal* 1 [1994]), Nechaev views contemporary conspiracies within the tradition of the Decembrist and Polish uprisings (86).

Editors of the academic collection of Dostoevsky's works find echoes of the first issue of the Bakunin-Nechaev journal *Popular reprisal* in the speech of the revolutionary Petr Verkhovensky (*Pss*, 12:209).

12. M. P. Pogodin, *Pol'skii vopros: Sobranie razsuzhdenii, zapisok i zamechanii (1831–1867)* (Moscow: V tipografii gazety "Russkii," 1867), 78.

13. Katkov, *1863 god.*, 162, 273.

14. Leslie, *Reform and Insurrection in Russian Poland*, 224–26.

15. Anna Grigorevna records "We saw a bridge, and then a chapel on George's Square, built in honor of the suppression of the Poles and very beautiful (indecipherable) and simple, which I liked a lot" (*Dnevnik 1867 goda*, 5–6).

16. Dostoevskaia, *Dnevnik 1867 goda*, 178.

17. Ashimbaeva, "A. N. Maikov," 74.

18. For more on Turgenev in *Demons*, see Frank, *Dostoevsky: The Miraculous Years*, 461–65; Dolinin, *Dostoevskii i drugie*, 163–86. Turgenev's reaction to the novel may be found in a December 1872 letter to M. A. Miliutina in *Polnoe sobranie sochinenii i pisem v dvadtsati vos'mi tomakh*, 10.2:39.

19. Cochrane, *The Collaboration of Nečaev, Ogarev and Bakunin*, 45, 177.

20. Gagarin's Parisian publication of Chaadaev's writings, *Oeuvres choisies de Pierre Tchadaïef* (Paris: A. Franck, 1862), likely brought the dissident's name to Dostoevsky's attention in the 1860s.

21. Statistical analysis in Jerzy Borejsza's *Emigracja polska po powstaniu styczniowym* establishes this (25–27).

22. Andrzej Walicki, *Philosophy and Romantic Nationalism: The Case of Poland* (Notre Dame, Ind.: University of Notre Dame Press, 1982), 371.

23. In *Philosophy and Romantic Nationalism*, Andrzej Walicki describes briefly the careers of General Hauke-Bosak, Dąbrowski, and Wróblewski (372–73). More detailed information on the London and Genevan circles of Polish exiles is available in Borejsza, *Emigracja polska po powstaniu styczniowym*.

24. Ashimbaeva, "A. N. Maikov," 74; Borejsza, *Emigracja polska po powstaniu styczniowym*, 364–65. As the Polish lover of the infamous Princess Obolenskaya, who financed Bakunin's conspiratorial activities in Vevey, Mroczkowski occupied an important place in Bakunin's subversive International Brotherhood.

25. Victor Hugo, "Viktor Giugo russkomu voisku," *Kolokol* 156 (February 15, 1863): 1301. In her diary, Anna Grigorevna records that he sponsored a dinner on the final day (241), but Frank in *Dostoevsky: The Miraculous Years* notes that the dinner did not take place (234).

26. Nikolai Barsukov, *Zhizn' i trudy M. P. Pogodina*, vol. 20 (St. Petersburg: Tipografiia M. M. Stasiulevicha, 1907), 131.

27. "the fall of the papacy as the most injurious of sects"; "God's religion, that is to say, the religion of truth and reason"; "Confédération suisse," *Journal*

de Genève 212 (September 10, 1867): 1. *Le temps: Archives historiques,* http://www.letempsarchives.ch/Default/Skins/LeTempsFr/Client.asp?Skin=LeTemps Fr&enter=true&AppName=2&AW=1340325799323; Dostoevskaia, *Dnevnik 1867 goda,* 248.

28. "that in which he calls the moral of Christ there are two morals, a *pagan one* which is the good one, his and that of his friends, with another which is Christian and which brings *war and not peace* to family and peoples, according to the words of Christ himself"; "Confédération suisse," *Journal de Genève* 213 (September 11, 1867), 1. *Le temps: Archives historiques,* http://www.letemps archives.ch/Default/Skins/LeTempsFr/Client.asp?Skin=LeTempsFr&enter =true&AW=1340375421916&AppName=2.

29. Lead articles on the first page of Fazy's *Journal de Genève* for September 11, 12, and 13 show that this frustration over the chaos at the league's meetings was shared by other participants.

30. A. Askariants and Z. Kemenova, eds., "Pis'ma N. P. Ogareva A. I. Gertsenu," *Literaturnoe nasledstvo* 39–40 (1941): 470–71. James Fazy led the opposition of the Swiss Diet to the Sonderbund and dominated the political scene in Geneva after the new Constitution of 1848 was composed. Gustave de Molinari was a Belgian economist and journalist who promoted laissez-faire capitalism and opposed the spread of socialism in nineteenth-century Europe. Carlo Gambuzzi, who fought alongside Garibaldi in 1862, was the lover of Bakunin's wife Antonia Kwiatkowska and one of the members of his alliance.

31. Askariants and Kemenova, "Pis'ma N. P. Ogareva A. I. Gertsenu," 470. In her diary, Dostoevskaya records that she listened to an Italian (who could have been Gambuzzi) speaking on the theme of "Away with the papacy" (*Dnevnik 1867 goda,* 249).

32. "the country of the great citizen of this J.-J. Rousseau, who found the first of the rights of man buried by despotism"; "M. Dupont loudly demanded that all religions with their permanent armies be destroyed and that a tabula rasa be made of the churches as well as the barracks"; "Confédération suisse," *Journal de Genève* 213:1.

33. Dostoevsky's use of the term "Russian Christ" (*russkii Khristos*) here may also signify a return to the Russian monarchy, since Bakunin uses the term to describe the people's ideal tsar in his 1862 pamphlet "The People's Affair: Romanov, Pugachev, or Pestel?"

34. M. Bakunin, "Narodnoe delo: Romanov, Pugachev, ili Pestel'?" in *Polnoe sobranie sochinenii,* vol. 1 (Izdanie I. Balashova, 1907), 221, 215.

35. "There was no solidarity, even of national patriotism, between Russians devoted to the cause of liberty and their government"; "Confédération suisse," *Journal de Genève* 213:1. In *Dostoevskii,* Leonid Grossman erroneously concludes that Dostoevsky was at the second session of the congress when Bakunin spoke (416–18), but Frank's comparative analysis of the diary kept by

Dostoevsky's wife and the conference proceedings indicate the likelihood that he attended the third section (*Dostoevsky: The Miraculous Years*, 236).

36. Dostoevsky's use of the term "united states [*soiuznye shtaty*]" also echoes the organ of the league, *Les États-Unis de l'Europe*.

37. "Some Words to My Young Brothers in Russia"; Michel Bakounine, "Quelques paroles à mes jeunes frères en Russie," in *Michel Bakounine et ses relations slaves 1870–1875*, ed. Arthur Lehning (Leiden: E. J. Brill, 1974), 11–16.

38. I. Stekov records in *Mikhail Aleksandrovich Bakunin: Ego zhizn' i deiatel'nost'*, vol. 2 (Moscow: Gosudarstvennoe izdatel'stvo, 1927) that after an 1864 visit to Bakunin in Florence, artist Nikolai Ge recalled meeting Bakunin's beautiful Polish wife in addition to "an entire circle of Polish and Russian emigrants" (299).

39. E. H. Carr, *Michael Bakunin* (New York: Vintage Books, 1937), 329.

40. Mroczkowski—along with another Polish member of Bakunin's Italian circle, Jan Zagórski—was a member of the IWA. Mroczkowski directed the Lausanne Commune, all of whose Polish members belonged to the league, according to Borejsza (*Emigracja polska po powstaniu styczniowym*, 361).

41. The dating of Maikov's letter indicates that he may be referring to the first (September) issue of this journal edited by Bakunin, but his younger rival in the Genevan section of the IWA, Utin, subsequently seized the editorship of this journal after Bakunin failed to form an alliance between the League and the IWA at the latter's Brussels Congress in 1868.

42. D'iakov et al., eds., *Vosstanie 1863 goda*, 1:XXIX; Koz'min, "Aleksandr Serno-Solov'evich," 699–700. Herzen believed that, with the help of local members of the subversive group Land and Will, the significant population of schismatics in Kazan could help instigate a popular rebellion.

43. N. P. Mitina and T. F. Fedosova, "K voprosu o russko-pol'skikh revoliutsionnykh sviaziakh v 1864–1866 gg.," in *Sviazi revoliutsionerov Rossii i Pol'shi*, ed. V. A. D'iakov, et al., 98–101 (Moscow: Izdatel'stvo Nauka, 1968). For further information about the arrests of Serno-Solovevich and Chernyshevsky after the correspondence with Herzen, Ogarev, and Bakunin was seized, see I. E. Barenbaum, *N. A. Serno-Solov'evich 1834–1866: Ocherk knigotorgovoi i knigoizdatel'skoi deiatel'nosti* (Moscow: Izdatel'stvo vsesoiuznoi knizhnoi palaty, 1961), 27–30.

44. M. P. Dragomanov, ed., *Pis'ma M. A. Bakunina k A. I. Gertsenu i N. P. Ogarevu*, Slavistic Printings and Reprintings, vol. 111 (The Hague: Mouton, 1968), 319. Correspondence reveals that Bakunin is disappointed in the way that Herzen is responding to Alexander Serno-Solovevich's attacks and that Bakunin's ideas are not as far removed from the younger generation as Herzen's.

45. E. I. Kiiko in the notes to Dostoevsky's complete works identifies this collection (*Pss*, 21:379).

46. Bakunin, who protests against the Swiss cooperation with Russia in the

pursuit of Nechaev in a March pamphlet, "Les ours de Berne et l'ours de St-Pétersbourg" ("The Bears of Berne and the Bears of St. Petersburg"), states in a May letter to Mroczkowski and Princess Obolenskaya that the Swiss police were aggressively searching for Nechaev, because they were offering an award of 20,000 francs (Bakounine, *Michel Bakounine et ses relations avec Sergej Nečaev 1870–1872*, 80). In "Otkliki na smert' Gertsena po materialam inostrannoi pechati i 'Prazhskoi kollektsii,'" *Literaturnoe nasledstvo* 63 (1956), L. P. Lanskii provides a summary of various announcements of Herzen's death in the Western press (523–30).

47. M. N. Katkov, "Moskva, 5go ianvaria," 1–2. Parts of the article are cited in Grossman's *Dostoevskii* (452).

48. Lehning dates a French edition of the leaflet "Quelques paroles à mes jeunes frères en Russie" to September 1869.

49. Michel Bakounine, "Nécrologie d'Alexandre Herzen," in *Michel Bakounine et ses relations slaves 1870–1875*, 22.

50. M. Pogodin, "A. I. Gertsen," *Zaria* 2 (1870): 76.

51. Kiiko identifies this citation in the notes to this 1873 entry in Dostoevsky's collected works (*Pss*, 21:374).

52. In *1863 god*, Katkov discusses this proclamation distributed by Land and Will but he attributes it to Polish agitators (25).

53. For the dispute between Leonid Grossman and Vyacheslav Polonsky over the importance of Bakunin, see *Spor o Bakunine i Dostoevskom: Stat'i L. P. Grossmana i Viach. Polonskogo* (Leningrad: Tip. Pechatnyi dvor, 1926). For a recent evaluation of their debate that favors the presence of Bakunin in the novel, see James Goodwin's *Confronting Dostoevsky's Demons: Anarchism and the Specter of Bakunin in Twentieth-Century Russia* (New York: Peter Lang, 2010). For a discussion of Herzen's presence in *Demons*, see E. N. Dryzhakova, "Dostoevskii i Gertsen: U istokov romana 'Besy,'" *Dostoevskii: Materialy i issledovaniia* 1 (1974): 219–39.

54. The restoration of Poland's pre-partition borders, advocated by patriots in the wake of 1863, was regarded by many moderates as extreme; yet Dostoevsky uses it again to depict Polish patriots in *The Brothers Karamazov*.

55. Here, especially considering his common use of diminutives to refer to radicals, Dostoevsky may be making a veiled reference to Utin or Marx, who strongly promoted Polish independence through the IWA while Dostoevsky was in Geneva and Vevey.

56. In *Confronting Dostoevsky's Demons*, Goodwin discusses the later conflict between Utin and Bakunin, which Dostoevsky did not witness but may have read about in the press (38–42).

57. Armin Gebhardt's recent history of the May uprising in *Die Dresdner Mairevolution 1849* (Marburg: Tectum Verlag, 2006) likewise records Bakunin's placement of the *Sistine Madonna* on the barricade: "In fact, Bakunin is to

have proposed transporting the Sistine Madonna and another famous painting from the nearby gallery and installing them on the top of the barricade" (41); Borisenok, *Mikhail Bakunin i "pol'skaia intriga,"* 268–72.

58. As editor of *Epoch,* Dostoevsky defends Pushkin against the utilitarians' preference for boots in his debates with the *Russian Word (Russkoe slovo)* in 1864. He revives this debate in *The Idiot* through Lebedev's rejection of the "bread" (*Pss,* 8:311–12), which Herzen in *My Past and Thoughts* equates with science in a debate with the Redemptorist priest, Vladimir Pecherin, who fears "the triumph of social ideas": "What is there to fear? . . . Could it be the noise of the wheels, bringing daily bread to the hungry and half-dressed crowd" (*Ss* 11:402). See the notes to *The Idiot* in the academic collection of Dostoevsky's works for further discussion of Herzen's and Pecherin's arguments (*Pss,* 9:393).

59. Dostoevsky no doubt appreciated the irony that Stepan's ideal of the *Sistine Madonna* had little impact on Granovsky, who wrote, "if it had not been pointed out to me, I would have walked by," according to A. V. Stankevich in *Timofei Nikolaevich Granovskii: Biograficheskii ocherk* (Moscow: Tipografiia Gracheva i K., 1869), 77.

60. Świderska, *Studien zur literaturwissenschaftlichen Imagologie,* 326–27.

61. Levin, *Shekspir i russkaia literatura XIX veka,* 112–13.

62. N. F. Budanova, in the commentary to *Demons* in Dostoevsky's collected works, outlines the Stepan-Granovsky connection and traces Dostoevsky's knowledge of Granovsky both to Alexander Stankevich's biography and to Strakhov's articles on the historian (*Pss,* 12:169–76).

63. The quotation also appears without attribution to Herzen in Stankevich, *Timofei Nikolaevich Granovskii,* 136. Yet, owing to his knowledge of Granovsky and Herzen, Dostoevsky likely recognized the quotation from Herzen's article on the historian, "O Publichnykh chteniiakh g-na Granovskogo" ("About the Public Readings of Mr. Granovsky"; *Ss,* 2:123).

64. D. C. Offord discusses how Granovsky's links underscore Stepan's chivalry in "The Devils in the Context of Contemporary Russian Thought and Politics," in *Dostoevsky's "The Devils": A Critical Companion,* ed. W. J. Leatherbarrow (Evanston, Ill.: Northwestern University Press, 1999), 75–76.

65. Yury Levin maintains that Prince Harry and Stavrogin "start out in the same way" but diverge over a sense of duty, since Stavrogin's sense of duty resembles that of the aimless Hamlet in "Dostoevskii and Shakespeare," in *Dostoevskii and Britain,* ed. W. J. Leatherbarrow (Providence, R.I.: Berg, 1995), 65.

66. Maurice Hunt, *Shakespeare's Religious Allusiveness: Its Play and Tolerance* (Burlington, Vt.: Ashgate, 2004), 30.

67. Turgenev, "Gamlet i Don-Kikhot," 8:190.

68. V. G. Belinskii, "'Gamlet,' drama Shekspira: Mochalov v roli Gamleta," in *Polnoe sobranie sochinenii,* 2:313, 276, 284, 325.

69. Świderska, *Studien zur literaturwissenschaftlichen Imagologie,* 340–41.

70. Levin mentions that the Polish uprisings of 1831 and 1863 are connected in Herzen to the call for vengeance by Hamlet's father in act 1, scene 5 of the tragedy (*Shekspir i russkaia literatura,* 154).

71. Udartsev, "Rukopis' M. A. Bakunina 'Gamlet,'" 55–57.

72. Udartsev, "Rukopis' M. A. Bakunina 'Gamlet,'" 61. The stage presence of Fortinbras's retinue is mentioned in *Netochka Nezvanova* (*Pss,* 2:167).

73. Udartsev, "Rukopis' M. A. Bakunina 'Gamlet,'" 62.

74. Ibid., 61.

75. According to Edward Carr in *Michael Bakunin,* Bakunin owes his involuntary tour of duty on the Polish frontier in 1834 (during the aftermath of the 1831 uprising) to his failure to thrive at artillery school (17). In "'What's in a Name?': Shakespeare's Poland," *English Studies* 81, no. 3 (June 2000), Terence McCarthy proposes Fortinbras is likewise allowed to pursue a military expedition because Poland is "the obvious country for a belligerent young man to test his strength on" (207).

76. William Shakespeare, *Hamlet,* ed. Harold Jenkins (London: Methuen, 1982), 346, 415. Also, historical links of Henry IV to Poland may be found in Terence McCarthy's "'What's in a Name?'" 205.

77. For this reading of Shakespeare's *Hamlet,* see Linda Kay Hoff, *Hamlet's Choice: Hamlet—A Reformation Allegory,* Studies in Renaissance Literature 2 (Lewiston, N.Y.: Edwin Mellen), 310–12. In addition, McCarthy addresses some of the geographic confusion surrounding Denmark, Poland, Norway, and Sweden in *Hamlet* ("'What's in a Name?'" 210–11).

78. See the beginning of the introduction for a discussion of Turgenev's article.

79. For example, see R. M. Davison, "Dostoevsky's *The Devils:* The Role of Stepan Trofimovich Verkhovensky," in *Dostoevsky's "The Devils": A Critical Companion,* ed. W. J. Leatherbarrow, 125; Ivanits, *Dostoevsky and the Russian People,* 129; Nancy K. Anderson, *The Perverted Ideal in Dostoevsky's "The Devils"* (New York: Peter Lang, 1997), 151.

80. Martinsen, *Surprised by Shame,* 188. In *Holy Foolishness,* Harriet Murav places his novel about pretending within the Russian chronicle tradition (101–23).

81. Alexander II's April manifesto may be found in M. N. Katkov, *1863 god,* 67. Soon after the manifesto, the gentry of St. Petersburg province sent Alexander II an address of support in which they use the phrase "Polish troubles" (Katkov, *1863 god,* 93).

82. Dostoevsky's interest in Bakunin's pamphlets is evident from a pamphlet, *L'Internationale, Karl Marx, Mazzini et Bakounine,* that survived in his library as noted in Budanova, *Biblioteka F. M. Dostoevskogo,* 230. Additional pamphlets may have been among the papers that Dostoevsky burned before returning to St. Petersburg out of fear that he would be searched upon reentering Russia.

83. N. I. Kostomarov, *Smutnoe vremia Moskovskogo gosudarstva v nachale XVII stoletiia, 1604–1613* (Moscow: Charli, 1994), 795.

84. This popular belief was challenged by the conservative Russian historian Pogodin in an 1858 article, "Must One Consider Boris Godunov the Founder of Serfdom?" ("Dolzhno li schitat' Borisa Godunova osnovatelem krepostnogo prava?"), to which Kostomarov quickly responded in an article with the same title, which is mentioned on note 6 of the introduction. The response sparked one of many heated debates between the two historians, including several on the Time of Troubles.

85. "The communes had risen up en masse against the tyranny of the tsar, the clergy, the nobility, and the Muscovite bureaucracy in the first years of the 17th century, and this memorable revolution had failed to destroy the Empire"; Bakounine, "Quelques paroles à mes jeunes frères en Russie," 14.

86. "Man educated, civilized, chivalrous"; see the introduction for the Polish connection to Herzen's work.

87. Michel Bakounine, "K ofitseram russkoi armii," 33–34. Dostoevsky may have been familiar with this booklet, especially since its publication in March 1870 coincided with his interest in Herzen.

88. Nechaeva, *Zhurnal M. M. i F. M. Dostoevskikh "Vremia,"* 197. See note 25 in chapter 3 for a more thorough discussion of the article.

89. Michel Bakounine, "Nauka i nasushchnoe revoliutsionnoe delo," in Bakounine, *Michel Bakounine et ses relations slaves 1870–1875,* 67. This pamphlet, too, was published in March 1870 in Geneva under the imprint of Herzen's longtime Polish collaborator, Ludwik Czerniecki.

90. For a more thorough list of Kostomarov's publications in *The Herald of Europe,* which include materials later published as *The Time of Troubles of the Muscovite State* and *The Last Days of the Commonwealth of Poland (Poslednie gody Rechi Pospolitoi,* 1869–70), see his "Bibliograficheskii ukazatel' sochinenii N. I. Kostomarova" in *Literaturnoe nasledie: Avtobiografiia* (St. Petersburg: Tipografiia M. M. Stasiulevicha, 1890), 504–11.

91. Several Time of Troubles dramas written in the nineteenth century are discussed in O. A. Derzhavina, "Istoricheskie deiateli i sobytiia kontsa XVI—nachala XVII veka v izobrazhenii sovremennikov i v russkoi literature XIX veka," in *Drevniaia Rus' v russkoi literature XIX veka (Siuzhety i obrazy drevnerusskoi literatury v tvorchestve pisatelei XIX veka)* (Moscow: Akademiia Nauk SSSR, 1990), 143–79.

92. Murav, *Holy Foolishness,* 119–20.

93. This quote is discussed in Murav, *Holy Foolishness,* 112; and in Saraskina, *Besy,* 271.

94. In "Dostoevskii i Gertsen," Dryzhakova, thoroughly investigates Stepan's connection to Herzen (219–39).

95. Apollonio, *Dostoevsky's Secrets,* 124; Martinsen, *Surprised by Shame,* 251.

96. Świderska, *Studien zur literaturwissenschaftlichen Imagologie,* 332. Apollonio provides a more demonic reading of this parentage in *Dostoevsky's Secrets* (110).

97. Herzen says this of Bakunin in *My Past and Thoughts.*

98. For some discussion of the tsar-in-hiding in *Demons,* see Ivanits, *Dostoevsky and the Russian People,* 119–121; Goodwin, *Confronting Dostoevsky's Demons,* 30–31.

99. Bakunin, "Narodnoe delo," 234. In *Spor o Bakunine i Dostoevskom,* Leonid Grossman identifies Bakunin's theory of the robber-revolutionary (Stenka Razin) with Nikolai Stavrogin (13) and believes that Dostoevsky draws on his concept of the populist tsar from "Narodnoe delo: Romanov, Pugachev, ili Pestel'?" in *Diary of a Writer* (211). Goodwin provides an analysis of Grossman's argument in *Confronting Dostoevsky's Demons* (30–31, 74, 137–38).

100. It is difficult to isolate a single source for Dostoevsky's reference to Razin, since his name appears in several writings by those affiliated with *The Bell* and in the thick journals of the day, especially after the 1858 publication of Kostomarov's history, *The Revolt of Stenka Razin.*

101. For a brief summary of the work, see Thomas M. Prymak, *Mykola Kostomarov: A Biography* (Toronto: University of Toronto Press, 1996), 80–81. All the same, Kostomarov encourages a harsh critique of historical and present Polish unrest, particularly after 1863.

102. Saraskina, *Besy,* 141.

103. Murav, *Holy Foolishness,* 114.

104. In *A Devil's Vaudeville: The Demonic in Dostoevsky's Major Fiction* (Evanston, Ill.: Northwestern University Press, 2005), W. J. Leatherbarrow links Petr to the demonic, owing in part to his arrival in town in the chapter "The Wise Serpent" (119). On the other hand, Victor Terras in *Reading Dostoevsky* (Madison: University of Wisconsin Press, 1998) views Petr as a "clever demon" and reserves the serpentine imagery for Stavrogin (89, 92).

105. The assertion by the Prince in the notebooks that a belief in the Immaculate Conception is a prerequisite for Christian faith demonstrates the doctrinal importance of the ever-Virgin Mary (here given the same significance as the raising of Lazarus) for *Demons* (*Pss,* 11:180). Also, Leatherbarrow in *A Devil's Vaudeville* discovers other strong apocalyptic imagery in *Demons* (138–39).

106. Susanne Fusso discusses the connection of the Marias through the imagery of the *Sistine Madonna* in "'Maidens in Childbirth': The Sistine Madonna in Dostoevskii's *Devils,*" *Slavic Review* 54, no. 2 (Summer 1995): 264–65, 268–70. In *Dostoevsky's Secrets,* Apollonio, in dialogue with Fusso, connects them to an *"image of motherhood"* in the novel (115–16).

107. In *Holy Foolishness,* Murav provides an insightful discussion of Maria's connection to the tradition of saintly folly (113–15).

108. Leonid S. Chekin, "Notes of Images of the Time of Troubles in *The Devils* and *The Brothers Karamazov*," *Dostoevsky Studies*, n.s., 2, no. 1 (1998): 90.

109. Such jesuitical reasoning by an unlearned disciple to motivate a murder anticipates the Ivan-Smerdyakov relationship in Dostoevsky's final novel.

110. Murav, *Holy Foolishness*, 115. Murav provides an interesting overview of "the ways in which imposture, demonic play, and social chaos were coded in the seventeenth century" (103–6).

111. Leatherbarrow, *A Devil's Vaudeville*, 131–35.

112. Ashimbaeva, "A. N. Maikov," 74.

113. Ibid., 74.

114. Martinsen, *Surprised by Shame*, 188–89.

115. Editors of the academic collection of Dostoevsky's works find echoes of the first issue (1869) of the Bakunin-Nechaev journal *Popular Reprisal* in the speech of the revolutionary Petr Verkhovensky (*Pss*, 12:209).

116. This quotation is taken from Herzen's protest against tsarist terror tactics in a May 1866 article, "Irkutsk i Peterburg," in *The Bell*.

117. This citation is taken from chapter 6 of *My Past and Thoughts*. In the Russian Shakespearean tradition, Hamlet is closely linked to suicide (perhaps owing to the suicidal conclusion of Sumarokov's *Hamlet*), a tradition continued by Turgenev in "Hamlet and Don Quixote" when he analyzes a citation from the tragedy's second scene of the first act ("Gamlet i Don-Kikhot," 8:197).

118. Herzen uses the image of Don Quixote to refer to those revolutionaries inspired by 1789 who against reason sought an earthly Kingdom of God in the building of republics in Europe, especially France and Italy (*Ss*, 16:150–53). He remains optimistic, particularly in the chapter "Vixerunt!" of *From the Other Shore* (*S togo berega*, 1850), that the success of a young Fortinbras will vindicate the aspirations of such revolutionaries in the expanse of history (*Ss*, 6:69).

119. Given Dolinin's discussion regarding the presence of Turgenev's "Specters" ("Prizraki") in the novel, this use of "specters" does not appear accidental (*Dostoevskii i drugie*, 165–73).

120. Feofan Prokopovich, the advisor chosen by Peter to draft the eighteenth-century spiritual reforms abolishing the patriarchate in favor of the Ecclesiastical College, is credited with having introduced Latinizing elements from the West into Russian Orthodoxy, owing to his connection with a Kievan school of theology.

121. Robert Louis Jackson, *Dostoevsky's Quest for Form: A Study of His Philosophy of Art* (New Haven, Conn.: Yale University Press, 1966), 11.

122. See James Scanlan's *Dostoevsky the Thinker* for a discussion of Dostoevsky's consistent search for "a panhuman ideal" (160–61).

123. Leatherbarrow, *A Devil's Vaudeville*, 132.

124. As the following chapter will discuss, Dostoevsky's development of the "Roman idea" betrays the influence of Granovsky, who identifies ancient Rome

with the concept of "universal monarchy [*vsemirnaia monarkhiia*]" in "Lektsii iz srednei istorii T. N. Granovskogo," 9.

125. For example, in her diary Anna Grigorevna recalled visiting a cathedral in Basel, Switzerland—an important Renaissance center and a haven for the Reformation's Protestant refugees—where she and her husband were shown the casket of the Catholic Renaissance humanist Desiderius Erasmus of Rotterdam, and the Salle de Conseils where the Ecumenical Council of Basel met to debate ecclesiastical authority with Pope Eugene IV (*Dnevnik 1867 goda,* 232). This council is also significant for the East, because it was at this council (later moved to Ferrara and then to Florence) that the decree of union with the Greek church was reached in 1439.

126. Budanova, *Biblioteka F. M. Dostoevskogo,* 230.

127. "It's a revolution a thousand times more tremendous than the one which, starting with the Renaissance and the seventeenth century above all, had overturned the scholastic doctrines and the ramparts of the Church, of the absolute monarchy, and of the feudal nobility in order to replace them with the metaphysical dogmatism of supposedly pure reason"; [Michel Bakounine,] *L'Internationale, Karl Marx, Mazzini et Bakounine,* 2nd ed. (Brussels: Libraire Cosmopolite Vital Puissant, 1871), 14.

128. Davison, "Dostoevsky's *The Devils,*" 125–26.

129. Ivanits, *Dostoevsky and the Russian People,* 128–30.

130. George E. Ganss, S.J, ed., *Ignatius of Loyola: The Spiritual Exercises and Selected Works* (N. Y.: Paulist, 1991), 10.

131. Michel Bakounine, "Vsesvetnyi revoliutsionnyi soiuz sotsial'noi demokratii, russkoe otdelenie: K russkoi molodezhi," in *Michel Bakounine et ses relations slaves 1870–1875,* 76.

132. "the last great priest of religious, metaphysical, and political idealism"; "faith in the Messianic predestination of Italy, the queen of nations, with Rome, the capital of the world"; [Bakounine,] *L'Internationale,* 5.

133. Michel Bakounine, "Vsesvetnyi revoliutsionnyi soiuz sotsial'noi demokratii," 76.

134. Goodwin, *Confronting Dostoevsky's Demons,* 54.

135. Katkov, *1863 god,* 283.

136. Nikolai's indifference to Fedka's theft and sale of this icon (*Pss,* 10:220–21) indicates further distancing from this potential namesake, whose "coincidence of name" is noted by Leatherbarrow in *A Devil's Vaudeville* (130).

CHAPTER FIVE

1. The English translation of the epigraph for this chapter is: "God will have too much consideration for the estate and will not give Hell the malicious pleasure of sending it a priest."

2. Also, Janik compares the actions of the Muscovite authorities in Vilnius following the arrest of Konarski to "the Spanish Inquisition [*hiszpańska inkwizycja*]" in *Dzieje Polaków* (130).

3. James Cracraft, *The Church Reform of Peter the Great* (Stanford, Calif.: Stanford University Press, 1971), 193, 229.

4. Samarin, *Iezuity i ikh otnoshenie*, 9.

5. *Sbornik protokolov Obshchestva liubitelei dukhovnago prosveshcheniia*, S.-Peterburgskii otdel, 5 vols. (St. Petersburg: Tipografiia F. G. Éleonskago i K., 1873–77), 4:49–50. All five volumes are in Dostoevsky's library (Budanova, *Biblioteka F. M. Dostoevskogo*, 128). *La Civiltà Cattolica* was an Italian periodical published by the Society of Jesus in Rome.

6. Sandoz provides a biblical history of the quotation in *Political Apocalypse*, 131–32. For additional discussion of its Pauline intertext within the context of the novel, see Nina Perlina, *Varieties of Poetic Utterance: Quotation in "The Brothers Karamazov"* (Lanham, Md.: University Press of America, 1985), 98–99.

7. Vrangel', *Vospominaniia o F. M. Dostoevskom*, 105. He cites a Latin phrase used cross-culturally to recognize the severity of certain laws, that is, "The law is harsh, but it is the law."

8. With a thorough discussion of *Diary of a Writer*, Evnin's "Dostoevskii i voinstvuiushchii katolitsizm 1860–1870-kh godov" demonstrates that the clergy loyal to the pope in Germany and the rise of the Clerical Party in France encourage Dostoevsky to believe in the militant nature of Catholicism (31, 33). In *Dostoevsky and the Catholic Church*, Dirscherl highlights the importance of ultramontanism for the discussion of Ivan's article on church and state in *The Brothers Karamazov* (116–17).

9. V. A. Viktorovich, "Dostoevskii v Obshchestve liubitelei dukhovnogo prosveshcheniia," *Dostoevskii i mirovaia kul'tura* 20 (2004): 9, 16–20. *Edinoverie* was a process by which Old Believers could return to the Russian Orthodox Church. For the debate between Filippov and Ivan Nilsky, a professor at the Petersburg Spiritual Academy (Peterburgskaia dukhovnaia akademiia), see *Sbornik protokolov*, 2:86–241, 256–424.

10. In his recollections "Vospominaniia o F. M. Dostoevskom," in Tiun'kin and Tiun'kina's *F. M. Dostoevskii v vospominaniiakh sovremennikov*, Solovev remembers having met Dostoevsky in January of 1873 (201–2). After the Society meeting on January 30, at which Dostoevsky's attendance is confirmed (Budanova and Fridlender, *Letopis'*, 2:338), Dostoevsky describes him as a "rather warm soul" (*Pss*, 29.1:259). Dostoevsky also invites him to one of the regular meetings at Meshchersky's attended by Pobedonostsev and Filippov (Budanova and Fridlender, *Letopis'*, 2:329). For additional information on the Dostoevsky-Solovev friendship during this period, see Frank's *Dostoevsky: The Mantle of the Prophet, 1871–1881* (Princeton, N.J.: Princeton University Press, 2002), 49–53, 61–63.

11. For a partial listing of Pobedonostsev's articles published in the 1873 issues of *The Citizen*, see Robert F. Byrnes, *Pobedonostsev: His Life and Thought* (Bloomington: Indiana University Press, 1968), 429.

12. See Thompson, *"The Brothers Karamazov" and the Poetics of Memory*, for further discussion of the novel's Reformation context (282).

13. *Sbornik protokolov*, 4:46–47.

14. Osinin's name is mentioned in the introduction to the aforementioned summary by Dostoevsky in *The Citizen* (*Pss*, 21:291).

15. The editor of *Contemporary News* (*Sovremennye izvestiia*), Nikita Gilyarov-Platonov, reports on Osinin's lectures in December 1871 in the series "O miunkhenskom kongresse starokatolikov," in which he mentions an article on Osinin's lectures that appeared in *Voice*. For the articles, see the collection of Gilyarov-Platonov's writings published by the Synod Press at Pobedonostsev's request: *Voprosy very i tserkvi: Sbornik statei 1868–1887 gg*, ed. N. V. Shakhovskii, vol. 1 (Moscow: Sinodal'naia Tipografiia, 1905), 316–21, 324–29.

16. John Basil, "The Russian Theological Academies and the Old Catholics, 1870–1905," in *Religious and Secular Forces in Late Tsarist Russia: Essays in Honor of Donald W. Treadgold*, ed. Charles E. Timberlake (Seattle: University of Washington Press, 1992), 96.

17. *Sbornik protokolov*, 1:7.

18. Leonid Grossman, "Dostoevskii i pravitel'stvennye krugi 1870–kh godov," *Literaturnoe nasledstvo* 15 (1934): 152. Filippov's appeal drew *The Citizen* and its editor into the contentious issue of the canonicity of the Holy Synod, which the ecclesiastical hierarchy defended as a permanent church council. Filippov thus encouraged those challenging the Russian church's authority to address doctrine in the absence of a Russian Orthodox church council, which had not been held since the seventeenth century. For Dostoevsky's biting criticism of Nilsky and his supporters, see his articles in the April and May 1873 issues of *The Citizen* (*Pss*, 21:139–42, 278–80).

19. Grossman, "Dostoevskii i pravitel'stvennye krugi," 152. For further discussion of the Schism and the OLDP, see the series of articles "Chtenie T. I. Filippova v zasedanii peterburgskogo Obshchestva liubitelei dukhovnogo prosveshcheniia 26 fevralia" and "Chtenie T. I. Filippova v zasedanii peterburgskogo Obshchestva liubitelei dukhovnogo prosveshcheniia 13 marta," *Grazhdanin* 11–16 (March 18, 25, 1874; April 8, 15, 22, 1874): n. pag. *Philolog.ru Biblia*, http://www.philolog.ru/filolog/grajdanin.htm.

20. [K. P. Pobedonostsev], "Tserkov' i gosudarstvo," *Grazhdanin* 17–19 (April 23, 30, 1873; May 7, 1873): n. pag. *Philolog.ru Biblia*, http://www.philolog.ru/filolog/grajdanin.htm. This is among those articles attributed to Pobedonostsev by Byrnes in *Pobedonostsev* (429).

21. I. A. Chistovich, "Po povodu starokatolicheskogo dvizheniia," in *Sbornik protokolov*, 2:3–26.

22. [K. P. Pobedonostsev], "K voprosu o vozsoedinenii tserkvei," *Grazhdanin* 33 (August 13, 1873): n. pag. *Philolog.ru Biblia*, accessed May 20, 2010, http://smalt/karelia.ru/~filolog/grazh/1873/13auN33.htm. Based on his correspondence with Dostoevsky, Valentina Vetlovskaya identifies the pseudonyms "V.," with which the article is signed, and "Z. Z." as Pobedonostsev's (*Pss*, 21:533–34).

23. For his discussion of the churches in Germany under the pseudonym Z. Z., see "Bor'ba gosudarstva s tserkov'iu v Germanii," *Grazhdanin* 34 (August 20, 1873): n. pag. *Philolog.ru Biblia*, http://smalt/karelia.ru/~filolog /grazh/1873/20auN34.htm; "Bor'ba gosudarstva s tserkov'iu v Germanii," *Grazhdanin* 40 (October 1, 1873): n. pag. *Philolog.ru Biblia*, http://smalt /karelia.ru/~filolog/grazh/1873/1ocN40.htm; "Tserkovnye dela v Germanii," *Grazhdanin* 51 (December 17, 1873): n. pag. *Philolog.ru Biblia*, http://smalt /karelia.ru/~filolog/grazh/1873/17deN51.htm; "Tserkovnye dela v Germanii," *Grazhdanin* 5 (February 4, 1874); n. pag. *Philolog.ru Biblia*, http://smalt/ karelia .ru/~filolog/grazh/1874/74n05.htm.

24. [Pobedonostsev], "K voprosu o vozsoedinenii tserkvei."

25. As was reported in *The Citizen,* the OLDP at its October 31, 1873 meeting (at which Dostoevsky may have been in attendance) agreed to cooperate closely with the Old Catholic Commission formed at the Congress of Constance to investigate the potential for union (Budanova and Fridlender, *Letopis'*, 430). For further detail, see "Peterburgskoe obozrenie," *Grazhdanin* 45 (November 5, 1873): n. pag. *Philolog.ru Biblia*, http://smalt/karelia.ru/~filolog/grazh/1873/5nN45 .htm#a6. For more on Dean Stanley's address and Pobedonostsev's introduction, see "Protokol piatogo zasedaniia" in *Sbornik protokolov* (2:242–50) or "Peterburgskoe obozrenie," *Grazhdanin* 5 (February 4, 1874): n. pag. *Philolog.ru Biblia*, http://smalt/karelia.ru/~filolog/ grazh/1874/74n05.htm. In "Redaktorskaia deiatel'nost' F. M. Dostoevskogo v zhurnale 'Grazhdanin' i religiozno-nravstvennyi kontekst 'Brat'ev Karamazovykh,'" *Russkaia literatura* 3 (1996), Irene Zohrab, before describing the novel's dialogue with Dean Stanley, provides a summary of articles on and by Dean Stanley that appeared in *The Citizen* in January, February, and March of 1874 (61–62).

26. Aleksandr Kireev, "Otchet o deiatel'nosti S. Peterburgskago otdela Obshchestva liubitelei dukhovnago prosveshcheniia 1873–1874," in *Sbornik protokolov*, 2:453–62.

27. A. L. Katanskii, "Chtenie pr. Katanskago 'Kratkii Ocherk istorii i kharakteristika popytok k soedineniiu Tserkvei Greko-Vostochnoi i Rimsko-Katolicheskoi za ves' vos'mivekovoi period razdeleniia Tserkvei,'" in *Sbornik protokolov*, 1:127–28.

28. T. I. Filippov, "Chtenie T. I. Filippov o bonskoi konferentsii," in *Sbornik protokolov*, 4:187.

29. In an October 1873 article, Dostoevsky directs his reader to Pobedonostsev's series entitled "Bor'ba gosudarstva s tserkov'iu v Germanii" discussed in note 23 above (*Pss*, 21:191).

30. [Pobedonostsev], "K voprosu o vozsoedinenii tserkvei."

31. N. P. Giliarov-Platonov, "Voinstvuiushchee ul'tramontantstvo," in *Voprosy very i tserkvi*, 397–400.

32. Several studies of Schiller and Dostoevsky effectively link *Don Carlos* to Ivan's poem. For example, Alexandra H. Lyngstad, in *Dostoevskij and Schiller* (The Hague: Mouton, 1975), concludes that "both the setting and the main character of the tale indubitably derive from Schiller's *Don Carlos*" (84). N. Vilmont finds that "from Schiller Ivan Karamazov borrowed both the spirit and philosophical basis of his poem" in his study *Velikie sputniki: Literaturnye étiudy* (Moscow: Sovetskii pisatel', 1966), 247.

33. Vladimir Kerenskii, *Starokatolitsizm: Ego istoriia i vnutrennee razvitie* (Kazan: Tipo-Litografiia Imperatorskago Universiteta, 1894), 98–99.

34. Ibid., 99–100.

35. A. A. Kireev, "Pis'mo A. A. Kireeva k I. T. Osininu," in *Sbornik protokolov*, 1:102–3.

36. Dostoevsky recovers from this initial impression and has contact with Tachalov during his visits to Ems in 1875 and 1876, so he may have received additional information on the Old Catholics from him during his period.

37. In "Plachevnye razmyshleniia o despotizme i o vol'nom rabstve mysli," in *Vospominaniia* (Moscow: Academia, 1930), Apollon Grigorev characterizes this as "the formula of despotism of 1792"—a date that corresponds to the beginning of the Terror in France when Parisian prisoners of the nobility and clergy were summarily executed in order to eradicate enemies of the state (343).

38. *Sbornik protokolov*, 1:33.

39. Filippov, "Chtenie T. I. Filippov o bonskoi konferentsii," 188.

40. V. S. Solov'ev, "Tri sily," in *Sobranie sochinenii V. S. Solov'eva*, 2nd ed., 12 vols. (St. Petersburg, 1911–13; reprint, Brussels: Foyer Oriental Chrétien, 1966), 1:227.

41. V. S. Solov'ev, "Chteniia o Bogochelovechestve (1877–1881)," in *Sobranie sochinenii V. S. Solov'eva*, 3:12. The date and location of the lecture as well as Dostoevsky's attendance at some of the lectures is established in Budanova and Fridlender, *Letopis'*, 3:249, 278–79.

42. The articles "Soglashenie s Rimom i moskovskie gazety" and "O tserkovnom voprose po povodu starokatolikov" may be found in the fourth volume of *Sobranie sochinenii V. S. Solov'eva* (117–32, 123–32).

43. In "The Russian Theological Academies," Basil finds that Russian participation in the Old Catholic movement waned by 1876 owing to the Russians' recognition that the Old Catholics were only a sect (92), whereas C. B. Moss in *The Old Catholic Movement: Its Origin and History* (Eureka Springs, Ark.: Episcopal Book Club, 1964) attributes the decline to growing political tensions over the Russo-Turkish War (270).

44. *Sbornik protokolov*, 1:104. For a more detailed discussion of the theo-

logical significance of the council, see Timothy Ware, *The Orthodox Church,* rev. ed. (London: Penguin Books, 1993), 34–35.

45. For a discussion of the entry, see Budanova, *Biblioteka F. M. Dostoevskogo,* 283.

46. Granovskii, "Lektsii iz srednei istorii," 5.

47. Granovskii, "Lektsii iz srednei istorii," 9. In his study "The Categories of Law and Grace in Dostoevsky's Poetics," Esaulov traces law *(pravo)* as a theological category in the Russian Orthodox tradition to Ilarion's *Sermon on Law and Grace (Slovo o zakone i blagodati)* and finds that Dante's presence in Ivan's discussion links Dante's "poetic encyclopedia of the medieval Catholic worldview" to a legalistic Roman theology (116, 122).

48. K. Pobedonostsev, *Istoricheskiia izsledovaniia i stat'i* (St. Petersburg: Tipografiia Ministerstva putei soobshcheniia, 1876), 280. Dostoevsky discusses the new study in a letter to Vsevolod Solovev in 1876 *(Pss,* 29.2:73).

49. Grossman, "Dostoevskii i pravitel'stvennye krugi 1870–kh godov," 137.

50. Thompson, *"The Brothers Karamazov" and the Poetics of Memory,* 285.

51. Granovsky's article on the Inquisition, "Ispanskaia inkvizitsiia," in *Sochineniia T. N. Granovskago,* vol. 2 (Moscow: V Tipografii V. Got'e, 1856), highlights its fame in literature by noting that the auto-da-fé is probably known to the reader "if not from historical works then from novels" (443).

52. Mikhail Vasil'evich Butashevich-Petrashevskii, "Pokazanie," in *Filosofskie i obshchestvenno-politicheskie proizvedeniia petrashevtsev,* ed. V. E. Evgrafov (Moscow: Gosudarstvennoe izdatel'stvo politicheskoi literatury, 1953), 456.

53. Granovskii, "Ispanskaia inkvizitsiia," 440. Similarly, Granovsky concludes that Ferdinand and Isabella stood at the head of the Inquisition "with an aim more political than religious"—the protection of their own privilege (440).

54. "Very little."

55. In *Istoricheskiia izsledovaniia i stat'i,* Pobedonostsev lists the five basic forms of Roman torture shared by Russia and the West as *verbera, equuleus, fidiculae, ungulae,* and *laminae* (284).

56. Deborah A. Martinsen, "Shame's Rhetoric, or Ivan's Devil, Karamazov Soul," in *A New Word on "The Brothers Karamazov,"* ed. Robert Louis Jackson (Evanston, Ill.: Northwestern University Press, 2004), 61.

57. Robin Feuer Miller, *"The Brothers Karamazov": Worlds of the Novel* (New York: Twayne, 1992), 62–63; Martinsen, "Shame's Rhetoric," 61–62.

58. This stands in marked contrast to another conversion in *House of the Dead,* in which a Kalmyk, Alexander, seeking to receive a reduced sentence, opportunistically decides to convert *(Pss,* 4:145).

59. S. S. Averintsev and A. N. Meshkov, eds., *Khristianstvo: Ėntsiklopedicheskii slovar' v 3 tomakh,* 3 vols. (Moscow: Nauchnoe izdatel'stvo "Bol'shaia Rossiiskaia ėntsiklopediia," 1995), 3:7.

60. Gregory L. Freeze, *The Parish Clergy in Nineteenth-Century Russia:*

Crisis, Reform, Counter-Reform (Princeton, N. J.: Princeton University Press, 1983), 7. This was not confined to the Orthodox Church, as Dostoevsky likely knew from the Omsk conspiracy, which was rumored to have been discovered owing to a Tobolsk pastor informing authorities about a soldier's disclosure. For more detail, see Bogusławski, "Wspomnienia Sybiraka," 282:1; Włodzimierz Djakow, "Polscy zesłańcy," 62; Janik, *Dzieje Polaków*, 155.

61. See, for example, Sergei Durov's testimony in Desnitskii, *Delo Petrashevtsev*, 3:193. In *The Parish Clergy in Nineteenth-Century Russia*, Freeze reports that the faithful regularly received these sacraments as late as 1916 (xxix). It is also significant that Granovsky discusses the Spanish Inquisition's use of informants to elicit confessions from impressionable co-conspirators in "Ispanskaia inkvizitsiia" (439).

62. Vrangel', *Vospominaniia o F. M. Dostoevskom*, 52.

63. "The 'pop [Russian priest]' lost all his influence because of his greed, drunkenness, and intimate relations with the police."

64. See note 120 of the fourth chapter for a discussion of the link between Peter and Catholicism.

65. Granovskii, "Ispanskaia inkvizitsiia," 443.

66. Already in 1863, Dostoevsky associates bread with mass manipulation when describing the "prattling loudmouths and whistlers, whistling for their bread" in the article "A Necessary Literary Explanation Concerning Various Cereal and Non-Cereal Questions" ("Neobkhodimoe literaturnoe ob"iasnenie po povodu raznykh khlebnykh i nekhlebnykh voprosov"; *Pss*, 20:50).

67. Thomas Bokenkotter, *Church and Revolution: Catholics in the Struggle for Democracy and Social Justice* (New York: Doubleday, 1998), 26.

68. See Ivanits's discussion of the Lord's Prayer and the flogging in *Dostoevsky and the Russian People* (27). This prayer is also uttered by Edmond Dantès while he was imprisoned in the château d'If in Alexandre Dumas's *Le Comte de Monte-Cristo*.

69. Bakhtin, *Problems of Dostoevsky's Poetics*, 168.

70. N. M. Iadrintsev, *Russkaia obshchina v tiur'me i ssylke* (St. Petersburg: Tipografiia A. Morigerovskogo, 1872), 113.

71. Pobedonostsev, *Istoricheskiia izsledovaniia i stat'i*, 292.

72. Bakhtin, *Problems of Dostoevsky's Poetics*, 118.

73. Elizabeth Blake, "Sonya, Silent No More: A Response to the Woman Question in Dostoevsky's 'Crime and Punishment,'" *Slavic and East European Journal* 50, no. 2 (Summer 2006): 261–65.

74. Malcolm V. Jones, "'The Legend of the Grand Inquisitor': The Suppression of the Second Temptation and Dialogue with God," *Dostoevsky Studies* 7 (1986): 125.

75. Thompson, *"The Brothers Karamazov" and the Poetics of Memory*, 195.

76. Ibid., 128.

77. Bakhtin, *Problems of Dostoevsky's Poetics*, 97–98.

78. In *Dostoevsky the Thinker,* Scanlan concludes from this passage that these figures "represented not conviction defeating conscience but an evil *conscience*" (98).

79. Cochrane, *The Collaboration of Nečaev, Ogarev and Bakunin in 1869*, 177.

80. In *Russia, Poland and the West,* Lednicki discusses Dostoevsky's objection to Mickiewicz's praise of the traitor Wallenrod (347–48).

81. For more on Dostoevsky's familiarity with Herzen's *Endings and Beginnings,* see E. I. Kiiko's discussion of its presence in *Winter Notes on Summer Impressions* (*Pss*, 5:358–60).

82. Perlina, *Varieties of Poetic Utterance*, 125–35.

83. Ivan's reference to "Young Russia" links his argument to the 1860s, when Herzen published the article "Young and Old Russia" ("Molodaia i staraia Rossiia") in response to the proclamation "Young Russia" which was distributed in Moscow and St. Petersburg in 1862 (*Ss*, 16:411).

84. Anthony J. Cascardi, *The Bounds of Reason: Cervantes, Dostoevsky, and Flaubert* (New York: Columbia University Press, 1986), 68, 70.

85. "the last great priest of religious idealism"; Mazzini and Bakounine, *L'Internationale: Karl Marx,* 5. See the final section of chapter 4 for a more detailed discussion of this pamphlet.

86. See the second section of chapter 4 for a fuller discussion of this 1873 *Diary of a Writer* entry.

87. Victor Terras, *A Karamazov Companion: Commentary on the Genesis, Language, and Style of Dostoevsky's Novel* (Madison: University of Wisconsin Press, 2002), 245. Terras concludes from the narrator's characterization that "while the narrator is very fond of Dr. Herzenstube, he also likes to make fun of him" (245).

88. See the first section of chapter 2 for additional discussion of this citation.

89. Granovskii, *Lektsii po istorii srednevekov'ia,* 8–9.

90. Ibid., *Lektsii po istorii srednevekov'ia,* 256.

91. He makes this characterization during his introductory comments at his reading of the chapter for a benefit performance in 1879.

92. For a discussion of Dostoevsky's praise for Pushkin's monk in an 1880 issue of *Diary of a Writer,* see the introduction to chapter 6.

93. For a summary of Bellyustin's case, see Freeze's *The Parish Clergy in Nineteenth-Century Russia,* 205–16.

94. Freeze, *The Parish Clergy in Nineteenth-Century Russia,* 394.

95. Copernicus stands alongside Cicero and Shakespeare in the tradition of men persecuted for their talent in the notes to *Demons* (*Pss*, 11:270).

96. For a discussion of the Inquisition's judgment of Galileo, see Maurice A. Finocchiaro's *Retrying Galileo, 1633–1992* (Berkeley: University of California Press, 2005), 37–42.

97. Finocchiaro, *Retrying Galileo*, 222. Finocchiaro describes Napoleon's desire to publish Galileo's file, the debate over torture in the 1840s, the search of the Inquisition archives for materials on Galileo by "republican officials" after the establishment of the Roman Republic in the 1840s, and the publications in the 1870s on the proceedings with material preserved in the archives (241, 246). Dostoevsky may have read about the proceedings in Grube, *Biografcheskie kartinki*, 40–43.

98. Sandoz, *Political Apocalypse*, 16.

99. Miguel de Cervantes, *Don Quixote*, ed. Joseph R. Jones and Kenneth Douglas (New York: W. W. Norton, 1981), 431.

100. Ivan tells Alesha that it was not "the devil" but "an impostor" (*Pss*, 15:86). Nina Perlina concludes that this remark draws on the "aesthetically related . . . tradition of Karamzin and Pushkin and alludes to the Time of Troubles with its Boris Godunov and Grigory Otrep'ev" (*Varieties of Poetic Utterance*, 143).

101. Here the Devil alludes both to Herzen's work and to "Specters [*Prizraki*]" (which Dostoevsky published in *Epoch*)—a work written by Ivan Turgenev, that is, Herzen's intended audience for *Endings and Beginnings*. See a discussion of the background of Herzen's *Endings and Beginnings* in his collected works for further details (*Ss*, 16:403–5).

102. Terras, *A Karamazov Companion*, 387.

103. See the notes to Dostoevsky's collected works for a discussion of the Devil's history of the human conscience, in which he distinguishes Voltairean ethics from an earlier age (*Pss*, 15:592).

CHAPTER SIX

1. Tokarzewski, *Siedem lat*, 61.

2. Kloczowski, *A History of Polish Christianity*, 239. Dostoevsky knew from an 1873 article in *The Citizen* criticizing Rome and its clergy for promoting pilgrimages to Lourdes and La Salatte that recent Marian apparitions were inspiring popular venerations in Europe. For further details, see [K. P. Pobedonostsev], "Frantsiia," *Grazhdanin* 35 (August 27, 1873): n. pag. *Philolog.ru Biblia*, http://smalt/karelia.ru/~filolog/grazh/1873/ 27auN35.htm.

3. This is an imprecise quotation of Pimen who says: "There is still one final account" (*PssP*, 7:17).

4. Emerson, *Boris Godunov*, 122.

5. Bakhtin, *Problems of Dostoevsky's Poetics*, 133.

6. The connection of Mitya to Demeter through the Eleusinian Mysteries— ancient Greek ceremonies dedicated to Demeter and her daughter—is made by several scholars, including Terras, *A Karamazov Companion*, 117; Perlina, *Varieties of Poetic Utterance*, 26, 56.

7. For a discussion of lying in Dostoevsky, see Martinsen, *Surprised by Shame* (30–35).

8. This is a likely reference to Vibulenus Agrippa who killed himself so as not to lose his property by state execution. For more, see Paul Plass, *The Game of Death in Ancient Rome: Arena Sport and Political Suicide* (Madison: University of Wisconsin Press, 1995), 95–96.

9. In *Dostoevsky and the Catholic Church,* Dirscherl notes the "crucial" role of France in Dostoevsky's understanding of the "Catholic idea" (104–5). In "Dostoevskii i voinstvuiushchii katolitsizm 1860—1870–kh godov," Evnin also discusses how Pius IX's interference in French internal affairs in 1877 encourages Dostoevsky to associate France with the papacy (32–34).

10. "Otchet o bonskoi konferentsii," in *Sbornik protokolov,* 4:114.

11. Ibid., 111–12.

12. Richard Blanke, *Prussian Poland in the German Empire (1871–1900)* (Boulder, Colo.: East European Monographs, 1981), 9.

13. Ibid., 10.

14. [K. P. Pobedonostsev], "Delo Ledokhovskago," *Grazhdanin* 49 (December 3, 1873): n. pag. *Philolog.ru Biblia,* http://www.philolog.ru/filolog/grajdanin.htm.

15. "Peterburg 25-go oktiabria," *Sankt-Peterburgskie vedomosti* 296 (October 26, 1877), 1. This newspaper is often cited by Dostoevsky.

16. A. D. Gradovskii, "Po povodu pol'skago legiona," *Sankt-Peterburgskie vedomosti* 121 (May 3, 1877), 2. In the article "In Latest Intelligence: The War," *The Times* 28,933 (May 4, 1877), the Prussian correspondent from *The Times* reports that the *Poznan Daily (Dziennik Poznański)* published a telegram from the Turkish sultan approving the formation of a Polish legion (5).

17. *The War Correspondence of the "Daily News" 1877 with a Connecting Narrative Forming a Continuous History of the War Between Russia and Turkey to the Fall of Kars* (London: Macmillan, 1878), 539.

18. For a response by a Polish émigré, see "Pis'mo k professoru Gradovskomu," *Sankt-Peterburgskie vedomosti* 149 (May 31, 1877), 1–2. For a commentary from Belarus, see "Peterburg, 3-go (15-go) iiunia," *Sankt-Peterburgskie vedomosti* 152 (June 4, 1877), 1–2. The debate between Gradovsky and the Polish émigré continues in issues 160 (June 12, 1877), 1–2, and 172 (June 24, 1877), 2.

19. For more details, see the untitled lead article in *Golos* 246 (October 15, 1877): 1–2, and the article "Sanktpeterburg 16-ogo marta," *Golos* 76 (March 17, 1877): 1–2.

20. V. S. Solov'ev, "Vstuplenie—Pol'sha i vostochnyi vopros, 1883," in *Sobranie sochinenii V. S. Solov'eva,* 4:14–15.

21. For a more lengthy discussion of Dostoevsky's "jingoistic call for world conquest," see Scanlan, *Dostoevsky the Thinker,* 219–23.

22. Sergei Hackel, "Diaspora Problems of the Russian Emigration," in *Eastern Christianity*, vol. 5, *The Cambridge History of Christianity*, ed. Michael Angold (Cambridge: Cambridge University Press, 2006), 542.

23. Scanlan, *Dostoevsky the Thinker*, 223.

24. Robin Feuer Miller, *Dostoevsky's Unfinished Journey* (New Haven, Conn.: Yale University Press, 2007), 77. She builds here on Jackson's model of the "triple vision" in "The Peasant Marei," which he outlines in *The Art of Dostoevsky* (20–32).

25. Miller, *Dostoevsky's Unfinished Journey*, 76.

26. Jackson, *The Art of Dostoevsky*, 32.

27. In *The Art of Dostoevsky*, Jackson reads the entry as a genuine *profession de foi* (22), and Miller similarly refers to the passage as his *profession de foi* in *Dostoevsky's Unfinished Journey* (75, 156).

28. Leikina-Svirskaia, "Zapiska o dele Petrashevtsev," 181, 182.

29. See the end of chapter 3 for further discussion of this scene.

30. Tokarzewski, *Siedem lat*, 150. Since Tokarzewski italicizes *mužik*, places it in quotation marks, and follows it with the Polish translation *chłop* in parentheses, it is clear that he understands it to be a Russian term, even though the pejorative *mužik* exists in Polish. Tokarzewski describes how Polish political prisoners were stripped of their rank and made into peasants directly preceding the execution of their corporal punishment by the tsar's officers in Modlin (62).

31. Although Dostoevsky writes that the earliest recollection takes place when he is nine in 1830, Budanova and Fridlender point out in *Letopis'* that the events that happen twenty years later are inaccurate, because Mirecki could have shared only one Easter (1851) with Dostoevsky (186). During the two years that their terms overlapped (1850–51), Dostoevsky spent the first Easter in the hospital.

32. Gary Saul Morson, "Introductory Study: Dostoevsky's Great Experiment," in *A Writer's Diary* by Fyodor Dostoyevsky, vol. 1 (Evanston, Ill.: Northwestern University Press, 1993), 24, 25.

33. Harriet Murav, *Russia's Legal Fictions* (Ann Arbor: University of Michigan Press, 1998), 131. Murav notes that the "theme of childhood" runs throughout "The Peasant Marei" and Dostoevsky's discussion of the case (136).

34. Murav, *Russia's Legal Fictions*, 129.

35. V. D. Spasovich, "Vospominaniia o K. D. Kaveline," in *Sobranie sochinenii K. D. Kavelina*, vol. 2 (St. Petersburg, n.p., 1904): x–xi. *Bayerische StaatsBibliothek*, http://daten.digitale-sammlungen.de/~db/bsb00005552/images/index.html?id=00005552&fip =yztsyztseayaenqrseayafsdreayaweaya&no =14&seite=16.

36. Spasovich, "Vospominaniia o K. D. Kaveline," xi.

37. Maciej Jankowski, *Być liberałem w czasie trudnym: Rzecz o Włodzimierzu Spasowiczu* (Lodz: Ibidem, 1996), 35.

38. Spasovich, "Vospominaniia o K. D. Kaveline," x; Jankowski, *Być liberałem w czasie trudnym*, 95. For the Turgenev and Nechaev connections to Ohryzko, see the first section of chapter 4.

39. Jan Trochimiak, "Iwan Turgieniew a Polska," *Studia polono-slavica orientalia: Acta Litteraria* 6 (1980): 137–38. For more on Turgenev's role in the Ohryzko affair, see N. V. Berg, *Zapiski N. V. Berga o pol'skikh zagovorakh i vozstaniiakh, 1831–1862* (Moscow: Tipografiia Gracheva, 1873), 152–56. An 1858 protest against anti-Semitism signed by Spasovich, Turgenev, Kavelin, and Ohryzko further attests to a long-term political affinity between Turgenev and Spasovich (*Ss*, 15:472).

40. V. Spasovich, "Razbor": 2–i chasti 'Kursa Grazhdanskago Prava K. Pobedonostseva': O pravakh semeistvennykh," in *Za mnogo let (1859–1871): Stat'i, otryvki, istoriia, kritika, polemika, sudebnyia rechi i proch* (St. Petersburg: Tipografiia F. Sushchinskago, 1872).

41. Tokarzewski, *Ciernistym szlakiem*, 119.

42. Robert Louis Jackson, "Dostoevsky and the Marquis de Sade: The Final Encounter," in *Dialogues with Dostoevsky: The Overwhelming Questions* (Stanford, Calif.: Stanford University Press, 1993), 148.

43. Robert Belknap, *The Genesis of "The Brothers Karamazov": The Aesthetics, Ideology, and Psychology of Making a Text* (Evanston, Ill.: Northwestern University Press, 1990), 63–65; Frank, *Dostoevsky: The Mantle of the Prophet*, 154.

44. See Belknap's *The Genesis of "The Brothers Karamazov"* for a history of the competing accounts of Ilinsky's story (57–63).

45. Dostoevsky's reference to the transfer of Bogusławski, Tokarzewski, and Żochowski to Omsk owing to clandestine correspondence in *House of the Dead* points to his intentional use of the message to radicalize the image of Grushenka's Pole (*Pss*, 4:210).

46. Terras, *A Karamazov Companion*, 277.

47. D'iakov, *Deiateli russkogo i pol'skogo osvoboditel'nogo dvizheniia*, 15.

48. Ibid., 10.

49. See notes 8 and 25 of chapter 4 for references to Hugo's "Viktor Giugo russkomu voisku" and Bakunin's "K ofitseram russkoi armii." Herzen discusses Potebnya's participation in the 1863 unrest in *My Past and Thoughts* (*Ss*, 11:304, 365, 372–73). Petr Slivitsky and Ivan Arngoldt were shot in 1862 for spreading treason within the army ranks.

50. Perlina, *Varieties of Poetic Utterance*, 166. In "The Temptation of Miracle," *Slavic and East European Journal* 36, no. 2 (1992), Curt M. Whitcomb also finds a similarity between Otrepev's dream and Mitya's confession to Alesha which connotes an "element of risk" entailed by "jumping from a precipice" (195).

51. Mart'ianov, "V perelome veka," 446.

52. Tokarzewski, *Siedem lat*, 125, 185.

53. Ibid., 133, 192.

54. In *Literature and Nationalism in Partitioned Poland,* Eile finds this Polish title more typical of Polish magnates (4).

55. Tokarzewski, *Siedem lat,* 167–68.

56. Śliwowska, *Zesłańcy polscy,* 409. Musiałowicz's significance as a prototype for Mussyalovich has been established by a number of scholars, but a paucity of biographical information on their mutual acquaintance has thwarted attempts to motivate Dostoevsky's selection of the surname. See, for example, Lednicki, *Russia, Poland, and the West,* 286; Budanova and Fridlender, *Letopis',* 1:184; Świderska, *Studien zur literaturwissenschaftlichen Imagologie,* 405.

57. Dostoevsky uses the easily identifiable abbreviations A—chukovsky and B—m for these two Poles. Out of the four only he and Korczyński served the remainder of Dostoevsky's sentence, because Anczykowski and Bem, who are mentioned by name in *House of the Dead,* received shorter sentences.

58. Bogusławski, "Wspomnienia Sybiraka," 282:2. It is also telling that Dostoevsky chose the name of someone, whom Janik writes, "showed weakness of character at the last minute" (*Dzieje polaków,* 155). Janik bases this on the account of Franciszek Knoll, who was also punished in connection with the affair and describes how Wróblewski tried to implicate him during the investigation (242). For additional details, see Knoll's "Spisek omski: Męczeństwo księdza Sierocińskiego i współtowarzyszy," in *Zesłanie i katorga na Syberii w dziejach Polaków 1815–1914* by Anna Brus et al. (Warsaw: Wydawnictwo Naukowe PWN, 1992), 239–45.

59. Jerzy W. Borejsza, *Patriota bez paszportu* (Warsaw: Czytelnik, 1970), 13; Maria Złotorzycka, *Walery Wróblewski (1836–1908): Szkic Biograficzny* (Warsaw: Państwowe Zakłady Wydawnictw Szkolnych, 1948), 7. There is a remote possibility Dostoevsky knew of the uncle through Mombelli's ties to the Cyril and Methodius Brotherhood described in Sokhan', *Kyrylo-mefodiïvs'ke tovarystvo* (6).

60. In *Patriota bez paszportu,* Borejsza posits that Walery Wróblewski may have seen this spectacle based on his presence in Vilnius during this very public event (12, 229).

61. Borejsza, *Patriota bez paszportu,* 19; Złotorzycka, *Walery Wróblewski,* 7–8. Złotorzycka mentions in a general manner that Ohryzko's Polish journal *Word* was being published during this period (8).

62. In *Dostoevsky's "The Devils": A Critical Companion,* J. Leatherbarrow addresses the significance of the bird imagery in *Demons* for the "apocalyptic coloring" of the novel (40). In *Dostoevsky and the Russian People,* Ivanits focuses on the way in which this imagery is applied to Maria Timofeevna and Stavrogin (113–14, 118).

63. Świderska, *Studien zur literaturwissenschaftlichen Imagologie,* 404–5.

Also, in *Literaturno-kriticheskie stat'i* (Moscow: Gosudarstvennoe izdatel'stvo khudozhestvennoi literatury, 1961), M. A. Antonovich maintains that Mussyalovich resembles Pan Kopychinsky from Zagoskin's *Yury Miloslavsky* "in that the former is presented as stupid, shallow, and cowardly in the same way that the latter is in Zagoskin" (412).

64. M. N. Zagoskin, *Iurii Miloslavskii ili russkie v 1612 godu* (Moscow: Panorama, 1991), 85.

65. Ibid., 87.

66. Gradovskii, "Po povodu pol'skago legiona," 2. Gradovsky writes, "Before my imagination still rushes Poland of 1863, the incorrigible conspirator longing for the borders of 1772, loitering about all the Western courts and preaching a crusade against Russia."

67. A quotation from this poem ("there is no tsaritsa on earth more beautiful than a Polish maiden") appears in a draft of this scene in Dostoevsky's notes (*Pss*, 15:291).

68. Also, his marriage in Smolensk places him on the western edge of Russia's 1771 border in an area seized by the Poles in 1611 and brutally attacked by Napoleon Bonaparte's troops (including Polish allies) in 1812. Zagoskin's *Yury Miloslavsky* opens with the devastating loss of Smolensk, while Tolstoy's *War and Peace* devotes significant space to the bloody battle over the city.

69. Dostoevsky's *Siberian Notebook* records an anecdotal remark about Poles (*Pss*, 4:244). Also, Iadrintsev, in *Russkaia obshchina v tiur'me i ssylke*, records a well-known prison song based on Lord Byron's "Childe Harold's Pilgrimage," so the presence of Byron in anecdote provides an additional Siberian reference (*Russkaia obshchina v tiur'me i ssylke*, 107).

70. In his *Vospominaniia o F. M. Dostoevskom*, Baron Wrangel describes in a general manner the subversive significance of Gogol whose work one of his "highly-placed relatives" describes as "the muck of functionaries entrusted with the authority and trust of the government" (32). However, Wrangel more pointedly discusses Dostoevsky's love of reciting Pushkin's "Egyptian Nights" and cites the lines: "The tsaritsa by voice and by gaze / Her magnificent feast revived" (33). Given Maximov's anecdote, the title "tsaritsa" here is also a likely allusion to Pushkin's poem "Budrys and His Sons."

71. Goryanchikov relates his own anecdotes about the prison beatings in the first three chapters of the second part of *House of the Dead*. The reference to Piron is also made by Fedor who believes that Zosima, the Russian Jesuit, has a little of Piron in him as well (*Pss*, 14:124).

72. See the third section of chapter 2 for a more detailed discussion of Pan Podvysotsky's story within the context of Dostoevsky's gambling history.

73. In *Nikolai Gogol*, Bojanowska discusses the author's "anti-Polish" tendencies within his creation of "a paradigm of Ukrainian history that nourished

Ukrainian nationalism while simultaneously laying an offering to Russian imperialism" (161).

74. To read about Spasovich in the novel, see for example, Lednicki, *Russia, Poland, and the West,* 292–94; Świderska, *Studien zur literaturwissenschaftlichen Imagologie,* 414–20; and Rosenshield, *Western Law, Russian Justice,* 175–76, 180, 185–87.

75. In this speech, which further juxtaposes this image with that of the Orthodox, Lednicki in *Russia, Poland, and the West* finds Dostoevsky's intent to malign Spasovich's reputation (293).

76. Lednicki, *Russia, Poland, and the West,* 292–94. Lednicki emphasizes Spasovich's ties to Catholicism, but in *Być liberałem w czasie trudnym* Jankowski outlines his father's conversion to Orthodoxy from the Uniate Church and shows Spasovich graduating from a Minsk gymnasium during a period of Russification in Belarus in the aftermath of the Szymon Konarski affair (16, 19). He then attends the university in St. Petersburg, where he begins a bilingual publishing career in Polish and Russian but also writes on "Little Russian" identity (20–23).

77. Rosenshield, *Western Law, Russian Justice,* 180–81.

78. V. Spasovich, "Delo o gosudarstvennom prestuplenii, tak nazyvaemoe: 'Nechaevskoe,'" in *Za mnogo let,* 447.

79. V. Spasovich, "Period iezuitsko-makaronicheskii," in *Za mnogo let,* 210; V. Spasovich, "Vzgliad na russkuiu literaturu, na eia glavnye organy i partii v kontse 1858 goda," in *Za mnogo let,* 323.

80. His citation from a poem ("he lived among us [*on mezhdu nami zhil*]," 1834), which Pushkin wrote in dialogue with Mickiewicz, reinforces this connection (*Pss,* 15:599).

81. Belinskii, "Pis'mo k N. V. Gogoliu," 212.

82. Ibid., 214.

83. Ibid., 213.

84. Both *Hippolytus* by the Greek dramatist Euripides and *Phaedra* by the Roman playwright Seneca are considered sources for this text.

85. The axle creaks and breaks. The intrepid Hippolyte
sees shattered his whole smashed chariot;
Entangled in the reins he himself falls. . . .
They stop not far from the ancient tombs
Where the kings, his ancestors, are cold relics.
I, sighing, run there, and his guard follows me,
The trail of his noble blood leads us,
The rocks are stained with it; the brambles dripping
tufts of hair carry the bloodied skin.

J. Racine, "Phèdre, tragédie," in *Oeuvres de J. Racine,* ed. Paul Mesnard, vol. 3 (Paris: Librairie de L. Hachette, 1865), 390–93. For Dostoevsky's discussion of

Racine's tragedy, see an 1840 letter to his brother Mikhail in which he calls the play "the highest, pure nature and poetry" (*Pss*, 28.1:70).

86. Wallace Fowlie, "Racine, Poet of Grace," *French Review* 12, no. 5 (March 1939): 397. Jansenist reformers challenged the Jesuits in the seventeenth century by embracing a more austere practice of faith that may be attributed to a belief in predestination and the elect. Racine comes from a family famous for its Jansenist traditions.

87. Trochimiak, "Iwan Turgieniew a Polska," 138–39; Frank, *Dostoevsky: The Mantle of the Prophet*, 418–19. Although Turgenev declined Spasovich's invitation to attend a banquet in Kraszewski's honor, he nevertheless published in *The Herald of Europe* a congratulatory letter, "For the Jubilee of Iu. I. Krashevsky: A Letter to V. D. Spasovich [K iubileiu Iu. I. Krashevskogo. Pis'mo k V. D. Spasovichu]" (*Polnoe sobranie sochinenii i pisem v dvadtsati vos'mi tomakh*, 15:180).

88. V. Semevskii, "Petrashevtsy: Studenty Tolstov, G. P. Danilevskii, Meshchanin P. G. Shaposhnikov, literator Katenev i B. I. Utin," *Golos Minuvshago* 12 (December 1916): 115–17.

89. Turgenev, *Polnoe sobranie sochinenii i pisem v dvadtsati vos'mi tomakh*, 5.2:382, 691; D'iakov, *Deiateli russkogo i pol'skogo osvoboditel'nogo dvizheniia*, 163. Turgenev insisted in a letter to Alexander II that he was not guilty of any political activities in 1863 and was allowed to provide only written testimony in the prominent case that sent Serno-Solovevich and his co-conspirators to Siberia.

90. Semevskii, "Petrashevtsy: Studenty," 114.

CONCLUSION

1. "The Russian People and Socialism"; "two steps from the Winter Palace."

2. Vrangel', *Vospominaniia o F. M. Dostoevskom*, 35–36.

3. D. Dashkov, "Stikhi i skazaniia pro Aleksiia Bozhiia cheloveka," in *Besedy v obshchestve liubitelei rossiiskoi slovesnosti*, 2nd ed. (Moscow: V Universitetskoi tipografii, 1868), 25.

4. In *Dostoevsky the Thinker*, Scanlan, disagreeing with Ward, finds that Dostoevsky's "Russian idea" includes a significant armed component, and Scanlan uses the language of the Crusades to describe a "wresting" of "the East from the Mohammedans by force" (226). Although Scanlan does not differentiate between Dostoevsky's enthusiastic support for Russia during the Russo-Turkish War and his postwar discussions of Europe, he nevertheless effectively demonstrates that Ward underestimates Dostoevsky's acceptance of the need for force in geopolitics. For Ward's analysis, see *Dostoyevsky's Critique of the West* (187–88).

5. T. N. Granovskii, "O Fiziologicheskikh priznakakh chelovecheskikh porod i ikh otnoshenii k istorii," in *Sochineniia T. N. Granovskago*, vol. 1 (Moscow: V Tipografii V. Got'e, 1856), 59.

6. [W. Spasowicz], *Polityka samobójstwa: Uwagi nad pisemkiem Polska i Rossya w 1872* (Poznan: W księgarni J. K. Żupańskiego, 1872), 37.

7. Cochrane, *The Collaboration of Nečaev, Ogarev and Bakunin in 1869,* 170.

8. For a discussion of the growing importance of the Jewish Question in Dostoevsky, see Susan McReynolds, *Redemption and the Merchant God: Dostoevsky's Economy of Salvation and Antisemitism* (Evanston, Ill.: Northwestern University Press, 2008), 52–53.

9. Here Dostoevsky paraphrases a line uttered by Griboedov's Repetilov in act 4, scene 6 of *Woe from Wit* (*Gore ot uma; Pss,* 27:350).

10. Hayden White, *Metahistory: The Historical Imagination in Nineteenth-Century Europe* (Baltimore: Johns Hopkins University Press, 1973), 15.

11. For a discussion of Hegel on tragedy and world history, see White's *Metahistory* (108–11).

12. White, *Metahistory,* 116.

13. Marx and Engels, *Werke,* 4:466.

14. Ibid., 3:378.

15. Apollon Grigor'ev, "Moi literaturnye i nravstvennye skital'chestva," in *Vospominaniia,* 91. This work, parts of which were published in *Time* and *Epoch,* is dedicated to Dostoevsky's older brother.

16. Grigor'ev, "Moi literaturnye i nravstvennye skital'chestva," 136.

17. Ibid., 137–40. For a discussion of Radcliffe's influence on Dostoevsky, see Robin Feuer Miller, "Dostoevsky and the Tale of Terror," in *The Russian Novel from Pushkin to Pasternak,* ed. John Garrard (New Haven, Conn.: Yale University Press, 1983), 103–21.

18. Turgenev, "Gamlet i Don-Kikhot," 8:173; Erich Auerbach, *Mimesis: The Representation of Reality in Western Literature* (Princeton, N.J.: Princeton University Press, 1953), 333.

19. Karl Marx, *Karl Marx, Friedrich Engels Gesamtausgabe* (*MEGA*), vol. 2 (Berlin: Dietz Verlag, 1982), 254.

20. See *Werke* 3:186–221 for Marx's application of this model to Max Stirner (Sancho Panza) and Franz Szeliga Zychlin von Zychlinsky (Don Quixote) in *The German Ideology* (*Die deutsche Ideologie,* 1846).

21. Zaccone, *Histoire des sociétés secrètes, politiques et religieuses,* 4.

22. Apollon Grigor'ev, "Stikhotvoreniia N. Nekrasova," in *Sochineniia v dvukh tomakh,* vol. 2 (Moscow: Khudozhestvennaia literatura, 1990), 305.

23. Apollon Grigor'ev, "Kriticheskii vzgliad na osnovy, znachenie i priemy sovremennoi kritiki iskusstva," in *Sochineniia v dvukh tomakh,* 2:42. Grigorev here juxtaposes "stilted French Classicism" with Shakespeare.

24. "Time often enough renders legitimate / that which initially seemed impossible without crime"; Pierre Corneille, *Oeuvres de P. Corneille,* ed. M. Ch. Marty-Laveaux, vol. 3 (Paris: Librairie de L. Hachette, 1862), 197.

25. In vain against le Cid a minister conspires,
All Paris for Chimene has Rodrigue's eyes
L'Académie as a body is fine to censure it,
The rebel-public insists on admiring it.

Nicolas Boileau-Despréaux, "Satire IX," in *Oeuvres de Boileau, à l'usage de la jeunesse,* 115. Dostoevsky writes the second line in his 1876–77 notebook, in which another notation—"Corneille and revolution"—suggests that his tragedies inform Dostoevsky's discussion of the European struggle between Catholic and Protestant (Lutheran) ideas in a January 1877 entry to *Diary of a Writer* (*Pss,* 24:239; 25:227, 7–8, 11).

26. Corneille, *Oeuvres de P. Corneille,* 3:361–64.

27. Corneille and Molière were educated by the Jesuits, while Racine was educated by followers of Jansenism, and Boileau studied theology before focusing on law.

28. Alekseev, "O dramaticheskikh opytakh Dostoevskogo," 57–61; Roger L. Cox, "Dostoevsky and the Ridiculous," *Dostoevsky Studies* 1 (1980): 105–7; Tartuffe's mores were so scandalous for seventeenth-century French society that Louis XIV banned public performances of the play.

29. Because Krylov wrote subversive fables in the tradition of *Fables* by the seventeenth-century fabulist Jean de la Fontaine, Maximov's citation recalls the friendly circle of Boileau, Racine, la Fontaine, and Molière.

30. See the introduction for further discussion of Pushkin's dialogue with Bunyan's *The Pilgrim's Progress.*

31. Dunning, "The Problem of *Boris Godunov:* A Review of Interpretations and the So-Called Canonical Text," in *The Uncensored Boris Godunov,* 37–40.

32. Caryl Emerson, "Tragedy, Comedy, Carnival and History on Stage," in *The Uncensored Boris Godunov,* 182.

33. Dunning, "The Problem of *Boris Godunov,*" 39. The tolerant Henri IV is famous for the phrase "Paris vaut bien une messe [Paris is well worth a mass]," which he reportedly uttered to account for his conversion from Protestantism to Catholicism.

34. See footnote 46 of the third chapter for Ivan's and Dostoevsky's discussions of the parallel lines meeting in eternity.

Bibliography

Adler, John, ed. *Responses to Shakespeare, 1830–1859.* Vol. 6. London: Routledge/Thoemmes, 1997.

Aksakov, I. S. *Otchego tak nelegko zhivetsia v Rossii?* Moscow: Rosspén, 2002.

Alekseev, M. P. "O dramaticheskikh opytakh Dostoevskogo." In *Tvorchestvo Dostoevskogo, 1821–1881–1921: Sbornik statei i materialov,* edited by L. P. Grossman, 41–62. Odessa: Vseukrainskoe gosudarstvennoe izdatel'stvo, 1921.

Anderson, Nancy K. *The Perverted Ideal in Dostoevsky's "The Devils."* Middlebury Studies in Russian Language and Literature 8. New York: Peter Lang, 1997.

Antonovich, M. A. *Literaturno-kriticheskie stat'i.* Moscow: Khudozhestvennaia literatura, 1961.

Apollonio, Carol. *Dostoevsky's Secrets: Reading Against the Grain.* Evanston, Ill.: Northwestern University Press, 2009.

Ashimbaeva, N. T. "A. N. Maikov: Pis'ma k F. M. Dostoevskomu 1867–1878." *Pamiatniki kul'tury. Novye otkrytiia* 8 (1982): 60–98.

Askariants, A., and Z. Kemenova. "Pis'ma N. P. Ogareva A. I. Gertsenu." *Literaturnoe nasledstvo* 39–40 (1941): 365–573.

Aston, Nigel. *Religion and Revolution in France, 1780–1804.* Washington, D.C.: Catholic University of America Press, 2000.

Auerbach, Erich. *Mimesis: The Representation of Reality in Western Literature.* Princeton, N.J.: Princeton University Press, 1953.

Averintsev, S. S., and A. N. Meshkov, eds. *Khristianstvo: Ėntsiklopedicheskii slovar' v 3 tomakh.* 3 vols. Moscow: Nauchnoe izdatel'stvo "Bol'shaia Rossiiskaia ėntsiklopediia," 1995.

Bakhtin, Mikhail. *Problems of Dostoevsky's Poetics.* Edited and translated by Caryl Emerson. Theory and History of Literature 8. Minneapolis: University of Minnesota Press, 1984.

———. *Rabelais and His World.* Translated by Hélène Iswolsky. 1968. Reprint, Bloomington: Indiana University Press, 1984.

[Bakounine, Michel.] *L'Internationale, Karl Marx, Mazzini et Bakounine.* 2nd ed. Brussels: Librairie cosmopolite, 1871.

Bakounine, Michel. *Michel Bakounine et ses relations avec Sergej Nečaev 1870–1872.* Edited by Arthur Lehning. Leiden: E. J. Brill, 1971.

———. *Michel Bakounine et ses relations slaves 1870–1875.* Edited by Arthur Lehning. Leiden: E. J. Brill, 1974.

Bakunin, M. "Narodnoe delo: Romanov, Pugachev, ili Pestel'?" In *Polnoe sobranie sochinenii.* Vol. 1. St. Petersburg: Izdanie I. Balashova, 1907.

———. *Sobranie sochinenii i pisem, 1828–76.* Edited by Iu. M. Steklov. 4 vols. Moscow: Izdatel'stvo Vsesoiuznogo obshchestva politkatorzhan i ssyl'noposelentsev, 1934–35.

Barbéris, Pierre. "Napoléon: Structures et signification d'un mythe littéraire." *Revue d'histoire littéraire de la France* 5–6 (September-December 1970): 1031–58.

Barenbaum, I. E. *N. A. Serno-Solov'evich 1834–1866: Ocherk knigotorgovoi i knigoizdatel'skoi deiatel'nosti.* Moscow: Izdatel'stvo vsesoiuznoi knizhnoi palaty, 1961.

Barsukov, Nikolai. *Zhizn' i trudy M. P. Pogodina.* Vol. 20. St. Petersburg: Tipografiia M. M. Stasiulevicha, 1907.

Basil, John. "The Russian Theological Academies and the Old Catholics, 1870–1905." In *Religious and Secular Forces in Late Tsarist Russia: Essays in Honor of Donald W. Treadgold,* edited by Charles E. Timberlake, 90–104. Seattle: University of Washington Press, 1992.

Bazanov, V. G., and G. M. Fridlender, eds. *Dostoevskii i ego vremia.* Leningrad: Nauka, 1971.

Bel'chikov, N. F. *Dostoevskii v protsesse Petrashevtsev.* Moscow: Nauka, 1971.

Belinskii, V. G. *Polnoe sobranie sochinenii.* 13 vols. Moscow: Akademiia Nauk SSSR, 1953–59.

Belknap, Robert. *The Genesis of "The Brothers Karamazov": The Aesthetics, Ideology, and Psychology of Making a Text.* Evanston, Ill.: Northwestern University Press, 1990.

Bilinkis, Ia. S. "Romany Dostoevskogo i tragediia Pushkina 'Boris Godunov': K probleme edinstva puti russkoi literatury XIX stoletiia." *Dostoevskii: Materialy i issledovaniia* 2 (1976): 164–68.

Blake, Elizabeth. "Portraits of the Siberian Dostoevsky by Poles in the *House of the Dead.*" *Dostoevsky Studies,* New Series 10 (2006): 56–71.

———. "Sonya, Silent No More: A Response to the Woman Question in Dostoevsky's 'Crime and Punishment.'" *Slavic and East European Journal* 50, no. 2 (Summer 2006): 252–71.

Blanke, Richard. *Prussian Poland in the German Empire (1871–1900).* Boulder, Colo.: East European Monographs, 1981.

Bloom, Harold, ed. *Bloom's Major Literary Characters: Raskolnikov and Svidrigailov.* Philadelphia: Chelsea House, 2004.

Bogusławski, Józef. "Wspomnienia Sybiraka: Pamiętniki Józefa Bogusławskiego."

Nowa reforma 249:1; 250:1; 251:1; 252:1; 253:1; 254:1; 255:1; 256:1; 257:1; 258:1; 259:1; 260:1; 261:1; 262:1; 263:2; 264:1; 275:1; 281:1; 282:2; 285:1; 286:1; 294:1; 297:1 (1896).

Boileau-Despréaux, Nicolas. *L'Art poétique.* In *Oeuvres de Boileau, à l'usage de la jeunesse,* 244–92. Brussels: La Société Nationale, 1837.

Bojanowska, Edyta M. "Empire by Consent: Strakhov, Dostoevskii, and the Polish Uprising of 1863." *Slavic Review* 71, no. 1 (Spring 2012): 1–24.

———. *Nikolai Gogol: Between Ukrainian and Russian Nationalism.* Cambridge, Mass.: Harvard University Press, 2007.

Bokenkotter, Thomas. *Church and Revolution: Catholics in the Struggle for Democracy and Social Justice.* New York: Doubleday, 1998.

Bonhoeffer, Dietrich. *Discipleship.* Vol. 4 of *Dietrich Bonhoeffer Works.* Translated by Barbara Green and Reinhard Krauss and edited by Geffrey B. Kelly and John D. Godsey. Minneapolis, Minn.: Fortress, 2001.

Bordet, Gaston. *La Pologne, Lamennais et ses amis (1830–34).* Paris: Éditions du Dialogue, 1985.

Borejsza, Jerzy. *Emigracja polska po powstaniu styczniowym.* Warsaw: Państwowe Wydawnictwo Naukowe, 1966.

———. *Patriota bez paszportu.* Warsaw: Czytelnik, 1970.

Borisenok, Iu. A. *Mikhail Bakunin i "pol'skaia intriga": 1840–e gody.* Moscow: Rosspėn, 2001.

Brody, Ervin C. *The Demetrius Legend and Its Literary Treatment in the Age of the Baroque.* Rutherford, N.J.: Fairleigh Dickinson, 1972.

Brus, Anna, et al. *Zesłanie i katorga na Syberii w dziejach Polaków 1815–1914.* Warsaw: Wydawnictwo Naukowe PWN, 1992.

Budanova, N. F. *Biblioteka F. M. Dostoevskogo: Opyt rekonstruktsii: Nauchnoe opisanie.* St. Petersburg: Nauka, 2005.

Budanova, N. F., and G. M. Fridlender, eds. *Letopis' zhizni i tvorchestva F. M. Dostoevskogo v trekh tomakh 1821–1881.* 3 vols. St. Petersburg: Gumanitarnoe agentstvo "Akademicheskii proekt," 1995.

Bury, J. B. *History of the Papacy in the 19th Century: Liberty and Authority in the Roman Catholic Church.* New York: Schocken Books, 1964.

Butashevich-Petrashevskii, M. V. *Delo Petrashevtsev.* 3 vols. Moscow: Akademiia Nauk SSSR, 1937–51.

Byrnes, Robert F. *Pobedonostsev: His Life and Thought.* Bloomington: Indiana University Press, 1968.

Carr, E. H. *Michael Bakunin.* London: Macmillan, 1937.

Cascardi, Anthony J. *The Bounds of Reason: Cervantes, Dostoevsky, and Flaubert.* New York: Columbia University Press, 1986.

Catteau, Jacques. "De la structure de *La maison des morts* de F. M. Dostoevskij." *Revue des études slaves* 54, nos. 1–2 (1982): 63–72.

Cervantes, Miguel de. *Don Quixote.* Edited by Joseph R. Jones and Kenneth Douglas. New York: W. W. Norton, 1981.

———. *El ingenioso hidalgo Don Quijote de la Mancha.* 36th ed. Madrid: Espasa-Calpe, 1991.

Chaev, N. A. "Dimitrii Samozvanets (Drama v piati deistviiakh)." *Ėpokha* (January 1865): 5–104.

Chekin, Leonid S. "Notes of Images of the Time of Troubles in *The Devils* and *The Brothers Karamazov.*" *Dostoevsky Studies,* n.s., 2, no. 1 (1998): 83–92.

Cherniavsky, Michael. "The Old Believers and the New Religion." In *The Structure of Russian History,* edited by Michael Cherniavsky, 140–88. New York: Random House, 1970.

"Chtenie T. I. Filippova v zasedanii peterburgskogo Obshchestva liubitelei dukhovnogo prosveshcheniia 13 marta." Parts 1, 2, and 3. *Grazhdanin* 13–14 (April 8, 1874): n. pag.; 15 (April 15, 1874): n. pag.; 16 (April 22, 1874): n. pag. *Philolog.ru Biblia,* http://www.philolog.ru/filolog/grajdanin.htm.

"Chtenie T. I. Filippova v zasedanii peterburgskogo Obshchestva liubitelei dukhovnogo prosveshcheniia 26 fevralia." Parts 1 and 2. *Grazhdanin* 11 (March 18, 1874): n. pag.; 12 (March 25, 1874): n. pag. *Philolog.ru Biblia,* http://www.philolog.ru/filolog/grajdanin.htm.

Chulkov, G. I. *Kak rabotal Dostoevskii.* Moscow: Sovetskii pisatel', 1939.

Clayton, J. Douglas. *Dimitry's Shade: A Reading of Alexander Pushkin's "Boris Godunov."* Evanston, Ill.: Northwestern University Press, 2004.

Cochrane, Stephen T. *The Collaboration of Nečaev, Ogarev and Bakunin in 1869: Nečaev's Early Years.* Giessen, W. Ger.: Wilhelm Schmitz, 1977.

Collins, Daniel. "The Tower of Babel Undone in a Soviet Pentecost: A Linguistic Myth of the First Five-Year Plan." *Slavic and East European Journal* 42, no. 3 (Fall 1998): 423–43.

"Confédération suisse." *Journal de Genève* 213 (September 11, 1867): 1. *LE TEMPS: Archives historiques,* http://www.letempsarchives.ch/Default/ Skins /LeTempsEn/Client.asp?Skin=LeTempsEn&enter=true&AW=1327038975 959 &AppName=2.

Corneille, Pierre. *Oeuvres de P. Corneille.* Edited by M. Ch. Marty-Laveaux. Vol. 3. Paris: Librairie de L. Hachette, 1862.

Cottrell, Charles Herbert. *Recollections of Siberia, in the Years 1840 and 1841.* London: John W. Parker, 1842.

Cox, Roger L. "Dostoevsky and the Ridiculous." *Dostoevsky Studies* 1 (1980): 103–9.

Cracraft, James. *The Church Reform of Peter the Great.* Stanford, Calif.: Stanford University Press, 1971.

Dashkov, D. "Stikhi i skazaniia pro Alekseia Bozhiia cheloveka." In *Besedy v Obshchestve liubitelei rossiiskoi slovesnosti,* 2nd ed., 20–52. Moscow: V Universitetskoi tipografii, 1868.

Derzhavin, G. R. *Stikhotvoreniia.* Edited by G. R. Gukovskii. Leningrad: Izdatel'stvo pisatelei, 1933.

Derzhavina, O. A. "Istoricheskie deiateli i sobytiia kontsa XVI—nachala XVII veka v izobrazhenii sovremennikov i v russkoi literature XIX veka." In *Drevniaia Rus' v russkoi literature XIX veka (Siuzhety i obrazy drevnerusskoi literatury v tvorchestve pisatelei XIX veka)*, 143–79. Moscow: Akademiia Nauk SSSR, 1990.

D'iakov, V. A. *Deiateli russkogo i pol'skogo osvoboditel'nogo dvizheniia v tsarskoi armii 1856–1865 godov: Biobibliograficheskii slovar'*. Moscow: Nauka, 1967.

———— [Djakow, Włodzimierz]. *Piotr Ściegienny i jego spuścizna*. Warsaw: Państwowe Wydawnictwo Naukowe, 1972.

———— [Djakow, Włodzimierz]. "Polscy zesłańcy w Syberii Zachodniej i północnym Kazachstanie (1830–1862)." In *Polacy w Kazachstanie: Historia i współczesność*, edited by Stanisław Ciesielski and Antoni Kuczyński, 45–68. Wrocław: Wydawnictwo Uniwersytetu Wrocławskiego, 1996.

D'iakov, V. A., et al., eds. *Sviazi revoliutsionerov Rossii i Pol'shi*. Moscow: Nauka, 1968.

————. *Vosstanie 1863 goda: Materialy i dokumenty*. 2 vols. Moscow: Akademiia Nauk SSSR, 1963.

Dickens, Charles. *The Pickwick Papers*, edited by James Kinsley. Oxford: Oxford University Press, 2008.

————. *A Tale of Two Cities*. Oxford: Oxford University Press, 1998.

Dirscherl, Denis, S.J. *Dostoevsky and the Catholic Church*. Chicago: Loyola University Press, 1986.

Dolinin, A. S. *Dostoevskii i drugie: Stat'i i issledovaniia o russkoi klassicheskoi literature*. Leningrad: Khudozhestvennaia literatura, 1989.

————, ed. *F. M. Dostoevskii: Materialy i issledovaniia*. Leningrad: Akademiia Nauk SSSR, 1935.

————. *Poslednie Romany Dostoevskogo: Kak sozdavalis' "Podrostok" i "Brat'ia Karamazovy."* Moscow: Sovetskii Pisatel', 1963.

Dombrovskii, Iaroslav. "Dva pis'ma Iaroslava Dombrovskago." *Kolokol* 200 (July 15, 1865): 1639–40.

Dorovatovskaia-Liubimova, V. S. "Frantsuzskii burzhua: Dostoevskii i Aleksandr Diuma." *Literaturnyi kritik* 9 (September 1936): 202–17.

Dostoevskaia, A. G. *Dnevnik 1867 goda*. Moscow: Nauka, 1993.

————. *Vospominaniia*. Edited by S. V. Belov and V. A. Tunimanov. Moscow: Khudozhestvennaia literatura, 1971.

Dostoevskii, Andrei. *Vospominaniia*. Moscow: Agraf, 1999.

Dostoevskii, F. M. *Polnoe sobranie sochinenii v tridtsati tomakh*. 30 vols. Leningrad: Nauka, 1972–90.

Dowler, Wayne. *Dostoevsky, Grigor'ev, and Native Soil Conservatism*. Toronto: University of Toronto Press, 1982.

Dragomanov, M. P., ed. *Pis'ma M. A. Bakunina k A. I. Gertsenu i N. P. Ogarevu*. Slavistic Printings and Reprintings 111. The Hague: Mouton, 1968.

Dryzhakova, E. N. "Dostoevskii i Gertsen: U istokov romana 'Besy.'" *Dostoevskii: Materialy i issledovaniia* 1 (1974): 219–39.

Dulov, A. V. *Petrashevtsy v Sibiri*. Irkutsk: Izdatel'stvo Irkutskogo universiteta, 1996.

Dumas, A. *Le Comte de Monte-Cristo*. Vol. 1. Paris: Nelson Éditeurs, n.d.

Dunning, Chester S. L. *Russia's First Civil War: The Time of Troubles and the Founding of the Romanov Dynasty*. University Park: Pennsylvania State University Press, 2001.

Dunning, Chester, et al. *The Uncensored Boris Godunov: The Case for Pushkin's Original Comedy, with Annotated Text and Translation*. Madison: University of Wisconsin Press, 2006.

Dwyer, Anne. "Of Hats and Trains: Cultural Traffic in Leskov's and Dostoevskii's Westward Journeys." *Slavic Review* 70, no. 1 (Spring 2011): 67–73.

Eile, Stanislaw. *Literature and Nationalism in Partitioned Poland, 1795–1918*. New York: St. Martin's, 2000.

Emerson, Caryl. *Boris Godunov: Transpositions of a Russian Theme*. Bloomington: University of Indiana Press, 1986.

———. *The First Hundred Years of Mikhail Bakhtin*. Princeton, N.J.: Princeton University Press, 1997.

———. "Pretenders to History: Four Plays for Undoing Pushkin's *Boris Godunov*." *Slavic Review* 44, no. 2 (Summer 1985): 257–79.

Emerson, Caryl, and Robert William Oldani. *Modest Musorgsky and Boris Godunov: Myths, Realities, Reconsiderations*. Cambridge: Cambridge University Press, 1994.

Esaulov, Ivan A. "The Categories of Law and Grace in Dostoevsky's Poetics." In *Dostoevsky and the Christian Tradition*, edited by George Pattison and Diane Oenning Thompson, 116–33. Cambridge: Cambridge University Press, 2001.

Evgrafov, V. E., ed. *Filosofskie i obshchestvenno-politicheskie proizvedeniia petrashevtsev*. Moscow: Gosudarstvennoe izdatel'stvo politicheskoi literatury, 1953.

Evnin, F. "Dostoevskii i voinstvuiushchii katolitsizm 1860–1870-kh godov (K genezisu 'Legendy o velikom inkvizitore')." *Russkaia literatura* 10, no. 1 (1967): 29–41.

———. "Roman 'Prestuplenie i nakazanie.'" In *Tvorchestvo F. M. Dostoevskogo*, edited by N. L. Stepanov, 128–72. Moscow: Akademiia Nauk SSSR, 1959.

Finocchiaro, Maurice A. *Retrying Galileo, 1633–1992*. Berkeley: University of California Press, 2005.

Flaubert, Gustave. *Madame Bovary: Mœurs de province*. Vol. 8 of *Oeuvres complètes de Gustave Flaubert*. Paris: Louis Conard, Libraire-Éditeur, 1921.

Fowlie, Wallace. "Racine, Poet of Grace." *French Review* 12, no. 5 (March 1939): 391–400.

Fox, Soledad. *Flaubert and Don Quijote: The Influence of Cervantes on Madame Bovary.* Brighton, Eng.: Sussex Academic, 2008.

Frank, Joseph. "Dostoevsky: The Encounter with Europe." *Russian Review* 22, no. 3 (July 1963): 237–52.

———. *Dostoevsky: The Mantle of the Prophet, 1871–1881.* Princeton, N.J.: Princeton University Press, 2002.

———. *Dostoevsky: The Miraculous Years, 1865–1871.* Princeton, N.J.: Princeton University Press, 1995.

———. *Dostoevsky: The Seeds of Revolt, 1821–1849.* Princeton, N.J.: Princeton University Press, 1976.

———. *Dostoevsky: The Stir of Liberation, 1860–1865.* Princeton, N.J.: Princeton University Press, 1986.

———. *Dostoevsky: The Years of Ordeal, 1850–1859.* Princeton, N.J.: Princeton University Press, n.d.

———. "*The Gambler:* A Study in Ethnopsychology." In *Freedom and Responsibility in Russian Literature: Essays in Honor of Robert Louis Jackson,* edited by Elizabeth Cheresh Allen and Gary Saul Morson, 69–85. Evanston, Ill.: Northwestern University Press; New Haven, Conn.: Yale Center for International and Area Studies, 1995.

Freeze, Gregory L. *The Parish Clergy in Nineteenth-Century Russia: Crisis, Reform, Counter-Reform.* Princeton, N.J.: Princeton University Press, 1983.

Freidenfel'd, F. "Listovka A. A. Serno-Solov'evicha protiv N. P. Ogareva." *Literaturnoe nasledstvo* 41–42 (1963): 111–16.

Fülöp-Miller, René. *The Power and the Secret of the Jesuits.* New York: Viking, 1930.

Fusso, Susanne. "'Maidens in Childbirth': The Sistine Madonna in Dostoevskii's *Devils.*" *Slavic Review* 54, no. 2 (Summer 1995): 261–75.

Gallagher, Catherine, and Stephan Greenblatt. *Practicing New Historicism.* Chicago: University of Chicago Press, 2000.

Ganss, George E., S.J., ed. *Ignatius of Loyola: The Spiritual Exercises and Selected Works.* New York: Paulist, 1991.

Gebhardt, Armin. *Die Dresdner Mairevolution 1849.* Marburg, Ger.: Tectum Verlag, 2006.

Gertsen, A. I. *Sobranie sochinenii v tridtsati tomakh.* 30 vols. Moscow: Akademiia Nauk SSSR, 1954–65.

Gibson, Ralph. *A Social History of French Catholicism 1789–1914.* New York: Routledge, 1989.

Giliarov-Platonov, N. P. *Voprosy very i tserkvi: Sbornik statei 1868–1887 gg.* Edited by N. V. Shakhovskii. Vol. 1. Moscow: Sinodal'naia Tipografiia, 1905.

Goodwin, James. *Confronting Dostoevsky's Demons: Anarchism and the Specter of Bakunin in Twentieth-Century Russia.* Middlebury Studies in Russian Language and Literature 33. New York: Peter Lang, 2010.

Gough, Austin. *Paris and Rome: The Gallican Church and the Ultramontane Campaign 1848–1853.* Oxford: Clarendon, 1986.

Gradovskii, A. D. "Po povodu pol'skago legiona." *Sankt-Peterburgskie vedomosti* 121 (May 3, 1877): 2–3.

Granovskii, T. N. "Lektsii iz srednei istorii T. N. Granovskogo." *Vremia* 9 (September 1862): 5–39.

———. *Lektsii po istorii srednevekov'ia.* Moscow: Nauka, 1986.

———. *Sochineniia T. N. Granovskago.* 2 vols. Moscow: V Tipografii V. Got'e, 1856.

Grigor'ev, Apollon. *Sochineniia v dvukh tomakh.* Vol. 2. Moscow: Khudozhestvennaia literatura, 1990.

———. *Vospominaniia.* Moscow: Academia, 1930.

Grossman, Leonid. *Dostoevskii.* Moscow: Molodaia Gvardiia, 1965.

———. "Dostoevskii i pravitel'stvennye krugi 1870–kh godov." *Literaturnoe nasledstvo* 15 (1934): 83–162.

———. "Gorod i liudi 'Prestuplenie i nakazanie.'" In *F. M. Dostoevskii: Prestuplenie i nakazanie,* 5–52. Moscow: Goslitizdat, 1935.

Grossman, L. P., and V. Polonskii. *Spor o Bakunine i Dostoevskom: Stat'i L. P. Grossmana i Viach. Polonskogo.* Leningrad: Tip. Pechatnyi dvor, 1926.

Grube, A. V. *Biograficheskie kartinki.* Moscow: Izdanie knigoprodavtsa A. L. Vasil'eva, 1877.

Gus, M. *Idei i obrazy F. M. Dostoevskogo.* 2nd ed. Moscow: Khudozhestvennaia literatura, 1971.

Hackel, Sergei. "Diaspora Problems of the Russian Emigration." In *Eastern Christianity.* Vol. 5 of *The Cambridge History of Christianity,* edited by Michael Angold, 539–57. Cambridge: Cambridge University Press, 2006.

Hegel, Georg Wilhelm Friedrich. *The Philosophy of History.* Translated by J. Sibree. New York: Dover, 1956.

Hoff, Linda Kay. *Hamlet's Choice: Hamlet—A Reformation Allegory.* Studies in Renaissance Literature 2. Lewiston, N.Y.: Edwin Mellen, 1989.

The Holy Bible: New Revised Standard Version. Oxford: Oxford University Press, 1977.

Hugo, Victor. *Napoléon le Petit.* Paris: J. Hetzel, 1870.

———. "Viktor Giugo russkomu voisku." *Kolokol* 156 (February 15, 1863): 1301.

Hunt, Maurice. *Shakespeare's Religious Allusiveness: Its Play and Tolerance.* Burlington, Vt.: Ashgate, 2004.

Iadrintsev, N. M. *Russkaia obshchina v tiur'me i ssylke.* St. Petersburg: Tipografiia A. Morigerovskogo, 1872.

"In Latest Intelligence: The War." *The Times* 28.933 (May 4, 1877), 5.

Ivanits, Linda. *Dostoevsky and the Russian People.* Cambridge University Press, 2008.

Jackson, Robert Louis. *The Art of Dostoevsky: Deliriums and Nocturnes*. Princeton, N.J.: Princeton University Press, 1981.

———. *Dialogues with Dostoevsky: The Overwhelming Questions*. Stanford, Calif.: Stanford University Press, 1993.

———. *Dostoevsky's Quest for Form: A Study of His Philosophy of Art*. New Haven, Conn.: Yale University Press, 1966.

———. "Napoleon in Russian Literature." *Yale French Studies* 26 (1960): 106–18.

Janik, Michał. *Dzieje polaków na Syberji*. Krakow: Krakowska Spółka Wydawnicza, 1928.

Jankowski, Maciej. *Być liberałem w czasie trudnym: Rzecz o Włodzimierzu Spasowiczu*. Lodz: Ibidem, 1996.

Jastrzębski, Jan. "Memuar Petrashevtsa." *Minuvshie gody* 1 (January 1908): 20–37.

Jones, Malcolm V. "'The Legend of the Grand Inquisitor': The Suppression of the Second Temptation and Dialogue with God." *Dostoevsky Studies* 7 (1986): 123–34.

———. "Some Echoes of Hegel in Dostoevsky." *Slavonic and East European Review* 49 (October 1971): 500–520.

Jonsen, Albert R., and Stephen Toulmin. *The Abuse of Casuistry: A History of Moral Reasoning*. Berkeley: University of California Press, 1988.

Karamzin, N. M. *Istoriia gosudarstva Rossiiskago*. Vol. 5. St. Petersburg: Voennaia Tipografiia Glavnago Shtaba Ego Imperatorskago Velichestva, 1817.

Katkov, M. N. "Moskva, 5go ianvaria." *Moskovskie vedomosti* 4 (January 6, 1870): 1–2.

———. *1863 god. Sobranie statei po pol'skomu voprosu*. Moscow: V Universitetskoi tipografii, 1887.

Kerenskii, Vladimir. *Starokatolitsizm: Ego istoriia i vnutrennee razvitie*. Kazan: Tipo-Litografiia Imperatorskago Universiteta, 1894.

Khomiakov, A. S. *Zapiski o vsemirnoi istorii*. Vol. 7 of *Polnoe sobranie sochinenii*. Moscow: Tipo-litografiia T-va I. N. Kushnerev, 1906.

Kirpotin, Valerii. *Dostoevskii v shestidesiatye gody*. Moscow: Khudozhestvennaia literatura, 1966.

———. *Razocharovanie i krushenie Rodiona Raskol'nikova: Kniga o romane F. M. Dostoevskogo "Prestuplenie i nakazanie."* Moscow: Sovetskii Pisatel', 1970.

Kloczowski, Jerzy. *A History of Polish Christianity*. Cambridge: Cambridge University Press, 2000.

Knapp, Bettina L. *Gambling, Game, and Psyche*. Albany: State University of New York Press, 2000.

Kokorev, A. V. *Khrestomatiia po russkoi literature XVIII veka*. Moscow: Izdatel'stvo "Prosveshchenie," 1965.

Komarovich, V. "Dostoevskii i Geine." *Sovremennyi mir* 10 (1916): 97–107.

Kostomarov, N. I. "Dolzhno li schitat' Borisa Godunova osnovatelem krepostnago prava." In *Istoricheskiia monografii i izsledovaniia Nikolaia Kostomarova,* vol. 1, 393–428. St. Petersburg: Tipografiia Tovarshchestva "Obshche-stvennaia pol'za," 1863.

———. *Literaturnoe Nasledie: Avtobiografiia.* St. Petersburg: Tipografiia M. M. Stasiulevicha, 1890.

———. *Smutnoe vremia Moskovskogo gosudarstva v nachale XVII stoletiia. 1604–1613.* Moscow: Charli, 1994.

Koz'min, B. P. "Aleksandr Serno-Solov'evich: Materialy dlia biografii." *Literaturnoe nasledstvo* 67 (1959): 698–733.

Kridl, Manfred. *Mickiewicz i Lamennais: Studyum porównawcze.* Warsaw: Księgarnia E. Wende i S-ka, 1909.

———. "Two Champions of a New Christianity: Lamennais and Mickiewicz." *Comparative Literature* 4, no. 3 (Summer 1952): 239–67.

Lanskii, L. R., ed. "Dostoevskii v neizdannoi perepiske sovremennikov (1837–1881)." *Literaturnoe nasledstvo* 86 (1973).

———. "Otkliki na smert' Gertsena po materialam inostrannoi pechati i 'Prazhskoi kollektsii.'" *Literaturnoe nasledstvo* 63 (1956): 523–30.

Latimer, Elizabeth Wormeley. *Russia and Turkey in the Nineteenth Century.* Chicago: A. C. McClurg, 1897.

Lawrence, D. H. *Reflections on the Death of a Porcupine and Other Essays.* Edited by Michael Herbert. Cambridge: Cambridge University Press, 1988.

Leatherbarrow, W. J. *A Devil's Vaudeville: The Demonic in Dostoevsky's Major Fiction.* Evanston, Ill.: Northwestern University Press, 2005.

———, ed. *Dostoevskii and Britain.* Providence, R.I.: Berg, 1995.

———, ed. *Dostoevsky's "The Devils": A Critical Companion.* Evanston, Ill.: Northwestern University, 1999.

Lednicki, Wacław. *Russia, Poland, and the West: Essays in Literary and Cultural History.* Port Washington, N.Y.: Kennikat, 1966.

Leikina-Svirskaia, V. R., ed. "Zapiska o dele Petrashevtsev: Rukopis' F. N. L'vova s pometkami M. V. Butashevicha-Petrashevskogo." *Literaturnoe nasledstvo* 63, no. 1 (1956): 165–90.

Leites, Edmund, ed. *Conscience and Casuistry in Early Modern Europe.* Cambridge: Cambridge University Press, 1988.

Le Panthéon: Symbole des révolutions. [Paris]: Picard Éditeur, 1989.

Leslie, R. F. *Reform and Insurrection in Russian Poland 1856–1865.* London: Athlone, 1963.

Levin, Iu. D. *Shekspir i russkaia literatura XIX veka.* Edited by M. P. Alekseev. Leningrad: Nauka, 1988.

Love, Jeff. "Narrative Hesitation in *The Gambler.*" *Canadian Slavonic Papers* 46, nos. 3–4 (September-December 2004): 361–80.

Lukács, Georg. "Dostoevsky." In *Dostoevsky: A Collection of Critical Essays,* edited by Rene Wellek, 146–58. Englewood Cliffs, N.J.: Prentice-Hall, 1962.

Lyngstad, Alexandra H. *Dostoevskij and Schiller.* The Hague: Mouton, 1975.

Maikov, A. N. *Polnoe sobranie sochinenii.* 4 vols. St. Petersburg: Izdanie T-va A. F. Marks, 1914.

Marcilly, Ch. *Satyre Ménippée de la vertu du catholicon d'Espagne et de la tenue des estatz de Paris.* Paris: Garnier Frères, Libraires-Éditeurs, 1889.

Mart'ianov, P. K. "V perelome veka. (Otryvki iz staroi zapisnoi knizhki)." *Istoricheskii vestnik* 11 (November 1895): 434–63.

Martinsen, Deborah A. "Shame's Rhetoric, or Ivan's Devil, Karamazov Soul." In *A New Word on "The Brothers Karamazov,"* edited by Robert Louis Jackson, 53–67. Evanston, Ill.: Northwestern University Press, 2004.

———. *Surprised by Shame: Dostoevsky's Liars and Narrative Exposure.* Columbus: Ohio State University Press, 2003.

Marx, Karl. *Karl Marx, Friedrich Engels Gesamtausgabe (MEGA).* Vol. 2. Berlin: Dietz Verlag, 1982.

Marx, Karl, and Friedrich Engels. *L'Alliance de la Démocratie Socialiste et l'Association Internationale des Travailleurs.* In *Sochineniia,* vol. 18. 2nd ed., 325–438. Moscow: Gosudarstvennoe izdatel'stvo politicheskoi literatury, 1961.

———. *Werke.* 43 vols. Berlin: Dietz Verlag, 1958–90.

McCarthy, Terence. "'What's in a Name?': Shakespeare's Poland." *English Studies* 81, no. 3 (June 2000): 199–216.

McReynolds, Susan. *Redemption and the Merchant God: Dostoevsky's Economy of Salvation and Antisemitism.* Evanston, Ill.: Northwestern University Press, 2008.

Mérimée, Prosper. *Correspondance générale: 1847–1849.* Edited by Maurice Parturier. Vol. 5. Paris: Le Divan, 1946.

Meshcherskii, Kniaz'. *Vospominaniia.* Moscow: Zakharov, 2001.

Meyendorff, John. *Byzantine Theology: Historical Trends and Doctrines.* New York: Fordham University Press, 1979.

Michelet, J. *Le Prêtre, la femme, et la famille.* Paris: Ernest Flammarion, Éditeur, 1895.

Mickiewicz, Adam. *Pan Tadeusz czyli Ostatnie zajazd na Litwie: Historia szlachecka z roku 1811 i 1812.* Kraków: Wydawnictwo Zielona Sowa, 2000.

Miliukov, A. P. "Fedor Mikhailovich Dostoevskii." *Russkaia starina* 31, no. 5 (May 1881): 33–52.

Miller, Orest F. *Biografiia, pis'ma i zametki iz zapisnoi knizhki F. M. Dostoevskogo.* St. Petersburg: Tipografiia A. S. Suvorina, 1883.

Miller, Robin Feuer. *"The Brothers Karamazov": Worlds of the Novel.* Twayne's Masterwork Series 83. New York: Twayne, 1992.

———. *Dostoevsky and "The Idiot": Author, Narrator, and Reader.* Cambridge, Mass.: Harvard University Press, 1981.

————. "Dostoevsky and the Tale of Terror." In *The Russian Novel from Pushkin to Pasternak*, edited by John Garrard, 103–21. New Haven, Conn.: Yale University Press, 1983.

————. *Dostoevsky's Unfinished Journey*. New Haven, Conn.: Yale University Press, 2007.

Morson, Gary Saul. "Introductory Study: Dostoevsky's Great Experiment." In *A Writer's Diary* by Fyodor Dostoyevsky. Vol. 1. Evanston, Ill.: Northwestern University Press, 1993.

————. "Paradoxical Dostoevsky." *Slavic and East European Journal* 43, no. 3 (Fall 1999): 471–94.

Moss, C. B. *The Old Catholic Movement: Its Origin and History*. Eureka Springs, Ark.: Episcopal Book Club, 1964.

Mucha, Bogusław. "Syberyjskie wiersze Dostojewskiego." *Zeszyty naukowe Uniwersytetu Jagiellońskiego: Prace historycznoliterackie* 36 (1977): 93–104.

Murav, Harriet. *Holy Foolishness: Dostoevsky's Novels and the Poetics of Cultural Critique*. Stanford, Calif.: Stanford University Press, 1992.

————. *Russia's Legal Fictions*. Ann Arbor: University of Michigan Press, 1998.

Napoléon III, S. M. I. *Histoire de Jules César*. New York: D. Appleton, Libraires-Éditeurs, 1865.

Nechaev, S. G. "Ot Russkogo Revoliutsionnogo Komiteta." *Narodnaia rasprava* 1 (Summer 1869). Reprint, *Novyi Zhurnal* 1 (1994): 77–90.

Nechaeva, V. S. *Zhurnal M. M. i F. M. Dostoevskikh "Èpokha," 1864–1865*. Moscow: Nauka, 1975.

————. *Zhurnal M. M. i F. M. Dostoevskikh "Vremia," 1861–1863*. Moscow: Nauka, 1972.

Nikitina, F. G. "Idei Lamenne v Rossii." *Dostoevskii i mirovaia kul'tura* 8 (1997): 201–26.

————. "Petrashevtsy i Lamenne." *Dostoevsky: Materialy i issledovaniia* 3 (1978): 256–59.

Oeler, Karla. "The Dead Wives in the Dead House: Narrative Inconsistency and Genre Confusion in Dostoevskii's Autobiographical Prison Novel." *Slavic Review* 61, no. 3 (Fall 2002): 519–34.

Ogarev, N. "Razbor osnovnykh polozhenii preobrazovaniia sudebnoi chasti v Rossii." *Kolokol* 151 (December 1, 1862): 1247–52.

Pascal, Blaise. *Oeuvres complètes*. Edited by Michel le Guern. 2 vols. Paris: Gallimard, 1998–2000.

Passage, Charles E. *Character Names in Dostoevsky's Fiction*. Ann Arbor, Mich.: Ardis, 1982.

Peace, Richard. *Dostoyevsky: An Examination of the Major Novels*. Cambridge: Cambridge University Press, 1971.

Perlina, Nina. *Varieties of Poetic Utterance: Quotation in "The Brothers Karamazov."* Lanham, Md.: University Press of America, 1985.

"Peterburg, 3-go (15-go) iiunia." *Sankt-Peterburgskie vedomosti* 152 (June 4, 1877), 1–2.

"Peterburg 25-go oktiabria." *Sankt-Peterburgskie vedomosti* 296 (October 26, 1877), 1.

"Peterburgskoe obozrenie." *Grazhdanin* 5 (February 4, 1874). n. pag. *Philolog.ru Biblia.* http://smalt/karelia.ru/~filolog/grazh/1874/74n05.htm.

"Peterburgskoe obozrenie." *Grazhdanin* 45 (November 5, 1873). n. pag. *Philolog.ru Biblia.* http://smalt/karelia.ru/~filolog/grazh/1873/5nN45.htm#a6.

Piotrowski, Rufin. "Souvenirs d'un Sibérien." Translated by Julien Klaczko. *Revue des deux mondes* 38 (1862): 850–78.

Plass, Paul. *The Game of Death in Ancient Rome: Arena Sport and Political Suicide.* Madison: University of Wisconsin Press, 1995.

Pobedonostsev, K. *Istoricheskiia izsledovaniia i stat'i.* St. Petersburg: Tipografiia Ministerstva Putei Soobshcheniia, 1876.

[Pobedonostsev, K. P.] "Bor'ba gosudarstva s tserkov'iu v Germanii." *Grazhdanin* 34 (August 20, 1873). n. pag. *Philolog.ru Biblia.* http://smalt/kareliaru/~filolog /grazh/1873/20auN34.htm; 40 (October 1, 1873). n. pag. *Philolog.ru Biblia.* http://smalt/karelia.ru/~filolog/grazh/1873/1ocN40. htm.

———. "Delo Ledokhovskago." *Grazhdanin* 49 (December 3, 1873). n. pag. *Philolog.ru Biblia.* http://www.philolog.ru/filolog/grajdanin.htm.

———. "K voprosu o vozsoedinenii tserkvei." *Grazhdanin* 33 (August 13, 1873). n. pag. *Philolog.ru Biblia.* http://smalt/karelia.ru/~filolog/grazh/1873 /13auN33.htm.

———. "Tserkov' i gosudarstvo." *Grazhdanin* 17–19 (April 23, 30, 1873; May 7, 1873). n. pag. *Philolog.ru Biblia.* http://www.philolog.ru/filolog/grajdanin .htm.

———. "Tserkovnye dela v Germanii." *Grazhdanin* 51 (December 17, 1873). n. pag. *Philolog.ru Biblia.* http://smalt/karelia.ru/~filolog/grazh/1873 /17deN51 .htm; 5 (February 4, 1874). n. pag. *Philolog.ru Biblia.* http://smalt/karelia .ru/~filolog/grazh/1874/74n05. htm.

Poddubnaia, R. N. "Dvoinichestvo i samozvanstvo." *Dostoevskii: Materialy i issledovaniia* 11 (1994): 28–40.

Pogodin, M. "A. I. Gertsen." *Zaria* 2 (1870): 75–95.

———. "Eshche za Minina." *Grazhdanin* 4 (January 1873): 101–5.

———. *Pol'skii vopros: Sobranie rassuzhdenii, zapisok i zamechanii (1831–1867).* Moscow: V tipografii gazety *Russkii,* 1867.

———. "Za Kniazia Pozharskogo." *Grazhdanin* 29 (July 1872): 369–72.

———. "Za Susanina." *Grazhdanin* 46 (November 1873): 1230–33; 47 (November 1873): 1257–59.

Pollard, A. F. *The Jesuits in Poland.* New York: Haskell House, 1971.

Prévost, Abbé. *Histoire du Chevalier des Grieux et de Manon Lescaut.* Paris: Éditions Garnier Frères, 1957.

Prymak, Thomas M. *Mykola Kostomarov: A Biography*. Toronto: University of Toronto Press, 1996.

Pushkin, A. S. *Polnoe sobranie sochinenii*. 19 vols. 1937–59. Reprint, Moscow: Voskresen'e, 1994–97.

Racine, J. *Phèdre, tragédie*. In *Oeuvres de J. Racine*, edited by Paul Mesnard, vol. 3. Paris: Librairie de L. Hachette, 1865.

Ransel, David L., and Bozena Shallcross, eds. *Polish Encounters, Russian Identity*. Bloomington: Indiana University Press, 2005.

[Razin, A. E.] "Chto takoe pol'skie vosstaniia." *Épokha* 1–2 (January/February 1864): 393–420.

———. "Nashi domashnie dela: Sovremennye zametki." *Vremia* 4 (April 1863): 164–209.

———. "Politicheskoe obozrenie." *Vremia* 2 (February 1863): 2:183–93.

———. "Politicheskoe obozrenie." *Vremia* 3 (March 1863): 2:128–47.

———. "Politicheskoe obozrenie: Obshchie polozheniia." *Vremia* 4 (April 1863): 2:210–20.

Rosenshield, Gary. *Western Law, Russian Justice: Dostoevsky, the Jury Trial, and the Law*. Madison: University of Wisconsin Press, 2005.

Rousseau, Jean-Jacques. *Oeuvres complètes de Jean-Jacques Rousseau*. Vol. 3. Paris: Éditions Gallimard, 1964.

Rusin. "Zametka na odnu gazetnuiu stat'iu: Po povodu pol'sko-rusinskogo voprosa." *Vremia* 9 (September 1862): 42–54.

Ruttenburg, Nancy. *Dostoevsky's Democracy*. Princeton, N.J.: Princeton University Press, 2008.

Said, Edward W. *Reflections on Exile and Other Essays*. Cambridge, Mass.: Harvard University Press, 2000.

Samarin, Iu. F. *Iezuity i ikh otnoshenie k Rossii: Pis'ma k Iezuitu Martynovu*. Moscow: Tipografiia Lazarevskago Instituta, 1866.

Sandoz, Ellis. *Political Apocalypse: A Study of Dostoevsky's Grand Inquisitor*. 2nd ed. Wilmington, Del.: ISI Books, 2000.

"Sanktpeterburg 16-ogo marta." *Golos* 76 (March 17, 1877): 1–2.

Saraskina, Liudmila. *Besy: Roman-Preduprezhdenie*. Moscow: Sovetskii pisatel', 1990.

Sartre, Jean-Paul. *Qu'est-ce que la littérature?* Paris: Gallimard, 1948.

Sbornik protokolov Obshchestva liubitelei dukhovnago prosveshcheniia, S.-Peterburgskii otdel. 5 vols. St. Petersburg: Tipografiia F. G. Éleonskago i K., 1873–77.

Scanlan, James P. *Dostoevsky the Thinker*. Ithaca, N.Y.: Cornell University Press, 2002.

Scirocco, Alfonso. *Garibaldi: Citizen of the World*. Translated by Allan Cameron. Princeton, N.J.: Princeton University Press, 2007.

Scott, Sir Walter. *Waverly.* London: Thomas Nelson and Sons, n.d.

Segel, Harold B. *The Literature of Eighteenth-Century Russia.* 2 vols. New York: E. P. Dutton, 1967.

————. *Stranger in Our Midst: Images of the Jew in Polish Literature.* Ithaca, N.Y.: Cornell University Press, 1996.

Semevskii, V. I. "M. V. Butashevich-Petrashevskii." *Golos minuvshago* 8 (August 1913): 51–86.

————. *M. V. Butashevich-Petrashevskii i Petrashevtsy.* Vol. 2 of *Sobranie sochinenii.* Moscow: Zadruga, 1922.

————. "Petrashevtsy: Kruzhok N. S. Kashkina I. Kashkin. Khanykov. Debu." *Golos Minuvshago* 2 (February 1916): 41–61.

————. "Petrashevtsy: Studenty Tolstov, G. P. Danilevskii, Meshchanin P. G. Shaposhnikov, literator Katenev i B. I. Utin." *Golos Minuvshago* 12 (December 1916): 97–118.

Serman, I. Z. "Paradoxes of the Popular Mind in Pushkin's *Boris Godunov.*" *Slavonic and East European Review* 64, no. 1 (January 1986): 25–39.

Shakespeare, William. *Hamlet.* Edited by Harold Jenkins. London: Methuen, 1982.

Shcheglov, F. "Semeistvo v rabochem klasse vo Frantsii." *Vremia* 11 (November 1861): 287–324.

Sheddon, J. H. *The Petrashevtsy: A Study of the Russian Revolutionaries of 1848.* Manchester: Manchester University Press, 1985.

Slight, Camille Wells. *The Casuistical Tradition in Shakespeare, Donne, Herbert and Milton.* Princeton, N.J.: Princeton University Press, 1981.

Śliwowska, Wiktoria. *Ucieczki z Sybiru.* Warsaw: Wydawnictwo Iskry, 2005.

————. *Zesłańcy polscy w Imperium Rosyjskim w pierwszej połowie XIX wieku.* Warsaw: Wydawnictwo DiG, 1998.

Sokhan', P. S., ed. *Kyrylo-mefodiïvs'ke tovarystvo u tr'okh tomakh.* Vol. 2. Kiev: Naukova dumka, 1990.

Solov'ev, V. S. *Sobranie sochinenii V. S. Solov'eva.* 12 vols. 1911–13. Reprint, Brussels: Foyer Oriental Chrétien, 1966–69.

Sorokine, Dimitri. *Napoléon dans la littérature russe.* Paris: L'Association langues et civilisations, 1974.

Spasovich, V. *Za mnogo let (1859–1871): Stat'i, otryvki, istoriia, kritika, polemika, sudebnyia rechi i proch.* St. Petersburg: Tipografiia F. Sushchinskago, 1872.

[Spasowicz, W.] "Polityka samobójstwa: Uwagi nad pisemkiem Polska i Rossya w 1872." Poznan: W księgarni J. K. Żupańskiego, 1872.

Stankevich, A. V. *Timofei Nikolaevich Granovskii.* Moscow: Tipografiia Gracheva i K., 1869.

Stempowski, Jerzy. "Polacy w powieściach Dostojewskiego." *Przegląd Współczesny* 109 (1931): 180–98.

Stone, M. W. F. "The Adoption and Rejection of Aristotelian Moral Philosophy in Reformed 'Casuistry.'" In *Humanism and Early Modern Philosophy*, edited by Jill Kraye and M. W. F. Stone, 59–90. London: Routledge, 2000.

Strakhov, N. N. "Rokovoi vopros." *Vremia* 4 (April 1863): 2:158.

Sue, Eugène. *Le Juif errant*. Vol. 1. Verviers, Belg.: Gerard, n.d.

Suslova, Apollinariia. *Gody blizosti s Dostoevskim*. Edited by A. S. Dolinin. New York: Serebrianyi vek, 1982.

Sužiedėlis, Saulius. *Historical Dictionary of Lithuania*. European Historical Dictionaries 21. Lanham, Md.: Scarecrow, 1997.

Sužiedėlis, Simas, and Antanas Kučas, eds. *Encyclopedia Lituanica*. Vol. 5. Boston, Mass.: Juozas Kapočius, 1976.

Świderska, Małgorzata. *Studien zur literaturwissenschaftlichen Imagologie: Das literarische Werk F. M. Dostoevskijs aus imagologischer Sicht mit besonderer Berücksichtigung der Darstellung Polens*. Munich: Verlag Otto Sagner, 2001.

Tchaadaev, Pierre. *Lettres philosophiques: Adressées a une dame*. Paris: Librairie des Cinq Continents, 1970.

Terras, Victor. *A Karamazov Companion: Commentary on the Genesis, Language, and Style of Dostoevsky's Novel*. Madison: University of Wisconsin Press, 2002.

———. *Reading Dostoevsky*. Madison: University of Wisconsin Press, 1998.

Thackeray, William Makepeace. *The Kickleburgs on the Rhine*. Vol. 17 of *The Complete Works of William Makepeace Thackeray*. New York: Harper & Brothers, 1903.

Thompson, Diane Oenning. *"The Brothers Karamazov" and the Poetics of Memory*. Cambridge: Cambridge University Press, 1991.

Tikhomirov, B. N. "K voprosu o 'prototipakh obraza idei' v romanakh Dostoevskogo." *Dostoevskii: Materialy i issledovaniia* 10 (1992): 42–55.

Tiun'kin, K., and M. Tiun'kina, eds. *F. M. Dostoevskii v vospominaniiakh sovremennikov v dvukh tomakh*. 2 vols. Moscow: Khudozhestvennaia literatura, 1990.

Tokarzewski, Szymon. *Ciernistym Szlakiem: Pamiętniki Szymona Tokarzewskiego z więzień, robót ciężkich i wygnania*. Warsaw: Druk L. Bilińskiego i W. Maślankiewicza, 1909.

———. *Katorżnicy: Obrazki syberyjskie*. Warsaw: G. Gebethner i Spółka, n.d.

———. *Siedem lat katorgi: Pamiętniki Szymona Tokarzewskiego 1846–1857 g.* 2nd ed. Warsaw: Gebethner i Wolff, 1918.

Tolstoi, Dmitrii A. *Rimskii katolitsizm v Rossii: Istoricheskoe issledovanie*. 2 vols. St. Petersburg: Izdanie i tipografiia V. F. Demakova, 1876.

Tolstoi, L. N. *Sobranie sochinenii v dvadtsati dvukh tomakh*. 22 vols. Moscow: Khudozhestvennaia literatura, 1979.

Trochimiak, Jan. "Iwan Turgieniew a Polska." *Studia polono-slavica orientalia: Acta Litteraria* 6 (1980): 125–43.

Bibliography

Turgenev, I. S. *Polnoe sobranie sochinenii i pisem v dvadtsati vos'mi tomakh.* 28 vols. Moscow: Izdatel'stvo Akademii Nauk SSSR, 1960–68.

Twain, Mark. *Adventures of Huckleberry Finn.* Edited by Susan K. Harris. Boston: Houghton Mifflin, 2000.

Udartsev, S. F. "Rukopis' M. A. Bakunina 'Gamlet.'" In *Pamiatniki kul'tury: Novye otkrytiia,* 55–63. Leningrad: Nauka, 1986.

Urban, William. *The Livonian Crusade.* Washington, D.C.: University Press of America, 1981.

Vainerman, V. S. "Omskoe okruzhenie Dostoevskogo." *Dostoevskii: Materialy i issledovaniia* 6 (1985): 174–91.

Viktorovich, V. A. "Dostoevskii v Obshchestve liubitelei dukhovnogo prosveshcheniia." *Dostoevskii i mirovaia kul'tura* 20 (2004): 9–21.

Vil'mont, N. *Velikie sputniki: Literaturnye ètiudy.* Moscow: Sovetskii pisatel', 1966.

Vrangel', A. E. "Pis'ma A. E. Vrangelia k Dostoevskomu." *Dostoevskii: Materialy i issledovaniia* 3 (1978): 258–85.

———. *Vospominaniia o F. M. Dostoevskom v Sibiri 1854–56 gg.* St. Petersburg: Tipografiia A. S. Suvorina, 1912.

Walicki, Andrzej. *Philosophy and Romantic Nationalism: The Case of Poland.* Notre Dame, Ind.: University of Notre Dame Press, 1994.

The War Correspondence of the "Daily News" 1877 with a Connecting Narrative Forming a Continuous History of the War Between Russia and Turkey to the Fall of Kars. London: Macmillan, 1878.

Ward, Bruce K. *Dostoevsky's Critique of the West: The Quest for the Earthly Paradise.* Waterloo, Can.: Wilfrid Laurier University Press, 1986.

Ware, Timothy. *The Orthodox Church.* Rev. ed. London: Penguin Books, 1993.

Wasiolek, Edward. Introduction to *The Gambler, with Polina Suslova's Diary,* by Fyodor Dostoevsky. Chicago: University of Chicago Press, 1972.

Waugh, Evelyn. *Brideshead Revisited: The Sacred and Profane Memories of Captain Charles Ryder.* Boston: Back Bay Books, 1999.

Wesling, Molly W. *Napoleon in Russian Cultural Mythology.* The Age of Revolution and Romanticism: Interdisciplinary Studies 29. New York: Peter Lang, 2001.

White, Hayden. *Metahistory: The Historical Imagination in Nineteenth-Century Europe.* Baltimore: Johns Hopkins University Press, 1973.

Zaccone, Pierre. *Histoire des sociétés secrètes, politiques et religieuses.* Paris: Arthême Fayard, Editeur, n.d. *Google Books,* https://play.google.com/books /reader ?id=GyAVAAAAQAAJ&printsec=frontcover&output=reader&auth user=0&hl=en_US&pg=GBS.PP1.

Zagoskin, M. N. *Iurii Miloslavskii ili russkie v 1612 godu.* Moscow: Panorama, 1991.

Żakiewicz, Zbigniew. "Polacy u Dostojewskiego." *Twórczość* 24, no. 6 (June 1968): 75–89.

Złotorzycka, Maria. *Walery Wróblewski (1836–1908): Szkic Biograficzny.* Warsaw: Państwowe Zakłady Wydawnictw Szkolnych, 1948.

Żochowski, Józef. *Życie Jezusa Chrystusa, ozdobione rycinami, według obrazów pierwszych mistrzów przedstawiającymi główne zdarzenia z życia Zbawiciela.* Warsaw: Nakład Gustawa Leona Glücksberga, 1847. *Polska Biblioteka Internetowa.* http://www.pbi.edu.pl/book_reader.php?p=54617.

Zohrab, Irene. "Redaktorskaia deiatel'nost' F. M. Dostoevskogo v zhurnale 'Grazhdanin' i religiozno-nravstvennyi kontekst 'Brat'ev Karamazovykh.'" *Russkaia literatura* 3 (1996): 55–77.

Zola, Émile. *Germinal.* Paris: Fasquelle, 1983.

Index

Gilyarov-Platonov, Nikita, 152
Godunov, Boris, 5, 9, 89, 132, 134, 245n84.
    See also under Pushkin, Alexander
Goethe, Johann von, 205
Gogel, N. V., 119, 161
Gogol, Nikolai, 7, 11, 36–37, 40, 189, 193,
    204, 209–10, 221n73, 230n7, 261n70,
    261n73
Gorchakov, Mikhail, 64
Gorchakov, Petr, 52
Gorgey, Artur, 25, 44
Granovsky, Timofei, 5, 6–7, 100–101, 114–
    15, 120, 127–28, 130, 154, 158, 166, 200,
    212n14, 243n59, 247n124
Grave, Anna de, 45
Gregory XVI, 10, 11
Griboedov, Alexander, 70, 209, 264n9
Grigorev, Apollon, 204, 205, 233n32

Hauke-Bosak, Józef, 120, 183
Hegel, Georg Wilhelm Friedrich, 5–6, 7,
    93–94, 99–100, 105, 110, 113, 143, 203,
    235n64
Heine, Heinrich, 61, 205, 225n22
Henri IV, 87, 208 265n33
Herald of Europe, The, 133
Herzen, Alexander, 6, 16, 17, 57, 65, 92,
    114, 116, 119–20, 123–32, 184, 195, 196,
    202, 214n47, 225nn23–24; on Alexander
    II, 42–43; on Bakunin, 133; in The
    Brothers Karamazov, 164; on Catholic
    Europe, 59, 100, 116–18, 157; chivalric
    imagery, 161–62, 204–5; in Diary of
    a Writer, 164; on Don Quixote ideal,
    18, 70, 140, 162–63, 165, 247n118; on
    French Revolution, 163; on Hamlet,
    233n38; historical understanding, 7,
    11–12, 48, 51, 56, 139, 147, 169–70, 198;
    on Jesuits, 230n5; on Lord's Prayer, 158;
    on Napoleon, 100, 103; on Piotrowski,
    48; Polish interests, 15, 43, 64, 125, 164,
    167; Turgenev and, 212n8; in Winter
    Notes, 59, 62, 224n13
Hirschfeld, Józef, 43
Hoffmann, E. T. A., 205
Hofmeister, Apolin, 26, 187
Hugo, Victor, 19, 35, 38, 57, 61, 80, 120,
    173, 205, 210, 217n78

Ignatius of Loyola, 142, 205
Iliad, 199

Ilinsky, D. N., 183
Inquisition, 4, 5, 8, 104, 118, 155, 156, 158,
    169, 202, 254n61; Dostoevsky's Grand
    Inquisitor, 8, 17, 19, 60, 104, 116, 147–
    49, 151–52, 154–71, 201
International Workingmen's Association,
    116, 125
Islam, 41, 52, 153, 197, 235n60
Ivan IV, 86
Ivanits, Linda, 81

Jackson, Robert L., 69, 70, 141, 178, 182,
    221n75
Jan III Sobieski, 31
Janik, Michał, 26
Jansenism, 57, 85, 87, 101, 175, 263n86
Jastrzębski, Jan, 12, 28
Jesuitism, 4, 12–13, 57, 87–91, 102, 103,
    106, 110, 113, 142–43, 147–48, 175,
    199, 201–2, 205; in Boris Godunov,
    234n47; in The Brothers Karamazov,
    8, 170–71, 172, 183, 192; in Crime and
    Punishment, 8, 13, 85–86, 89–90, 94–97,
    107–9; in Demons, 115, 116, 118, 134,
    138, 142–43; in The Double, 8, 12–13,
    215n58; in House of the Dead, 23; Polish
    revolutionaries and, 14–15, 23, 50, 67,
    118; Russian politics and, 7, 17, 216n73;
    socialism and, 18. See also casuistry
Jesus, 11, 14, 16, 116, 121, 123, 155–61,
    164, 170, 191, 192, 197, 201, 202, 208
Jones, Malcolm, 160
Journal de Genève, 121, 123
Judaism, 37, 41, 201

Kamieński, Henryk, 26
Karakozov, Dimitry, 119, 139
Karamzin, Nikolai, 9, 88, 108–9
Katansky, Alexander, 151, 153, 154
Katkov, Mikhail, 55, 64–65, 82, 107, 118–
    19, 125, 131, 143
Kavelin, Konstantin, 181
Kelsiev, Vasily, 123–24
Kepler, Johannes, 96, 102, 210
Kireev, Alexander, 150–51
Klaczko, Julian, 48
Kloczowski, Jerzy, 32
Konarski, Szymon, 26, 109
Konrad von Wallenrode, 118, 161. See also
    under Mickiewicz, Adam
Korczyński, Ludwik, 26, 28, 33, 186

Index

Kościuszko, Tadeusz, 64
Kostomarov, Mykola, 6, 8, 131–32, 133, 134, 136, 212n20
Kraśnicki, Tomasz, 43
Kraszewski, Józef, 196
Krivtsov, Major, 27, 28, 29–30, 33, 45, 179, 219n26
Kronenberg, S. L., 179–82
Krylov, Ivan, 207, 265n29
Krzyżanowska, Natalya, 45
Krzyżanowski. Karol, 45
Kudryavtsev, Petr, 7
Kwiatkowska, Antonia, 43, 240n30

Lacordaire, Jean-Baptiste Henri, 11
Lamennais, Félicité de, 10–11, 13
Lamotte (doctor), 43
Land and Will, 124, 138, 183–84, 241n42
Lannes, Jean, 61
Lamartine, Alphonse de, 181
Latimer, Elizabeth Wormeley, 52
Lawrence, D. H., 6
Leatherbarrow, W. J., 137, 141
Lednicki, Wacław, 41, 44, 192, 222n102
Ledóchowski, Mieczysław, 175–76
Lelewel, Joachim, 119
Lent, 8, 160
Levin, Yury, 128
Libelt, Karol, 43
Lorrain, Claude, 17, 141, 168
Louis XIV, 40, 87, 175
Louis XV, 194
Louis-Philippe, 58
Luther, Martin, 5, 6, 7, 16, 59, 130, 169–70
Lvov, Fedor, 12, 179

Machiavelli, Niccolò, 166
Maikov, Apollon, 14, 52, 119, 120, 123, 124, 138–39, 149
Malczewski, Franciszek, 221n66
Marian Devotion, 168, 173, 195, 256n2; Immaculate Conception, 154, 172, 246; Sistine Madonna, 127, 167, 168, 242, 243, 246
Marseillaise, La, 125
Martinsen, Deborah, 98, 156, 228n90
Martyanov, Petr, 27, 29, 38, 46, 50, 185
Martynov, Ivan, 86, 229n5
Marx, Karl, 5, 16, 54, 56, 63, 119, 120, 138, 203–5; and Engels, 186
Mazzini, Giuseppe, 117, 129, 142, 165

Menippean satire, 159
Mérimée, Prosper, 58, 135–36, 211n6, 224n9
Meshchersky, Vladimir, 149
Michelet, Jules, 87, 198
Mickiewicz, Adam, 12, 205; WORKS: *Books of the Polish Nation and the Polish Pilgrims*, 10; *Forefathers' Eve*, 28; "Konrad Wallenrod," 160–61; "To My Muscovite Friends," 18; *Pan Tadeusz*, 36–37, 85; "To the Polish Mother," 30; "The Three Budryses," 188–89
Mierosławski, Ludwik, 26, 43, 187
Miller, Robin Feuer, 81, 156, 178
Milyukov, Alexander, 9, 10, 23
Minin, Kuzma, 8, 88, 139, 203, 212n19
Mirecki, Aleksander, 23, 26, 27, 33–34, 36, 43, 44, 46, 49, 50–51, 78, 112, 178–79, 181, 183, 200
Mochalov, Pavel, 204
Molière, 207, 208, 209, 210
Molinari, Gustave de, 121, 240n30
Mombelli, Nikolai, 12, 260n59
Morning Post, 177
Moscow News, 16, 64–65, 101, 107
Mroczkowski, Walery, 120, 123, 239n24, 241n40
Murav, Harriet, 7–8, 133, 135, 137, 180
Muravev, Mikhail, 118
Murillo, Bartolomé Esteban, 127
Musiałowicz, Jan, 27–28, 33, 69, 186, 190, 260n56

Napoleon (I) Bonaparte, 17, 18–19, 79, 85, 86–87, 109, 111–12, 168, 175, 199–200, 203; and Catholicism, 3; in *Crime and Punishment*, 8, 62, 94, 97, 98–103, 105–6, 110–11, 139, 169; in *The Double*, 232n30; and Poland, 5; popularity among Russians, 57, 92–93, 101, 105, 237n95
Napoleon III, 3, 13, 14, 31, 39, 55, 58–59, 61, 63, 77, 86, 100–103, 106, 161, 225n21, 235n70
Nechaev, Sergei, 114–16, 118, 119, 124–25, 132, 134, 139, 140, 201; Nechaevists, 114, 131, 137–38, 140, 180, 192, 198
Nechaeva, Vera, 64, 223n5, 232n25
Newton, Isaac, 96, 102, 210
Nicholas I, 4, 11, 18, 25, 32, 34, 109, 164, 193, 196, 199
Nilsky, Ivan, 150

Index

Oates, Titus, 87
Oeler, Karla, 47
Offord, Derek, 128
Ogarev, Nicolai, 121–22, 124, 226n49
Ohryzko, Jozafat, 118, 119, 161, 181, 201
Old Believers, 37, 40–41, 69, 92, 124, 148, 150, 154, 208, 232nn25–26, 232n28
OLDP (Society of Lovers of Spiritual Enlightenment), 147, 148–53, 174–75, 251n25
Orsini, Felice, 161, 225n21
Osinin, I. T., 149
Ostrovsky, Alexander, 133, 209
Otrepev, Grigory, 6–7, 8, 18, 86, 99, 105, 110, 132, 141, 167–68, 173, 208, 224n9; in *Boris Godunov*, 57, 88–90, 96–98, 101, 106, 134–37, 211n6; in *The Brothers Karamazov*, 169, 256n100; in *Demons*, 115, 130, 136–38; in *The Double*, 12–13, 90–91, 115

papal infallibility, 3, 4, 15, 16, 115, 147, 148–49, 172, 201
Pascal, Blaise, 85, 96, 101, 103, 207, 229n3, 233nn44–45
Paskevich, Ivan, 25, 50, 64
Pecherin, Vladimir, 62, 225n23
People's Affair, 123
Perlina, Nina, 30, 49, 158, 162
Pestel, Pavel, 134
Peter the Great, 140, 147, 157–58, 198
Petipa, Marius, 204
Petrashevsky, Mikhail, 11, 12, 26, 74, 80, 87, 92, 155, 180, 232n26
Petrashevsky Circle, 7, 9, 11–13, 29, 35, 43, 65, 132, 140, 157, 179, 195–97, 198, 213n26; Catholic presence in, 12–13, 86; gambling and, 74
phyletism, 178, 201
Piotrowski, Rufin, 48
Pius VII, 3, 99, 102
Pius IX, 3–4, 9, 12, 15, 16, 59, 72, 116–17, 143, 152, 164, 172, 257n9
Pleshcheev, Alexei, 7, 212n14
Pobedonostsev, Konstantin, 149–51, 154–56, 159, 175, 181–82, 197, 208
Poddubnaya, R. N., 230n7
Pogodin, Mikhail, 8, 121, 125, 131–32, 212n19
Poland: agrarian reforms, 42–43, 45–46;

characterization of Poles in Dostoevsky's work, 23–28, 35, 40–42, 44–47, 50–53, 54–55, 63, 66–68, 74, 76–78, 110–12, 124, 127, 133–34, 172–79, 182–91, 201, 207, 219n28, 242n54, 259n45; marginalization of Poles in Russia, 69; nationalism and revolutionary activities, 3–5, 10–12, 14–15, 23, 25–28, 30–32, 36, 42–43, 62–68, 76, 121, 125–27, 138–40, 161–62, 183, 200–201; the Polish Question, 42, 66, 71, 119, 125, 126–27, 129–30, 177, 196; Polish uprising of 1863, 4, 5, 14, 25, 31, 41, 50, 55–56, 59, 63–64, 68, 71, 76, 86, 106, 110, 117, 118, 125–26, 129, 131–32, 143, 170. *See also under* Catholicism; Jesuitism
Polonsky, Yakov, 56, 67
Popular Reprisal, 118
Potebnya, Andrei, 184
Prévost, Antoine-François, 72–73
Prokopich, Feofan, 247n120
Protestantism, 7, 14, 15, 16, 48, 59, 62, 85, 87, 89, 130, 132, 141, 149, 150, 151, 156, 170, 175, 178, 192–93, 199–201, 208, 229nn2–3, 248n125, 265 nn25, 33
Proudhon, Pierre-Joseph, 55, 57, 126, 224n8
Pugachev, Yemelyan, 92, 132, 134
Pushkin, Alexander, 57, 127, 153, 168, 184, 203, 204, 206, 209–10, 243n58; WORKS: "The Anniversary of Borodino," 111; "Before the Sainted Tomb," 111; *Boris Godunov*, vii, 6–7, 9, 88–90, 96–99, 101, 106, 134–37, 167, 172, 173, 196, 199, 208–9, 210, 211n6, 230n7; "Budrys and His Sons," 188–89, 261n70; "In the Depths of Siberian Mines," 183; "Egyptian Nights," 189, 261n70; *Eugene Onegin*, 17, 57; "The Queen of Spades," 98; "There Lived on Earth a Poor Knight," 79–80; "To the Slanderers of Russia," 14, 111, 216n64; "The Wanderer," 6, 208

Quinet, Edgar, 122

Raciborski, Hipolit, 26
Racine, Jean, 7, 57, 73, 101, 194, 206–7, 262n85
Radcliffe, Ann, 204

Index

Raphael, 127, 140–41, 168, 195, 204
Razin, Alexei, 59, 64, 223n5, 224n10
Razin, Stenka, 92, 103, 132, 134
Reformation, 5–7, 15–16, 59, 96,
   141–43, 204, 206–8; and *The Brothers*
   Karamazov, 147–57, 163, 165–66,
   168–71, 172
Renaissance, 7, 97, 141, 142, 165, 168, 169,
   210, 234n52, 248n125
Reuchlin, Johann, 166
Richelieu, Cardinal, 206–7
Risenkampf, A. E., 88–89
Robespierre, Maximilien de, 204
Röhr, Jan, 26
Rosenshield, Gary, 106
Rousseau, Jean–Jacques, 10, 15, 54, 61,
   122, 156, 204, 216n67, 216n69
Ruprecht, Karol, 26
Russian Herald, 101
Russian Messenger, 66
Russian Orthodoxy, 4–5, 8, 10, 11, 14, 17,
   32, 37, 41, 60, 88, 97, 147, 150–51, 157–
   58, 178, 181, 199, 202, 250n18; in *The*
   Brothers Karamazov, 166; in *Crime and*
   Punishment, 92, 109; in *Demons*, 128,
   136–37, 173. *See also* Old Believers
Russian womanhood ideal, 184
Russo-Turkish War, 174, 176–77
Ruttenburg, Nancy, 47

Sa, Emmanuel, 87
Sade, Marquis de, 39, 182, 210
Said, Edward, 215n63
Saint Petersburg News, 176–77
Saint-Simon, Henri de, 11, 181
Samarin, Yury, 86, 89, 95, 101, 147–48,
   230n5
Sand, George, 55, 205, 210
Sandoz, Ellis, 169
Saraskina, Lyudmila, 7–8, 133, 134
Scanlan, James P., 17, 178, 263n4
Schiller, Friedrich, 6, 89, 152, 173, 195,
   204, 205, 231n17
Ściegienny, Piotr, 10–11, 26, 31
Scott, Walter, 5, 80, 81, 204, 228n92
serfdom, 6, 11, 42, 67, 72, 82, 125, 132,
   134, 165–66, 203
Serno-Solovevich, Alexander and Nikolai,
   124, 125, 137, 226n49
Shakespeare, William, 19, 168, 197, 204–6,

207, 208, 209, 243n65; *Hamlet*, 6, 18,
   93–94, 104, 128–31, 140–42, 172,
   194–95, 196–97, 198, 204, 207, 210,
   233nn33–34, 233n37, 244n70,
   247n117
Shchapov, Afansy, 92, 109, 232n26
Shcheglov, F., 57
Shidlovsky, Ivan, 89
Sierakowski, Zygmunt, 187
Sierociński, Jan, 48–49, 186
Siéyès, Emmanuel Joseph, 60
Slavophilism, 72, 181, 192–93, 202
Śliwowska, Wiktoria, 24
Smith, F., 66
Society of Lovers of Spiritual
   Enlightenment. *See* OLDP
Solovev, Vladimir, 153, 177
Solovev, Vsevolod, 149, 253n48
Sommerville, Johann P., 229n2
Sorokine, Dmitri, 111
Spasovich, Uladzimir, 174, 180–82, 191–92,
   195–96, 200–201, 262nn75–76
Speshnev, Nikolai, 12, 13, 26, 141
Stanley, Arthur, 151
Stobnicki, Ksawery, 26, 43
Strakhov, Nikolai, 64, 112, 114, 125, 128,
   131
Strauss, David, 29
Sue, Eugène, 12, 35–36, 38, 57, 118, 202,
   221n68
Sumarokov, Alexander, 88, 231n15
Susanin, Ivan, 8, 212n19
Suslova, Apollinaria, 71, 72, 75
Suvorov, Alexander, 63
Švitrigaila, Prince, 108–9, 237n87
Świderska, Małgorzata, 63, 71–72, 76–77,
   128, 133, 188

Tachalov, Arseny, 152, 252n36
Telescope, 120
Terras, Victor, 183
Thackeray, William Makepeace, 70, 205,
   227n61
Thierry, Amédée, 200
Thompson, Diane Oenning, 16
Tikhon of Zadonsk, 114, 129
Time, 14, 42, 46, 53, 56–57, 59, 62, 92, 100,
   109, 125; anti-Polish stance, 55, 64–65
Time of Troubles, 5, 7–8, 9, 58, 88, 114,
   130, 131–33, 139, 187, 231n17

291